70 YEARS FOR EVERY CHILD

THE STATE OF THE WORLD'S CHILDREN 2016

A fair chance for every child

Contents

01

unicef ✿ 70 YEARS
FOR EVERY CHILD

Contents, continued

02

03

04

Contents, continued

unicef   70 YEARS FOR EVERY CHILD

Contents, continued

The state of the world's children

Inequity imperils millions of children and threatens the future of the world

Pupils play at an early childhood development (ECD) centre in Gulu District, Uganda.

© UNICEF/UN03308/Ose

As we look around the world today, we're confronted with an uncomfortable but undeniable truth: Millions of children's lives are blighted, for no other reason than the country, the community, the gender or the circumstances into which they are born.

And, as the data in this report show, unless we accelerate the pace of our progress in reaching them, the futures of millions of disadvantaged and vulnerable children – and therefore the future of their societies – will be imperilled.

Before they draw their first breath, the life chances of poor and excluded children are often being shaped by inequities. Disadvantage and discrimination against their communities and families will help determine whether they live or die, whether they have a chance to learn and later earn a decent living. Conflicts, crises and climate-related disasters deepen their deprivation and diminish their potential.

But it need not be so. As this report also illustrates, the world has made tremendous progress in reducing child deaths, getting children into school and lifting millions out of poverty. Many of the interventions behind this progress – such as vaccines, oral rehydration salts and better nutrition – have been practical and cost-effective. The rise of digital and mobile technology, and other innovations have made it easier and more cost-effective to deliver critical services in hard-to-reach communities and to expand opportunities for the children and families at greatest risk.

For the most part, the constraints on reaching these children are not technical. They are a matter of political commitment. They are a matter of resources. And they are a matter of collective will – joining forces to tackle inequity and inequality head-on by focusing greater investment and effort on reaching the children who are being left behind.

The time to act is now. For unless we accelerate our progress, by 2030:

- Almost 70 million children may die before reaching their fifth birthdays – 3.6 million in 2030 alone, the deadline year for the Sustainable Development Goals.

- Children in sub-Saharan Africa will be 10 times more likely to die before their fifth birthdays than children in high-income countries.

unicef 70 YEARS FOR EVERY CHILD

- Nine out of 10 children living in extreme poverty will live in sub-Saharan Africa.

- More than 60 million primary school-aged children will be out of school – roughly the same number as are out of school today. More than half will be from sub-Saharan Africa.

- Some 750 million women will have been married as children – three quarters of a billion child brides.

These vast inequities and dangers do more than violate the rights and imperil the futures of individual children. They perpetuate intergenerational cycles of disadvantage and inequality that undermine the stability of societies and even the security of nations everywhere.

More than ever, we should recognize that development is sustainable only if it can be carried on – sustained – by future generations. We have an opportunity to replace vicious cycles with virtuous cycles in which today's poor children – if given a fair chance at health, education and protection from harm – can, as adults, compete on a more level playing field with children from wealthier backgrounds. Thus making not only their own lives better, but their societies richer in every sense of the word.

For when we help a boy access the medicine and nutrition he needs to grow up healthy and strong, we not only increase his chances in life, we also decrease the economic and social costs associated with poor health and low productivity.

When we educate a girl, we not only give her the tools and knowledge to make her own decisions and shape her own future, we also help raise the standard of living of her family and her community.

When we provide education, shelter and protection for children caught in conflicts, we help mend their hearts and their minds – so that someday, they will have the ability and the desire to help rebuild their countries.

This report concludes with five ways to strengthen our work, building on what we have learned over the last 25 years – and what we are still learning: Increasing information about those being left behind. Integrating our efforts across sectors to tackle the multiple deprivations that hold so many children back. Innovating to accelerate progress and drive change for the most excluded children and families. Investing in equity and finding new ways of financing efforts to reach the most disadvantaged children. And involving everyone, beginning with communities themselves, and with businesses, organizations and citizens around the world who believe we can change the outcome for millions of children.

We can. Inequity is not inevitable. Inequality is a choice. Promoting equity – a fair chance for every child, for all children – is also a choice. A choice we can make, and must make. For their future, and the future of our world.

Anthony Lake
Executive Director, UNICEF

REACHING EVERY CHILD
THE PROMISE OF EQUITY

INTRODUCTION

Reaching every child

The promise of equity

If the soul of a society can be judged by the way it treats its most vulnerable members, then by a similar measure, a society's future – its long-term prospects for sustainable growth, stability and shared prosperity – can be predicted by the degree to which it provides every child with a fair chance in life. Providing every child with that fair chance is the essence of equitable development. And as this edition of *The State of the World's Children* argues, promoting equity is more than a moral obligation. It is both a practical and a strategic imperative, helping to break intergenerational cycles of disadvantage and thus reducing the inequalities that undermine all societies.

Musamat (sitting and facing camera), 6, plays a game at the Bakchora pre-primary school in Satkhira Sadar, Bangladesh.

© UNICEF/UN016332/Gilbertson VII Photo

Every child is born with the same inalienable right to a healthy start in life, an education and a safe, secure childhood – all the basic opportunities that translate into a productive and prosperous adulthood. But around the world, millions of children are denied their rights and deprived of everything they need to grow up healthy and strong – because of their place of birth or their family of origin; because of their race, ethnicity or gender; or because they live in poverty or with a disability.

How do these deprivations manifest themselves in the life of a child, on the journey to adulthood?

An infant deprived of post-natal care may not survive her first days. A child deprived of immunization or safe water may not live to see his fifth birthday, or may live a life of diminished health. A child deprived of adequate nutrition may never reach his full physical or cognitive potential, limiting his ability to learn and earn. A child deprived of quality education may never gain the skills she needs to succeed someday in the workplace or send her own children to school. And a child deprived of protection – from conflict, violence or abuse, from exploitation and discrimination, from child labour, or early marriage and motherhood – may be physically and emotionally scarred for life, with profound consequences.

How do such inequities manifest themselves in the countries and communities where these children grow up?

The evidence is all around us, in the form of cycles of deprivation that are transmitted from one generation to the next, deepening inequality that threatens societies everywhere. Children who do not have the opportunity to develop the skills they will need to compete as adults can neither break these vicious cycles in their own lives nor give their children a chance to fulfil their potential. Their societies, too, are deprived of the full contribution they might have made. Left unaddressed, gaps will grow wider and cycles more vicious, affecting more children. This is especially true in a world increasingly beset by violent conflict, chronic crises and other humanitarian emergencies caused by natural disasters and the growing effects of climate change – all of which affect children disproportionately, and the most disadvantaged and vulnerable children most of all.

This report's call to action is, therefore, motivated by a sense of urgency and the conviction that a different outcome, and a better world, are possible. Children born into poverty and deprivation are not doomed to live lives of despair. Inequity is not inevitable, if governments invest in expanding opportunity for every child – shifting policies, programming and public spending priorities so the most disadvantaged have a chance to catch up with the most advantaged.

As the report shows, the good news is that there are more effective – and cost-effective – ways to reach the hardest-to-reach children, families and communities. New technology, the digital revolution, innovative ways to finance critical interventions and citizen-led movements are all helping to drive change for the most disadvantaged. Investing in these interventions and initiatives, and fuelling these emergent movements, will yield both short- and long-term benefits for millions of children and their societies.

The arithmetic of equity is relatively simple, and it is not a zero-sum game. Everyone should move forward, in rich and poor countries alike. But with greater investment and effort focused on reaching the children and families who have made the least progress, advances in child survival, health and education can be more equally shared to the benefit of all. To realize our global development goals, we must invest first in the children who are furthest behind.

Investing in the most disadvantaged is not only right in principle. Evidence shows that it is also right in practice. In a 2010 study,[1] UNICEF demonstrated that an equity-focused approach would accelerate progress towards global health goals faster than could be achieved by the current path and would be especially cost-effective in low-income, high-mortality countries.

The study was based on a simulation that tested two scenarios for achieving maternal and child health goals. One approach emphasized a greater effort to reach children who were worse off. The other was a stay-the-course method that did not place special emphasis on the disadvantaged.

Two key findings emerged: First, by addressing the concentration of various forms of inequity in the most disadvantaged populations, an equity approach accelerated progress towards realizing the health goals faster than the stay-the-course path. Second, by averting more deaths with the same financial investments, the equity approach was considerably more cost-effective and sustainable than the alternative.

So investing in equity is not only a moral necessity. It is a practical and strategic imperative as well.

unicef ❤ | 70 YEARS FOR EVERY CHILD

Unless the world tackles inequity today, in 2030:

167 million children will live in **extreme poverty**

69 million children under age 5 **will die** between 2016 and 2030

60 million children of primary school age will be **out of school**

unicef 🏛️ 🔷 70 YEARS FOR EVERY CHILD

Why focus on equity now?

As governments around the world consider how best to meet their commitment to achieve the Sustainable Development Goals (SDGs) by 2030, the lessons of global efforts over the past 15 years are instructive.

Progress achieved towards the Millennium Development Goals (MDGs) between 2000 and 2015 demonstrated the power of national action, backed by international partnerships, to deliver transformative results. Children born today are significantly less likely to live in poverty than those born at the start of the new millennium. They are over 40 per cent more likely to survive to their fifth birthday[2] and more likely to be in school.

Governments and communities around the world have rightly celebrated these advances. Yet in the midst of progress, millions of children continue to live – and die – in unconscionable conditions. In 2015, an estimated 5.9 million children died before reaching age 5, mostly as a result of diseases that can be readily and affordably prevented and treated.[3] Millions more children are still denied access to education simply because their parents are poor or from a stigmatized group, because they were born female, or because they are growing up in countries affected by conflict or chronic crises. And even though poverty is falling globally, nearly half of the world's extreme poor are children, and many more experience multiple dimensions of poverty in their lives.

In many cases, equity gaps have narrowed over the past 25 years. For example, in all regions, the poorest households experienced greater absolute declines in child mortality than the richest. Four regions achieved gender parity in primary education.[4] But in far too many other cases, overall progress did little to narrow deep and persistent disparities. Governments failed to track the equity gaps separating the most disadvantaged children from the rest of society. National averages marking overall progress masked glaring – and sometimes growing – gaps between children from the poorest households and those from the richest households.

We cannot afford to let that history repeat itself.

To meet the 2030 goals, the pace of progress in the next 15 years will have to outpace that of the MDG period. The consequences and costs of failure are enormous. In fact, if the trends of the past 15 years continue for the next 15 years, by 2030, an estimated 167 million children, the great majority in sub-Saharan Africa, will still be living in extreme poverty. Approximately 3.6 million children under age 5 will die that year, still from mostly preventable causes. And there could still be more than 60 million primary-school-aged children out of school.[5]

Far more than the MDGs that preceded them, the 2030 goals recognize the critical importance of promoting equity. The 17 goals and 169 associated targets that the world's governments have committed to achieving are universal, linked by a pledge "that no one will be left behind … and we will endeavour to reach the furthest behind first."[6]

Redeeming that pledge must begin with delivering progress for the *children* who have been left behind. And the need to do so is urgent.

The United Nations has projected increasing humanitarian needs and a grim outlook for children in 2016.[7] The United Nations High Commissioner for Refugees estimated that by 2015, at least 60 million people had fled their homes because of conflict and violence.[8] Half of them are children.[9] The number of children experiencing prolonged and complex disasters, such as the conflict in the Syrian Arab Republic, is growing.[10]

The intensifying effects of climate change are also exacerbating the risks to the most disadvantaged children. Globally, more than half a billion children live

A group of young girls eat lunch at Salam #9 Primary School for Girls in the Abu Shouk camp for internally displaced people, Sudan.

© UNICEF/UNI165741/Noorani

Chinmaya Shrestha warms her three-day-old grandson at the primary health centre in Gorkha District, Nepal.

© UNICEF/UN016489/Shrestha

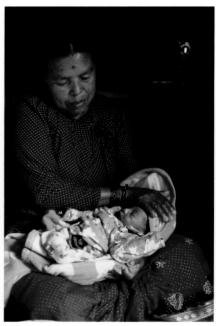

unicef ❤   70 YEARS FOR EVERY CHILD

OUR NEW TARGETS FOR
CHILDREN CANNOT BE ACHIEVED
UNLESS WE MAKE THE MOST
DISADVANTAGED CHILDREN A
PRIORITY.

in zones where the occurrence of flooding is extremely high, and nearly 160 million live in zones where the severity of drought is high or extremely high.[11] The World Health Organization has projected that approximately 250,000 additional deaths will occur annually through 2030 from malnutrition, malaria, diarrhoea and heat stress attributable to climate change.[12]

The challenges of reaching these children with essential services and protection are considerable, but so are the benefits to be gained. And we must reach them. For if we do not, we are likely to see hard-won development gains slip away and watch the consequences of this failure play out across the world.

There is no question that progress for the most disadvantaged children and families is the defining condition for delivering on the 2030 goals and determining the future opportunities of generations to come. The time to act is now.

Meeting the equity imperative

Thirty-five years ago, the first *State of the World's Children* report commented on an earlier set of development goals. The question arises, the authors wrote, "as to whether these goals are ... launched with no more than a wing and a prayer or are they validated by hard evidence that they can be achieved?"[13] This report contends that our new targets for children cannot be achieved unless we make the most disadvantaged children a priority, shifting policies, programmes and public spending to promote greater equity.

The areas in which children experience inequity are many, but in this report we focus specifically on three areas that exemplify both the magnitude of the challenge and the immensity of the opportunity to improve the lives of millions of children.

The report begins with the most glaring inequity of all – disparities in child survival – and goes on to explore the underlying determinants of preventable

Aida, 16, and her baby, born prematurely in Bwaila Hospital in Lilongwe, Malawi.

© UNICEF/UN018540/Chikondi

child mortality. It argues that to meet the 2030 child survival target, we must urgently address persistent disparities in maternal health, the availability of skilled birth attendants, adequate nutrition and access to basic services, as well as other factors such as discrimination, exclusion and a lack of knowledge about child feeding and the role of safe water, adequate sanitation and hygiene in preventing childhood disease.

CHILD POVERTY IS ABOUT MORE THAN INCOME.

The discussion continues with a look at one of the most effective drivers of development and the greatest equalizer of opportunity: education. Without quality education, disadvantaged children are far more likely to be trapped as adults in low-skilled, poorly paid and insecure employment, preventing them from breaking intergenerational cycles of disadvantage. But a greater focus on early childhood development, on increasing education access and quality, and on providing education in emergencies will yield cascading benefits for both this generation and the next.

Having discussed two of the most glaring deprivations children face, this report then examines child poverty in all its dimensions – and the role social protection programmes play in reducing it. Arguing that child poverty is about more than income, it presents a case for combining measures to reduce income poverty with integrated solutions to the many deprivations experienced by children living in poverty.

Finally, as a call to action, the report concludes with a set of principles to guide more equity-focused policy, planning and public spending. These broad principles include expanding **information** about who is being left behind and why; improving **integration** to tackle the multiple dimensions of deprivation; fostering and fuelling **innovation** to reach the hardest-to-reach children; increasing **investment** in equity-focused programmes; and driving **involvement** by communities and citizens around the world.

These principles are a guide more than a blueprint, but they can help shape policy, frame priorities and inform the debate about the best way to deliver on the promise of the 2030 goals and secure a better future not only for the most disadvantaged children, but for us all.

Lunchtime at Kotingli Basic School, Northern Region, Ghana.

© UNICEF/UN04350/Logan

BOX 1. EQUITY DEFINED

The term 'equity' may mean different things in different contexts, but when UNICEF uses it, in this report and elsewhere, it refers to all children having the same opportunities to survive, develop and attain their full potential. Fundamentally, it is about fairness and opportunity – a fair chance for every child.

The conviction that all children possess the same right to grow up healthy, strong, well-educated and capable of contributing to their societies is a cornerstone of every international agreement to recognize and protect children's rights. It culminated, in 1989, with the adoption of the Convention on the Rights of the Child, the most rapidly and widely ratified human rights treaty in history.

Inequity occurs when certain children are unfairly deprived of the basic rights and opportunities available to others. It is frequently rooted in complex cultural, political and systemic factors that shape societies and the socio-economic status of individuals. Ultimately, these factors determine a range of outcomes, including children's well-being.

Society's institutions play a critical role in determining these outcomes for children, most notably in health and education. Where policies, programmes and public spending priorities are equitable, targeting those in greatest need, they can lead to good results for the most disadvantaged children. Where they are inequitable, they effectively preselect children for heightened risks of disease, hunger, illiteracy and poverty based on their country, community or family of origin, their gender, race or ethnicity and other factors. This can perpetuate intergenerational cycles of disadvantage, harming individual children and undermining the strength of their societies as inequality deepens.

An 'equity approach' to development begins with learning more about who is being left behind and why, identifying the children at greatest risk and analysing the structural determinants of inequity – poverty, geography and discrimination, for example – and the complex interplay among them. It requires asking hard questions about how deficient public policies, discriminatory practices, inefficient delivery systems and other obstacles that prevent children from realizing their rights, and finding innovative solutions to these problems. It requires an integrated approach to closing the gaps, working across development and humanitarian sectors, at national, local and community levels, to reach every child.

And, as much as anything else, it demands that the global community recognize the critical connection between the well-being of the most disadvantaged children and the future of our shared world.

Children attend a remedial class, held inside a building sheltering displaced families in Homs, in the Syrian Arab Republic.

© UNICEF/UNI137681/Morooka

CHILD HEALTH:
A FAIR START
IN LIFE

CHAPTER 1

Child health:

A fair start in life

When it comes to children realizing their right to survive and develop, the odds are stacked against those from the poorest and most disadvantaged households. That any child should face diminished prospects of survival or decent health because of the circumstances of his or her birth is grossly unfair and a violation of that child's rights. It is also costly in human, economic, social and political terms. Sustainable progress for today's children and future generations requires a focus on equity – giving every child a fair chance. Reaching the most marginalized children is more than an ethical imperative; it is a precondition for meeting the 2030 goals on child health and well-being.

Prisca, 18, and her baby, in Bwaila Hospital in Lilongwe, Malawi.

© UNICEF/UN018535/Chikondi

Disparities in the survival and health prospects of children from different backgrounds are not random. They systematically follow the contours of social disadvantage linked not only to wealth but also to ethnicity, education and rural-urban divides, among other factors.

One of the most important lessons learned from efforts to improve child – and maternal – health in the past 15 years is that approaches focusing on overall progress will not eliminate the disparities that leave the poorest women and children at the highest risk. While even the poorest countries have achieved considerable progress, inequities persist.

In terms of child survival, while the absolute gap has substantially narrowed since 1990, great inequities remain between rich and poor countries. The relative child mortality gap between sub-Saharan Africa and South Asia on one side and high-income countries on the other has barely changed in a quarter of a century. Children born in sub-Saharan Africa are 12 times more likely than their counterparts in high-income countries to die before their fifth birthday, just as they were in 1990.[14]

A child born in Sierra Leone today is about 30 times more likely to die before age 5 than a child born in the United Kingdom. Women in sub-Saharan Africa face a 1-in-36 lifetime risk of maternal mortality, compared to 1 in 3,300 in high-income countries. The lifetime risk in Chad is 1 in 18.[15]

Narrowing the gaps between rich and poor countries is one of the defining challenges of our time. The starting point for achieving that outcome in child survival is to work towards bringing mortality rates among the poorest to the levels of the wealthiest *within* countries.

Prospects for the survival and good health of all children in every society, rich and poor, should advance as quickly as possible. But the prospects of the children left furthest behind need the most rapid improvement. In other words, accelerated gains must be achieved among those facing the highest risks of death and disease. An effective approach to this challenge will have to address the wider social determinants of inequity, including poverty, discrimination and unequal access to basic services.

Patterns and risks of child mortality

For approximately 1 million children in 2015, their first day of life was also their last. Globally, the neonatal mortality rate (probability of dying during the first 28 days of life) is declining less rapidly than the mortality rate for children between 1 month and 5 years of age. This means that the share of under-five deaths occurring during the neonatal period is increasing. In 2015, neonatal deaths accounted for 45 per cent of total deaths, 5 per cent more than in 2000.[16]

THE SHARE OF UNDER-FIVE DEATHS OCCURRING DURING THE NEONATAL PERIOD IS INCREASING.

The rising share of deaths in the neonatal period reflects the faster decline in mortality of children aged 1 to 59 months than of newborns. Still, of the 5.9 million under-five deaths in 2015, almost half were caused by infectious diseases and conditions such as pneumonia, diarrhoea, malaria, meningitis, tetanus, measles, sepsis and AIDS. Pneumonia and diarrhoea remain leading causes of death in the three regions with the highest under-five mortality: Eastern and Southern Africa, South Asia and West and Central Africa. The burdens of both disease and mortality are often highest among the most disadvantaged.[17]

There are marked regional variations around the broad neonatal trend. In sub-Saharan Africa, newborn deaths account for about one third of the deaths of children under age 5. In regions with lower levels of child mortality, neonatal deaths comprise approximately half of the total. South Asia, on the other hand, has both high overall child mortality and a high share of neonatal deaths.[18]

The geographical distribution of the burden of child mortality is also changing. Globally, child deaths are highly concentrated. In 2015, about 80 per cent of these deaths occurred in South Asia and sub-Saharan Africa, and almost half occurred in just five countries: the Democratic Republic of the Congo, Ethiopia, India, Nigeria and Pakistan.[19] Children living in fragile states and conflict-affected countries face elevated risks. According to the World Development Report 2011, they are more than twice as likely to be undernourished as children in low- and middle-income countries, and twice as likely to die before age 5.[20] Among the 20 countries with the highest child mortality rates, 10 fall into the World Bank's list of fragile contexts.[21]

In countries affected by conflict, damage to health systems threatens children's lives. The Syrian Arab Republic, for instance, had made impressive progress in reducing under-five mortality prior to the current conflict there. Since 1990, the rate fell from 37 to 13 deaths per 1,000 live births. Since 2012, however, the country's *excess crisis mortality* – that is, the under-five mortality attributable to crisis conditions – has been an estimated one to two deaths per 1,000 live births.[22]

Compared to the richest children, the **poorest children** are:

1.9 times

as likely to **die before age 5**

Destruction of infrastructure and lack of personnel, equipment and medicines have hindered access to maternal and newborn health services, leading to a large increase in unassisted births in a country where 96 per cent of deliveries in 2009 were attended by skilled personnel.[23] Crisis conditions have also sparked a rise in vaccine-preventable and infectious diseases, including diarrhoea and pneumonia, among children under age 5.[24]

Globally, access to land, credit and property rights has a further impact on child survival prospects. Marginalized groups living in informal settlements, illegal dwellings or urban slums are vulnerable to health threats because of overcrowding, unsanitary conditions, high transportation costs, discriminatory practices and lack of access to basic services. These factors also create barriers to demand, impeding the initial and continued use of services by the most disadvantaged. When combined with low rates of immunization, this situation exacerbates the transmission of diseases such as pneumonia, diarrhoea, measles and tuberculosis.[25]

Climate change brings added risks. When water becomes scarce because of drought, the poorest children and families are most likely to resort to unsafe water sources, making them more vulnerable to diseases such as cholera and diarrhoea. Climate change is also associated with an increased incidence of vector-borne infectious diseases such as malaria, as well as with food insecurity, rising air pollution, diarrhoeal disease and malnutrition.[26]

Failure to mitigate these and other background risks associated with ill health in childhood will dampen the benefits of any progress countries make towards universal health coverage. Sanitation provides a case in point, illustrating how the 2030 goals are interconnected.

In low- and middle-income countries in 2012, inadequate drinking water, sanitation and hygiene accounted for around 1,000 under-five deaths per day.[27] Research in Nigeria suggests that lack of access to improved water and sanitation facilities may elevate the risk of mortality among children aged 1 to 11 months by as

much as 38 per cent.[28] Use of unimproved sanitation facilities and, specifically, the prevalence of open defecation are also implicated in stunting because they expose children to health problems that can interfere with normal growth.

While progress on sanitation has been slow in many countries, there are encouraging indications that more rapid progress is possible. In Nepal, a Social Movement for Sanitation has mobilized local communities and civic authorities in some of the poorest parts of the country, creating 27 open defecation-free districts.[29] Such initiatives have the potential to generate large returns for child survival. One evaluation in Mali found a 57 per cent reduction in diarrhoea-related deaths of children under age 5, and a 13 per cent reduction in child stunting, in open defecation-free communities.[30]

Prospects for child survival

The 2030 goals have set a high bar for progress on maternal, newborn and child survival and health. Among the targets for Goal 3 is the aim to reduce neonatal mortality to at least as low as 12 deaths per 1,000 live births and under-five mortality to at least as low as 25 deaths per 1,000 live births in every country. Universal health coverage, another 2030 target, is one of the conditions for reaching the above outcomes.

These targets are achievable, but only if governments keep a relentless focus on the most disadvantaged children. The deepest and earliest cuts in child and maternal mortality must benefit those facing the highest risks.

THESE TARGETS ARE ACHIEVABLE, BUT ONLY IF GOVERNMENTS KEEP A RELENTLESS FOCUS ON THE MOST DISADVANTAGED CHILDREN.

Since 1990, the global under-five mortality rate has been cut by 53 per cent.[31] The global annual rate of reduction in under-five mortality from 2000 to 2015 was more than double the rate achieved in the 1990s. Between 2000 and 2015, every region registered major progress in child survival. Sub-Saharan Africa has increased the average annual rate of decline in under-five mortality from 1.6 per cent during the 1990s to 4.1 per cent since 2000.[32]

Maternal mortality rates are also falling. Since 1990, the annual number of maternal deaths has decreased by 43 per cent. Between 2005 and 2015, the global annual rate of reduction was more than twice the 1990–2000 rate.[33] Of the 75 countries accounting for more than 95 per cent of maternal, newborn and child deaths, about three quarters made accelerated gains.[34]

Some of the world's poorest countries have made extraordinary progress. While the world missed the MDG target of a two-thirds reduction in under-five mortality between 1990 and 2015, 24 low-income and lower-middle-income countries achieved it.[35] Some of these countries – such as Ethiopia, Liberia, Malawi, Mozambique and Niger – started out with very high mortality rates,[36] in excess of 200 deaths per 1,000 live births. Egypt and Yemen achieved respective declines of 72 per cent and 67 per cent in under-five mortality despite chronic conflict and economic hardships.[37] Meanwhile, China has experienced a rapid and considerable decline in under-five mortality – 80 per cent since 1990.[38]

The diversity of national experiences demonstrates that dramatic reductions in child mortality are possible in countries whose social, political and economic contexts vary widely. The same is true for maternal health, given that a range of countries with different contexts and starting points achieved the MDG target of a 75 per cent reduction in maternal mortality.

While child mortality generally declines as average income increases, many poorer countries are outpacing richer neighbours in reducing their under-five mortality rates (see Figure 1.1). Yet some countries in the fast lane for global economic growth

unicef ◆   70 YEARS FOR EVERY CHILD

– including India and Nigeria – have been in the slower lane for child mortality reduction. The policy lesson: Economic growth can help but does not guarantee improved child survival, and a country's income need not hinder progress.

Inequities in child survival

Disparities in maternal, newborn and child health in high-mortality countries represent a major barrier to sustained progress towards every child's right to survive and thrive. On average, children born into the poorest 20 per cent of households are almost twice as likely to die before age 5 as those born into the richest 20 per cent.[39]

Behind this global average is an array of diverse national patterns. For example, children born into the poorest 20 per cent are almost twice as likely to die during their first five years as those from the richest 20 per cent in Bangladesh and three times as likely in India, Indonesia and the Philippines.[40]

Some countries have registered rapid progress since 2000 while also enhancing equity *(see Figure 1.2, blue dots)*. Other countries have achieved dramatic progress without improvements in equity *(see Figure 1.2, yellow dots)*. In the latter countries, the survival gap between rich and poor children has slightly widened.

These disparities have serious consequences. The combination of demography (poorer households having more children) and inequality in survival prospects (children in poor households facing higher mortality rates) means that the poorest children account for a greater share of child deaths than the wealthiest.

FIGURE 1.1

Countries with limited economic growth can still reduce child mortality

Annual rate of reduction in under-five mortality, 2000–2015, and annual rate of change in GDP, 2000–2014, by country

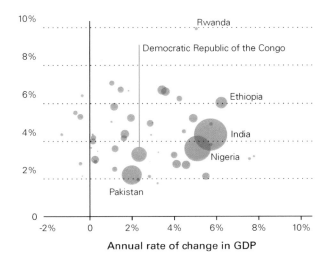

Annual reduction in under-five mortality rate

Bubble size indicates the estimated number of under-five deaths in 2015

1,000,000

100,000

10,000

Annual rate of change in GDP

Note: Countries selected had an under-five mortality rate above 40 deaths per 1,000 live births in 2015, 10,000 or more live births in 2015, and available GDP data, for 2000–2014 or most recent available year. Each bubble represents a country.

Source: World Bank, World Development Indicators (update of 22 December 2015), and United Nations Inter-agency Group for Child Mortality Estimation, *Levels & Trends in Child Mortality: Report 2015.*

But it also means that equivalent percentage reductions in child mortality rates save more lives among the poor. An analysis of survey data covering 51 high-mortality countries found that reducing the neonatal mortality rate of the poorest 20 per cent to the rate of the richest 20 per cent would have averted some 600,000 deaths in 2012.[41]

Under-five mortality should continue to decline for all children. But in order to reach the child survival targets, mortality rates for children from the poorest households will have to fall much more rapidly than the rates for those from the wealthiest households *(see Figure 1.3)*. To make that happen, governments will have to address a range of critical factors affecting the poorest and most disadvantaged children.

FIGURE 1.2

Progress in under-five mortality does not necessarily come with greater equity

Change in ratio of under-five mortality rate by household wealth and change in overall under-five mortality rate

Percentage change in ratio of under-five mortality rate among children in poorest versus richest households

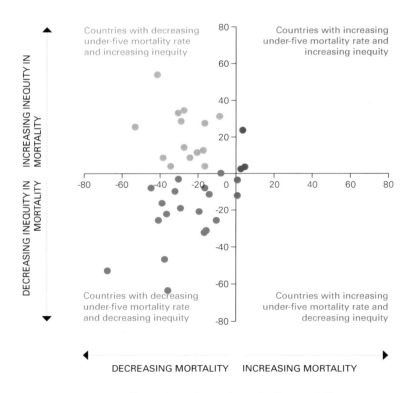

Percentage change in under-five mortality

Note: Using surveys conducted in the years 2005–2009 and 2010–2014 with respective midpoints of the reference years in 2000–2004 and 2005–2012.

Source: UNICEF analysis based on Demographic and Health Surveys (DHS), Multiple Indicator Cluster Surveys (MICS) and other nationally representative sources of data for 37 countries.

FIGURE 1.3

The poor will need to make faster progress to reach the 2030 goal

Required annual rate of reduction in under-five mortality to achieve the SDG target by 2030, by poorest and richest wealth quintiles, 2015–2030

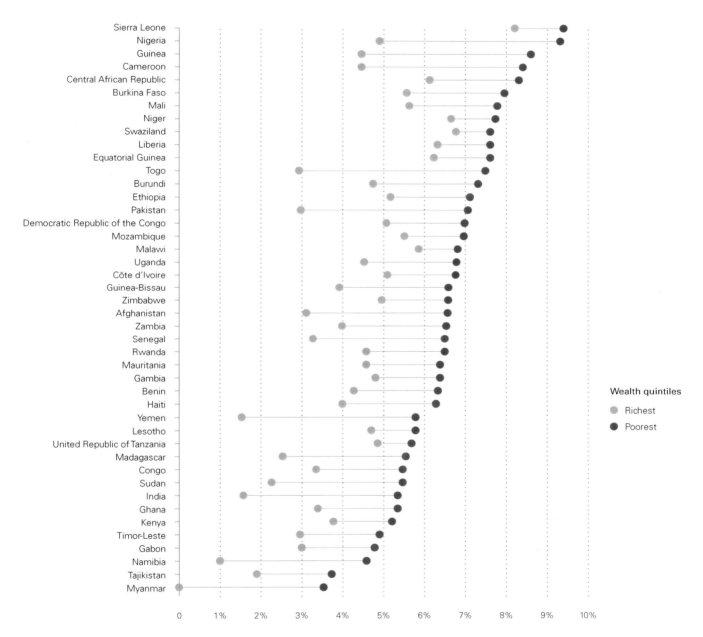

Required annual rate of reduction to reach an under-five mortality rate
of 25 deaths per 1,000 live births by 2030

Note: Most recent available survey data in countries with an under-five mortality rate above 40 deaths per 1,000 live births in 2015 using United Nations Inter-agency Group for Child Mortality Estimation (UN IGME) 2015 estimates.

Source: UNICEF analysis based on DHS, MICS and other nationally representative sources from the most recent survey conducted since 2006.

Achieving substantial improvements in nutrition – a target within Goal 2 – will be key to boosting child survival rates. Half of all deaths of children under age 5 are attributable to undernutrition, and large disparities exist in related indicators such as stunting. An analysis of 87 countries with recent available data shows that stunting rates among the poorest children are more than double those among the richest.[42] In West and Central Africa, progress on stunting has been slow, with less than a 25 per cent reduction between 1990 and 2014. And in over one third of low-income countries with available trend data, the gap between the richest and poorest households in stunting reduction has been widening.[43]

Household wealth is one determinant of a child's chance to survive, but maternal education is also a strong predictor. Across much of South Asia and sub-Saharan Africa, children with mothers who received no education are almost three times as likely to die before age 5 as children of mothers with secondary education.[44] Education enables women to delay and space births, secure access to maternal and child health care and seek treatment for children when they fall ill.

If all mothers achieved secondary education, there would be 1.5 million fewer annual deaths of children under age 5 in sub-Saharan Africa and 1.3 million fewer in South Asia.[45]

Child marriage and women's reproductive health management also influence child mortality patterns. While child marriage rates are decreasing, each year about 15 million girls are married before the age of 18.[46] These girls represent a highly vulnerable group: They are denied their childhood, face limited opportunities for education and often begin childbearing too early. Girls in the poorest 20 per cent of the population, as well as those living in rural areas, face the greatest risks.[47] In Africa, the level of child marriage among the poorest has remained unchanged since 1990.[48]

A smiling boy with his mother, in Bangladesh.

© UNICEF/UNI78184/Siddique

Around the world, child brides are less likely than adult women to receive adequate medical care while pregnant. The lack of care, and the fact that girls are not physically mature enough to give birth, put both mothers and their babies at risk. Complications during pregnancy and childbirth are the second leading cause of death for girls between ages 15 and 19.[49] And babies born to mothers under age 20 are 1.5 times more likely to die during the first 28 days than babies born to mothers in their twenties or thirties.[50]

When a woman is denied opportunities to manage her reproductive health, she and her children suffer. Short birth spacing, for example, is a risk factor for preterm birth,[51] and limited access to contraception is one barrier to safe spacing. Globally, an estimated 216 million married women need, but lack, access to modern contraceptive methods.[52] If women who want to avoid pregnancy had access to these methods, unintended pregnancies would drop by 70 per cent.[53] Reducing the number of unintended pregnancies, in turn, could avert 60 per cent of maternal deaths and 57 per cent of under-five child deaths.[54]

The rural-urban divide also contributes to unequal chances in child survival. Children born in rural areas are 1.7 times more likely to die before age 5 than children in urban areas.[55]

Looking specifically at disparities linked to wealth and residence, a new comparison *(see Figure 1.4)* uses household survey data to chart child survival trajectories between 2015 and 2030 in a group of eight countries starting out from different positions. These projections illustrate the need for the fastest progress among the worst-off groups. Reaching the most marginalized households is more than an ethical imperative; it is a precondition for ending the preventable deaths of newborns, children under age 5 and their mothers.

FIGURE 1.4

Progress must accelerate for the least advantaged children

Required reduction in under-five mortality rate (deaths per 1,000 live births) from 2015–2030 to achieve the SDG target, by subgroups in selected countries

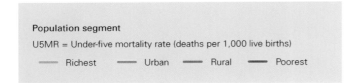

Population segment

U5MR = Under-five mortality rate (deaths per 1,000 live births)

—— Richest   —— Urban   —— Rural   —— Poorest

Nigeria and Pakistan. In both countries, the under-five mortality rate (U5MR) in the wealthiest and the poorest households is above the SDG target, and marked disparities persist between regions. In the North-West region of Nigeria, for example, U5MR was double that of the South-West. And while the richest 20 per cent will have to cut mortality by more than half to achieve the target by 2030, the poorest 20 per cent must achieve a reduction of three quarters.

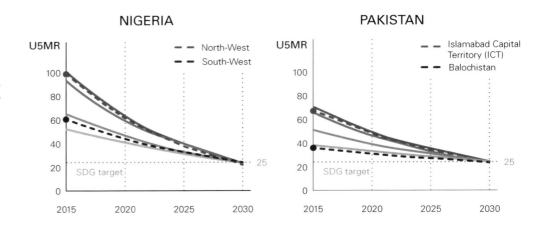

Ethiopia and Mozambique. Both countries achieved MDG 4 (reducing U5MR by two thirds between 1990 and 2015). For Ethiopia to achieve the SDG target by 2030, U5MR in Addis Ababa – the country's best performer – will have to fall by more than one third. The worst performing region, Benishangul-Gumuz, will have to cut mortality by more than two thirds from 2015 to 2030.

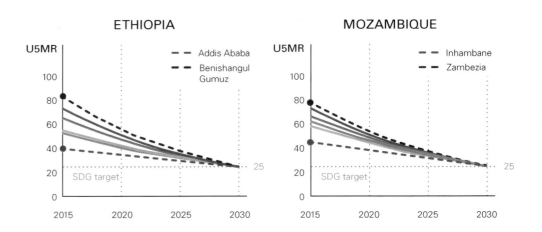

Note: Required annual rate of reduction to achieve the SDG target of 25 deaths per 1,000 live births by 2030 calculated from reference year (mid-year of reference period of 10 years preceding the survey) of the under-five mortality rate in the survey data. Subgroups that have already achieved the target are kept constant. Selected subgroups are by best and worst performing region, richest and poorest wealth quintiles and urban and rural residence. Groups may overlap.

Source: UNICEF analysis based on DHS, MICS and other nationally representative sources.

unicef ● | 70 YEARS FOR EVERY CHILD

Population segment

U5MR = Under-five mortality rate (deaths per 1,000 live births)

— Richest   — Urban   — Rural   — Poorest

Indonesia and the Philippines.
In both countries, the wealthiest 20 per cent and the most advantaged regions have already met the 2030 target. In the Philippines, while both the richest quintile and urban areas have reached the 2030 target, the poorest 20 per cent and the Autonomous Region in Muslim Mindanao will have to reduce mortality rates by about two fifths to do so.

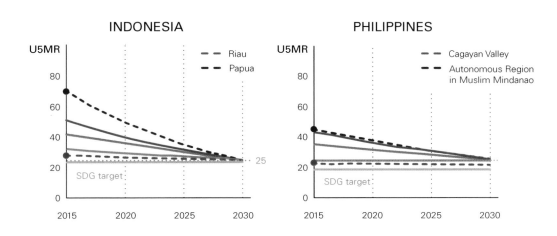

INDONESIA

U5MR
- - Riau
- - Papua
SDG target

PHILIPPINES

U5MR
- - Cagayan Valley
- - Autonomous Region in Muslim Mindanao
SDG target

Bangladesh and Cambodia.
Cambodia is one of the world's most striking post-2000 child survival success stories: In 2015, U5MR was close to the SDG target. However, two provinces inhabited mainly by ethnic minorities reported rates of 79 or 80 deaths per 1,000 live births. Compared to the level in Phnom Penh, children born in these two provinces faced about 3.5 times the risk of dying before their fifth birthday. Bangladesh will have to reduce disparities linked to household wealth and high levels of mortality in regions such as Sylhet in order to maintain progress.

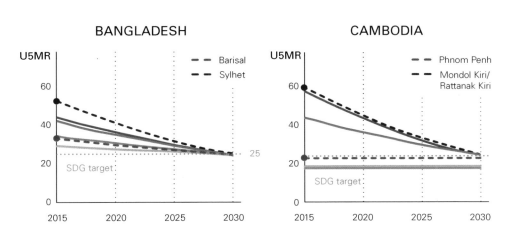

BANGLADESH

U5MR
- - Barisal
- - Sylhet
SDG target

CAMBODIA

U5MR
- - Phnom Penh
- - Mondol Kiri/ Rattanak Kiri
SDG target

Disparities in access and quality of care

Providing all women with antenatal care, skilled care at birth and essential newborn care can dramatically improve prospects for safe pregnancy and child survival. Unfortunately, these areas are marked by extreme disparity – not just in access to care but also in the quality of care. Evidence shows that unequal access starts before birth and continues into the critical early years.

Disparities in utilization of antenatal care and skilled birth attendance mirror social disparities in child survival. Globally, women from the richest 20 per cent of households are still more than twice as likely as those from the poorest 20 per cent to have a skilled attendant at birth.[56] And a modest increase in antenatal care coverage since 2000 has done little to narrow disparities in the antenatal period.[57] Rural-urban divides have also remained intact. In 2015, just over half of pregnant women benefited from the recommended minimum of four antenatal care visits; the vast majority of those who do not receive the minimum are poor and live in rural areas.[58]

At the regional level, glaring disparities in antenatal care and skilled birth attendance exist in South Asia and sub-Saharan Africa. In both Bangladesh and Pakistan, women from the richest households are respectively four and six times more likely to receive antenatal care (at least four visits) than those from the poorest. On the other hand, some of the largest gaps in skilled birth attendance are in Eastern and Southern Africa. In Eritrea, women from the richest households are 10 times more likely to benefit from skilled birth attendance than those from the poorest households.[59]

Mothers and newborns in the poorest households are also less likely to receive a post-natal check-up. As a result, they are exposed to elevated risks associated with undetected hypothermia, infection and post-birth complications.

Such large and avoidable inequities cost children's lives and cause immense suffering. The lack of adequate health facilities in poor communities plays a role in these outcomes, and so do the social attitudes of some health providers. Women from socially excluded groups often experience hostile treatment or a lack of responsiveness from the health system and health providers. Even when health facilities serving the poor are accessible and affordable, discriminatory practices can be an obstacle to equal treatment.

In the case of pneumonia, early diagnosis and effective case management by trained health providers can save lives. Yet children from the poorest households who develop symptoms of pneumonia, and face the greatest risks, are the least likely to be taken to a health facility. Children from the wealthiest households are 1.5 times as likely as those from the poorest to be taken to a health facility in Madagascar,[60] and approximately four times as likely in Ethiopia.[61] Similar patterns apply to the treatment of diarrhoea, another major killer.

Marginalized communities such as the Roma population in Central and Eastern Europe, for example, face inequities in access to and utilization of health services at every turn. In both Serbia and Bosnia and Herzegovina, one in five Roma children are moderately or severely stunted. As of 2012, only 4 per cent of Roma children 18 to 29 months old in Bosnia and Herzegovina had all the recommended vaccinations, compared to 68 per cent of non-Roma children.[62]

Achieving equity is not only relevant in the poorest countries. In some rich countries, children from different backgrounds face starkly unequal prospects. The United States,

SUCH LARGE AND AVOIDABLE INEQUITIES COST CHILDREN'S LIVES AND CAUSE IMMENSE SUFFERING.

unicef ❤   70 YEARS FOR EVERY CHILD

for instance, has a higher reported infant mortality rate than most high-income countries in the OECD. For babies born here, the odds of survival are closely linked to ethnicity: In 2013, infants born to African American parents were more than twice as likely to die as those born to white Americans.[63]

As in other countries, factors such as income, mother's education and birthplace also continue to determine a child's chances of surviving to age 5 in the United States. These disparities are reflected dramatically at the state level. The infant mortality rate of the state of Mississippi in 2013, for example, was double that of the state of Massachusetts.[64] Combining home visits by health workers with wider measures aimed at narrowing inequalities in education and income could play a vital role in addressing the situation.

Low-cost interventions can make a difference

The overwhelming majority of child deaths could be prevented through well known, low-cost and easily deliverable interventions. This is true for deaths that occur both in the neonatal period and after the first month. Quality care during pregnancy, labour and birth, and in the immediate post-natal period, not only prevents the onset of complications but expedites their early detection and prompt management. Early post-natal care is particularly important in reducing mortality in the first few days day of life.

The rising proportion of neonatal deaths points to the more difficult challenges ahead in sustaining and accelerating progress on child survival. The interventions needed to address the major causes of neonatal mortality are closely linked to those that protect maternal health *(see Figure 1.5)*, so it is vitally important to increase coverage of interventions before, during and after pregnancy.

40 PER CENT OF NEONATAL DEATHS COULD BE AVERTED WITH KEY INTERVENTIONS AROUND THE TIME OF BIRTH.

Research published in *The Lancet* estimates that 40 per cent of neonatal deaths could be averted with key interventions around the time of birth. These include care by a skilled birth attendant, emergency obstetric care, immediate newborn care (including breastfeeding support and clean birth practices, such as cord and thermal care) and newborn resuscitation. Another 30 per cent could be saved through 'kangaroo mother' care with skin-to-skin contact starting from birth, prevention or management of neonatal sepsis, treatment of neonatal jaundice and prevention of brain damage caused by birth-related oxygen deprivation.[65]

The benefits of breastfeeding are still under-recognized in many countries. Starting within the first hour of birth, longer-duration breastfeeding is associated with protection against childhood infections, increases in intelligence and reductions in the prevalence of overweight and diabetes. Research found that if breastfeeding were scaled up to near universal levels, the lives of 823,000 children under age 5 would be saved annually in 75 low- and middle-income countries. For nursing women, breastfeeding protects against breast cancer and improves birth spacing.[66]

Reaching the most vulnerable

National leadership, backed by international cooperation, has played a critical role in driving global achievements in child survival over the past 15 years. Economic growth, rising incomes and poverty reduction have certainly contributed, by both improving living standards and generating resources for investment in health. But in many

unicef   70 YEARS FOR EVERY CHILD

low- and middle-income countries, much of the impetus for progress has come from strengthened health systems and community-based health interventions. Community health workers have expanded the reach of care, linking vulnerable people to high impact, low-cost interventions for maternal, newborn and child health.[67]

One striking example comes from Ethiopia. Between 2004 and 2010, the Government of Ethiopia trained and deployed 38,000 health extension workers to local posts across the country, where they delivered basic antenatal and post-natal care, reaching populations previously not covered by the health system.[68] Similarly, Health Surveillance Assistants in Malawi have provided an essential link between the formal health system and the community, contributing to one of the world's most accelerated national declines in child mortality.[69]

FIGURE 1.5

Accelerated progress in neonatal mortality is key to meeting the SDG target

Required annual rate of reduction 2015–2030 versus the observed annual rate of reduction in neonatal mortality

Annual rate of reduction required from 2015 to reach a neonatal mortality rate of 12 deaths per 1,000 live births by 2030 (%)

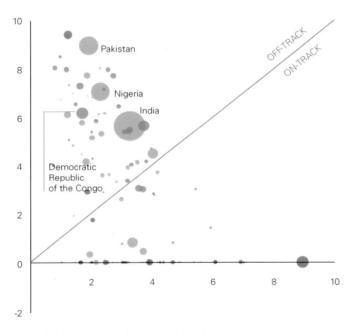

Observed annual rate of reduction in neonatal mortality during 2000–2015 (%)

● Low-income countries ● Lower-middle-income countries ● Upper-middle-income countries ● High-income countries

Bubble size indicates estimated number of neonatal deaths in 2015   ● 1,000,000 ● 100,000 · 10,000

Note: Countries above the diagonal line need faster rates of reduction (i.e., accelerated progress) to achieve the target. Countries below the diagonal line will be able to achieve the target at their current rates of reduction. Those on the horizontal axis had already reached the target in 2015.

Source: UNICEF analysis based on UN IGME, 2015.

unicef ● 70 YEARS FOR EVERY CHILD

BOX 1.1 FEMALE VOLUNTEERS HELP HEALTH WORKERS REACH THE MARGINALIZED IN NEPAL

Nepal, one of the world's poorest countries, has registered one of the most rapid reductions in maternal mortality since 1990. This progress is the result of sustained policy reform stretching over two decades, including a period marked by conflict.

Health system development played a critical role in Nepal's success. Safe motherhood policies, introduced in the 1990s and strengthened since then, have greatly increased the number of community-level health workers and skilled birth attendants. In addition, the government made maternal health and family planning priorities within an expanding health budget, and health spending per capita doubled between 1995 and 2011. During roughly the same period, antenatal care coverage increased five-fold. The number of births assisted by skilled attendants doubled between 2006 and 2011, to 36 per cent of the total.

Alongside the formal health system, Nepal developed a network of female community health volunteers. After receiving 18 days of basic training and being provided with medical equipment, the volunteers liaise closely with health workers, a model that has extended the reach of the health system into some of the country's most marginalized areas.

Health sector plans have aimed to build the professionalism of health staff, improve training and expand delivery of basic services across political cycles. The current National Safe Motherhood and Newborn Health Long Term Plan (2010–2017) emphasizes the development of obstetric care and referral systems. Reframing maternal and child care as health rights or entitlements, meanwhile, has empowered women, who can now hold providers to greater account for delivering interventions related to safe motherhood, neonatal health, nutrition and reproductive health.

Developments outside the health system have also fostered equitable progress in Nepal. Behaviour change, access to reproductive health care and increased access to education have contributed to a steep decline in fertility rates. In addition, the proportion of the population living in poverty has dropped sharply, from 68 per cent in the mid-1990s to 25 per cent in 2011.

Source: Engel, Jakob, et al., 'Nepal's Story: Understanding improvements in maternal health', Case Study, Overseas Development Institute, July 2013.

Around 70 per cent of the global decline in under-five deaths since 2000 can be traced to the prevention and treatment of infectious diseases. The annual number of under-five deaths from pneumonia, diarrhoea, malaria, sepsis, pertussis, tetanus, meningitis, measles and AIDS declined from 5.4 million to 2.5 million from 2000 to 2015.[70] Malaria deaths among children under age 5 have fallen by 58 per cent globally since 2000,[71] largely through the use of insecticide-treated mosquito nets and the antimalarial drug artemisinin. And vaccination programmes resulted in a 79 per cent drop in measles deaths between 2000 and 2014, preventing the deaths of an estimated 17.1 million children.[72]

Innovation is also accelerating progress for the hardest-to-reach children. In Malawi – where 130,000 children under 14 were living with HIV in 2014 – the government, together with partners, is testing the use of drones as a cost-effective way of reducing waiting times for HIV-testing of infants, for whom early diagnosis is critical to quality care.

Currently, dried blood samples are transported by road from local health centres to the central laboratory for testing, taking an average of 16 days to reach the lab, and another eight weeks to deliver the results. Challenges such as the cost of fuel and poor state of roads result in delays, which present a significant problem for effective treatment. If successful, the innovation using drones could cut both costs and the time families wait to receive results from months to weeks.[73]

What if the gaps are not closed?

The pace of progress on child and maternal health and survival can increase or decrease as a result of policy choices made by governments and the international community in the coming years. However, if current trends continue, in 2030:

- There will be 3.6 million deaths of children under age 5 in that year alone. A total of 69 million such deaths will have occurred between 2016 and 2030,[74] with sub-Saharan Africa accounting for around half of these and South Asia for another third.[75]

- Five countries will account for more than half of the global burden of under-five deaths: India (17 per cent), Nigeria (15 per cent), Pakistan (8 per cent), the Democratic Republic of the Congo (7 per cent) and Angola (5 per cent).[76]

- All but five of the 30 countries with the highest under-five mortality rates will be in sub-Saharan Africa.[77] Some 620 million children will have been born in that region between 2016 and 2030[78] – about 30 per cent of the world total.[79] It is the only region expected to see growth in its under-five population, which is likely to expand by over 40 million.[80] Nigeria alone will account for around 6 per cent of all births globally.[81]

- The global maternal mortality rate will be around 161 deaths per 100,000 live births – still five times the level for high-income countries in 1990.[82]

- Pneumonia will remain the second biggest killer of children under age 5, and preterm birth complications will remain the first.[83]

ACHIEVING THE SDG CHILD SURVIVAL TARGET WOULD SAVE THE LIVES OF 38 MILLION CHILDREN.

Based on current trends, then, prospects for universal achievement of the 2030 targets for neonatal and under-five survival are bleak. Unless the trends change, dozens of countries will miss the mark by a wide margin *(see Figures 1.5 and 1.6)*. South Asia will not achieve the neonatal target until 2049 and sub-Saharan Africa will reach it after mid-century.[84] The average annual rate of reduction in neonatal mortality required for India to reach the target is almost double the current level.

Compared to staying at the 2015 survival rate for children under age 5, achieving the SDG child survival target would save the lives of 38 million children worldwide in the next 15 years. If each country matched its top regional performer's trend, an additional 7 million lives could be saved. If each country matched or fell below the current average rate of under-five mortality in high-income countries, an additional 21 million lives could be saved.[85] The latter scenario – again, compared to staying at the 2015 rate – would save 59 million children's lives between now and 2030.

In an analysis of 75 high-burden countries, only eight are expected to reach the SDG target. If each country scaled up intervention coverage as fast as the best performer in each area of intervention (e.g., skilled birth attendance, exclusive breastfeeding for the first six months, etc.), 33 countries could reach the target by 2030. The annual number of children dying before age 5 in those countries would drop by almost two thirds — from 5.5 million in 2015 to 2 million in 2030.[86]

These and other scenarios for 2030 point to the urgent need to scale up proven interventions. Closing the gap between the current trajectory and the rate of progress needed to achieve the 2030 child survival goal would save the lives of 13 million children under age 5, almost half of them newborn. Around four in every five lives saved would be in sub-Saharan Africa.[87]

FIGURE 1.6

Many countries will miss the under-five mortality target, some by a wide margin

Projected under-five mortality rate, at current trends, in countries that are expected to miss the SDG target by 2030

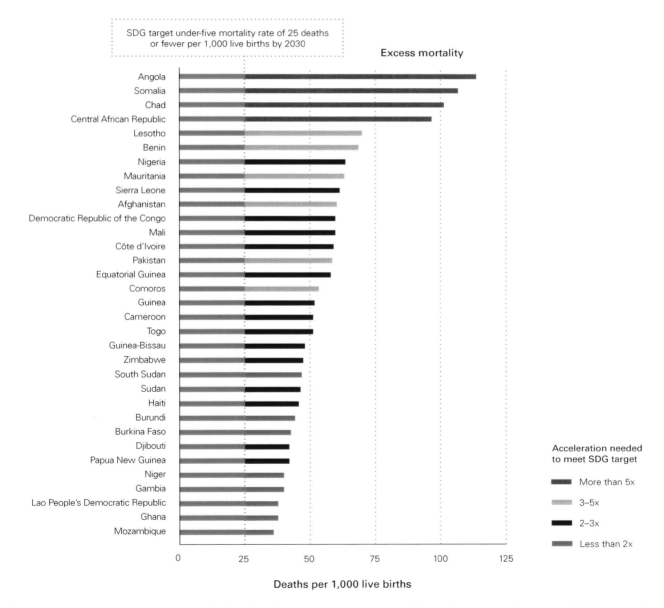

Deaths per 1,000 live births

Note: The countries shown had 10,000 or more live births in 2015 and are expected to miss the SDG target by more than 10 deaths per 1,000 live births, if current trends continue.

Source: UNICEF analysis based on UN IGME, 2015.

Equity objectives

Interim equity objectives – or 'stepping stone' targets – linked to achievement of the 2030 goals could play a valuable role in guiding policy on child and maternal well-being. National strategies aimed at halving disparities in child survival in five to seven years, for example, would help put the most vulnerable women and children at the centre of policy. The strategies could focus on inequities associated with household wealth, education levels, rural-urban divides and differences between regions or ethnic groups.

Translating these interim targets into outcomes would require fundamental changes in how child and maternal health services are financed and delivered, and in policies aimed at lowering background risks. But interim equity objectives could act as a powerful catalyst towards meeting the 2030 commitments.

The objectives would also provide a reference point for monitoring and reporting. In effect, they would serve as milestones on the road to 2030. This is a key link in the chain of accountability. Objectives become meaningful only when they provide a benchmark, backed by data, against which performance can be measured. Currently, there are large gaps in both coverage and quality of the data available. Civil registration systems cover only a small fraction of global births, and coverage is mostly limited in countries with the highest child and maternal death rates. Coverage of deaths is even sparser.[88]

Globally, the births of nearly one in four children under age 5 have not been recorded.[89] Of the 74 countries reviewed by the Commission on Information and Accountability for Women's and Children's Health, only two registered more than half of all deaths.[90] In low- and middle-income countries, up to 80 per cent of deaths occur outside of health facilities, and many are not reported accurately.[91] This means that critical information on the deaths of newborns, children and mothers is incomplete.

Because of deficits in these areas, data on child and maternal deaths have to be extrapolated and interpolated through modelling. As child and maternal deaths decline and become more statistically rare, the importance of observational data increases – especially for the most marginalized and hard-to-reach populations.

High return on health investments

The investments needed to end preventable child and maternal deaths offer high returns. The scale of the returns reflects the hidden costs of health risks. Childhood illness not only claims lives and causes suffering, but also undermines the potential of children, their communities and countries. Malnutrition and childhood illness compromise cognitive development and reduce adult productivity. When health systems fail to prevent illness, society pays a price in the form of treatment costs and lost productivity. Conversely, improved maternal and child health and nutritional status can create a positive cycle, enabling children to realize their potential and helping their communities and countries to prosper.

What would it cost to effectively end preventable deaths among children and mothers? Detailed financial costings developed under the Global Investment Framework for Women's and Children's Health provide valuable insights.[92]

unicef ✿ 70 YEARS FOR EVERY CHILD

Six core investment packages for 74 high-mortality countries would cost about US$30 billion in additional annual spending, an increase of 2 per cent above current levels. The spending packages would cover maternal and newborn health, child health, immunization, family planning, HIV/AIDS and malaria, with nutrition as a cross-cutting theme. Between 2013 and 2035, this investment would avert an estimated 147 million child deaths, 32 million stillborn deaths and 5 million maternal deaths.

In effect, such an approach would bring the level of essential maternal and child health coverage available to the poorest 20 per cent of the population in the 74 countries towards the coverage available to the richest 20 per cent.

BOX 1.2 EVERY CHILD COUNTS: THE IMPORTANCE OF QUALITY DATA ON CHILD SURVIVAL

Accurately counting births and deaths is the first step towards making sure that every child's rights are recognized and respected. Yet more than 100 developing countries lack the civil registration and vital statistics (CRVS) systems needed to generate accurate birth and death data.

Around the world, 230 million children currently under age 5 were not registered at birth. That figure includes 39 per cent of children in sub-Saharan Africa and 44 per cent of children in South Asia. In the absence of reliable data, estimates for child mortality in countries lacking CRVS systems are based on a sophisticated statistical model using survey responses, census information and other sources. But no model can compensate for high-quality input data based on birth and death registration.

Household surveys provide valuable information on differences in child mortality by socio-economic characteristics – including parental wealth, location, education and others. But greater disaggregation of data on various population groups is required to provide a detailed picture of localities marked by high levels of childhood disadvantage. That means collecting, synthesizing and speeding up data reporting on these social groups and localities.

The situation is further complicated by large information gaps on cause-specific mortality. For example, estimates of the global burden of acute lower respiratory infection (ALRI) among young children have to rely on hospital-based data, but those numbers underestimate influenza-associated ALRI incidence in low-income communities because of poor families' limited access to specialized care. And the best global estimates for severe bacterial infection among neonatal children range from 5.5 million to 8.3 million – a large margin reflecting uncertainties in the underlying data.

Despite considerable progress resulting from increased surveys, there are still major gaps in data tracking the coverage of health interventions as well. Such data are central to accountability, providing information on reach and disparities. While not every country has the capacity to report on all indicators, existing survey tools could be modified to focus more sharply on quality of care.

In the end, however, there is no substitute for CRVS systems. The cost of achieving universal CRVS coverage by 2024 has been put at US$3.8 billion for 73 countries (excluding China and India). In the interim, expanding health system coverage and applying new information and communication technologies can generate critical birth and death registration information, along with vital information on specific diseases.

Source: World Bank/World Health Organization, *Global Civil Registration and Vital Statistics: Scaling up investment Plan 2015–2024*, World Bank, Washington, D.C., 28 May 2014, p. 2. United Nations Children's Fund, *Every Child's Birth Right: Inequities and trends in birth registration*, UNICEF, New York, 2013. pp. 6, 36. Nair, Harish, et al., 'Global burden of respiratory infections due to seasonal influenza in young children: A systematic review and meta-analysis', *The Lancet*, vol. 378, no. 9807, 3 December 2011, p. 1925. Seale, Anna, et al., 'Estimates of possible severe bacterial infection in neonates in sub-Saharan Africa, South Asia, and Latin America for 2012: A systematic review and meta-analysis', *The Lancet*, vol. 14, no. 8, pp. 731–741, August 2014.

The projected social and economic returns on this investment – in terms of productivity, increased output and wider benefits associated with improved health – are also impressive, totalling nine times the cost.[93]

Other projected returns on investments in ending child and maternal mortality include:

- At least a 10-fold return on health and nutrition spending through better educational attainment, workforce participation and social contributions.[94]

- Returns of US$16 for every US$1 invested in immunization. Even with the introduction of new, more costly vaccines, immunization remains one of the most cost-effective buys in health planning.[95]

- Returns of US$16 for every US$1 invested in nutrition interventions.[96] Child undernutrition can cost between 1.9 per cent (Egypt) and 16.5 (Ethiopia) per cent of a country's GDP.[97]

- Savings totalling US$302 billion annually through protection, promotion and support for breastfeeding.[98]

The spending identified by the Global Investment Framework would address the problem of insufficiently resourced health systems that provide low coverage of cost-effective interventions. More than US$10 billion of the additional annual cost would support enhanced delivery of reproductive, maternal, newborn and child health care – including provision of an additional 544,000 community health workers and 675,000 nurses, doctors and midwives.[99]

Nang Doy and her four-month-old child, Thao Nga, sit for growth monitoring vaccinations administered by the District Mother and Child outreach team, in Lao People's Democratic Republic.

© UNICEF/UNI76591/Holmes

Benefits of universal health coverage

Sustained progress will also require health systems that are equipped both to deliver quality care across a continuum of services and to reach all women and children, beginning with the most disadvantaged.

The combination of high quality antenatal care, care during labour and around birth and the first week of life, and care for the small and sick newborn are essential to improve child and maternal health outcomes. Effective antenatal care, for example, provides early identification of complications in pregnancy and offers women the micronutrient supplements they need for their own health and normal foetal development. Educated and equipped health workers can deliver obstetric care and essential newborn care, in addition to promoting and supporting breastfeeding, identifying and treating infections, and providing potentially life-saving immunization.

The association between antenatal care, skilled birth attendance and child survival is not automatic *(see Figure 1.7)*, in part because the quality of care provided is highly variable within and among countries. Nevertheless, expanded provision in both of the former has been central to progress in child survival. As the share of neonatal mortality rises as a proportion of total child deaths, the urgency of achieving universal coverage of quality antenatal care and skilled birth attendance increases.

FIGURE 1.7

Antenatal care and skilled attendance at birth save newborn lives

Association between antenatal care (four or more visits), skilled attendance at birth and the neonatal mortality rate

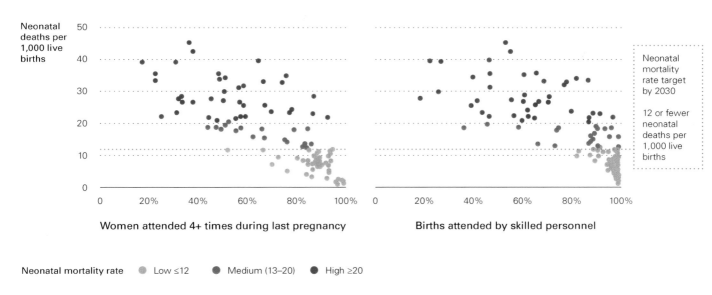

Neonatal mortality rate   ● Low ≤12   ● Medium (13–20)   ● High ≥20

Source: For neonatal mortality rate, UN IGME 2015 estimates. For antenatal care and skilled attendance at birth, UNICEF global databases, 2015, based on MICS, DHS and other national sources.

FIGURE 1.8

In 63 countries, equity in intervention coverage could reduce under-five mortality rates by almost 30 per cent

Impact on the under-five mortality rate of increasing national coverage to the level of the top wealth quintile

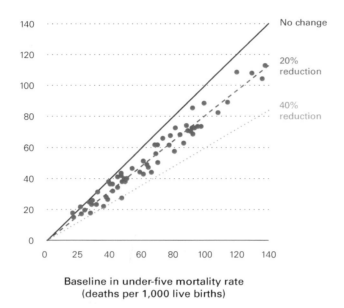

Under-five mortality rate with scaled-up interventions (deaths per 1,000 live births)

Baseline in under-five mortality rate (deaths per 1,000 live births)

Note: Health services in the scaled-up model included interventions such as skilled birth attendance, vitamin A supplementation and vaccinations. The 63 countries represent 88 per cent of global under-five deaths. The LiST analyses were carried out by Adrienne Clermont, Yvonne Tam and Neff Walker at the Institute for International Programs, Johns Hopkins Bloomberg School of Public Health.

Source: Lives Saved Tool (LiST) analysis by Johns Hopkins University, 2015.

Strategies to deliver universal, quality health care by 2030 have to embrace two closely-related goals: expanding coverage *while* narrowing equity gaps. Here again, coverage rates for the poorest 20 per cent of the population must increase much faster than rates for the wealthiest 20 per cent in order to reach universal coverage. In 63 high-mortality countries, scaling up national coverage of health interventions to the level of the wealthiest 20 per cent could prevent one in four under-five deaths and decrease average under-five mortality rates in countries by almost 30 per cent *(see Figure 1.8)*.

Another strategy – set out by the World Health Organization (WHO) and UNICEF in the integrated Global Action Plan for Pneumonia and Diarrhoea – identifies the measures needed to eliminate avoidable deaths from pneumonia and diarrhoea by 2025. Simply scaling up existing interventions would cut deaths by two thirds at a cost of US$6.7 billion under the plan.[100]

In child nutrition, a study of 34 high-burden countries, where 90 per cent of the world's children who suffer stunting live, identified 10 proven interventions with the potential to avert 900,000 under-five deaths. They range from treatment of acute malnutrition to complementary feeding, breastfeeding, and vitamin A and

unicef ✿ 70 YEARS FOR EVERY CHILD

zinc supplementation. The additional annual cost of scaling up present nutrition coverage to meet 90 per cent of the need in the 34 countries would be about US$9.6 billion, according to the study.[101]

As compelling as such estimates are, they sometimes divert attention from the critical importance of strengthening health systems' capacity to deliver services.

Properly trained and motivated health workers are the lifeblood of efficient, equitable and resilient health systems. The interventions needed to diagnose, prevent and treat the causes of child and maternal deaths are not stand-alone technologies. They have to be delivered by skilled community-level health workers, midwives, nurses and doctors.

Chronic shortages of health workers represent major obstacles to accelerated progress. In many countries, health workers are concentrated in urban areas or facilities serving more advantaged populations. They may be reluctant to work in remote areas because of low remuneration, lack of continuing educational opportunities, difficult working conditions, shortages of supplies and equipment, or a lack of social services for their own families.

WHO has estimated that a minimum of 23 health workers for every 10,000 people is required in countries seeking relatively high levels of health system coverage for the basic needs of their populations.[102] Countries falling below this

A health worker administers a dose of oral polio vaccine to a child at the entrance to his home in Baghdad's Sadr City, Iraq.

© UNICEF/UNI199369/Khuzaie

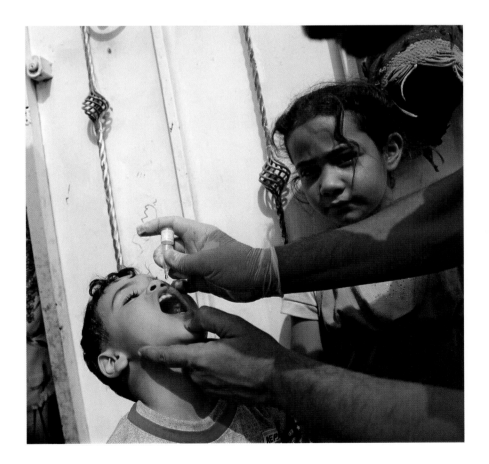

FIGURE 1.9

Many countries do not have enough health providers

Number of physicians, nurses and midwives per 10,000 population and WHO minimum threshold

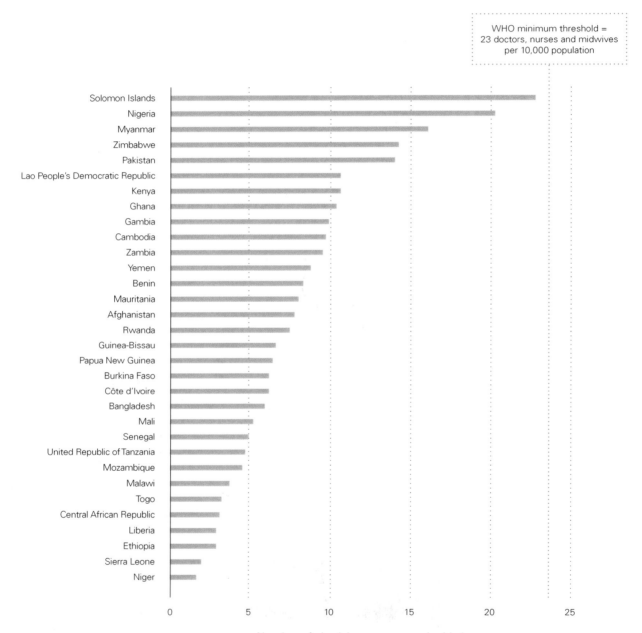

WHO minimum threshold =
23 doctors, nurses and midwives
per 10,000 population

Number of physicians, nurses and midwives

Source: World Health Organization, Global Health Workforce Statistics, 2014.

threshold struggle to provide skilled care at birth, as well as emergency and specialized services for newborn and young children. Most countries in sub-Saharan Africa and many high-mortality countries in South Asia fall well below the threshold *(see Figure 1.9)*.

By 2035, the world will need an additional 12.9 million health workers. Already today, sub-Saharan Africa has a health worker deficit of 1.8 million, and unless there is concerted action, that figure will rise to 4.3 million over the next 20 years as population rises.[103] The additional cost of providing sub-Saharan Africa with just another 1 million community health workers would be US$3.1 billion per year, according to an estimate by the Earth Institute at Columbia University. The return on that investment, in addition to the lives saved and suffering reduced, would be an estimated US$19.4 billion per year from enhanced productivity.[104]

The Ebola crisis in West Africa graphically illustrated the fragility of under-resourced and under-staffed health systems. On the eve of the outbreak, Sierra Leone and Liberia had fewer than three health workers for every 10,000 people.[105] Liberia had approximately 50 doctors for a country of 4.3 million.[106] Deaths among health workers during the crisis depleted the affected countries' already limited number of skilled providers. One of the lessons from the Ebola crisis is that strong health systems are needed not only to contain epidemics and deliver vital interventions, but to help countries and communities become more resilient.

For its part, Indonesia has an overall health worker-to-population ratio close to WHO's recommended level, but health workers are unequally distributed throughout the country. Facilities serving the poor often lack basic amenities and trained staff. Thus, approximately half the women in Maluku and Papua provinces deliver their babies without skilled attendance – more than double the level in Sumatera – and urban women are more than three times more likely than their rural counterparts to have skilled attendance at birth.[107]

Countries with some of the world's lowest health worker-to-population ratios also face equity issues. In Liberia, the ratio of skilled birth attendants to population in the best-covered county is over three times higher than in the county with the least coverage.[108]

An attendant wipes the face of a preterm baby in the Special Care Newborn Unit at Tangail Medical College Hospital, Bangladesh.

© UNICEF/UNI195711/Mawa

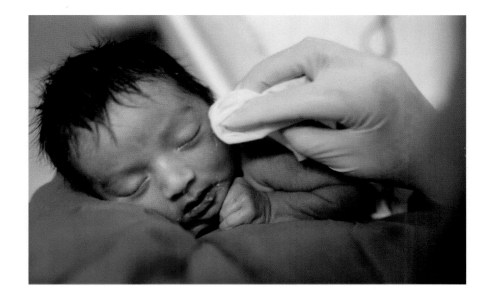

Adequate and equitable financing

By one estimate from 2012, financing a health system equipped to provide a minimal level of essential services on a universal basis would cost about US$86 per capita annually. This is more than double the average level of health system spending in low-income countries.[109]

Even when services are available, formal and informal charges for maternal and child health care create affordability barriers for the poor. Like other obstacles – including distance, time and costs associated with using services, poor awareness, quality concerns, and social and cultural impediments – these charges reduce demand for vital services, often with fatal consequences in the case of maternal, newborn and child health. They deplete assets and trap poor households in cycles of ill health and poverty.

When public health spending does not cover the costs of provision, inadequate service coverage and imposition of user fees invariably hit the poorest households hardest. According to the World Health Report of 2010, *Health Systems Financing: The path to universal coverage*, each year, about 150 million people suffer financial catastrophe while 100 million are forced into poverty as a result of health-related expenses.[110] The risk of impoverishment rises sharply once out-of-pocket payments exceed 15 to 20 per cent of health expenses.[111]

Increased public spending on health is a feature of many of the countries with the best performance in child survival. While there are no hard-and-fast rules, evidence suggests that governments should aim at allocating around 5 per cent of GDP for health spending.[112] Yet many countries with high mortality rates in South Asia spend less than 3 per cent of GDP on health, and in many cases, that spending is skewed towards services that do not reach the poor.[113]

Even with concerted efforts to allocate funding towards health, many of the world's poorest countries would fall short of the US$86 per capita spending target. One exercise estimated a financing gap of about US$74 billion under a

A health worker marks a boy's finger to indicate that he has been vaccinated during a measles immunization campaign, at a health outreach post in Lishiko Village, Lusaka, Zambia.

© UNICEF/UNI91597/Nesbitt

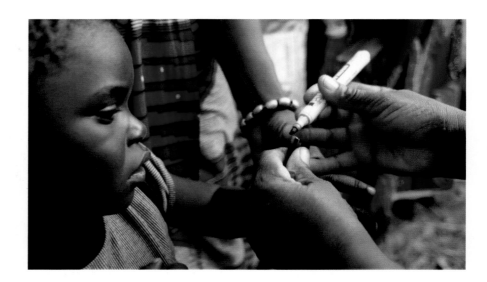

unicef ✿ 70 YEARS FOR EVERY CHILD

scenario in which all low-income countries meet more stringent standards for revenue allocation and health sector financing. While only indicative in nature, this estimate provides a valuable ballpark figure for the additional international public financing that would be needed to bring the 2030 child and maternal health targets within reach.[114]

Targeted schemes to finance services for the poor, exempt them from user fees and provide them with insurance have a mixed record of success. Experience shows that targeted financing often has a negligible impact on service utilization. Financing the entry of poor households into existing national health insurance programmes, which pool risk across populations, has produced more positive results.[115]

Brazil's Family Health Programme, for example, expanded coverage from 10.6 million to 100 million people between 1998 and 2010, with an initial focus on disadvantaged areas. The programme provides access to health care – free at the point of use – to more than 90 per cent of the country's municipalities.[116]

Thailand's Universal Coverage Scheme (UCS) enhanced equity by bringing a large uninsured population under the umbrella of a national programme, greatly reducing 'catastrophic' health payments among the poor and improving

BOX 1.3 BANGLADESH SHOWS THE CHALLENGE OF SUSTAINED PROGRESS IN CHILD SURVIVAL

In recent years, Bangladesh has made solid progress in reducing mortality rates among children under age 5. Part of its success can be traced to the expansion of community-level health interventions. Accelerated progress will depend on expanded and more equitable provision of antenatal care and skilled birth attendance.

Starting from a low base, the country has already achieved a rapid expansion of coverage in both areas. The proportion of babies delivered in health facilities increased from 8 per cent to 37 per cent between 2000 and 2014. Antenatal coverage by skilled providers also rose, from 33 per cent to 64 per cent.

Nevertheless, large disparities remain. The wealth gap in access to skilled antenatal care has declined only marginally. Coverage is 36 per cent for the poorest women and 90 per cent for the wealthiest. The ratio of poor-to-rich women benefitting from skilled birth attendance in 2014 was about one to four, with two of the country's divisions – Sylhet and Barisal – lagging far

behind the rest of the country. And fewer than one third of women received the recommended minimum of four antenatal care visits in 2014.

On a more positive note, Bangladesh has been making progress towards equity in terms of deliveries that take place in health facilities. In 2004, the ratio of poorest-to-richest women delivering in a health facility was 1 to 12. By 2014, the ratio had improved to one to four.

Recognizing that sustained improvements in maternal and child health will require a greater reduction in disparities between different social and economic groups, the government has introduced a range of equity targets for key interventions. The targets form the basis for monitoring coverage in low-income communities, urban slum areas, poor-performing districts and areas with ethnic minorities, such as the Chittagong Hill Tracts in south-eastern Bangladesh. Taken together, they represent a potential pathway to equity for the country's most disadvantaged mothers and children.

Source: National Institute of Population Research and Training (NIPORT), Mitra and Associates, and ICF International, Bangladesh Demographic and Health Survey 2014: Key indicators, Dhaka, Bangladesh, and Rockville, Maryland, USA, 2015.

BOX 1.4 HEALTH EQUITY FUNDS PROVIDE FREE HEALTH CARE TO THE POOR

Cambodia has witnessed extraordinary advances in child survival and other health indicators. Between 2000 and 2015, under-five mortality fell from 108 to 29 deaths per 1,000 live births, one of the most rapid rates of decline in the world. The same period saw a dramatic increase in utilization of child and maternal health facilities. Social insurance provided through the country's Health Equity Funds (HEFs) has played an important role in this success.

HEFs are multi-stakeholder initiatives in which non-governmental organizations reimburse public health facilities for treating poor patients, using a combination of government and donor financing. The mechanism has largely eliminated the practice of charging under-the-counter fees. It has also contributed to improving quality of care by providing cash incentives for staff and facilities to serve patients.

In essence, HEFs are a purchasing mechanism that provides free health care to the poor. As of 2013, they covered more than 2.5 million people in 51 of Cambodia's 81 districts, supporting more than a million health centre consultations.

Studies show that where HEFs operate they are a significant force for inclusion, improving access for the poor and reducing out-of-pocket payments. However, there are limits to what has been achieved. An estimated 40 to 50 per cent of the poor do not use HEFs, perhaps as a result of distance or the quality of care, and those just above the poverty line are excluded.

Source: Kelsall, Tim, and Seiha Heng, 'The Political Economy of Inclusive Healthcare in Cambodia', ESID Working Paper no. 43, 16 December 2014.

BOX 1.5 ELIMINATING MALNUTRITION CAN HELP BREAK THE CYCLE OF UNEQUAL OPPORTUNITY

In 2014, 159 million children under age 5 were stunted. Another 41 million children under age 5 were overweight – and their number is rising. Stunting and other forms of undernutrition reflect societal inequities; stunting can serve as a marker for poverty.

In Africa and Asia, 11 per cent of GNP is lost due to poor nutrition. Eliminating malnutrition in young children has several benefits. It could improve school attainment by at least one year, reduce poverty, empower women and, in turn, break the intergenerational cycle of poverty.

Everyone has a right to food and good nutrition. Realizing that right is critical to fulfilling children's rights, including the right to good health that is a prerequisite to expanded opportunities in life.

That is the principle behind the Scaling Up Nutrition (SUN) movement, which brings together governments, civil society, the United Nations, donors, businesses and scientists to eliminate all forms of malnutrition through nationally-driven processes. SUN countries are working to increase access to affordable and nutritious food, as well as demand for it.

As of March 2016, 56 countries had joined SUN, including the Democratic Republic of the Congo, Ethiopia, Haiti, Kyrgyzstan, Peru and Sri Lanka. This means that SUN has the potential to reach 82.8 million children.

In Peru, the national programme Incluir para Crecer (Inclusion for Growth) focuses on children and pregnant women in the poorest areas with the aim of reducing social inequities and poverty in order to reduce malnutrition and promote growth. Since 2006, stunting has fallen by half – from about 30 per cent in 2004–2006 to 15 per cent in 2014. Stunting prevalence among children from the poorest households declined from 54 per cent to 34 per cent over the same time period.

Source: United Nations Children's Fund, *Improving Child Nutrition: The achievable imperative for global progress*, UNICEF, New York, 2013, and UNICEF global nutrition database, 2016.

unicef ✿ | 70 YEARS FOR EVERY CHILD

access to essential health services.[117] Within a year of its launch, UCS covered 75 per cent of the Thai population, including 18 million previously uninsured people.[118]

In Rwanda, the national health insurance programme, Mutuelle de Santé, covers about 90 per cent of the population and provides free coverage for the very poor. Out-of-pocket spending fell from 28 per cent to 12 per cent of total health expenditures in the programme's first decade.[119] And Cambodia's Health Equity Funds have played a critical role in strengthening both the reach and the equity of the health system in that country *(see Box 1.4)*.

Power in partnerships

Many of the interventions needed for more children to enjoy good health are well known. The challenge is to implement them at scale so that there are enough community health workers, nurses and doctors to link the most disadvantaged people to high-quality services. Failure to mobilize the necessary resources will act as a brake on progress in child survival and health.

The challenge is great, but concrete and practical strategies such as the Every Newborn action plan offer a road map for equitable policy and financing. Movements such as Every Woman Every Child and A Promise Renewed (APR) provide a platform for action, bringing together governments, the private sector, international agencies and campaigners.

The APR movement was launched in June 2012, when the Governments of Ethiopia, India and the United States, in collaboration with UNICEF, convened the Child Survival Call to Action in Washington, D.C. Answering the call, 178 governments – as well as hundreds of civil society, private sector and faith-based organizations – signed a pledge under the APR banner vowing to do everything possible to stop women and children from dying of causes that are easily preventable.

Since then, more than 30 countries have deepened their commitments by launching sharpened national strategies for maternal, newborn and child survival based on APR's core principles: building political commitment, strengthening accountability and mobilizing societies and communities.

Current multilateral partnerships also provide a strong foundation for broadening and deepening cooperation to support national strategies on child and maternal health. One example comes from the GAVI Alliance. In collaboration with global companies involved in pharmaceutical development and supply-chain management, and represented in the International Federation of Pharmaceutical Wholesalers, the Alliance has developed a three-year partnership to immunize hard-to-reach children in 73 countries. Pharmaceutical companies themselves have an important role in developing affordable products to prevent and treat killer diseases, including rotavirus, pneumonia and sepsis.[120]

Effective implementation of the strategies outlined in this chapter will require stepped-up coordination and more robust leadership, both nationally and globally. National strategies to achieve universal health coverage and equitable, quality care for children and their mothers should set clear priorities, specifically, to reach the most disadvantaged groups with life-saving interventions. These strategies will have to include providing trained staff with incentives to work in hard-to-reach areas.

A fair chance for girls – End child marriage

By Angélique Kidjo, Award-winning artist and UNICEF Goodwill Ambassador

Child marriage exemplifies how the world's poorest girls bear the heaviest burden of disadvantage, especially those living in marginalized communities in rural areas of sub-Saharan Africa and South Asia, where the practice is most common.

Girls who are married have their childhoods stolen from them. I've seen this, and how it hurts them.

When I was growing up in Cotonou, Benin, several of my girlfriends from primary school were married at a very young age. Some I never even saw again – their married lives took them far away. Others I met up with later on, but they weren't the same. Their joy and enthusiasm were gone. They were no longer free to

act like children, but instead were forced to be grown-ups. I noticed they carried a sense of shame, a sharp awareness that they were different from the rest of us.

While there has been progress in reducing child marriage, it is uneven. Girls from the poorest households – and those living in rural areas – face twice the risk of being married before turning 18 as girls from the richest households or those living in urban areas.

With no progress, almost 950 million women will have been married as children by 2030, up from more than 700 million today. And by 2050, almost half of the world's child brides will be African.

The costs are too high – for the girls whose rights are violated when they are married, and for the societies that need those girls to grow up into productive, empowered adults.

Married girls are among the world's most vulnerable people. When their education is cut short, girls lose the chance to gain the skills and knowledge to secure a good job and provide for themselves and their families. They are socially isolated. As I observed among my former schoolmates who were forced to get married, the consciousness of their isolation is in itself painful.

Subordinate to their husbands and families, married girls are more vulnerable to domestic violence, and not in a position to make decisions about safe sex and family planning – which puts them at high risk of sexually transmitted infections, including HIV, and of pregnancy and childbearing before their bodies are fully mature. Already risky pregnancies become even riskier, as married girls are less likely to get adequate medical care. During delivery, mothers who are still children are at higher risk of potentially disabling complications, like obstetric fistula, and both they and their babies are more likely to die.

By robbing girls of their potential, child marriage robs families, communities and nations of the contributions these girls might have made as women. Child marriage hampers countries' efforts to improve the health of mothers and children, fight malnutrition and keep children in school. When girls are married as children, they cannot help but pass on poverty, low education and poor health – into which they themselves have been trapped – to the next generation.

Child marriage may seem like an intractable problem. It happens because societies often place a lesser value on girls – so they don't get the same chances as their brothers – and because poverty and other forms of disadvantage, like low levels of education, further constrain their opportunities, making marriage seem like the best option to secure a girl's future.

But there are proven strategies that can change girls' lives, preserve their childhoods and empower them to make better futures for themselves and their societies. These involve increasing girls' access to education, empowering girls with knowledge and skills, educating parents and communities, increasing economic

incentives and supporting families, and strengthening and enforcing laws and policies that set the minimum age of marriage at 18 for both girls and boys.

Education is a critical part of the solution. Girls who have little or no education are up to six times more likely to be married as children than girls who have secondary schooling. When a girl is in school, those around her are more likely to see her as a child, rather than as a woman ready to be a wife and mother. And the experience of going to school is empowering for girls, enabling them to develop skills and knowledge, and to forge social networks that equip them to communicate and stand up for their interests. Educated girls are better able to contribute to their countries' growth and development, and also to the prosperity and well-being of their future families.

Fifteen million girls are married as children every year, and the sheer numbers underline the importance of investing in solutions that can have an impact at scale, to speed up progress in ending the practice. Focused investments to reach and empower poor and marginalized girls through health, education, social protection and other systems can create alternative pathways for girls and their families.

No less critical is the slow, patient work of changing social norms. These kinds of long-lasting, fundamental changes come from within communities, and they depend on engaging both mothers and fathers in finding solutions that make a difference in their daughters' lives.

When child marriage is a thing of the past, we will have put an end to an inequity that takes away girls' fundamental rights and steals their childhoods. More girls and women will be able to make the most of their lives and give their best to their families, communities and societies – which will go a long way towards breaking intergenerational cycles of poverty and strengthening communities and nations. Ending child marriage unlocks possibilities that can transform life for girls and yield benefits for us all.

Florence, 14, at the Hope Secondary School, in Kinshasa, the Democratic Republic of the Congo.

© UNICEF/UNI199292/Dubourthoumieu

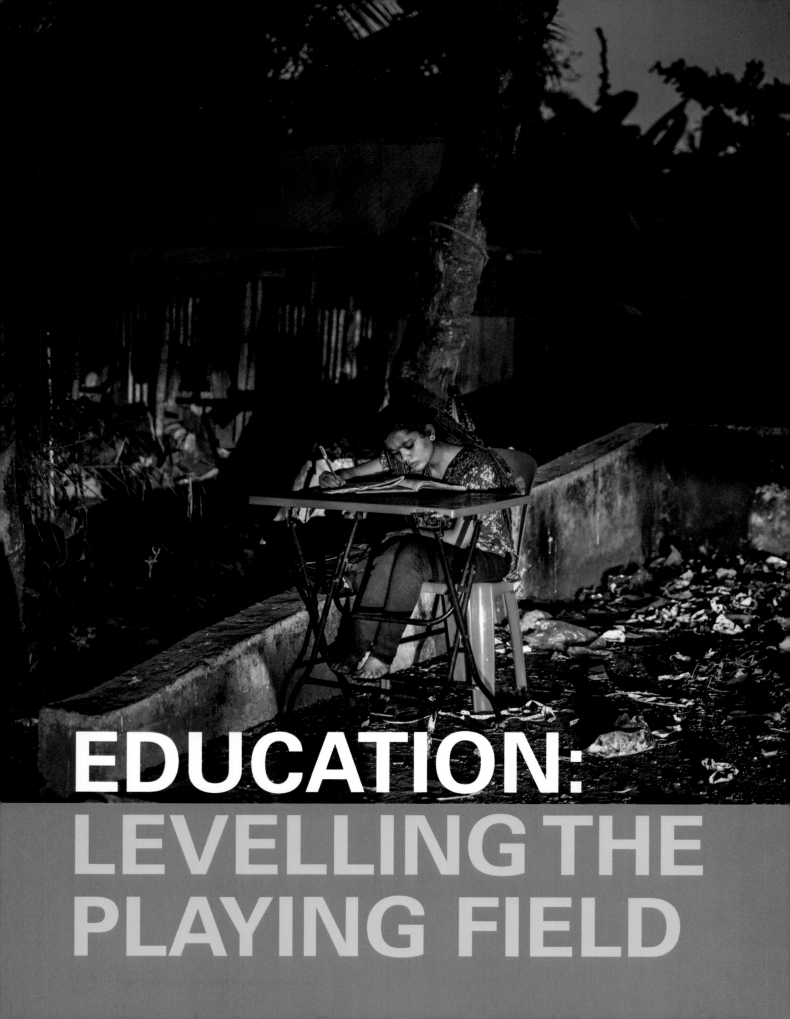

EDUCATION:
LEVELLING THE PLAYING FIELD

CHAPTER 2

Education:

Levelling the playing field

Quality education has the power to end intergenerational cycles of inequity, improving the lives of children and the societies in which they live. Education can provide children with the knowledge and skills they need to succeed in life. It is associated with increased incomes, reduced poverty and improved health. But for education to play this role, it must begin with early childhood development and continue with quality learning opportunities that provide all children, especially the most disadvantaged, with a fair chance to thrive.

Jhuma Akhter, 14, does her homework under the glow of a lamp post outside her home in Khulna, Bangladesh.

© UNICEF/UN016303/Gilbertson VII Photo

In rich and poor countries around the globe, education has long served as a great leveller of opportunity because it helps people realize their potential and contribute to their communities and the world. Good education increases knowledge, sparks innovation, builds skills that drive growth and prosperity, and fosters inclusive societies. For generations, quality and equitable education has provided children with a pathway out of deprivation. What has been true for the prospects of individual children has also held true for the future of nations.

And yet, millions of children around the world are still denied their right to education because of factors they do not control – factors such as poverty, gender, ethnicity, disability or geographical location. Armed conflict, natural disasters and the impacts of climate change also deprive children of the chance to go to school and learn. In addition, when public resources are not allocated on the basis of evidence pointing to the greatest need, education systems can entrench inequities rather than dismantle them.

This chapter will make the case that two challenges – lack of access to education and deficits in learning outcomes – must be overcome for education to fulfil its role as an agent of equity. To overcome these challenges, countries will be best served if they offer comprehensive early childhood care and learning opportunities, and if they focus on making the fastest progr furthest behind. This approach has the potential to narrow t outcomes between the richest and poorest children by 203

Access to education – from the start

The Convention on the Rights of the Child recognizes that every child has the right to go to school and learn. That right begins in early childhood, which is one reason why the Sustainable Development Goals (SDGs) call on governments to "ensure that all girls and boys have access to quality early childhood development, care and pre-primary education."

For education to fulfil its role as a catalyst for equity, it must begin with early childhood interventions that help mitigate the disadvantages faced by children born into poor and non-literate environments. Investment in quality early childhood care and education produces a double benefit: It is both fair and efficient.

One key to success is the provision of comprehensive interventions that cross development sectors to include nutrition, health, and water, sanitation and hygiene practices. This kind of holistic approach also takes child protection into account and focuses on the quality of care provided to infants and young children.

There are indications that a holistic approach can provide success. Comprehensive interventions that combine nutrition, protection and stimulation have been shown to produce marked gains in young children's cognitive development.[121] Improved nutrition and preparedness for learning translate into improved education outcomes – which, in turn, improve children's health and can raise their earning levels as adults. A long-term study in Jamaica found a 42 per cent increase in average adult earnings associated with early childhood stimulation.[122] Research in the United States puts the returns on early childhood investments at 7 to 10 per cent a year.[123]

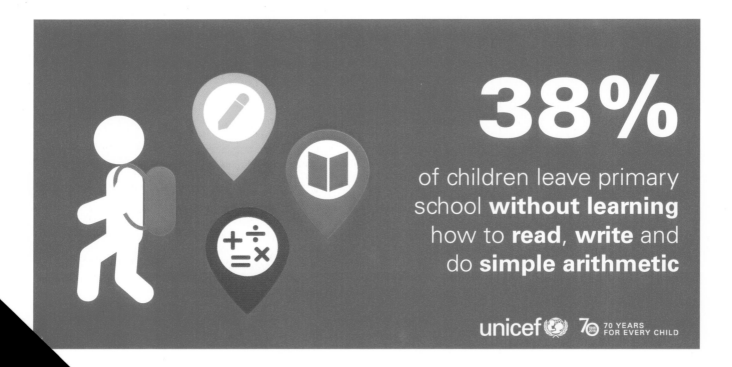

38% of children leave primary school **without learning** how to **read, write** and do **simple arithmetic**

unicef 70 YEARS FOR EVERY CHILD

Lunchtime at Kotingli Basic
School, Northern Region,
Ghana.

© UNICEF/UN04349/Logan

Efforts to protect and expand the right to education – starting from early childhood
– have been under way for decades. In many cases, they have led to great
success. But school enrolment figures indicate that the pace of progress is in
jeopardy. Since 2011, the global number of children who do not attend school has
increased.[124]

In most countries, less than half of children attend early childhood education
programmes.[125] About 124 million children and adolescents are denied
opportunities to enter and complete school – including around 59 million children
of primary school age *(see Figure 2.1)* and 65 million young adolescents of lower
secondary school age, according to figures from 2013.[126] More than half of the
primary-school-aged children who are not in school live in sub-Saharan Africa.[127] In
addition, gender gaps in enrolment continue to be a problem.

School enrolment trends do not bode well for achieving SDG 4, which, in addition
to an emphasis on early childhood development, calls for primary and secondary
education for all children in the next 15 years. Indeed, if current trends persist, by
2030:

- There could be over 60 million primary-school-aged children still out of school.[128]

- Low-income countries will have primary and lower secondary completion
  rates of about 76 per cent and 50 per cent, respectively.[129]

- Lower-middle-income countries will have completion rates of nearly 92 per
  cent for primary education and more than 80 per cent for lower secondary
  education *(see Figure 2.2)*.[130]

Also based on current trends, low-income countries in 2030 will not be on track to
achieve universal primary and lower secondary school completion until around the
turn of the next century.[131]

Charting a path towards universal access to primary and secondary schooling, along with effective learning for all, begins with identifying the children left behind. Those excluded from learning opportunities often face multiple kinds of disadvantage. Poor girls living in rural areas usually have the least access to education.[132] Children also face disadvantages and lack of services due to discrimination based on ethnic origin or disability.

Some out-of-school children never enter a classroom. Many children – especially those from the poorest households – arrive on the first day unprepared to succeed in school.[133] As they progress through the education system, some drop out well before completing primary school. For many others, the transition from primary into lower secondary education, or from lower to upper secondary school, remains an insurmountable hurdle *(see Figure 2.3)*.

FIGURE 2.1

More than half of the 59 million out-of-school children live in sub-Saharan Africa

Number and percentage of primary-school-aged children out of school for UNICEF regions for 2000 and 2013

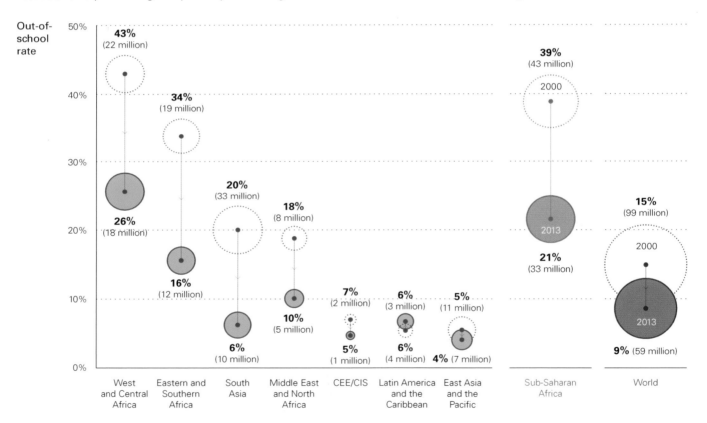

Bubble size indicates number of out-of school children

Source: UNICEF analysis based on data from the UNESCO Institute for Statistics global database, 2015.

FIGURE 2.2

If current trends persist, the world is off-track to reach primary and secondary education for all by 2030

Projected completion rates by country income group and level, 2010–2100

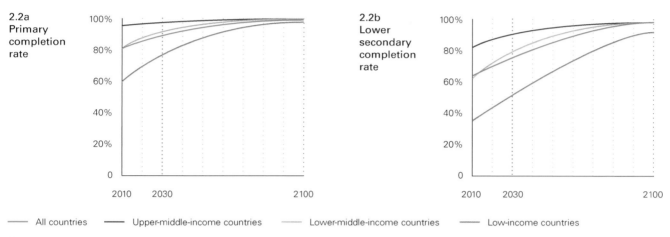

2.2a
Primary completion rate

2.2b
Lower secondary completion rate

—— All countries   —— Upper-middle-income countries   —— Lower-middle-income countries   —— Low-income countries

Note: Projections are based on current trends.

Source: United Nations Educational, Cultural and Scientific Organization, *EFA Global Monitoring Report*, 'How long will it take to achieve universal primary and secondary education?', Technical background note for the Framework for Action on the post-2015 education agenda, UNESCO, Paris, May 2015.

FIGURE 2.3

Many girls and boys drop out as they transition through education levels

Gross enrolment ratio (GER) in pre-primary, primary and secondary education in five UNICEF regions and sub-Saharan Africa, 2013

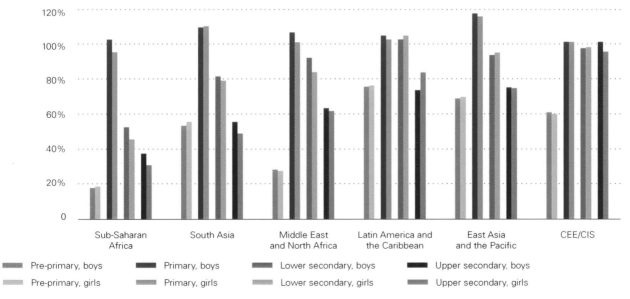

▮ Pre-primary, boys   ▮ Primary, boys   ▮ Lower secondary, boys   ▮ Upper secondary, boys

▮ Pre-primary, girls   ▮ Primary, girls   ▮ Lower secondary, girls   ▮ Upper secondary, girls

Source: UNESCO Institute for Statistics global database, 2015.

There are multiple reasons for disadvantage in education. In China, for example, migration from rural districts to urban centres affects whether children have access to education entitlements.[134] If they are living in cities but remain registered in rural areas, their entitlements may be severely limited.

Poverty is also an important part of the equation. The impact of poverty on education begins early, because the poorest children in any country are the least likely to attend early childhood education programmes.[135] And the disadvantages continue. In sub-Saharan Africa, nearly 60 per cent of 20- to 24-year-olds from the poorest fifth of the population have been through fewer than four years of schooling. By contrast, only 15 per cent in the richest quintile have been in school for less than four years.[136] In Egypt and the United Republic of Tanzania, being born poor nearly doubles the risk of missing out on basic education relative to the national average. For poor women in both countries, the risk is even higher.[137]

In recent years, wealth-based disparities in attendance rates have narrowed in many countries as primary school attendance has increased.[138] However, while children from the poorest households are now more likely to enter school, they are also more likely than their more advantaged peers to drop out.[139]

Pakistan has more than 5.6 million out-of-school children of primary school age.[140] There are also large wealth-related gaps in school attendance and retention *(see Figure 2.4)*. Children in the richest 20 per cent of the population get nearly nine more years of schooling, on average, than children in the poorest 20 per cent. This wealth gap is magnified by gender disadvantages among the poorest girls and by regional disparities. While Pakistan is making national progress in primary school completion, some groups – notably poor rural girls – have been left behind.[141]

Education pathway analysis helps to identify when disparities intensify as children progress in school. In Nigeria, disparities begin early. According to 2013 data, less than a third of poor Nigerian children between 15 and 17 years of age had entered primary school at the correct time, though nearly all of the children from richer households had *(see Figure 2.5)*. The gap continues to widen at the start of each level of education, as greater proportions of poor children drop out. By the start of upper secondary education, only 7 per cent of poor children enter school, compared to 80 per cent of wealthier children.

> EDUCATION IS NOT JUST ABOUT GETTING THROUGH SCHOOL; LEARNING IS WHAT COUNTS.

Equity and learning outcomes

Education is not just about getting through school; *learning* is what counts. But assessments of the knowledge and skills that children acquire in school indicate that education systems have failed millions of children. Worldwide, nearly 250 million children of primary school age – well over one third of the 650 million children in this age group – do not master basic literacy and numeracy, according to an estimate from 2013.[142] Some 130 million of them spend at least four years in school and still lack these skills.

Learning deficits begin early, sometimes even before primary school. In 28 countries or areas with available data, less than half of children between the ages of 3 and nearly 5 were developmentally on track in literacy and numeracy in 2014.[143]

The lack of learning in children's early years raises concerns at many levels. In early childhood and primary school, children acquire the foundational skills that allow them to develop problem-solving capabilities, flourish in secondary education and later succeed in employment markets.

unicef ● 70 YEARS FOR EVERY CHILD

FIGURE 2.4

In Pakistan, the level of education achieved depends on gender, residence and wealth

Average number of years of schooling of youth aged 20–24, 2013

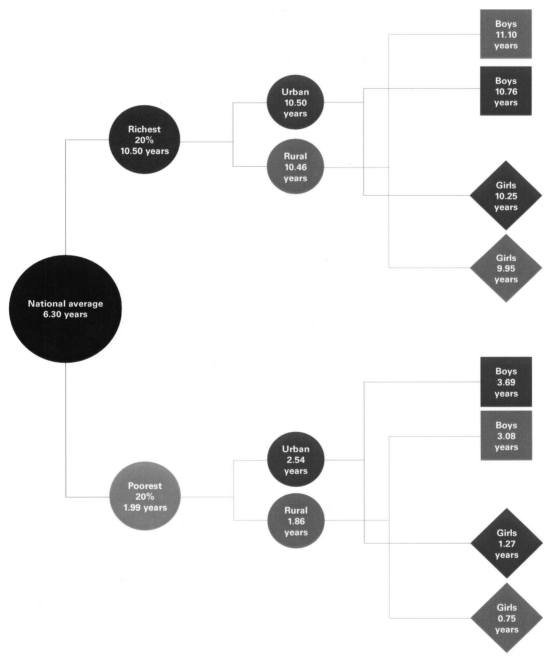

Note: Chart is not drawn to scale.

Source: UNESCO, Global Education Monitoring Report, World Inequality Database on Education (WIDE), 2013 DHS data.

FIGURE 2.5

Wealth, gender and residence affect education in Nigeria

Educational attainment of upper-secondary-school-aged adolescents by sex, residence and wealth quintile, 2013

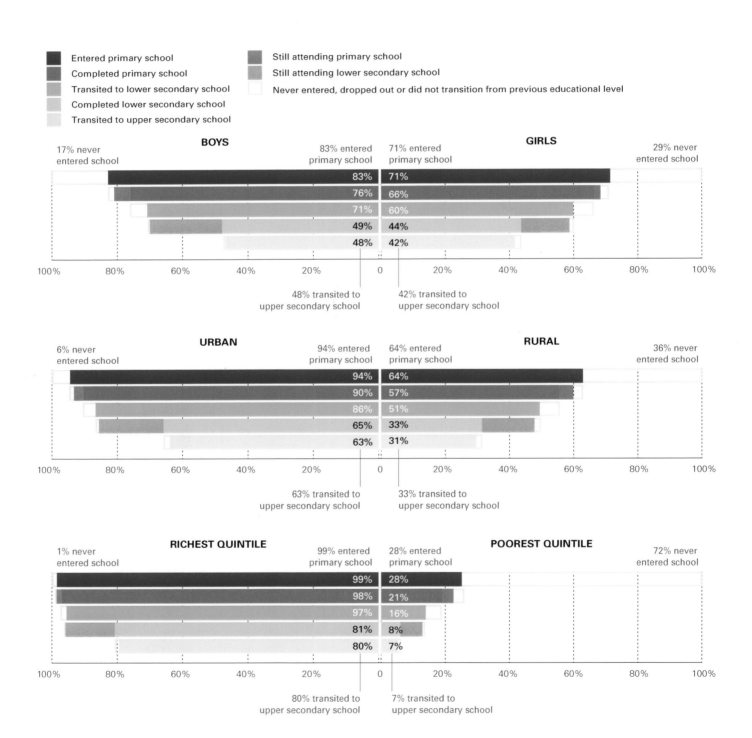

- ■ Entered primary school
- ■ Completed primary school
- ■ Transited to lower secondary school
- ■ Completed lower secondary school
- ■ Transited to upper secondary school

- ■ Still attending primary school
- ■ Still attending lower secondary school

- □ Never entered, dropped out or did not transition from previous educational level

BOYS

17% never entered school

83% entered primary school

| 83% |
| 76% |
| 71% |
| 49% |
| 48% |

48% transited to upper secondary school

GIRLS

71% entered primary school

29% never entered school

| 71% |
| 66% |
| 60% |
| 44% |
| 42% |

42% transited to upper secondary school

URBAN

6% never entered school

94% entered primary school

| 94% |
| 90% |
| 86% |
| 65% |
| 63% |

63% transited to upper secondary school

RURAL

64% entered primary school

36% never entered school

| 64% |
| 57% |
| 51% |
| 33% |
| 31% |

33% transited to upper secondary school

RICHEST QUINTILE

1% never entered school

99% entered primary school

| 99% |
| 98% |
| 97% |
| 81% |
| 80% |

80% transited to upper secondary school

POOREST QUINTILE

28% entered primary school

72% never entered school

| 28% |
| 21% |
| 16% |
| 8% |
| 7% |

7% transited to upper secondary school

unicef ✿ ⁊⃝ 70 YEARS FOR EVERY CHILD

Experiences at home set the stage for success in learning. While more than half of children aged 3 to nearly 5 in most countries are engaged by an adult in learning activities at home, less than half have access to three or more books at home.[144] Learning outcomes are also tied to the multiple kinds of advantages and disadvantages that children face. Evidence shows that poverty often leaves children with deficits in learning outcomes *(see Figure 2.6)*. Starting early in life, even before reaching age 5, children from poor households are more likely than their more affluent peers to present developmental delays in literacy and numeracy.[145] In India, being born into the poorest households carries a learning 'penalty' relative to children from the richest households. The penalty widens between ages 7 and 11, reaching a 19 per cent gap in students' ability to subtract.[146]

When children face wealth-related disadvantages and have parents who did not attend school, there are powerful multiplier effects – especially for young girls. By age 11 in India, girls and boys who come from the richest homes and have educated parents enjoy a huge academic advantage over other children. The most advantaged boys and girls are about six times more likely to learn basic reading and mathematics skills than girls from the poorest households whose parents were not educated.[147]

FIGURE 2.6

Wealth-based gaps in basic math skills start early and persist over time

Percentage of children able to subtract, by age, 2012

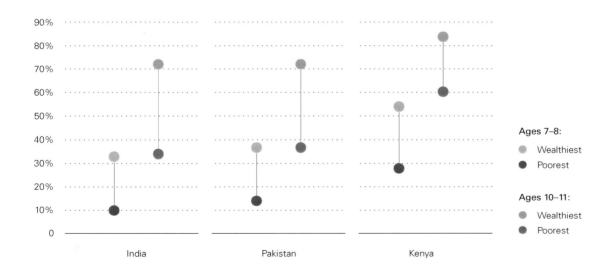

Note: While Indian and Kenyan children should have completed Grade 2 by age 8, Pakistani children should have completed Grade 3 by age 8.

Source: ASER India, ASER Pakistan and Uwezo Kenya survey data from 2012, in Rose, Pauline, and Benjamin Alcott, *How can education systems become equitable by 2030?: DFID think pieces – Learning and equity*, United Kingdom Department for International Development, London, August 2015.

BOX 2.1 THE DEVELOPING BRAIN: AN EARLY WINDOW OF OPPORTUNITY FOR LEARNING

Long before a child enters the classroom, inequities can create a lasting imprint on the architecture of the brain.

Recent research on brain development casts new light on the formative influence of early childhood experience. In the first few years of life, a child's brain creates 700 to 1,000 new neural connections every second, a pace that later diminishes. These early connections set the foundation on which later connections are built.

The new research shows that nutrition, health care and interaction between children and their caregivers can help with brain development in early childhood. Conversation, repeating and connecting words in meaningful contexts, and early exposure to literacy through reading and play are all positively associated with language skills.

Conversely, frequent exposure to chronically stressful events in infancy, including nutritional deprivation and violence, can affect children by damaging neurons in areas involved in learning and emotional development. In other words, these deprivations affect how the brain develops. Negative experiences in a child's life often manifest themselves later as difficulties with learning, emotional development and management of anxieties.

Because the first years of a child's life affect brain development so significantly, early childhood offers a critical window of opportunity to break intergenerational cycles of inequity. Early childhood care, protection and stimulation can jumpstart brain development, strengthen children's ability to learn, help them develop psychological resilience and allow them to adapt to change.

Early interventions can even affect future earnings. Research has shown, for example, that preventing undernutrition in early childhood leads to an increase in hourly earnings of at least 20 per cent later in a child's life.

Source: The World Bank, World Development Report 2015: Mind, society, and behavior, Washington, D.C., 2015, Chapter 5. Center on the Developing Child at Harvard University, 'Brain Architecture', <http://developingchild.harvard.edu/science/key-concepts/brain-architecture>, accessed 15 March 2016. Lake, Anthony, and Margaret Chan, 'Putting science into practice for early child development', The Lancet, vol. 385, no. 9980, 2014, pp. 1816–1817. International Food Policy Research Institute, Global Nutrition Report 2014: Actions and accountability to accelerate the world's progress on nutrition, Washington, D.C., 2014.

Although evidence is still limited and fragmented, a growing body of research appears to validate this pattern of substantial differences in key learning indicators between children from the poorest and richest households. Research from five countries in Latin America finds large wealth-related gaps on children's standardized test scores for language development. The gaps are evident by age 3, and there is no evidence of recovery once children enter school.[148]

The deficits continue as children progress through school. In Latin America, a region-wide assessment showed that more than one quarter of third-grade students were unable to recognize basic phrases or locate information in a simple text.[149] In India's rural schools, a 2014 study showed that just under half of children in fifth grade were able to read a basic second-grade text. In arithmetic, half of fifth graders could not subtract two-digit numbers, and only about one quarter could do basic division.[150]

The same issues arise in other countries. In Uganda, an enrolment success story, just over half of the children in Grade 5 were able to read a story at Grade 2 level, according to the results of a 2012 assessment.[151] In Kenya, a third of children in Grade 5 could not perform Grade 2 numeracy tasks. About 10 per cent of students in Grade 8 were unable to perform these tasks, according to a 2012 assessment.[152]

unicef ◆   70 YEARS FOR EVERY CHILD

And at the secondary level, international student achievement tests point to desperately low levels of learning in many low- and middle-income countries. In the most recent Programme for International Student Assessment (PISA), two thirds or more of secondary school students in Argentina, Brazil, Colombia, Indonesia, Jordan, Peru, Qatar and Tunisia were performing below Level 2, a marker of baseline proficiency in math. Less than 1 per cent were performing at the top two levels. In comparison, an average of 23 per cent of students in the high-income Organisation for Economic Co-operation and Development (OECD) countries were low-achieving, and 13 per cent performed at the top level.[153]

Evidence from Latin America underscores the interaction between inequity and low levels of learning achievement. Research on the 2012 PISA scores by the Inter-American Development Bank found that the average gap between the poorest and richest students of the same age in the region was equivalent to two years of schooling.[154]

Such failures in learning have repercussions for children's futures and for national prosperity. Many education systems fail to teach children the skills they need to become productively employed adults and contribute to national social development and economic growth. The costs of misalignment between skills and jobs are visible in many parts of the world.

AROUND ONE IN FIVE YOUNG PEOPLE IN OECD COUNTRIES DO NOT COMPLETE SECONDARY EDUCATION.

According to the International Labour Organization, the share of undereducated young workers in low-income economies is triple that of the share in upper-middle-income economies. In sub-Saharan Africa, three in five young workers do not have the level of education needed for their jobs.[155] Employer surveys in the Middle East and North Africa indicate a pervasive disconnect between the skills learned in school and those demanded by modern business.[156] That mismatch is one of the reasons for the persistently high levels of unemployment among educated youth in the region, and it is an issue facing young people worldwide.

As the high-level Commission for Quality Education for All in Latin America has summarized the problem: "Without significant improvements in learning levels, the rising levels of schooling will hardly turn into the improvements in quality of life to which Latin American citizens aspire."[157]

High-income countries also face learning challenges. The growth in the number of children with access to education in OECD countries has resulted in 80 per cent of young people achieving upper secondary qualifications and a quarter gaining tertiary education.[158] However, around one in five young people in OECD countries do not complete secondary education and have to make the transition to adulthood facing the prospect of lower wages, less secure employment and marginalization.[159] This education gap is an increasingly powerful determinant of wider inequalities in wealth and opportunity, hampering the development of more inclusive societies.[160]

For governments, addressing the problems at the source – within education systems – is the most cost-effective way to make sure that children and young people develop the skills and competencies they need. Efforts to narrow the learning gaps are under way. In Tunisia, for example, the government has embarked on a major reform process to improve learning outcomes for children in school and on a comprehensive programme for out-of-school children.[161]

At the same time, many young people are living with the consequences of the system's past failures. In 2012, UNESCO's *Global Education Monitoring Report* found that 200 million 15- to 24-year-olds had left school without basic skills. Tackling this backlog will require investment in second-chance education and skills training for adolescents and young adults through partnerships between governments and the private sector.[162]

Education in emergencies and protracted crises

Increasingly, complex emergencies and protracted crises are impeding the right to education. These emergencies do not just temporarily interrupt children's lives and educations, they close doors on education for the length of a childhood, or even a lifetime. Though an armed conflict, epidemic or natural disaster can devastate the life of any child, the poorest and most disadvantaged children are the most vulnerable.

Humanitarian emergencies and protracted crises can disrupt education. An estimated 75 million children aged 3 to 18 in 35 countries are in desperate need of education, according to a recent report. Of these children, 17 million are refugees, internally displaced or part of another population of concern *(see Box 2.2)*.[163] Notably, girls in conflict-affected contexts are 2.5 times more likely to be out of school than girls in more peaceful settings.[164]

Two boys carry chopped firewood in Kafar Batna village in Damascus, the Syrian Arab Republic.

© UNICEF/UN06854/Al Shami

In conflict situations, education is often under fire either directly or indirectly, as conflict damages schools and endangers the lives of teachers and students.[165] A study by the Global Coalition to Protect Education from Attack documented thousands of assaults on students, teachers and institutions in 70 countries in a five-year period ending in 2013. The incidents included bombings, kidnappings, illegal arrests, torture and killings of students and teachers.[166]

unicef ✪ 70 YEARS FOR EVERY CHILD

Specific examples are numerous. In Nigeria, the armed gro
abducted hundreds of women and girls in major attacks in
2012 and 2014, the group killed 314 children in schools in
Nigeria.[167] From the start of the group's insurgency to the end of
than 600 teachers had been killed and more than 1,200 schools damaged or
destroyed.[168]

Teachers and children also have been attacked, kidnapped and killed in Yemen,
the Syrian Arab Republic and many other countries. In 2014 alone, there were
163 attacks on schools in Afghanistan; nine schools were attacked in the Central
African Republic; and there were 67 reported attacks on schools in Iraq.[169]

Check for conference transcripts

BOX 2.2 THE DESTRUCTIVE IMPACT OF ARMED CONFLICT ON EDUCATION

Conflict has immediate and often life-threatening effects on children. It also holds back the development of the education systems that should be functioning to help them reach their full potential. Recent experience in the Syrian Arab Republic has shown how conflict can halt and even reverse progress on education.

In 2010, before the current crisis began, nearly all of the country's primary-school-aged children and 90 per cent of lower-secondary-school-aged children were enrolled in school. Five years later, some 2.1 million children aged 5 to 17 in the Syrian Arab Republic were not in school. In addition, about 700,000 school-age Syrian refugee children – half of the school-age refugee population – were out of school in neighbouring states.

More than half of the nearly 4.6 million refugees who have fled the conflict are children, many now facing a future without the hope that comes with education. Neighbouring states have struggled to cope with this influx. With support from donors, the Government of Lebanon has introduced an innovative system that accommodates large numbers of out-of-school refugee children by creating a two-shift system in public schools. About 150,000 refugee children have entered Lebanon's public school system in this way.

Yet there is still a large gap between the education needs of Syrian refugee children and the learning opportunities available to them. The language of instruction is a major factor hindering their ability to continue their education. In addition, in most countries where refugees settle, Syrian teachers are not employed in the public system.

But it is not just the Syrian Arab Republic where education is interrupted by conflict. In Gaza, nearly 500,000 children were unable to return to classrooms at the start of the 2014/15 school year because of damage to school infrastructure. In Yemen, conflict had closed thousands of schools and pushed 1.8 million children out of education as of August 2015, adding to the 1.6 million who were out of school before the violence there escalated. In the Sudan, war that has lasted decades in some areas has deprived more than 3 million children of an education. Armed conflicts in the Central African Republic, the Democratic Republic of the Congo and South Sudan have stalled progress in areas already marked by chronic deficits in education.

In DRC, where conflict has been ongoing since 1993, more than 3.5 million children of primary school age are out of school. Even so, recent data show primary school attendance has been increasing steadily – from 51 per cent in 2001 to 87 per cent in 2013. Meanwhile, the gaps in attendance between boys and girls, children living in urban versus rural areas, and those from the richest and poorest households have all been narrowing.[170]

Source: UNESCO Institute for Statistics and United Nations Children's Fund, *Fixing the Broken Promise of Education for All: Findings from the Global Initiative on Out-of-School Children*, UIS, Montreal, 2015, p. 49. United Nations Children's Fund, *Syria Crisis Education Strategic Paper*, London 2016 Conference paper, UNICEF, New York, January 2016, p. 1. United Nations High Commissioner for Refugees, 'Education Sector Situation Analysis' for November and December 2015, found on the Syria Regional Refugee Response website, <http://data.unhcr.org/syrianrefugees/country.php?id=122>, accessed 12 January 2016. United Nations Children's Fund Regional Office for the Middle East and North Africa, *Education under Fire: How conflict in the Middle East is depriving children of their schooling*, UNICEF, Amman, 3 September 2015, p. 6. Global Partnership for Education, Democratic Republic of Congo page, <http://www.globalpartnership.org/country/democratic-republic-of-congo>, accessed 8 April 2016; *MICS 2001 and 2010; DHS 2007 and 2013–2014.*

Conflict that drives children and families from their homes often leads to a state of persistent displacement. At the end of 2014, half of all refugees had been in exile for more than 10 years, and at least half of internally displaced people had a high probability of being uprooted for three years or longer.[171] For them, displacement has become the new normal.

But conflict is not the only cause of protracted crisis in children's lives. Climate change poses another growing danger, intensifying the risks associated with drought and floods. Climate-related disasters threaten children's lives and disrupt their education, creating conditions that leave them at increased risk of abuse, neglect, trafficking and child labour.[172]

These disasters can also inflict extensive damage on school infrastructure. When Cyclone Pam struck Vanuatu in 2015, for example, it affected about 80 per cent of schools. Some were damaged and others were turned into evacuation centres.[173] The problem exists throughout the Pacific region, where many schools in small island states are unavoidably located near coastal areas. Throughout the region, climate change and weather-related emergencies have hindered efforts to provide children with good-quality learning opportunities.[174]

Despite the challenges of conflict and climate change, education accounts for a small share of requests for humanitarian aid – and only a small fraction of those requests are funded. Less than 2 per cent of the funds raised by humanitarian appeals went to education.[175] This figure suggests that education is considered a low priority in humanitarian contexts, a viewpoint that is curiously out of step with the aspirations of parents and children affected by crises.[176] For them, a return to school can help restore a sense of security, normalcy and, above all, hope for a better future.

The deeper problem is that aid mechanisms are poorly aligned with real needs. It is not possible to finance education for children facing the prospect of long-term displacement through short-term (and invariably under-funded) emergency appeals. Rapid response has to be coupled with long-term financing. A holistic approach that bridges the traditional divide between development expertise and humanitarian response is required. By linking humanitarian and development efforts, education programmes in emergency or post-emergency contexts can provide children with the chance to bounce back and lead productive, peaceful and fulfilling lives.

unicef 🙂   70 YEARS FOR EVERY CHILD

Benefits of quality education

The inequities that deny children the right to quality education from early childhood through adolescence can trap young people in low-skilled, poorly paid, insecure employment, which holds back economic growth and fuels inequality.

Changing demographics underscore the importance of educating all children, especially those who have been excluded. In the next 15 years, the population of 15- to 24-year-olds worldwide will increase by nearly 100 million. The largest share of this cohort will be in Asia and Africa.[177]

If current trends continue through 2030, the poor-quality education and high levels of inequity in access to school compromising young people's future employment prospects and their countries' economic growth can also threaten stability and social cohesion. Indeed, in many low- and middle-income countries, growing disparities in education among different social groups already have increased the probability of conflict.[178]

Conversely, if this growing population enters adulthood with the skills needed to build secure livelihoods and make positive choices, the effects could be socially and economically transformative.[179]

Good quality and equitable education serves to unlock opportunity and undo intergenerational cycles of inequity: On average, each additional year of education a child receives increases her or his adult earnings by about 10 per cent. And for each additional year of schooling completed, on average, by young adults in a country, that country's poverty rate falls by 9 per cent.[180] The returns on education are highest in low-income and lower-middle-income countries.[181]

Some of the highest returns of all are associated with education for girls. Education empowers girls later in life to seek better health care during pregnancy, in childbirth and during their children's early years. The results are reflected in lower levels of under-five mortality, reduced fertility, improved health-care practices and later marriage and childbearing.[182] Children – especially girls – born to educated mothers are more likely to attend school, resulting in a cycle of opportunity that extends across generations. There is also evidence that education is associated with higher levels of civic engagement and participation in political processes.[183]

Education can also be a tool in the fight against child rights violations such as child labour, though stopping such violations will demand action on many fronts. Historically, enforcement of compulsory education has provided a powerful impetus towards ending child labour. In today's rich countries, that was a critical part of the largely successful effort to limit the practice in the late nineteenth and early twentieth centuries.[184] Backed by the right mix of anti-poverty measures and strategies for improving the quality of learning opportunities, compulsory education could play a similar role in the struggle to eliminate child labour in the low- and lower-middle-income countries of the twenty-first century.

The benefits of education are not solely the product of more years of schooling. Learning outcomes also matter and have a powerful effect on earnings, the distribution of income and long-term economic growth.[185] In lower-middle-income countries, if all children born today could be educated to a basic level of literacy and numeracy skills, there would be a 13-fold increase in GDP over their lifetimes.[186]

UNIVERSAL BASIC SKILLS CAN ALSO MAKE ECONOMIC GROWTH MORE INCLUSIVE.

Universal basic skills can also make economic growth more inclusive. Disparities in access to quality education are among the most powerful determinants of income disparities because of the effect learning and skills have on productivity, wages and employment. Narrowing the skills gap would create the conditions for more equitable patterns of growth, while increasing the size of the economy and reducing poverty.[187]

Reaching children throughout the learning process

As suggested previously in this chapter, quality education begins with interventions in early childhood. There is evidence that early childhood education can prepare children from the most disadvantaged homes for greater success when they enter primary school. However, not all children have access *(see Figure 2.7)*.

In Cape Verde, an assessment of children entering primary school demonstrated a 14 percentage point advantage for children who attended pre-primary school over the children who did not.[188] An evaluation published in 2009 from Argentina found that attending pre-primary school had a significant positive effect on standardized test scores in third-grade math and Spanish. It also improved classroom attention, effort, discipline and participation. And the benefits of preschool for children in neighbourhoods with high poverty levels were greater than for other Argentine children.[189]

Early childhood interventions for poor children in Bangladesh, Indonesia, the Plurinational State of Bolivia, and other countries have all shown results in reducing early learning gaps.[190] Unfortunately, attendance rates for pre-primary education are lowest in the poorest countries with the highest levels of child poverty.[191]

Early interventions thus build a foundation for making sure that all children complete school and learn essential knowledge and skills. But equity in education requires even more. It calls for a focus on the children who are left behind *throughout* the learning process. The progress these children make will have to be accelerated if their rates of school participation and their learning outcomes are to catch up with those of more advantaged children by 2030.

This acceleration can take different forms, depending on the national context. The Philippines, Senegal and Uganda, for instance, all have large out-of-school populations at different levels of school enrolment and completion. In the case of Senegal, while there are large disparities in primary school completion rates among different social groups, all groups are far from universal completion. The challenge is to accelerate overall progress with rapid advancement for disadvantaged groups. By contrast, in the Philippines and Uganda, children from the wealthiest households and the best-performing regions are close to universal school completion. Therefore, efforts in those countries would best be concentrated on the poorest and most disadvantaged children *(see Figure 2.8)*.

Disparities in access among different groups of children dictate the rate of progress needed in each group to achieve universal primary school completion. The needs of each group, in turn, will have far-reaching implications for how governments frame policies and allocate resources to specific regions, schools and children. To succeed, these policies must combine a commitment to equity in the schools with initiatives that tackle the determinants of inequity operating outside the classroom.

The Reaching Out-of-School Children programme in Bangladesh illustrates how governmental and non-governmental organizations can develop innovative strategies for reaching the most disadvantaged children. As part of the programme, Ananda (Joy of Learning) Schools have offered a second chance at

FIGURE 2.7

Early childhood education gaps vary by wealth and residence

Early childhood education attendance by wealth, residence and national average

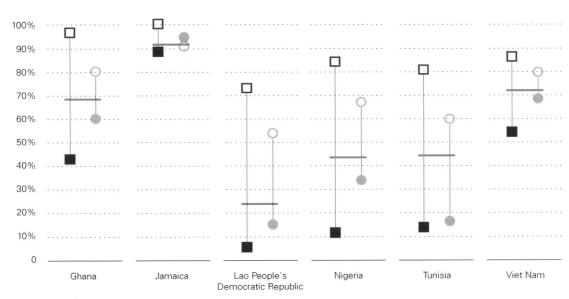

Note: Data are for 2011, except for the Lao People's Democratic Republic and Tunisia (2011–2012) and Viet Nam (2013–2014).

Source: UNICEF global databases, 2016.

FIGURE 2.8

Progress must accelerate for the least advantaged children

Speed of acceleration required for universal primary completion for all, by background

——— Richest   ——— Poorest   ——— Urban   ——— Rural

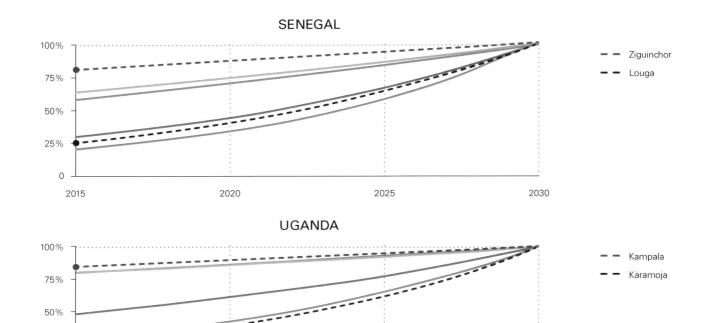

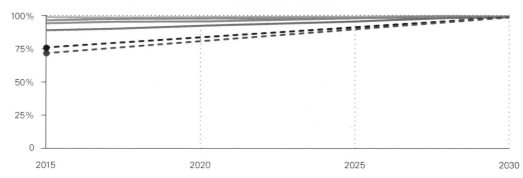

Note: Calculations use the survey year and the annual compound rate of change.

Source: DHS data, Overseas Development Institute calculations.

education for children in areas of high poverty and low school completion rates. Blending formal and non-formal methods to prepare students aged 8 to 14 for Grade 5 exams, the schools enrolled more than 790,000 children in 90 of the country's poorest *upazilas* (sub-districts) between 2005 and 2012 and achieved an 83 per cent pass rate.[192] The goal is to reach 148 sub-districts by 2017.

Initiatives like the one in Bangladesh demonstrate that the goal of reaching the hardest-to-reach children with quality education is not a matter of simply doing more of the same. It demands a commitment to trying something new.

From Argentina to Zimbabwe, new approaches to education are tested and scaled to meet local, national and global needs. Some innovations make use of new technology. EduTrac, for example, is a mobile phone-based data-collection system using SMS technology to encourage the flow of real-time information on education indicators in Uganda, among other countries.[193] Through eLearning Sudan, electronic tablets are used to instruct out-of-school children in remote villages of North Kordofan state, where traditional modes of education are not available.[194] Other innovations tackle the challenge of education in crisis situations with self-learning curricula that provide access to alternative education with adult guidance.

Attitudes and cultural norms will also have to change. In Montenegro, for example, national efforts have been under way to change attitudes that block access to education for children with disabilities. An intensive public awareness campaign, which started in 2010, is partially credited with generating greater public interest in the issue.[195] A poll in 2014 showed that 78 per cent of Montenegrins supported inclusive education.[196]

Equity targets

EQUITY TARGETS CAN PROVIDE A CLEAR SET OF PRIORITIES THAT SHINE A SPOTLIGHT ON A COUNTRY'S MOST EDUCATIONALLY DISADVANTAGED CHILDREN.

To accelerate progress for the hardest-to-reach children, national education policies may consider setting equity targets – calibrated to national circumstances – aimed at making sure all children have a fair chance to go to school and learn. Interim or 'stepping stone' equity targets on the road to meeting the 2030 goals for education would also be useful.

For instance, governments could set an interim target of halving disparities associated with wealth, gender, ethnicity and location in access to early childhood, primary and lower secondary education by 2022. Or they could decide on an interim target that places special emphasis on the poorest girls. Similar interim targets could be set to reduce disparities in learning outcomes.[197]

Equity targets will make a difference only if they are grounded in policy reform, and closing gaps in school participation will require detailed data on who is out of school or at risk of dropping out. Some equity targets can be achieved through the education system – for example, through learning assessment tools that identify which children are falling behind and guide resources towards them. Other targets can be reached by tackling disadvantages associated with poverty, gender, ethnicity and disability.

As a guide for policymakers, equity targets can provide a clear set of priorities that shine a spotlight on a country's most educationally disadvantaged children.

Teaching matters

Inextricably linked to issues of effective learning and equity are the women and men who interact with children in learning environments: teachers. Effective teachers can transform lives. Poorly trained, badly paid, ineffective teachers working in weakly governed education systems undermine opportunity and often reinforce inequities.

Problems associated with teachers and the governance systems in which they operate are evident worldwide. Among other issues, teacher absenteeism is endemic in many countries. For example, a 2013 survey of primary schools in Kenya reported teacher absenteeism rates of nearly 17 per cent for public primary schools.[198]

Other aspects of teaching and class planning have received insufficient attention. For example, a wave of first-generation learners – children whose parents did not have access to education – have entered primary school. These students are considered to be at risk of low learning levels. Yet teacher training systematically fails to equip educators with the skills needed to teach them.[199]

How teachers are distributed within a country can create difficulties with class size and quality of instruction for disadvantaged children in underserved districts. In countries with data on student-teacher ratios and qualifications of teachers, it is the early grades – ironically, the grades with the most students and the greatest needs – that have the largest classes and the least qualified teachers.[200]

Poorly trained and unmotivated teachers are hardly the only governance issue in underperforming schools. A lack of planning and financing becomes evident in the form of overcrowded classes, insufficient resources and poor infrastructure. For example, in sub-Saharan Africa, over half of the schools lack access to drinking water and toilets.[201] Not all have separate facilities for boys and girls. Few schools have access to electricity, which they need to take advantage of new learning technologies. Average class sizes in the United Republic of Tanzania and Malawi are 72 and 90 children, respectively.[202] In Uganda, there is one textbook for every three children.

As countries seek to climb the scale of educational performance, teachers – by definition – will play a critical role. Societies need to make sure teaching is considered a high-status profession in keeping with its critical role in shaping the future. With the future in mind, national equity goals should aim to connect the best teachers with the most disadvantaged pupils. Too often, career incentives have the inverse effect, guiding the best teachers towards the most advantaged students.

Research provides a number of clues to guide reform in this regard. In India, a programme run by Pratham, a non-governmental organization, provided remedial education to the lowest-performing children in public schools.[203] Hiring informal teachers from the local community to provide supplementary education, the programme achieved marked improvements in test scores. Targeted pedagogical training for teachers in Kenya, Mali and Niger similarly improved early grade reading among underperforming children.[204]

As these examples suggest, preschool and early grade teaching for first-generation learners and students needing remedial support – scaled up to a national level – could dramatically improve learning trajectories. The most effective route to scaling up these efforts is through national teacher training programmes.

59

THE WORLD'S CHILDREN 2016

unicef 70 YEARS FOR EVERY CHILD

There will also simply be a need for more teachers, now that the adoption of the SDGs has committed governments around the world to universal secondary schooling by 2030. Even achieving universal lower secondary education by then will require an additional 5.1 million teachers, 3.3 million of them for primary schools. Half of the new lower secondary school teachers and 63 per cent of the primary school teachers will be needed to serve the rapidly growing school-aged population in sub-Saharan Africa.[205]

Education financing

One of the lessons of the past decade is that more money, in itself, does not deliver better learning outcomes. How resources are allocated, however, does matter.

Many governments around the world have increased education spending. Average spending on education in low-income countries increased from 3.2 per cent of GDP in 1999 to 4 per cent in 2012.[206] But many governments continue to systematically underinvest in education, especially in South Asia. In 2012, India invested 3.9 per cent of its GDP in education.[207] The Government of Pakistan reports spending about 2 per cent of GDP on education.[208] These investment levels are below the estimated 5.5 per cent of GDP that will be required to provide education for all by 2030.[209]

How resources are allocated within countries has an important bearing on equity. Providing equal amounts of finance on a per pupil basis is not necessarily a formula for equitable funding. For a child who enters an education system carrying disadvantages associated with poverty, gender, disability or ethnicity, more resources may be needed to achieve opportunities equivalent to those enjoyed by more privileged children. Unfortunately, spending is often skewed in favour of the most privileged pupils.

This is partly because poor children are more likely to drop out of school early, thereby losing the benefits of public spending. UNICEF research on low-income countries overall shows that children from the richest 10 per cent of the population receive around 46 per cent of the benefits from public spending on education.[210]

A pre-school student, 5, traces a number on a flip chart, as part of a numeracy lesson in Timor-Leste.

© UNICEF/UN07789/Nazer

Several countries, including Brazil and Viet Nam *(see Box 2.3)*, have introduced reforms aimed at achieving more equitable spending patterns. In Chile, a school subsidy programme, Subvención Escolar Preferencial, provides a mechanism that makes flat-rate payments for each pupil, plus additional payments to schools that have high concentrations of disadvantaged students and students with learning difficulties.[211]

The global commitment to achieving universal secondary education reflects a growing awareness of the role of higher-level skills in driving economic growth. Yet in countries where a large share or even a majority of children fail to complete primary school, increasing spending on secondary education actually could have negative consequences for equity. The per-pupil costs of secondary schooling are far higher than those for primary school, and in many low-income countries, only a minority of poor children even enter secondary education.[212]

In addressing this important equity issue, governments should consider the sequencing and phasing of any expenditure increases. Broadly speaking, countries that are still some distance from universal primary completion should focus public spending at the pre-primary, primary and lower secondary levels. As progress towards universal access is achieved, spending can gradually shift to upper secondary education.

The role of aid

THE 2030 EDUCATION GOALS WILL REMAIN OUT OF REACH IF THE CHILDREN WHOSE LIVES ARE DISRUPTED BY CONFLICT ARE IGNORED.

Aid continues to play a critical role in mobilizing the resources needed to strengthen education systems for the world's poorest and most disadvantaged children, including children threatened by conflict and displacement.

When a political crisis led to a potentially shattering shortfall in Madagascar's budget for primary schools, for instance, an already fragile education system faced teacher strikes, a lack of resources and dropping school attendance. In 2013, a UNICEF programme provided teacher salaries and supplies that allowed primary school students to continue their studies.[213]

But the question of aid is much bigger than any single emergency. Providing universal pre-primary, primary and lower secondary education in low-income and lower-middle-income countries by 2030 will cost an estimated US$340 billion a year.[214] Much of the cost could be covered through a combination of economic growth and increased revenue collection. Even if governments meet minimum benchmarks in these areas, though, there will still be an annual education financing gap of US$39 billion in low-income and lower-middle-income countries.

In the case of low-income countries, the gap is equivalent to 42 per cent of the financing needed to meet the 2030 education goals.[215] Whichever way the equation is viewed, without an increase in aid, the gap will leave many countries far short of the goals, with fragile states experiencing some of the largest potential shortfalls.[216]

Recent developments in aid for education are not encouraging. Between 2010 and 2013, development assistance for basic education fell 11 per cent.[217] Several major bilateral donors have cut aid to education, and the international aid architecture is ill suited to address the plight of children affected by armed conflict and humanitarian emergencies.[218] But the 2030 education goals will remain out of reach if the children whose lives are disrupted by conflict are ignored.

To address this concern, a group of organizations and leaders – including UNICEF and the United Nations Secretary-General's Special Envoy for Global Education, Gordon Brown, launched Education Cannot Wait – A Fund for Education in Emergencies. Geared towards rapid disbursement in the immediate aftermath of a crisis *and* sustained support over the longer term, such a fund could help bridge the gap in education financing.

Two factors stand out as critical to its success. First, there is a global shortfall of around US$8.5 billion a year – an average of US$113 per child – in the funding needed to educate the estimated 75 million children affected by crises.[219] To make up that deficit, the fund for education in emergencies would need to involve regional governments in conflict-affected areas, the private sector and philanthropists. Second, governance arrangements would be needed for effective coordination across United Nations agencies, multilateral partnerships such as the Global Partnership for Education, and aid organizations. Coordination could give rise to partnerships that successfully bridge the divide between humanitarian responses and development expertise.

BOX 2.3 BRAZIL AND VIET NAM: MAKING THE GRADE

Brazil and Viet Nam offer valuable lessons on reforming education systems.

In 2012, students in Viet Nam achieved mathematics and reading scores in the Programme for International Student Assessment (PISA) that were far higher than expected given the country's income level. Fifteen-year-olds performed on a par with their peers in Germany and outperformed students in the United Kingdom and the United States. This achievement resulted from the country's commitment to measuring success and providing resources to achieve its education goals. By 2012, Viet Nam was allocating 21.4 per cent of its national budget to education. Teachers were capable and absenteeism was very low.

In Brazil, meanwhile, success was recorded in enrolment, increased equity and learning outcomes. Between 2003 and 2012, enrolment rates for 15-year-olds increased from 65 per cent to 78 per cent. Many of the children entering the school system were from socio-economically disadvantaged groups. Also between 2003 and 2012, Brazilian students' average PISA scores rose by 25 points; for disadvantaged pupils, the increase was 27 points.

Brazil's successes were driven by multiple reforms that began in the mid-1990s and included the establishment of an independent evaluation body, which became the Evaluation System for Basic Education. The system now serves as a transparent reporting mechanism and a common method for measuring learning achievements. High-performing schools are allowed greater autonomy, while underperforming schools receive support for improving standards.

Brazil also increased funding for education, which reached 6.3 per cent of GDP by 2012. The central government's financing facility targeted funds to schools in low-performing municipal education systems, and it now funds pre-primary education as well. Teacher training improved and equity was strengthened with Bolsa Escola, a programme that provided cash transfers to poor households.

The examples of Viet Nam and Brazil show that accelerating educational progress for the children left furthest behind can produce positive results.

Source: Bodewig, Christian, 'What explains Vietnam's stunning performance in PISA 2012?', East Asia & Pacific on the Rise, World Bank blogs, 11 December 2013, <http://blogs.worldbank.org/eastasiapacific/blogs/christian-bodewig>, accessed 22 January 2015. The World Bank, 'Government expenditure on education as % of GDP', <http://data.worldbank.org/indicator/SE.XPD.TOTL.GD.ZS>, accessed 12 February 2016. Hanushek, Eric A., and Ludger Woessmann, *Universal Basic Skills: What countries stand to gain*, OECD Publishing, 2015, pp. 31–33. Bruns, Barbara, David Evans and Javier Luque, *Achieving World-Class Education in Brazil: The next agenda,* The World Bank, Washington, D.C., 2012, pp. 7, 40, 11, 8. UNESCO Institute for Statistics, database, <http://data.uis.unesco.org/index.aspx?queryid=189>, accessed 10 February 2016.

Five years of conflict in the Syrian Arab Republic have illustrated the critical need to make education an integral part of the response to humanitarian crises. In this case, No Lost Generation, an initiative launched by UNICEF and partners, offers protection and learning opportunities for children and adolescents in the Syrian Arab Republic and the countries where millions of Syrian refugees have settled, including Egypt, Iraq, Jordan, Lebanon and Turkey.

Equitable progress is possible

Education has the power to end intergenerational cycles of inequity and improve the lives of children and the societies in which they live. However, achieving effective learning for all children regardless of their circumstances – from early childhood education through primary and secondary school – is a daunting challenge. A drive for greater equity is a condition for meeting the challenge by 2030, but will it run the risk of undermining the overall quality of school systems? Do the demands of equity and quality pull in different directions?

International experience provides an unequivocal answer: The highest-performing education systems in the world – such as those in Finland, the Republic of Korea and Japan – have been successful in combining equity with quality.[220] These systems strive to deliver quality education for all children, recognizing that the needs of the most disadvantaged pupils are as important as the accomplishments of the most advantaged. Recent evidence from the PISA learning assessments in the OECD countries is instructive. Of the 13 countries that were able to substantially increase their scores, nine did so from a starting point of strong equity and the other four increased equity.[221]

Fajer, 5, sits in a classroom at Teabat al Reah School in the Zumar sub-district of Ninewa, Iraq.

© UNICEF/UNI199908/Anmar

Universal primary and secondary schooling and improved learning outcomes are ambitious but achievable goals. Many countries have developed and tested innovative approaches to meeting these goals, and there have been some successes. Chile has been one of the world's fastest climbers in international and regional learning assessments, and the gaps in basic education test scores between the country's poorest and richest children have been narrowing.[222] As noted previously, Brazil and Viet Nam have succeeded in expanding access to education, improving learning outcomes and strengthening equity.

From these examples, some of the ingredients of successful reform emerge. Establishing equity as a central goal for access *and* learning can guide countries in reforming their education systems to make sure that the most disadvantaged children are not forgotten. Countries need to identify disadvantaged schools, pupils and regions, and direct more financial support to them. More spending on education also will be essential. While much of the impetus for change has to come from national governments, the international community has a vital role to play in supporting and financing education.

Success in providing quality education for every child depends on making learning an explicit objective in education policy and on investing in the development of strong national learning assessment institutions. It requires a strong commitment to the professionalization of teaching and improved teacher training and support systems. To help children from poor and marginalized groups overcome the disadvantages they start out with, early childhood care and universal pre-primary education should be priorities.

In addition, providing disadvantaged children with access to quality education requires integrated strategies to combat poverty and efforts to remove the financial barriers to education.

The benefits of investing in quality education for the most disadvantaged children are tremendous – for this generation of children, for the next generation and for the communities and societies in which they live. Education nourishes young minds, expands horizons and can break the cycle of disadvantage that traps generations in poverty. By investing in education systems and putting the needs of the most disadvantaged children first, nations can unlock education's potential to transform children's lives and the world.

Indigenous Awa children stand in line to enter the El Diviso school in Colombia.

© UNICEF/UN013357/LeMoyne

Give children a chance

By Gordon Brown, United Nations Special Envoy for Global Education

The voices of young people are at fever pitch. Technologically gifted, hungry for knowledge and with boundless energy, today's children and youth adapt quickly. They are connected. This is the generation that 'gets it'.

So global leaders should listen. But all too often, they don't. Somehow, our planet's future guardians – millions of them – continue to be underestimated, ignored and abused. Now, all that children are likely to see is a greedy world that denies them their right to equal opportunities and the chance to flourish.

Despite international laws designed to protect child rights, emergencies and protracted crises affected the education of an estimated 75 million children and young people 3 to 18 years of age. Many are living without proper access to food, shelter, health care and education. Many of them are victims of human trafficking and sexual exploitation.

Around 150 million children under the age of 14 are engaged in child labour, often in hazardous conditions. Child trafficking is on the rise and 5.5 million children are engaged in forced labour, with thousands more subject to abuse, forced into marriage and coerced into militias despite the prohibition of such practices under the Rome Statute of the International Criminal Court (ICC).

For decades, civil rights and liberation movements have fought the worst of oppression – from Western colonialism to South African apartheid, discrimination against African Americans and centuries-old prejudice against gay and lesbian adults. By comparison, children's rights have been neglected. They continue to be undermined even as world leaders commit to more ambitious targets for health, education and security under the newly adopted Sustainable Development Goals (SDGs).

While the number of out-of-school boys and girls of primary school age rose from about 56.6 million in 2010 to 59 million in 2013, for example, aid to basic education has been cut – yet again. It is down nearly 10 per cent since 2010.

The world's biggest challenge in the decade to come is bridging the gap between, on one hand, the opportunities young people have been promised, see others enjoying and expect, and on the other, the denial of those opportunities as doors are closed to them and the ladders of opportunity are kicked away.

The good news is that children across the world are participating in rights campaigns. In Bangladesh, young girls are forming child marriage-free zones. Child labourers have joined the Global March against Child Labour. And a girls' rights movement pressing for access to education has been inspired by Malala Yousafzai, the more than 200 still-missing Chibok girls of Nigeria and 1,000 global youth ambassadors from A World at School, a campaign working to get all children into school.

It is time for progressive minds everywhere to support these freedom struggles. Here is a set of short-term, practical proposals that can not only advance the SDGs but also support a global civil rights movement for children and young people.

Invest in children

Making sure children have the opportunities they need to flourish and realize their rights will take resources. We must focus on getting every child into school and also ensure that quality of learning is consistently high.

Education Cannot Wait – A Fund for Education in Emergencies can address the needs of the estimated 75 million children affected by crises and protracted emergencies. The fund, launched in May 2016, would help offset an annual funding shortfall of US$8.5 billion needed to maintain access to education for these children.

In addition to greater international aid, countries should adopt child-focused budgeting of their available resources. Under Article 4 of the Convention on the Rights of the Child, States parties are obligated to invest in children to the maximum extent of their available resources. As a result, increasing numbers of countries

are designing budgets with children specifically in mind. The Committee on the Rights of the Child, with the support of child advocacy organizations, is already drafting a General Comment on public spending to realize children's rights that will clarify the policy implications of Article 4.

Uphold child rights

But more resources, by themselves, will not suffice. What is to guarantee that children's rights will be upheld or even taken seriously?

No United Nations convention has been ratified in as many countries as the Convention on the Rights of the Child. But in too many areas, these rights are not being implemented. Similarly, the 1998 Rome Statute recognizes the need for special measures to protect children as victims and witnesses during judicial proceedings, and requires that judicial staff have expertise on children's issues. Yet criminal acts affecting children and within the province of the ICC – rape, sexual violence, trafficking and the use of children as soldiers – are not being properly investigated. Impunity remains widespread.

The Third Optional Protocol to the Convention on a Communications Procedure, which entered into force in April 2014, allows children to bring complaints about rights violations directly to the Committee on the Rights of the Child – but only if no solution is found at the national level. As of February 2016, only 26 countries had ratified the Protocol, and those most likely to violate it are the least likely to sign on.

An International Children's Court, along with a Children's Commissioner appointed to each country, is therefore vital to address these outstanding issues.

Listen to young voices

There is at least one other prerequisite for mustering the necessary resources to secure opportunities for children and establishing legal mechanisms to protect their rights. Namely, children and young people need a political mechanism through which they can debate these important issues. Young people's parliaments and other platforms for meaningful participation are a must.

An annual meeting of the United Nations Security Council as a Children's Rights Council would have a huge impact. Over the course of the year, a children's sub-council of the Security Council could examine the key issues that need to be raised.

To make this happen, the United Nations General Assembly should host a session for children and young people, preferably before its next session. Ideally, agreement on a United Nations Children's Council that reports to the Security Council could be reached in time for the 70th anniversary of the Universal Declaration of Human Rights in 2018. And by the 30th anniversary of the Convention on the Rights of the Child in 2019, we could see the establishment of a new International Children's Court.

The long-term goal is much simpler: Give children a chance. Give children a voice. The future is theirs.

Education activist Malala Yousafzai speaks with students at a school in the Za'atari camp for Syrian refugees in Mafraq Governorate, Jordan.

© UNICEF/UNI158222/Malhas

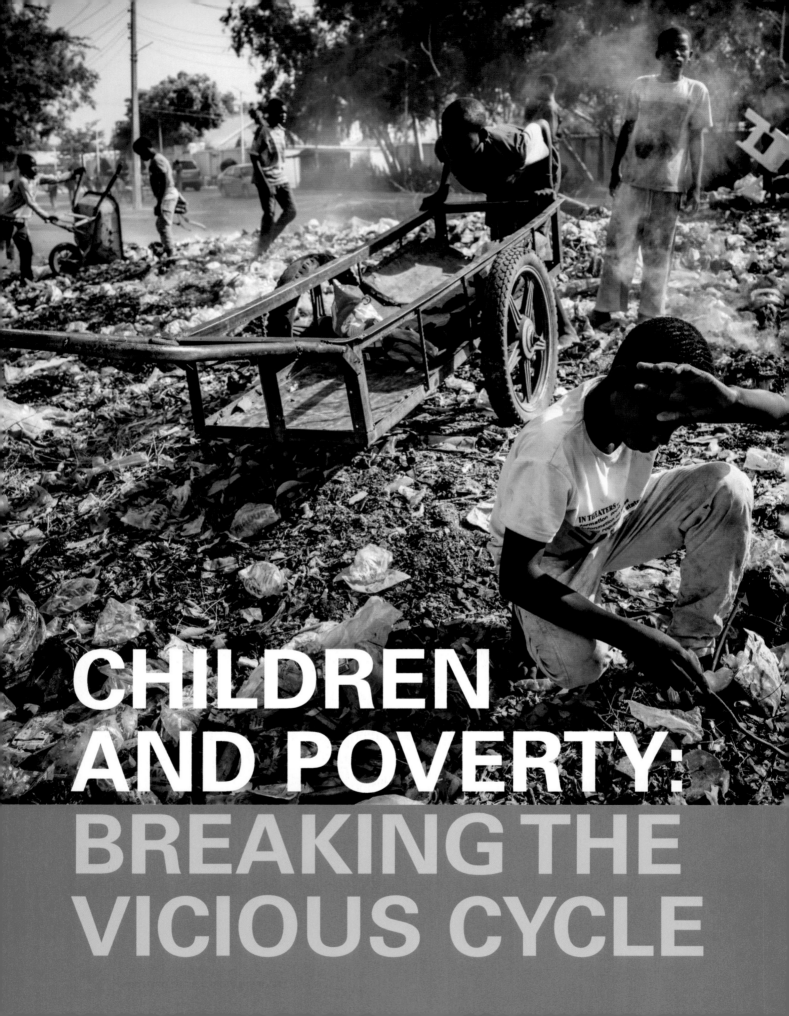

CHILDREN AND POVERTY:
BREAKING THE VICIOUS CYCLE

CHAPTER 3

Children and poverty:

Breaking the vicious cycle

No one is more vulnerable to poverty than children. Poverty perpetuates the cycle of disadvantage and inequity, which robs millions of children of their potential and causes irreparable damage that reverberates throughout a lifetime. Putting children at the heart of poverty reduction is one of the best ways to break that cycle and create a level playing field for every child.

Muhammad Modu, 15, internally displaced from Malori, digs through a rubbish dump for saleable items in Maiduguri, Nigeria.

© UNICEF/UN016293/Gilbertson VII Photo

The amount of money available in a household plays a crucial role in determining the opportunities a child may encounter in life. But for children, poverty is about more than money. It affects very real aspects of their lives – including whether they can attend school, be well nourished or have access to health care, safe drinking water and sanitation. Children from the poorest households are the most likely to die from preventable causes and the least likely to have access to quality education and health care.

Efforts to reduce child poverty must therefore go beyond moving households above a monetary threshold. A multidimensional approach is critical to respond to this multifaceted challenge.

This chapter begins by looking at how children experience poverty. It then asks how many of the world's children live in poverty, defined in terms of 'extreme', 'moderate' and 'relative' monetary poverty. It also explores the multiple and overlapping dimensions of poverty that further deprive children of their rights.

The chapter argues that the key to a more equitable world is reducing child poverty in all its dimensions and narrowing the gaps between those who are most and least advantaged. It notes that consistent measurement – and knowing who the most disadvantaged children are, where they live and how they are deprived – is essential to developing successful policies and programmes to end child poverty. Finally, the chapter examines the role of cash transfer programmes in reducing poverty and inequality and improving equitable access to nutrition, health, education and other services.

The effects of poverty in childhood

There is no universal interpretation of poverty in general, or of child poverty more specifically. While it may seem like a simple concept, poverty is not always easy to quantify. Some may understand poverty as the lack of adequate income to meet basic human needs. Others define it as the inability to keep up with the average standard of living in a given society. Still others take a wider view, interpreting poverty as a lack of access to basic services such as education, primary health care or safe drinking water.

Viewed from the perspective of a child, the exact definition becomes immaterial. Being deprived, by any measure, is damaging to a child's development, particularly when deprivations are experienced in early childhood. A child rarely has a second chance at a good start in life. Deprivations of health, nutrition or stimulation in the earliest months and years of life when the brain is developing at a rapid pace, can lead to damage that is difficult or even impossible to overcome later.

Undernutrition in early childhood, for instance, can result in stunting. Left unaddressed at that point, it can affect cognitive development, leading to learning difficulties and poor health in adolescence and adulthood. Poor health, beyond the physical and emotional consequences, also denies children the chance to play and learn. Missing out on education in early childhood or living in an environment that provides little stimulation or emotional support can severely restrict a person's productivity as an adult.

In these and many other ways, poverty, in the form of deprivations that begin in childhood, can be felt throughout a lifetime. Children who grow up deprived not only have limited opportunities to fulfil their potential; they often have no option but to raise their own children in poverty. To break this vicious cycle, poverty reduction must begin with a focus on children.

At current trends

9 out of **10**

of the world's children living in **extreme poverty** will live in **sub-Saharan Africa** in 2030

unicef 🅤 70 YEARS FOR EVERY CHILD

unicef 🅤 70 YEARS FOR EVERY CHILD

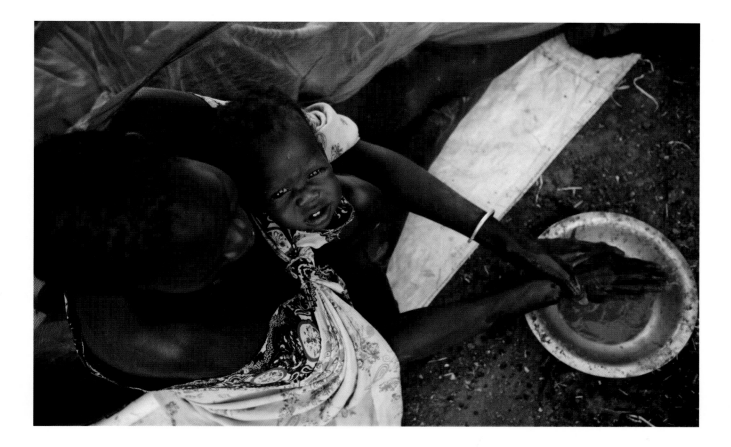

A woman washes her hands in dirty water while camping outside to register for a food ration card in Thanyang, South Sudan.

© UNICEF/UN016625/Holt

Measuring how many children live in poverty

The first step in reducing child poverty is measuring it. Methods to calculate monetary poverty provide a useful yardstick against which to measure social progress. While limited, these measures are the most widespread indicators used to capture the extent of poverty at the household level and can gauge the financial bottlenecks faced by disadvantaged children and their families *(see Box 3.1)*.

Monetary poverty lines are set at both national and international levels. They usually work by placing a value on a basket of goods and services considered the minimum requirement to live a non-impoverished life at current prices. Households lacking sufficient resources to afford that basket are considered poor.

Monetary poverty measures do not, however, take into account other crucial dimensions – such as lack of education, health, water or sanitation – that are extremely important for understanding how children experience poverty.

Relying on household-level measures may also mask the fact that individuals within the household, especially children, may not have adequate resources allocated to them and may be deprived in other dimensions. For these reasons, child poverty is best seen as a combination of monetary and non-monetary factors at both the household and individual levels.

Children living in extreme poverty

The measure most commonly used to calculate monetary poverty is the international poverty line developed by the World Bank and set at US$1.90 per day since October 2015. By this measure, in 2012, almost 900 million people struggling to survive below that line, were living in extreme poverty.[223] Because poorer families tend to be larger, children are disproportionately represented among the extreme poor. While children aged 17 and under account for about one third (34 per cent) of the total population in low- and middle-income countries, they make up nearly half (46 per cent) of the population living on less than US$1.90 per day *(see Figure 3.1)*.

Nevertheless, the last three decades have seen unprecedented progress in reducing extreme poverty. The overall proportion of people living in extreme poverty has fallen, and that trend is projected to continue. In 2012, the number of people living in extreme poverty worldwide was almost half of what it had been at the end of the 1990s.[224]

But particular attention to the pace of progress is warranted in some regions. In the Middle East and North Africa, for example, after years of progress, the rates of monetary poverty appear to be stagnant or, by some estimates, even on the rise.[225]

BOX 3.1 MONETARY CHILD POVERTY MEASURES

The most common indicators to measure monetary child poverty are:

The international extreme poverty line

The World Bank's 'extreme poverty' line identifies people living in households that have less than US$1.90 per person per day. It is calculated by converting the national poverty lines from a selection of the poorest countries in the world to a common currency – using purchasing power parity (PPP) exchange rates to adjust for the difference in cost of living across countries – and then taking an average of those lines.

This measure reflects a very low absolute poverty standard based on basic needs for survival. It was used to set targets for poverty reduction under the Millennium Development Goals and is now part of the Sustainable Development Goals, which aim to eradicate extreme poverty by 2030.

The World Bank also calculates higher international poverty thresholds, such as US$3.10 per person per day, using the same per capita approach. These measures represent levels of poverty above extreme poverty.

National poverty lines

Governments use national poverty lines to monitor monetary poverty within their own countries. According to these measures, a person is considered poor if he or she lives in a household with a consumption or income level below a nationally established threshold. National poverty lines are estimated in local currencies and reflect national standards.

While absolute poverty lines reflect the minimum level of income or consumption needed to fulfil basic requirements, some governments opt to use 'relative poverty' lines. These thresholds still allow for participation in the normal consumption and living standards of the country but measure poverty in relation to the national average income levels. (The European Union and Organisation of Economic Co-operation and Development also use relative poverty lines to compare levels of poverty among their members and with other countries.)

The great advantage of national poverty lines is that they are specific to the country, reflecting its specific characteristics and level of development. However, the methodology used varies greatly across countries and, therefore, doesn't allow for comparisons between them.

unicef ✿ 70 YEARS FOR EVERY CHILD

In the Syrian Arab Republic, data suggest the conflict that began there in 2011 caused a sharp increase in the rate of extreme poverty, measured by the proportion of the population living below a national poverty line. The rate increased from 12.3 per cent in 2007 to an estimated 43 per cent in 2013.[226] Poverty is also a concern for the millions of refugees who have fled the crisis. In 2014, the United Nations High Commissioner for Refugees estimated that 7 out of 10 registered Syrian refugees in Jordan and Lebanon could be considered poor.[227] Half of these refugees are children.

Another region of particular concern is sub-Saharan Africa, which accounts for a large and rising share of the world's extreme poor. Based on current trends, 9 out of 10 of the world's children surviving on less than US$1.90 a day will live in sub-Saharan Africa in 2030 (see Figure 3.2).

FIGURE 3.1

A disproportionate share of children live in extreme poverty

Percentage of children under 18 among the total population and the extreme poor, in low- and middle-income countries, 2012

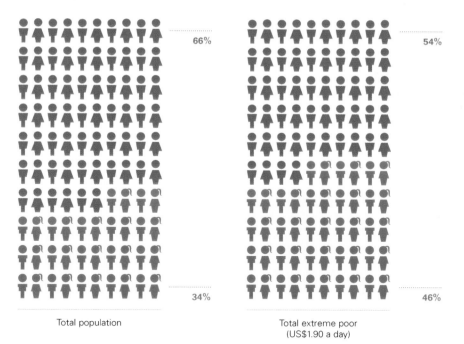

66%

34%

Total population

54%

46%

Total extreme poor
(US$1.90 a day)

Estimates are presented as the share of children among the total extreme poor. The analysis considers how the age profile of the extreme poor evolves depending on changes in the age composition of the population, and fertility rates by wealth quintile.

The analysis does not include the Middle East and North Africa or Europe and Central Asia due to lack of data and low poverty rates.

Percentages for all low- and middle-income countries are estimated based on World Bank data for Sub-Saharan Africa, South Asia, and the Latin America and Caribbean regions. Data for other regions were not available at the time of calculation.

Children under 18   Adults (18 and over)

Note: Poverty rates are derived from the World Bank's PovcalNet and *Global Monitoring Report 2015/2016*. Age-disaggregated population profiles are from the United Nations Department of Economic and Social Affairs 2012 estimates. Fertility rates by wealth quintile are derived from Demographic and Health Surveys (after 2005). Child poverty estimates were calculated based on regional poverty aggregates and demographic factors, and not household income or consumption survey analysis.

Estimates for children using the updated international poverty line of US$1.90 a day are not yet available. However, the latest profile of the world's extreme poor (based on the previous level of US$1.25 a day) revealed that 47 per cent of those living in extreme poverty were 18 years old or younger. Since the data used to calculate the first estimates relied on ranking profiles based on old surveys, the profile should provide a valid reference.

Source: Overseas Development Institute calculations for UNICEF (2016), based on data from the World Bank (2016), and the United Nations Department of Economic and Social Affairs (2013) and DHS (after 2005).

FIGURE 3.2

In 2030, 9 out of 10 children in extreme poverty will live in sub-Saharan Africa

Estimated percentage of children living in extreme poverty (US$1.90 a day), by World Bank region, in 2002, 2012 and projections for 2030

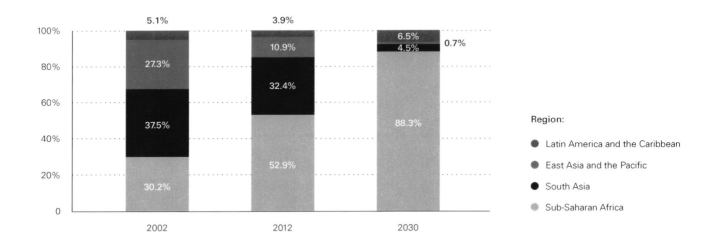

Note: Poverty projections are linear interpolations based on projections published in the World Bank's *Global Monitoring Report 2015/2016* and assume average growth over the past 10 years. The analysis does not include Middle East and North Africa, Europe and Central Asia due to lack of data and low poverty rates. The analysis considers how the age profile of the extreme poor evolves depending on changes in the age composition of the population and fertility rates by wealth quintile.

Source: Overseas Development Institute calculations for UNICEF (2016), based on data from the World Bank (2016) and United Nations Department of Economic and Social Affairs (2013) and DHS (after 2005).

BOX 3.2 MEASURING MULTIDIMENSIONAL CHILD POVERTY

Ideally, all countries should report on the number of children living in poverty using both monetary and multidimensional measures.

Monetary measures, such as the national and international poverty lines mentioned previously, are already widely used to report progress in reducing poverty. They can form the basis for estimating the number of children living in monetary poverty – that is, the child poverty rate – at the national, regional and global levels.

Multidimensional child poverty measures add depth and complexity to the data. They can be adapted and applied to each country's economic and social context, informing the development of national approaches to poverty reduction.

The Multidimensional Poverty Index (MPI) is one example of a tool designed to enhance poverty data. The index covers three dimensions of disadvantage – health, education and material deprivation – measured by 10 indicators. MPI data reports, which can be disaggregated for children, count individuals as poor when they are disadvantaged in relation to at least one third of the indicators.

The Multiple Overlapping Deprivation Analysis is another tool, developed by UNICEF, to sharpen the equity focus of child poverty and deprivation analyses around the world. It selects the child as the unit of analysis, rather than the household, since children experience poverty differently than adults.

This concentration is especially alarming given that sub-Saharan Africa is the world's youngest region, with children under age 18 accounting for around half the population.[228] Over the next 15 years, the region will account for almost the entire increase in the world's population of children. If current trends persist, 156 million children in sub-Saharan Africa will be struggling to survive on less than US$1.90 a day in 2030; as a group, they will comprise nearly half of the world's extreme poor.[229]

Poverty is not just more pervasive but also more intense in sub-Saharan Africa than in other regions. On average, poor people there are starting the journey towards the US$1.90 extreme poverty threshold from a lower base than their counterparts in other parts of the world. Some 89 million people in the region, or around 10 per cent of the population, lived on less than 80 cents a day in 2012. In sub-Saharan Africa, people who are below the extreme poverty threshold live on an average of US$1.20 a day, compared to US$1.50 for the extreme poor in South Asia.[230]

Children living in 'moderate' poverty

It is worth noting that the extreme poverty line of US$1.90 a day is not a hard-and-fast border dividing the poor from the non-poor. Millions of children living above this line still live in poverty, are vulnerable to it or experience deprivations in other dimensions of their lives.

Data using broader poverty lines give a sense of the global and universal nature of poverty (see Figure 3.3). In 2012, more than 2 billion people in low- and middle-income countries lived on less than US$3.10 a day, which is considered 'moderate' poverty. This total includes almost 900 million people in South Asia, some 500 million in East Asia and the Pacific, and about 72 million in Latin America and the Caribbean. About 50 million people in the Middle East and North Africa lived on less than US$3.10 a day in 2008, the latest year for which reliable surveys are available.[231] Worldwide, more than 3 billion people remained vulnerable to poverty in 2012, subsisting on less than US$5 a day.[232]

WORLDWIDE, MORE THAN 3 BILLION PEOPLE REMAINED VULNERABLE TO POVERTY IN 2012, SUBSISTING ON LESS THAN US$5 A DAY.

In many cases, these people – who represent more than half the population in low- and middle-income countries – are already subject to some dimensions of deprivation and remain well within the gravitational pull of extreme poverty. A drought, an illness, the outbreak of conflict or an economic downturn is all it might take to put them back under the US$1.90 a day level.

The experience of Latin America illustrates the need to look beyond poverty thresholds. Between the mid-1990s and 2011, extreme poverty in the region fell by half, thanks to rising incomes as well as pensions and other social transfers.[233] In 2012, there were more people in Latin America's middle class than in the ranks of the extreme poor. However, 38 per cent of the population lived on a daily income of between US$4 and US$10 a day in 2013, at risk of slipping back into extreme poverty.[234]

Poor children living in rich countries

Relative poverty, which is of particular relevance in richer countries, can also affect the lives of children. Having fewer opportunities to be educated, healthy or nourished compared to their peers puts children at a disadvantage and limits their life chances.

FIGURE 3.3

More than half of the population in low- and middle-income countries live on less than US$5 a day

Percentage of population living below various international poverty lines, by World Bank region, 2012

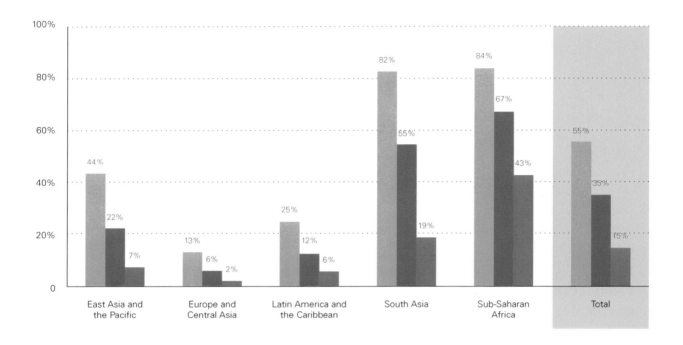

● People vulnerable to poverty (less than $5.00 a day)

● People living in moderate poverty (less than $3.10 a day)

● People living in extreme poverty (less than $1.90 a day)

Note: Total refers to low- and middle-income countries available in PovcalNet. Data were not available for the Middle East and North Africa at the time of calculation. All estimates are based on purchasing power parity figures (current international $) extrapolated from the 2011 International Comparison Program (ICP) benchmark estimates. US$5.00/day is not an official international poverty line used by the World Bank.

Source: The World Bank (2016).

Eight years after the onset of the 2008 financial crisis, the slow pace of economic recovery, high levels of unemployment, financial pressure and rising inequality are jeopardizing the hopes of a generation of children in high-income countries belonging to the Organisation for Economic Co-operation and Development (OECD).[235] At the same time, children and poor families are feeling the effects of deficit reduction programmes initiated by governments in response to the crisis.[236]

In the 41 most affluent countries, nearly 77 million children lived in monetary poverty in 2014.[237] Taking pre-crisis levels as an anchor point, child poverty rates increased in 23 OECD countries after 2008. In five countries, child poverty rates increased by more than 50 per cent.[238] In most countries in the European Union, the proportion of children in poverty is higher than the rate for adults *(see Figure 3.4)*.

unicef ● 70 YEARS FOR EVERY CHILD

FIGURE 3.4

In most European Union countries, children are at a higher risk of monetary poverty than adults

Percentage of population at risk of poverty in the European Union, by age group, 2014

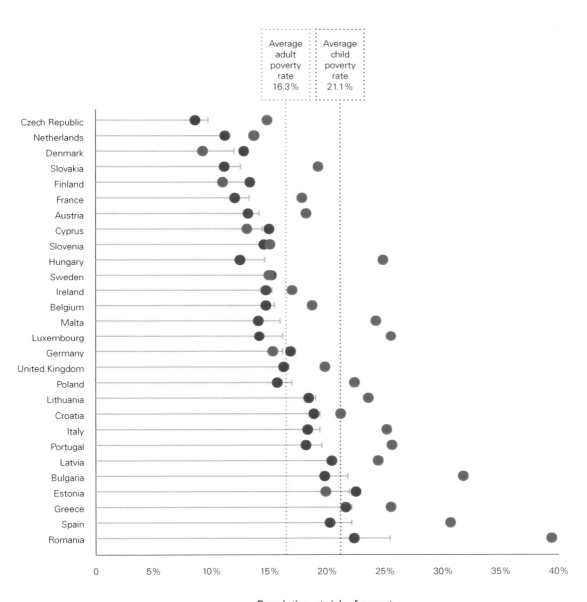

Population at risk of poverty

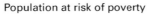

Note: 'At risk of poverty' is defined as living below the poverty threshold, which is 60 per cent of median equivalized income after social transfers.

Source: Eurostat (2016) based on European Union Statistics on Income and Living Conditions.

Child poverty in all its dimensions

Simply living in a household that is above the threshold of monetary poverty does not necessarily mean a child is out of poverty. Consider a family that meets the threshold defined by the national poverty line but still lacks access to shelter, food, water, sanitation, education, health care or information. According to a monetary interpretation of poverty, this family would not be considered poor. A wider interpretation, however, would consider a child living in that household as poor because of the deprivations faced by his or her family.

Several measures have been developed to better understand and monitor poverty in its multiple dimensions *(see Box 3.2)*. By looking at the different deprivations that children experience in crucial aspects of their lives, countries can better target policies and programmes that benefit the most disadvantaged.

Measures such as the Multidimensional Poverty Index aim to accurately estimate the extent of the problem. Its most recent findings indicate that 1.6 billion people lived in multidimensional poverty in 2015.[239]

Another study of multidimensional poverty focused on children in sub-Saharan Africa and returned alarming results. In the 30 countries for which comparable data were available, 247 million out of a total of 368 million children under age 18 experience two to five deprivations that threaten their survival and development.[240] A study in 2008–2009 found that 81 million children and adolescents in countries in Latin America and the Caribbean were affected by at least one moderate or severe deprivation of their rights to education, nutrition, housing, sanitation, drinking water or access to information.[241]

Disadvantages overlap and reinforce one another

When children experience poverty, poor health, malnutrition, stress, violence, abuse, neglect, inadequate care or a lack of learning opportunities, particularly during the first years of their lives, their ability to fulfil their potential is at risk.

A girl who must walk long distances to fetch water has less time to attend school. A child who is undernourished is more susceptible to diseases spread through poor sanitation. A baby who lacks nurturing, stimulation and interaction when the neural connections in the brain are forming might never have the chance to develop fully. Each deprivation exacerbates the effect of the others, and when two or more coincide, the effects on children can be catastrophic.

Deprivations are particularly magnified for children living in fragile and conflict-affected states. These children are more than twice as likely to be undernourished as children in other low- and middle-income countries. They are also more than three times as likely to be out of school, twice as likely to die before their fifth birthday and more than twice as likely to lack access to improved sources of drinking water, according to the *World Development Report 2011*.[242]

In addition to conflict, the impacts of climate change and environmental degradation create new risks and reinforce old social and economic vulnerabilities created by poverty and inequality. Some of the world's poorest children live in areas that are especially vulnerable to natural disasters such as flooding, drought or

A boy feeds a younger child in the Nyarugusu refugee camp, in Kigoma Region, United Republic of Tanzania.

© UNICEF/UNI186112/Calvin

unicef 🙼   70 YEARS FOR EVERY CHILD

Moses, 1, Sarah, 2, and Paul, 7,
stand with their mother Lucy
and cousin Joslyn, 7, outside
their home, destroyed by Super
Cyclone Pam, Tanna Island,
Vanuatu.

© UNICEF/UNI181237/Crumb

severe storms. More than 300 million children live in zones of very high flood occurrence that are also in countries where over half of the population gets by on less than US$3.10 a day.[243]

Children who are already deprived in many dimensions of their lives are likely to face some of the most immediate dangers of climate change as their families are most exposed to the potential harm and find it hardest to bounce back from climate-related shocks. As noted previously, many families living above the threshold of extreme poverty may be just one disaster away from falling into it. As climate hazards arise more frequently, the cumulative effect of repeated shocks will make it difficult for many of the most disadvantaged households to survive, recover, cope and adapt.

Urbanization is another force putting pressure on poverty reduction efforts and highlighting inequities. National poverty lines may not take into account all of the high costs of urban living – especially housing, transportation, water, sanitation, education and health services. And children in urban areas may lack access to essential services even when they live close to them. As a result, the risks for urban populations can exceed those in rural areas.

For example, a 2006 study in sub-Saharan Africa showed greater disparities in child nutrition between rich and poor urban communities than between urban and rural areas.[244] A 2012 study in Egypt found that rates of poverty and deprivation among some children in urban slums reached or exceeded those in the country's most deprived rural areas.[245] And for the many children in China who have migrated to cities with their families, holding a *hukou* household registration from a rural area often means they are not entitled to urban health, education and other critical services.[246]

The challenges facing children in poor urban communities are particularly relevant in light of the projection that 66 per cent of the world's population will be urban in 2050, with the fastest urbanization on the African and Asian continents.[247] Excluded from other opportunities, many of the urban poor have little choice but to take informal jobs that are outside of government regulation, taxation and observation. The most marginalized people – including women and people with disabilities – are often trapped in the informal economy because of discrimination, which limits their opportunities.[248]

There is a strong link between informal work and poverty.[249] Informal workers lack basic social protection, face unsafe working conditions and are subject to layoffs without compensation. They are locked in low-productivity activities with few opportunities for mobility and no protection in the event of non-payment of wages.

Race, ethnicity and social exclusion also often play a role in determining a child's life chances, even in some of the world's richest countries. In the United States in 2013, 39 per cent of African American children, 36 per cent of American Indian children and 32 per cent of Hispanic children lived in poor families, defined as having income below the established federal poverty level. That compares to 13 per cent of the country's white children and 13 per cent of its Asian children.[250]

In Europe, Roma people are the largest ethnic minority and are among the most deprived.[251] A 2011 study in 11 European Union countries found that around 41 per cent of Roma children lived in households where someone had to go to bed hungry at least once in the month prior to the survey because they could not afford to buy food.[252] Based on national thresholds, families with four or more children – practically all of the Roma households surveyed – were at risk of poverty.[253] The proportion of Roma children living in households that fell below the national 'at-risk-of-poverty' line was twice as high as that of non-Roma children living nearby.[254]

Migrant households in Europe are also especially vulnerable to poverty. In Spain, one in two children in migrant households lived in poverty in 2012.[255] In Greece, child poverty rates for migrant households increased by 35 per cent between 2008 and 2012, compared to 15 per cent for the general population.[256]

While the challenges are great, many of the solutions are at hand. An integrated approach that focuses on interventions in health, nutrition, water and sanitation, protection, and learning during the first years of children's lives can set a firm foundation for their entire lifetime.

THE NATIONS SIGNING ON TO THE 2030 GOALS HAVE MADE A COMMITMENT TO ADDRESS CHILD POVERTY IN ALL ITS DIMENSIONS.

Universal measurement of child poverty

The nations signing on to the 2030 goals have made a commitment to address child poverty in all its dimensions. Given this commitment, they need consistently updated data on who is poor and how they are poor in order to monitor progress, identify gaps and guide policies and programmes – all in the interest of making sure that vulnerable children are not left behind.

Efforts to measure child poverty are not new. Indeed, many countries have already taken steps to generate data on how many children are living in poverty, based on the international extreme-poverty threshold of US$1.90 a day, as well

unicef   70 YEARS FOR EVERY CHILD

Children attending the Traiko Simeonov primary school, where 90 per cent of students are Roma, in Shumen, northern Bulgaria.

© UNICEF/UNI154479/Pirozzi

as on national poverty lines. There are also well-established methodologies, mentioned previously, to capture the extent of multidimensional child poverty, and these measurements can complement the monetary measurements.

Still, the number of countries that report child poverty figures is limited. A recent internal analysis by UNICEF found that more than one third of countries are not measuring child poverty, and around half of those that are measuring it are not doing so routinely.[257]

Ideally, all countries should report on the number of children living in poverty using both monetary and multidimensional measures. Multidimensional child poverty measures give a fuller picture of how children experience poverty. These data can be adapted and applied to each country's economic and social context, informing the development of national approaches to poverty reduction.

International financial institutions, development agencies, donors and regional bodies could be cooperating more effectively to raise standards and strengthen national statistical capacity in these countries. Such a course would bring the world one step closer to the goal of eradicating extreme poverty in general, and child poverty in particular.

The role of cash transfers in reducing poverty and inequality

Reducing child poverty in all its dimensions is one of the world's most important and urgent tasks, requiring concerted and sustained efforts to put children first and give them what they need to have a fair chance to survive and thrive.

Because children experience poverty in multifaceted ways, it is critical not only to provide equitable services – including essential health care and quality education – but also to make sure the most disadvantaged children have access to those services. Social protection mechanisms such as pensions, fee waivers, child support grants and cash transfers are an effective approach that can reduce vulnerability to poverty and deprivation, strengthen families' capacity to care for their children and overcome barriers to accessing essential services.

Cash transfers can work as a 'safety net' to keep the poorest, most vulnerable households out of destitution in all settings, including humanitarian emergencies. At the same time, they offer families a ladder out of poverty by boosting incomes, increasing school attendance, improving nutrition, encouraging the use of health services and providing job opportunities. By one estimate, social protection initiatives keep some 150 million people out of poverty,[258] and they make a positive impact on children's lives across a range of indicators. Results from many regions demonstrate direct impacts such as increased income and consumption, increased access to goods and services, greater social inclusion and reduced household stress.

Because of their usually modest size, cash transfer programmes alone cannot directly lift most households above the monetary poverty threshold. But they can make a real difference in reducing the effects of poverty and bolstering families and economies. Cash transfers work by putting more money into the hands of the poor, strengthening local markets and creating a stream of social benefits that come with poverty reduction. As households spend the transfers they receive, their impact is multiplied in the local economy and the benefits transmitted to others in society.

Children in Supaul, a flood-prone district in the state of Bihar, India.

© UNICEF/UNI130498/Singh

Cash transfer programmes can reduce inequality while contributing to economic growth, productivity and job creation. In Brazil, for example, Bolsa Familia, one of the largest cash transfer programmes in the world, was paired with Beneficio de Prestação Continuada – a combination social pension and disability grant. Together, these programmes contributed to more than one quarter of the country's 2.7 per cent fall in inequality as measured by the Gini index between 1995 and 2004.[259]

In Ukraine, meanwhile, child allowances contributed to an estimated 1 per cent decrease in inequality between 2001 and 2007. The allowances were designed to take into account the specific vulnerabilities affecting households with more than one child, who faced the greatest risk of poverty.[260]

Cash transfer programmes also offer protection against shocks, helping households to weather downturns without having to sell off productive assets, take children out of school or cut vital spending on health and nutrition. Some programmes explicitly target families with children, but cash transfers need not be child oriented to benefit them.

Some evidence has shown that cash transfers can also increase women's role in making household spending decisions, allowing them more financial security and enabling them to engage in income-generating activities.[261]

In conflict-affected countries, fragile states and humanitarian emergencies, cash grants may be among the most efficient and effective ways of reaching the poorest households.[262] One recent example is a programme that, each month, has assisted around 56,000 children from 15,000 vulnerable Syrian refugee families living in host communities in Jordan. Cash transfers have given the families the means to cover basic needs and expenses specific to children.

Of the 500 families who participated in a survey about the programme, 88 per cent reported using the cash grant to cover at least one child-specific expense. The majority said they spent it on fresh foods for children (65 per cent), school-related expenses (56 per cent) and medicines for children (53 per cent).[263]

In Kenya, the Hunger Safety Net Programme provided cash transfers to poor households in four arid and semi-arid counties. In spite of a severe drought, households receiving the grant were 10 per cent less likely than non-recipients to fall into the poorest tenth of the population.[264] Beyond its effects on poverty, the transfer programme was found to improve food security and enable households to spend more on health care. It also had a positive impact on classroom performance for children already in school.

CASH TRANSFERS HAVE BEEN SHOWN TO HELP CHILDREN STAY IN SCHOOL LONGER AND ADVANCE TO HIGHER LEVELS OF EDUCATION.

Cash transfers and access to essential services

As some of these examples show, cash transfers address multiple deprivations and help children gain access to services that are critical to their well-being. For example, cash transfers for the most vulnerable households and children can be used to trigger eligibility for health coverage – an approach adopted by Ghana with its Livelihood Empowerment Against Poverty (LEAP) programme. A unique feature of LEAP is that, in addition to small, bimonthly cash payments, it provides beneficiaries with free health care coverage through the National Health Insurance Scheme.[265]

Cash transfers can also address some of the determinants of educational disadvantage, helping to break the link between poverty and school drop-out rates.[266] In Morocco, a cash transfer programme led to a significant improvement in school participation.[267] Evidence shows that cash transfers have increased demand for education[268] and improved school enrolment and attendance.[269]

In addition, cash transfers have been shown to help children stay in school longer and advance to higher levels of education. In Cambodia, an initiative providing scholarships to at-risk pupils from low-income households increased the average time they remained in school by more than half a grade.[270] In Colombia, Ghana and Pakistan, cash transfers programmes have helped improve rates of transition to higher levels of education.

In some cases, cash transfers and other social protection measures have had an impact on learning as well. For example, cash transfer programmes led to improved test scores for children in Burkina Faso and modest improvements in Morocco.[271] Meanwhile, school feeding programmes have been linked to increased learning and cognitive development. In Bangladesh, primary school students in a school meal programme showed a 15.7 per cent improvement in learning metrics, mostly in mathematics, compared with children who did not participate in the programme.[272]

Cash transfers have also proven to have some impact on child marriage and child labour and on the educational disadvantages these practices entail. While addressing these child rights violations is a complex challenge that demands action in multiple sectors, cash transfers can play a role in alleviating some of the financial pressures that force children into work or marriage and out of school.[273]

A cash transfer programme in Panama, for example, led to a nearly 16 per cent reduction in child labour among indigenous children aged 12 to 15 and to a nearly 8 per cent increase in elementary school enrolment in indigenous areas.[274] Pakistan's Female School Stipend Programme reduced girls' labour-force participation by as much as 5 per cent.[275] In Bangladesh, a cash transfer programme was successful in encouraging girls to enrol, particularly in secondary school, and in delaying marriage.

Expanding social protection – and looking ahead

Every country in the world has at least one social safety net programme in place, and specific child and family benefit programmes rooted in legislation exist in 108 countries. Yet these often cover only small groups of the population, and in 75 countries no such targeted programmes are available at all.[276]

Expanding social protection is critical to achieving the 2030 goals. In fact, the goals include a specific target on implementing nationally appropriate social protection systems and measures to achieve substantial coverage of the poor and vulnerable by 2030.

A universal approach to expanding social protection would not only increase coverage but would also reduce the chances of mistakenly excluding eligible households, create social solidarity and reduce the stigma that is sometimes

Children stand near their family's house in the Muhamasheen area of Mathbah, in Sana'a, Yemen.

© UNICEF/UN013965/Shamsan

A boy trying to earn money by weighing people in the street, in Sana'a, Yemen.

© UNICEF/UN018345/Altwaity

associated with targeting. However, countries can realize social protection by taking incremental approaches that work within their resource and capacity constraints – as well as their social and economic policy frameworks – towards the ultimate goal of universal coverage.

For rich countries, the immediate challenge is to repair and strengthen the safety nets and benefits that were eroded in the wake of the global financial crisis. For many middle-income countries, the architecture of existing cash transfer programmes provides a basis for further expansion. Governments in low-income countries face starker choices. With limited budgets and high levels of child poverty, there are tensions between targeted transfer approaches and universal approaches. These tensions have to be addressed on a case-by-case basis.

In the end, however, social protection programmes are just one tool in the wider effort to address the underlying issue of child poverty. In adopting the SDGs, world leaders recognized the central importance of that issue. Goal 1 aims to effectively end extreme poverty by 2030 (Target 1.1) and to reduce by at least half the proportion of men, women and children living in poverty in all its dimensions under national definitions (Target 1.2). The goals also emphasize that no country is immune to the impact of poverty, underscoring the fact that ending child poverty is a universal challenge.

Working towards the 2030 goals, governments will have to recognize and respond to the distinctive challenges of child poverty in all its dimensions and make explicit commitments to end it. Failing to do so in this generation will transmit the human, social and economic costs to future generations.

What are we waiting for? Sustainable societies begin with children

By Kailash Satyarthi, Nobel Peace Prize Laureate and founder, Kailash Satyarthi Children's Foundation

In the foothills of the Himalayas, many years ago, I met a small, skinny child labourer. He asked me: "Is the world so poor that it cannot give me a toy and a book, instead of forcing me to take a gun or a tool?" Another time, a child-mother from the streets of Colombia who had been trafficked, raped and enslaved, asked me this: "I have never had a dream. Can my child have one?" A Sudanese child, kidnapped by an extremist militia and forced to kill his friends and family, once asked me: "Is this my fault?"

Slavery did not end with abolition in the 19th century. Even in modern times and developed countries, it still exists in its cruellest forms. Most recent data show that there are still 150 million child labourers in the world; that 59 million children of primary school age are out of school; and that 15 million girls under 18 are forced into marriage each year. Millions of children live with a disability that makes them more likely to be marginalized or miss out on education.

Millions of undocumented immigrants and people on the margins of society are trafficked and forced into domestic labour or the sex trade. In crisis-affected areas, slavery is much more rampant, as children are given guns instead of toys and girls are sometimes sold for less than a pack of cigarettes. Unfortunately, 37 million children living in crisis-affected countries are out of primary or lower-secondary school. I have met children toiling on cocoa farms in Côte d'Ivoire, selling flowers in Colombia, sewing footballs in Pakistan, working in mica mines and brick kilns in India, and living unimaginable horrors in Nigeria.

All children deserve a fair and equal start in life. They deserve freedom and a childhood. They deserve comprehensive, well-rounded, quality education. These have to be viewed not just as basic rights but as a means towards a more inclusive and sustainable society.

In September 2015, more than 200 world leaders came together to adopt a 15-year plan for sustainable development. I applaud the United Nations for incorporating the need to eliminate child labour, forced labour, modern slavery and human trafficking, as well as a strong emphasis on inclusive and equitable quality education, into the Sustainable Development Goals (SDGs). For the first time, clear targets have been set to end these evils, and the relationship between them and sustainable growth has been recognized. My fellow activists and I had been calling for this for many years.

Sustainable societies can only have a prosperous future when their children are safe, educated and healthy. Put simply, ending child labour, slavery, trafficking and violence against children is directly tied to achieving most of the other development goals.

Together, we have framed a will for a better future. However, what matters most is the will in the words, not the words in the will.

Addressing the United Nations SDG Summit in New York, I, on behalf of the most marginalized children, demanded action, not promises. We know progress is possible: Since the last development agenda, both the number of people living in extreme poverty and the number of primary-school-aged children out of school have been halved successfully.

Our generation can be the one that puts a complete end to the evil of child slavery. We can provide an education for every last child. We have an opportunity to embrace peace, equality, inclusivity and sustainable development by ensuring freedom for all.

But we can only do so when governments, businesses, civil society and citizens unite, and when each carries out its role wilfully and effectively. We

unicef ♥ 70 YEARS FOR EVERY CHILD

need governments to make child-friendly policies and invest adequately in education and young people. Governments can no longer ignore the economic arguments against child labour. Increased child labour leads to higher unemployment. Today, for the 150 million children (5–14 years old) doing jobs meant for adults, there are 200 million unemployed adults. Through the right economic measures, governments should ensure decent living wages for parents so they can send their children to school.

The benefits of education are known to contribute to economic growth and poverty alleviation. Reports show that each dollar invested in quality education will return 15 times the amount in two decades. The rule of law should extend to every last child. Businesses must be more responsible and faith leaders must recognize that compassion for others is a central tenet for all faiths.

It is the responsibility of each and every one of us: We must build the world of our dreams with compassion for our fellow man and woman, regardless of ethnicity, race, religion, nationality, politics or anything else.

When we as citizens unite in holding governments, businesses and civil society accountable, anything will be possible. My colleagues and I have humbly done our part – drop by drop over the years. The result is that more than 85,000 children have been rescued from child labour and servitude and given back their childhood. It is not enough to extinguish the blaze represented by the millions of children who remain in slavery, but to those children and their families it has meant everything.

We can be and must be the generation that extinguishes that blaze once and for all.

We need to teach our bright, young, energetic and idealistic youth the value of compassion, so they don't become disillusioned or turn to violence at a time when both they and the world seem more susceptible than ever. Devli, an eight-year-old bonded labourer whom my colleagues and I once rescued from a stone quarry, perfectly captured the urgency upon which we must act. She asked me, "Why didn't you come earlier?"

Her question is for all of us. What are we waiting for? Each one of us has the potential to bring about

change if we channel our energies and our anger at injustices in the right way. Even a small spark can dispel darkness in a room. And each of us represents a small but critical spark if we act on the problems we see rather than just witness them.

Together we can ensure that the commitments for a sustainable world are kept and that slavery is relegated to the history books where it belongs. Let that be the legacy of our lives – our gift to the world.

A girl makes bricks at a factory in the Shahdra neighbourhood, north of Lahore, Pakistan.

© UNICEF/UNI44028/Pirozzi

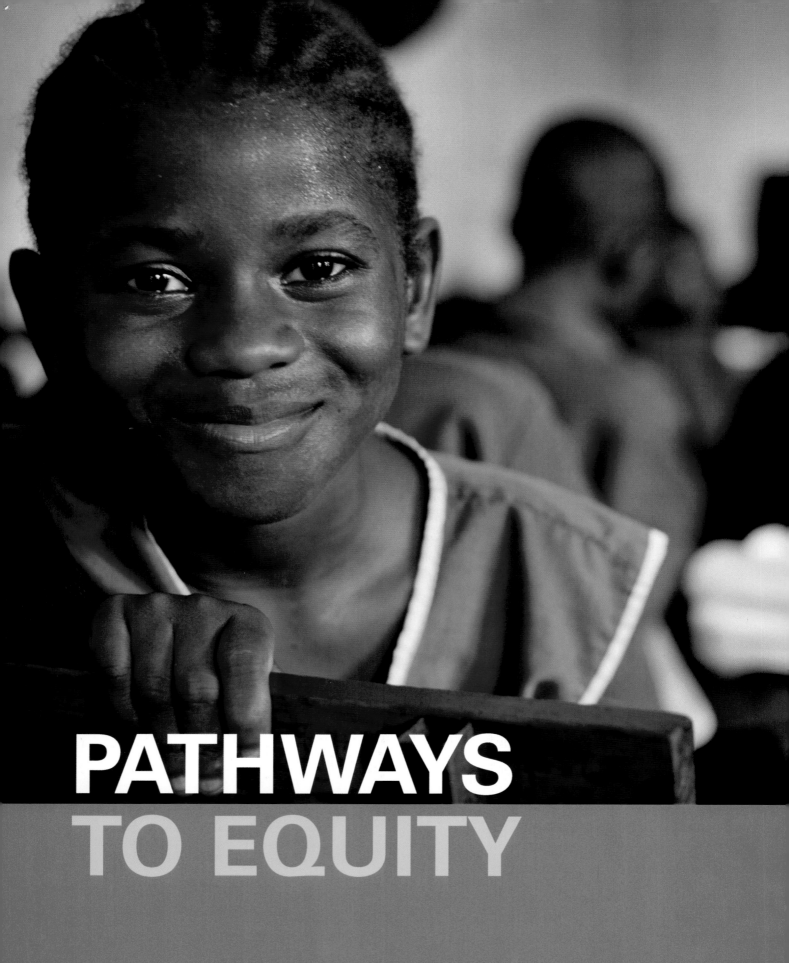

PATHWAYS
TO EQUITY

CHAPTER 4

Pathways to equity

Every child has the right to a fair chance – and every society has a stake in expanding opportunity, leaving no one behind. It's the right thing to do, and the smart thing to do. And now is the time to chart our course towards a more equitable world.

Fatuma, 10, lost both of her parents to Ebola. She attends primary school in Freetown, Sierra Leone.

© UNICEF/UN011612/Holt

A defining shift in this still-new century is the growing global understanding of the scope – and the cost – of an increasingly unequal world. This report has argued that, left unaddressed, inequities in childhood and adolescence will continue to generate unequal outcomes for families around the world, fuelling intergenerational cycles of disadvantage that threaten the strength and stability of societies everywhere.

Current rates of progress are insufficient to interrupt those cycles and close gaps in equity by 2030 – the target year for reaching the Sustainable Development Goals, which pledge to leave no one behind. If current trends continue until then, some regions and countries with growing populations and high levels of disadvantage, especially Africa and Asia, will have the same number of children out of school as there are today. Almost 120 million children will suffer from stunting, undermining their physical and cognitive development, with potentially irreversible consequences. Conflicts and chronic crises caused by the effects of climate change will increase risks to children's lives and futures, displacing more and more children and families, increasing vulnerability and deepening disadvantage.

But as this report shows, and as growing evidence clearly indicates, inequity is neither inevitable nor insurmountable. With the right investments, at the right time, disadvantaged children can realize their rights to a better life. By reducing the inequities that violate their rights today, such investments can help these children lead more productive lives as adults and enable them to pass on more opportunities to their children, thus replacing intergenerational cycles of deprivation with sustainable cycles of opportunity.

That is the promise – and the imperative – of equity.

Every child has the right to a fair chance, and all societies have a stake in expanding opportunity for their youngest members. Drawing from the work of UNICEF and partners, the five key areas that follow – information, integration, innovation, investment and involvement – represent broad, often overlapping, pathways to equity. They encompass operating principles and critical shifts that can help governments, development partners, civil society and communities shape policies and programmes with the potential to make that fair chance a reality for every child.

Information

Going beyond national averages to focus on the most excluded

Information – broadly encompassing data about who is being left behind and how programmes are reaching or failing to reach those in greatest need – is a first operating principle of equitable development.

One of the most significant drawbacks in the global effort to achieve the Millennium Development Goals (MDGs) was the fact that national averages showing overall gains towards certain goals sometimes masked persistent disparities, failing to reveal that the poorest were not always benefiting proportionately from overall progress. For example, the global target on safe drinking water was met five years ahead of schedule, even though gaps in access to safe sources of drinking water actually widened in some low-income countries.

Without solid data on the status of populations at the subnational level, communities unreached by the advance of progress may remain unnoticed. Improving the availability and quality of data about the children and families in greatest need is therefore critical, including by expanding efforts to measure child poverty in all of its dimensions. The Multiple Indicator Cluster Surveys programme, pioneered by UNICEF and conducted with partners, is helping to break down data on children by household wealth, geography, gender, ethnicity, language, religion, age and many other key factors. The more governments incorporate such disaggregated data into policy planning and public spending, the greater

1 in 4 of the world's school-aged children live in countries **affected by crises**

unicef 70 YEARS FOR EVERY CHILD

unicef 70 YEARS FOR EVERY CHILD

the chances of making a difference in the lives of the most disadvantaged, vulnerable and marginalized children.

Information not only helps shape programmes around community needs, it also helps governments and their development partners change course when programmes are not as efficient as they could be in meeting those needs. For example, M-Trac, an SMS-based disease surveillance and tracking system, provides real-time data, helping governments and development partners monitor stocks of essential medicines more efficiently. And in humanitarian emergencies and other critical situations, information can drive a more timely and targeted response, directing life-saving aid to where it is most needed.

But in itself, information about disparities and other factors that contribute to inequity is not sufficient. Inequities will persist without equity targets and tracking mechanisms to monitor the widening or narrowing of gaps. UNICEF and some partners already use a new system called the Monitoring Equity for Results System (MoRES) to track the progress of joint efforts to overcome bottlenecks that stand between children and families and the services they need. MoRES identifies both barriers to *supply* – for instance, not enough community health centres or skilled birth attendants to serve the needs of poor communities – and barriers to *demand* – for instance, the inability of poor families to pay for medical care, or insufficient understanding of the urgent importance of post-natal care.

Equipped with such data, governments and development partners can target programmes to expand opportunity – for instance, through cash transfers to help families pay school fees, or public awareness campaigns about the importance of birth registration, which provides children with an official identity that can expand their access to services and shield them from exploitation throughout their childhoods.

Governments can further accelerate progress towards the 2030 goals by establishing national equity targets to spotlight disparities, such as those affecting disadvantaged regions or ethnic groups. Governments can also adopt interim 'stepping stone' markers to measure progress towards achieving the overall equity targets – and thus towards achieving the SDGs' mandate to leave no one behind.

The data revolution can benefit the most disadvantaged and hardest to reach, but only if it is truly inclusive of those left behind and uncounted. Among the more exciting and promising shifts in recent years is the way in which communities are collecting and sharing information about local needs and the degree to which they are unmet. For example, U-Report, a real-time social messaging tool, is enabling young U-Reporters to share important information with their governments about pressing issues in their communities and lives – from whether girls are able to go to school to where health interventions are needed to halt the spread of epidemics.

Decision makers are listening. In Uganda, Members of Parliament voluntarily signed up for U-Report to find out what their youngest constituents have to say, and the system has helped strengthen immunization coverage there. In Zambia, it is raising awareness about HIV testing. With more than 2 million active users in 22 countries to date, U-Report shows that momentum around citizen-driven data collection and information sharing is a growing trend.

Integration

Taking a multidimensional approach to tackling multiple deprivations that deny children a fair chance in life

Integration – in how we approach solutions and how we deliver interventions – is a critical path towards equitable development.

The multiple threats to the survival and well-being of the most disadvantaged and vulnerable children are not neatly divided by sector. The enormous challenges that affect them – conflicts, climate change, extreme poverty and more – are all closely interconnected. The multiple deprivations that children suffer are also overlapping and all too often mutually reinforcing. So solutions must intersect as well.

Consider the earliest days of a child's life, a brief window of opportunity when brain development is at its peak. Whether children's brains reach the potential that *nature* has given them depends on how they are *nurtured* – whether children receive proper nourishment and stimulation, whether they are protected from violence and prolonged adversity. Early childhood development programmes must therefore be integrated, encompassing education, nutrition and protection.

Integrating interventions across these separate sectors is more effective than addressing them individually: Success in one area supports success in another. For example, the introduction of school feeding programmes to boost nutrition has been linked to increased learning and cognitive development. As noted earlier in this report, in Bangladesh, primary school students in a school meal programme showed a 15.7 per cent improvement in learning achievement, mostly in mathematics.[277]

Integrated strategies can also be more cost-effective, particularly where service providers share human resources[278] – for example, using immunization campaigns in remote areas to deliver critical micronutrients and measure children for stunting.

Most urgently for the hundreds of millions of children affected by conflict and chronic crises – including those caused by climate change – we need to break down the artificial barriers between development work and humanitarian action. No such distinction exists in the lives of the children these interventions are designed to help.

A lack of development can intensify the impact of conflict and worsen or even help trigger natural disasters, such as flooding and mudslides. Disasters and conflicts can interrupt, and sometimes roll back, years of development progress, risks that are now playing out in countries like the Central African Republic, the Syrian Arab Republic and Yemen, with tremendous short- and long-term consequences. Conversely, strong development reduces the impact and perhaps even the likelihood of future crises.

Immediate humanitarian action can also provide pathways to 'build back better' and advance development. For example, following the 2015 earthquake in Nepal, the government's social assistance programmes provided a platform to disburse cash transfers to approximately 400,000 of the people most affected. From a humanitarian standpoint, this assistance supported the immediate needs of people whose lives had been torn apart. From a development perspective, it prevented those families from spending their assets to cope with the aftermath of the disaster and spurred the government to establish a new monitoring system to strengthen future social assistance efforts.

Students whose education has been disrupted by conflict attend Curriculum B classes at the Hasan Zaiat school in Aleppo, the Syrian Arab Republic.

Similarly, during the worst of the Ebola crisis in West Africa, UNICEF and partners not only built new community care centres to help care for Ebola victims, but also worked to revitalize existing primary-health-care centres to treat those suffering from other ailments – an important investment in the future.

The SDGs explicitly recognize – as the MDGs did not – the inherent connections among economic development, social development, environmental protection and peacebuilding. We will not meet the global goals without an integrated approach to development and humanitarian action. Not when millions of children are bearing the brunt of climate-related disasters and chronic crises and nearly 250 million are living in countries and areas affected by armed conflict. Not when 24 million of the children in these places are out of school. Not when these countries account for nearly two thirds of the world's children who have not been immunized with basic vaccines.[279] And not when millions of children are on the move as families desperately flee their homes and embark on dangerous journeys that leave children more vulnerable and deepen deprivation.

Insisting on closer coordination among humanitarian and development organizations can help break down divisions between sectors. This includes joint planning, keeping humanitarian needs front and centre as we implement the SDGs, and integrating appeals for both humanitarian and development funding during specific crises. And it includes using more social protection tools like cash transfers in humanitarian emergencies to provide short-term support for families while strengthening social safety nets for the future.

Taken together, these practical, cost-effective measures, focusing on countries in crisis, will not only support emergency response in the short term but also map out a path to expanded opportunity for the most vulnerable and excluded children throughout their lives.

Innovation

Accelerating change for the most disadvantaged children by using new and different approaches to development

For UNICEF, innovation means doing our work in a different way that adds value to children's lives. Innovation is not a value in itself but, rather, a new approach to solving difficult problems.

UNICEF has a long history of supporting innovation for children. We have pioneered and collaborated on solutions such as the Mark II Handpump (to improve access to safe water) and ready-to-use therapeutic food (to treat severe acute malnutrition). And we found new ways of working with governments and other partners to increase global immunization rates of children under age 5, from 20 per cent to 76 per cent, in a single decade (1980–1990).

The evolving challenges now facing the world's children – from disease outbreaks to the migrant and refugee crisis, to the situation of millions of out-of-school children – have one thing in common: the great speed at which they are disrupting young lives. Meeting these challenges means, yet again, reinventing our ways of working. It means being agile and adaptable in how we build solutions. It means looking towards new partnerships – including collaborations with companies that might not be our traditional partners, and with young people themselves.

In an increasingly connected world, more and more people are accessing basic information services. As a result, the global drive for new solutions is engaging more and more young people not only as beneficiaries of solutions but also as problem-solvers in their own right.

A child receives ready-to-use therapeutic food as part of a package of services for the treatment of malnutrition, in Somalia.

© UNICEF/UNI201564/Rich

A woman is photographed for the Rapid Family Tracing and Reunification mobile phone application in the Nyarugusu refugee camp, in Kigoma Region, Burundi.

© UNICEF/UNI188792/Beechey

Innovation in the development and humanitarian sectors is also about being open about failures as well as successes. It is about using technology to get information in new ways, at new speeds.

In an emergency setting, social messaging tools now make it possible to get information from the affected populations in real time. For example, during the Ebola epidemic in West Africa, UNICEF was able to talk with young people directly using the U-Report system, our social messaging platform for communication between young people and decision makers. In Liberia, UNICEF and partners involved in the Ebola response polled more than 43,000 people in a single day via text messages to find out about their needs, aggregate that information and take action accordingly.

U-Report is now available in 22 countries and has more than 2.1 million users. It is one of the many new tools that are dramatically changing the way problems come to light – and the way solutions are discovered. These tools add urgency to the work of governments and the rest of the international community. When we get information in real time, we have an obligation to respond.

Technological innovations not only improve communication and collaboration, but they also provide new ways of gathering data. For instance, the Ugandan Bureau of Statistics is using the U-Report survey tool to create micro surveys that the government can distribute via mobile phone. Such digital tools complement paper-based surveys, which often reflect information obtained several months or even years in the past. Using real-time data gives governments and their development partners a quicker sense of critical issues as they arise and enables them to direct their responses strategically.

But innovative solutions are not only about technology; they also demonstrate how technology can support human behaviour as a key driver of success in solving complex, systemic problems in 2016 and beyond.

For UNICEF and partners, innovation means working with young people in new ways. In Blantyre, Malawi, our Innovation Lab works with the Polytechnic Institute and primary and secondary schoolchildren who are able to design solutions to their own problems. These young people are using modern design techniques and concepts to figure out how to best shape their world – including ways to create a school environment that is more conducive to learning.

In this relationship, UNICEF functions as a broker and a convener, not pushing ideas but working with young people and institutional partners to help them take good ideas to scale.

This approach points to a new way of doing business, with innovation opening up opportunities for new types of partnerships in areas such as personal data. For example, in collaboration with ARM, a leading digital technology company, UNICEF recently launched the Wearables for Good Challenge to accelerate the development of new wearable technologies that can help save and improve children's lives. More than 250 teams from around the world applied. Most of them consisted of young people who believed they could work together on open-source technologies providing mothers in rural environments with the information they need to keep themselves and their children safe.

Innovating for equity is also about how to fund this work and make it real. UNICEF's Innovation Fund, launched in 2015, is a novel instrument enabling us to support local entrepreneurs and designers in a very concrete sense. By creating a

hybrid with elements from the worlds of both venture finance and development, we are now in a position to build a network of companies working on open-source solutions for children who have been left behind.

The Innovation Fund pushes UNICEF to work with partners – including innovation labs, incubators and accelerators – in new ways. It allows for innovative ideas to more quickly permeate UNICEF's global system, and for us to test, evaluate and adapt them to the needs of the world's most vulnerable children.

In the end, our goal is to create real change for children. There is evidence that adopting new ways of doing business can help us do just that.

In Uganda, for instance, unpublished preliminary data indicate a substantial increase in national birth registration levels, stemming from policy change, legislation and community outreach – and the application of mobile technology. And in Liberia, more than 13,000 U-Reporters responded almost instantly to a question about sexual violence in schools, with 86 per cent saying it was a serious problem. They also provided ideas on how to address the issue. The government subsequently used their feedback to shape local and national policy changes and interventions.

Around the world, innovation is making a difference. Building up real-time, multi-directional information flows, creating communities of open-source change agents and funding them to take innovations to scale: These approaches and more have the potential to reduce inequities by accelerating results for the poorest and most disadvantaged children.

U-Reporter Michelle Abika (centre) helps raise community awareness about Ebola prevention, in Monrovia, Liberia.

© NICEF/UNI178336/Naftalin

Investment

Using equity-focused budgeting and innovative finance to reach the most excluded children and families

As this report has argued, investing in the most disadvantaged children and communities is more than a moral imperative. It is a smart, strategic investment that helps achieve results more effectively and more cost-effectively, in turn helping to break intergenerational cycles of deprivation and strengthening societies. The reverse is also true: When we fail to invest in the most marginalized children and families, we also fail their societies. Disparities in access to critical services and support cost hundreds of billions of dollars globally every year.[280]

Expanding opportunity for the most disadvantaged children should be a first priority in budget design and public spending. A country's budget reflects how well political commitments are being translated into direct actions to benefit the most excluded children. Such spending plays a crucial role in funding the systems that connect disadvantaged children and families with essential services and support, including social safety nets that protect families during crises and other shocks.

Prioritizing children in national budgets is not enough. All governments – whether they are in low-, middle- or high-income countries – also need to analyse the impact of their budget decisions on the most vulnerable children. In some cases, public spending is skewed in favour of the most, not the least, advantaged children. Perhaps the most glaring illustration of this injustice is the gap in per capita spending on education. In some low-income countries, nearly half of all public spending on education is dedicated to the best-educated students, representing only 10 per cent of the total student population. Similarly, in many countries, students growing up in the wealthiest households have access to up to 18 times more public educational resources, including textbooks and other materials, than students from the poorest households.[281]

But better coordination and planning between ministries of finance and development can help national budgets better serve the needs of the most disadvantaged. So can tracking expenditures more closely to understand whether the programmes they pay for are reaching the hardest to reach.

Better monitoring of the impact of public spending is critical to achieving virtually all of a government's priorities, and achieving equity for children is no exception. Several countries have mechanisms in place to provide a foundation for monitoring the impact of public spending on child poverty. Bangladesh, for example, has developed a child-focused budgeting framework that is used by the Ministry of Finance to review potential impacts on children. In South Africa, the Children's Institute is monitoring budgetary allocations aimed at implementing the provisions of the country's Children's Act of 2005.

At the same time, governments can increase the return on their investments by adopting more integrated planning and budget approaches, as well as more integrated programme delivery across sectors, as this chapter has already discussed.

In the midst of funding shortfalls and increasing competition for official development assistance and humanitarian aid, low- and middle-income countries and their development partners are finding new ways of filling gaps in funding and securing more predictable and diversified funding sources. While targeted, short-term investments can often break bottlenecks that prevent children and

families from accessing critical services and support, those achievements cannot be sustained over time without more sustainable financing.

Today, new partnerships are showing how public and private funding can be mobilized and targeted directly to the most disadvantaged – from cash grants for poor families so they can afford health care and education for their children, to financing for programmes that train front-line and community health workers, to support for expanded education programming in ethnic minority and indigenous communities.

Some of the most promising of these new partnerships are finding new ways to finance the development and provision of critical supplies such as vaccines, insecticide-treated mosquito nets and nutritional supplements to the most excluded children and communities. For instance, the Power of Nutrition partnership aims to raise US$1 billion for nutrition using an innovative matching mechanism that multiplies every dollar in private funding up to six times with new financing secured from other investors. Similarly, UNITLIFE uses micro levies from extractive industries to increase resources for the fight against malnutrition in sub-Saharan Africa; for example, the Republic of the Congo will contribute the equivalent of US$0.10 per barrel of oil sold by its national oil company. And UNITAID, a global health initiative to combat HIV/AIDS, tuberculosis and malaria, raised more than half its funds over the past five years through levies on air travel.

Among the most successful examples of such an innovative partnership is GAVI, the Vaccine Alliance, which helps shape markets and make vaccines more affordable for developing countries. GAVI has partnered with the World Bank, the World Health Organization, the Bill and Melinda Gates Foundation and UNICEF to speed up the development and availability of vaccines to prevent pneumococcal disease, one of the leading causes of mortality in children under age 5.

The need for more predictable funding and sustained investment is of more urgent importance when it comes to humanitarian emergencies. Humanitarian needs have grown exponentially as conflicts have become more protracted and crises both more frequent and more intense. With funding shortfalls growing, donors, governments and international organizations are exploring new ways to fund humanitarian action.

Investing in emergency-preparedness before emergencies happen improves the ability of governments and international organizations to respond to them – with high returns on investment. Prepositioning supplies in regions prone to droughts and floods and conducting training and simulations in-country can decrease the need to surge staff in emergencies, reduce procurement and transportation costs, speed up response time and even cut carbon dioxide emissions. Similarly, investing in improving local health systems and other critical infrastructure not only strengthens development, but also reduces the impact and the cost of responding to crises.

A joint research initiative by the World Food Programme and UNICEF, supported by the United Kingdom Department for International Development, calculated that investment for humanitarian preparedness in high-risk contexts yields an average financial return of 200 per cent – meaning that every US$1 spent on preparing is worth an average US$2 needed in the event of an emergency.[282]

Making resources work best for the most disadvantaged children – by securing more equitable investment – takes on ever increasing importance in the context of the Sustainable Development Goals. By encouraging governments to leave no one behind, the new global goals require deliberate shifts in policy, budget design and public spending to benefit those in greatest need.

Involvement

Achieving equity for children is everybody's business

By definition, equitable development is inclusive development. Traditional, top-down ways of promoting development – a vertical system led almost entirely by governments and international agencies – are beginning to shift. Development is becoming more horizontal, crossing sectors, geographies and age groups, and transcending traditional barriers to participation. Greater cooperation, coordination and collaboration among low- and middle-income countries is creating a robust exchange of resources, technology and knowledge to tackle common challenges. Social media and digital technology are organizing, increasing and sustaining public engagement more quickly and effectively, as groups share information, broaden their memberships and multiply the number of partners dedicated to the same causes.

These new opportunities and channels are giving citizens a way to raise their voices about urgent issues affecting their lives. They are providing governments with valuable insights into the lives and needs of those who have been left behind and uncounted. And, significantly, they are fuelling a new era of involvement and public engagement – ranging from local campaigns to broad movements that call for change and give people a powerful new way to demand accountability for the promises their leaders have made.

These loosely organized efforts can be local, national, regional or global – or cross the lines among them. In India, the I Paid a Bribe movement started out as a website for ordinary citizens to report instances of government corruption in their own lives, but it rapidly grew into a movement to combat government corruption in India and beyond.

In Nigeria, the #bringbackourgirls campaign – which has achieved global reach – began with a single tweet by a lawyer in Abuja protesting the abduction of hundreds of schoolgirls by the armed group Boko Haram.

As part of the Scaling Up Nutrition movement, women attend a nutrition demonstration in Burkina Faso.

© UNICEF/UNI189376/Hubbard

Mohammad Abdullah-Shariff, his wife, Shirin Aziz-Amah, and their five children. After fleeing Iraq, they received help from volunteers, near the village of Skala Eressos, Lesbos, Greece. At right, the family, at the Moria reception centre for refugees and migrants.

© UNICEF/UNI197504/Gilbertson VII Photo

In the United States, the Ice Bucket Challenge was started in 2014 by a group of college students after a friend was diagnosed with amyotrophic lateral sclerosis (ALS), an incurable degenerative disorder. Their online challenge to their friends to either dump a bucket of ice on their heads within 24 hours and challenge others to do the same, or make a contribution to the ALS Association. It raised US$115 million to date and engaged millions of people in finding a cure.[283]

Some movements are never meant to 'go viral' or to transform a national or local issue into a global call for action. But they can still have a tremendous impact on people's lives. For example, a movement to end open defecation in Nepal mobilized both citizens and civic authorities in some of the poorest parts of the country and, in a short time, resulted in 27 districts becoming open-defecation–free.

Movements can also be a powerful pillar of support for government efforts to benefit the most disadvantaged children. For example, the Scaling Up Nutrition (SUN) movement has succeeded in making the prevention of undernutrition a growing global priority – a success it owes to a powerful combination of government commitment and resources, supported by networks of activists and experts around the world using technology to draw attention to the scourge of stunting and organize for change.

Whatever form they take, movements require a different way of working and a new kind of leadership. True movements are led from *within*, not solely from the offices of decision makers in national governments or the United Nations. But governments, international organizations and civil society should see this as an opportunity to work together with communities to address common challenges, such as protecting the environment, ending extreme poverty, promoting women's rights and, fundamentally, expanding opportunity so that the most disadvantaged children can realize their right to a fair chance in life.

unicef   70 YEARS FOR EVERY CHILD

Equity for every child

Information and data help us identify the children and communities being left behind and monitor the effectiveness of our efforts to reach them. Integration across sectors addresses the overlapping deprivations and challenges children face. Innovation spurs new solutions to old problems, helping children and communities meet the challenges of a changing world. Investment, approached equitably, fuels more sustainable progress for the most disadvantaged. Involvement by communities, including by children and young people, is changing the way we set priorities and take action. All are pathways to building a more equitable world where every child has a fair chance for a better future.

Fulfilling the promise of equity is possible. Inequalities in opportunity for children can be drastically reduced within a generation.

As the world embarks on an ambitious new course of international development, the pledge to leave no one behind must become more than a slogan. Providing a fair chance for every child must be an operating principle for us all.

Achieving equity for children is a question of priorities, recognizing both the moral and strategic importance of investing in those in greatest need.

It is a practical challenge, overcoming barriers and bottlenecks that keep children from the support they need and block their access to critical opportunities.

It is a matter of political will, translating commitment into action through equity-focused policies, programmes and public spending to improve the lives of the most disadvantaged.

It is an investment, shifting how governments and donors finance development to better serve the most excluded.

It is a broader commitment, putting an end to conflict and violence that target children and following through on pledges to address the effects of climate change.

Finally, it is a call to action for all people to engage in building a more equitable world, knowing that a sustainable future – and our shared destiny – depend on it.

ENDNOTES

1. United Nations Children's Fund, *Narrowing the Gaps to Meet the Goals*, UNICEF, New York, September 2010.
2. United Nations Inter-agency Group for Child Mortality Estimation, *Levels & Trends in Child Mortality – Report 2015*, UNICEF, New York, September 2015, p. 3 (hereafter referred to as 'UN IGME 2015').
3. Ibid.
4. United Nations Children's Fund, *Progress for Children: Beyond averages – learning from the MDGs*, No. 11, UNICEF, New York, June 2015, pp. 22, 26.
5. The projections in this paragraph were calculated for UNICEF by the Overseas Development Institute, 2015.
6. United Nations, Transforming our world: the 2030 Agenda for Sustainable Development, General Assembly Resolution A/RES/70/1, paragraph 4, United Nations, New York, 25 September 2015.
7. United Nations Office for the Coordination of Humanitarian Affairs, *Global Humanitarian Overview 2016*, United Nations OCHA, New York 2015, p. 5.
8. United Nations High Commissioner for Refugees, *UNHCR Mid-Year Trends 2015*, UNHCR, Geneva, 2015, p. 3.
9. United Nations Office for the Coordination of Humanitarian Affairs, *Global Humanitarian Overview 2016*, United Nations OCHA, New York, December 2015, p. 3.
10. United Nations Children's Fund, *Humanitarian Action for Children 2016 – Overview*, UNICEF, New York, January 2016, pp. 3, 6–7.
11. United Nations Children's Fund, *Unless We Act Now: The impact of climate change on children*, UNICEF, New York, November 2015.
12. World Health Organization, Quantitative Risk Assessment of the Effects of Climate Change on Selected Causes of Death, 2030s and 2050s, WHO, Geneva, 2014.
13. Grant, James P., *The State of the World's Children 1980–81*, UNICEF, New York, n.d., p. 6.
14. UN IGME 2015.
15. World Health Organization, United Nations Children's Fund, United Nations Population Fund and the World Bank, *Trends in Maternal Mortality: 1990 to 2015 – Estimates by WHO, UNICEF, UNFPA, World Bank Group and the United Nations Population Division*, WHO, Geneva, November 2015.
16. United Nations Children's Fund, *Committing to Child Survival: A Promise Renewed – Progress report 2015*, UNICEF, New York, September 2015 (hereafter referred to as 'APR 2015'), p. 35.
17. United Nations Children's Fund, *Narrowing the Gaps to Meet the Goals*, UNICEF, New York, September 2010.
18. APR 2015, p. 35.
19. APR 2015, pp. 28, 29.
20. The World Bank, *World Development Report: Conflict, security, and development*, The World Bank, Washington, D.C., 2011, p. 62.
21. APR 2015, p. 32.
22. UN IGME 2015.
23. United Nations Children's Fund, *The State of the World's Children 2012: Children in an urban world*, UNICEF, New York, February 2012.
24. Save the Children, *A Devastating Toll: The impact of three years of war on the health of Syria's children*, Save the Children, London, March 2014, p. iv.

25. United Nations Children's Fund, *Unless We Act Now: The impact of climate change on children*, UNICEF, New York, November 2015, p. 8.
26. Ibid.
27. World Health Organization, *Preventing Diarrhoea through Better Water, Sanitation and Hygiene: Exposures and impacts in low- and middle-income countries*, WHO, Geneva, December 2014.
28. Ezeh, Osita K., et al., 'The Impact of Water and Sanitation on Childhood Mortality in Nigeria: Evidence from Demographic and Health Surveys, 2003–2013', *International Journal of Environmental Research and Public Health*, vol. 11, no. 9, September 2014, pp. 9256–9272.
29. Nepal National Sanitation and Hygiene Coordination Committee, 'Nepal Country Paper on Sixth South Asian Conference on Sanitation (SACOSAN-VI)', Dhaka, January 2016, p. 17.
30. United Nations Children's Fund, *Annual Results Report 2014: Water, sanitation and hygiene*, UNICEF, New York, June 2015, p. 3.
31. UN IGME 2015.
32. APR 2015, p. 19.
33. World Health Organization, United Nations Children's Fund, United Nations Population Fund and the World Bank, *Trends in Maternal Mortality: 1990 to 2015 – Estimates by WHO, UNICEF, UNFPA, World Bank Group and the United Nations Population Division*, WHO, Geneva, November 2015.
34. Victora, Cesar G., et al., 'Countdown to 2015: A decade of tracking progress for maternal, newborn, and child survival', *The Lancet*, October 2015, pp. 1–2.
35. You, Danzhen, et al., 'Global, Regional, and National Levels and Trends in Under-5 Mortality between 1990 and 2015, with Scenario-Based Projections to 2030: A systematic analysis by the UN Inter-agency Group for Child Mortality Estimation', *The Lancet*, vol. 386, no. 10010, pp. 2275–2286, December 2015.
36. Ibid.
37. United Nations Children's Fund, *Levels and Trends in Child Mortality*, UNICEF, New York, 2015, pp. 20, 26.
38. Wang, Yanping, et al., 'Under-5 mortality in 2851 Chinese Counties, 1996–2012: A subnational assessment of achieving MDG 4 goals in China', *The Lancet*, vol. 387, no. 10015, January 2016, pp. 273–283.
39. APR 2015, p. 9.
40. Bangladesh (DHS 2014), Indonesia (DHS 2012), India (DHS 2005–2006), Philippines (DHS 2013).
41. Lawn, Joy E., et al., 'Every Newborn: Progress, priorities, and potential beyond survival', *The Lancet*, vol. 384, no. 9938, July 2014, pp. 189–205.
42. UNICEF global databases, 2016.
43. United Nations Children's Fund, *Progress for Children: Beyond Averages – Learning from the MDGs*, No. 11, UNICEF, New York, June 2015.
44. APR 2015.
45. United Nations Educational, Scientific and Cultural Organization, *EFA Global Monitoring Report 2013/14 – Teaching and Learning: Achieving quality for all*, UNESCO, Paris, pp. 158–159.
46. United Nations Children's Fund, *Ending Child Marriage: Progress and prospects*, UNICEF, New York, 2014, p. 6.

47. Ibid. p. 4.
48. United Nations Children's Fund, *A Profile of Child Marriage in Africa*, UNICEF, New York, 2015.
49. World Health Organization, 'Adolescent pregnancy', Fact Sheet No. 364, WHO, Geneva, Updated September 2014.
50. United Nations Children's Fund, *Committing to Child Survival: A Promise Renewed – Progress report 2014*, UNICEF, New York, September 2014, p. 34.
51. DeFranco, Emily A., Shelley Ehrlich and Louis J. Muglia, 'Influence of interpregnancy interval on birth timing', *British Journal of Obstetrics & Gynaecology*, vol. 121, no. 13, December 2014, pp. 1633–1641.
52. United Nations, Department of Economic and Social Affairs, 'World Contraceptive Patterns 2015', United Nations, New York, 2015.
53. United Nations Population Fund, *Adding It Up: The costs and benefits of investing in sexual and reproductive health*, UNFPA, 2014, p. 4.
54. World Health Organization, *Every Newborn: An action plan to end preventable deaths*, WHO, Geneva, June 2014, p. 17.
55. UNICEF Global databases 2016.
56. United Nations Children's Fund, *The State of the World's Children 2016: A fair chance for every child*, Table 13, New York, 2016.
57. United Nations Children's Fund, *Progress for Children – Beyond Averages: Learning from the MDGs*, No. 11, UNICEF, New York, June 2015, p. 2
58. UNICEF Global databases 2016.
59. Bangladesh DHS 2014; Pakistan DHS 2012–2013; Eritrean Population and Health Survey 2010.
60. MDG survey 2012–2013.
61. Central Statistical Agency (Ethiopia) and ICF International, 2012; *Ethiopia Demographic and Health Survey 2011*, Addis Ababa, Ethiopia, and Calverton, Maryland, USA; Central Statistical Agency and ICF International, p. 143.
62. UNICEF Regional Office for CEE/CIS, 'Realizing the Rights of Roma Children and Women in Bosnia and Herzegovina, the former Yugoslav Republic of Macedonia, and Serbia: Summary analysis of key findings from MICS surveys in Roma settlements in the three countries', UNICEF Regional Office for CEE/CIS, issue 2, 2014.
63. Mathews, T. J., Marian F. MacDorman and Marie E. Thoma, 'Infant Mortality Statistics From the 2013 Period: Linked birth/infant death data set', Division of Vital Statistics, National Vital Statistics Reports, vol. 64, no. 9, August 2015, pp. 3–4.
64. Ibid. p. 6.
65. APR 2015, p. 12.
66. Victora, Cesar G., et al., 'Breastfeeding in the 21st Century: Epidemiology, mechanisms, and lifelong effect', *The Lancet*, vol. 387, no. 10017, pp. 475–490, January 2016.
67. John Hopkins University, the Office of the UN Special Envoy for the health-MDGs, the World Bank, Partners in Health, Last Mile Health, the Clinton Foundation, ALMA, the Governments of Ethiopia and Liberia, *Strengthening Primary Health Care through Community Health Workers: Investment case and financing recommendations*, New York, July 2015.
68. Ibid. p. 14.
69. Doherty, Tanya, et al, 'Assessment of Malawi's Success in Child Mortality Reduction through the Lens of the Catalytic Initiative Integrated

Health Systems Strengthening Programme: Retrospective evaluation', *Journal of Global Health*, vol. 5, no. 2, November 2015.

70. APR 2015, p. 39.
71. World Health Organization, *World Malaria Report 2015*, WHO, December 2015.
72. World Health Organization, 'Measles', Fact Sheet WHO/286, WHO, Geneva, Updated March 2016.
73. Email communication from UNICEF Malawi, 23 March 2016.
74. UNICEF projection, based on UN IGME 2015, p. 6.
75. UNICEF projection, based on APR 2015, pp. 61–64.
76. UNICEF projection, based on APR 2015, p. 64.
77. UNICEF analysis based on UN IGME 2015.
78. UNICEF projection, based on APR 2015, p. 63.
79. Calculation based on APR 2015, p. 63: Between 2016 and 2030, 2.1 billion children will be born around the world and sub-Saharan Africa will see 620 million births.
80. UNICEF projection based on APR 2015, p. 63.
81. United Nations, Department of Economic and Social Affairs, Population Division, *World Population Prospects: The 2015 revision*, United Nations, New York, 2015.
82. Alkema, Leontine, et al., 'Global, Regional, and National Levels and Trends in Maternal Mortality between 1990 and 2015, with Scenario-based Projections: A systematic analysis by the UN Maternal Mortality Estimation Inter-Agency Group', *The Lancet*, vol. 387, no. 10017, January 2016, p. 10; World Health Organization, United Nations Children's Fund, United Nations Population Fund and the World Bank, *Trends in Maternal Mortality: 1990 to 2015 – Estimates by WHO, UNICEF, UNFPA, World Bank Group and the United Nations Population Division*, WHO, Geneva, November 2015, p. 54.
83. Liu, Li, et al., 'Global, regional, and national causes of child mortality in 2000–13, with projections to inform post-2015 priorities: an updated systematic analysis', *The Lancet*, vol. 385, no. 9966, October 2014.
84. UNICEF analysis based on UN IGME 2015.
85. APR 2015, pp. 62–70.
86. APR 2015, p. 70.
87. APR 2015, p. 62.
88. Mikkelsen, Lene, et al., 'A Global Assessment of Civil Registration and Vital Statistics Systems: Monitoring data quality and progress', *The Lancet*, vol. 386, no. 10001, October 2015, pp. 1395–1406.
89. United Nations Children's Fund, *Every Child's Birth Right: Inequities and trends in birth registration*, UNICEF, New York, 2013.
90. World Health Organization, 'Working Group on Accountability for Results: Final Paper', Commission on Information and Accountability for Women's and Children's Health, WHO, May 2011.
91. World Bank/WHO, *Global Civil Registration and Vital Statistics Scaling up Investment Plan 2015–2024*, World Bank/WHO, May 2014.
92. Stenberg, Karin, et al., 'Advancing Social and Economic Development by Investing in Women's and Children's Health: A new Global Investment Framework', *The Lancet*, vol. 383, no. 9925, pp. 1333–1354, April 2014.
93. Ibid.

94. United Nations, *The Global Strategy For Women's, Children's and Adolescents' Health (2016–2030): Survive, thrive, transform, Every Woman Every Child*, United Nations, New York, 2015, p. 9.
95. Ozawa, Sachiko, et al., 'Return On Investment From Childhood Immunization In Low- And Middle-Income Countries, 2011–20', *Health Affairs*, vol. 35, no. 2, pp. 199–207, February 2016.
96. Ibid.
97. African Union Commission, NEPAD Planning and Coordinating Agency, UN Economic Commission for Africa, and UN World Food Programme, *The Cost of Hunger in Africa: Social and economic impact of child undernutrition in Egypt, Ethiopia, Swaziland and Uganda – Abridged Report*, UNECA, Addis Ababa, 2014, p. 4.
98. Rollins, Nigel C., et al., 'Why Invest, and What It Will Take to Improve Breastfeeding Practices?', *The Lancet*, vol. 387, no. 10017, pp. 491–504, January 2016.
99. Stenberg, Karin, et al., 'Advancing Social and Economic Development by Investing in Women's and Children's Health: A new global Investment framework', *The Lancet*, vol. 383, no. 9925, pp. 1333–1354, April 2014.
100. Chopra, Mickey, et al., 'Ending of Preventable Deaths from Pneumonia and Diarrhoea: An achievable goal', *The Lancet*, vol. 381, no. 9876, April–May 2013, pp. 1499–1506.
101. Black, Robert E., et al., 'Maternal and Child Nutrition: Building momentum for impact', *The Lancet*, vol. 382, no. 9890, August 2013.
102. World Health Organization, 'Achieving the Health-Related MDGs. It Takes a Workforce!', WHO, Geneva, February 2016.
103. Campbell, Jim, et al., 'A Universal Truth: No health without a workforce – Forum Report' (Third Global Forum on Human Resources for Health, Recife, Brazil), Global Health Workforce Alliance and World Health Organization, Geneva, 2013.
104. John Hopkins University, the Office of the UN Special Envoy for the health-MDGs, the World Bank, Partners in Health, Last Mile Health, the Clinton Foundation, ALMA, the Governments of Ethiopia and Liberia, *Strengthening Primary Health Care through Community Health Workers: Investment case and financing recommendations*, New York, July 2015.
105. World Health Statistics 2015, WHO, p. 116.
106. Boozary, Andrew S., et al., 'The Ebola Outbreak, Fragile Health Systems, and Quality as a Cure', *The Journal of the American Medical Association*, vol. 312, no. 18, pp. 1859–1860, November 2014.
107. Statistics Indonesia (Badan Pusat Statistik—BPS), National Population and Family Planning Board (BKKBN), and Kementerian Kesehatan (Kemenkes–MOH), and ICF International. 2013. Indonesia Demographic and Health Survey 2012. Jakarta, Indonesia: BPS, BKKBN, Kemenkes, and ICF International.
108. Liberia Health System Assessment, 2015, p. 28.
109. 'What Steps Countries Are Taking to Implement Pro-Poor Universal Health Coverage? – A background document prepared for The Bellagio Workshop on Pro-Poor Universal Health Coverage', Evans, David, Naomi Beyeler and Alix Beith, July 2015, p. 11.
110. World Health Organization, *The World Health Report – Health Systems Financing: The path to universal coverage*, WHO, Geneva, 2010.

111. Ibid.
112. The Royal Institute of International Affairs, *Shared Responsibilities for Health: A coherent global framework for health financing, Final Report of the Centre on Global Health Security Working Group on Health Financing*, Chatham House, London, May 2014.
113. Martin, Roma, et al., 'Addressing Inequality in South Asia', South Asia Development Forum, World Bank Group, Washington, D.C., 2015.
114. Greenhill, Romilly, et al., *Financing the Future: How international public finance should fund a global social compact to eradicate poverty*, Overseas Development Institute, London, April 2015.
115. Save the Children, The Rockefeller Foundation, UNICEF and the World Health Organization, *Universal Health Coverage: A commitment to close the gap*, Save the Children Fund, London, September 2013, p. 39.
116. Lindelow, Magnus, and Edson C. Araujo, Brazil – Universal Health Coverage for 'Inclusive and Sustainable Development: Country summary report', Working Paper 91214, The World Bank Group, Washington, D.C., September 2014.
117. Health Insurance System Research Office, *Thailand's Universal Coverage Scheme: Achievements and challenges – An Independent Assessment of the First 10 Years (2001–2010): Synthesis report*, Health Insurance System Research Office, May 2012, pp. 11,19.
118. Tangcharoensathien, Viroj, et al., 'Promoting Universal Financial Protection: How the Thai universal coverage scheme was designed to ensure equity', *Health Research Policy and Systems*, vol. 11, no. 25, August 2013, p. 12.
119. Makaka, Andrew, Sarah Breen and Agnes Binagwaho, 'Universal Health Coverage in Rwanda: A report of innovations to increase enrolment in community-based health insurance', *The Lancet*, vol. 380, Special Issue, S7, October 2012.
120. GAVI, The Vaccine Alliance, 'Immunisation Leaders Call for Increased Political Support for Immunisation in Pakistan', GAVI, The Vaccine Alliance Secretariat, Geneva, February 2015.
121. Behrman, Jere. R., Yingmei Cheng and Petra E. Todd, 'Evaluating Preschool Programs When Length of Exposure to the Program Varies: A nonparametric approach', *Review of Economics and Statistics*, vol. 86, no. 1, February 2004, pp. 108–132.
122. Gertler, Paul, et al., 'Labor Market Returns to Early Childhood Stimulation: A 20-year follow up to an experimental intervention in Jamaica', Policy Research Working Paper no. 6529, World Bank, Washington D.C., July 2013, p. 2.
123. Heckman, James J., 'The Economics of Inequality: The value of early childhood education', *American Educator*, Spring 2011, p. 32.
124. United Nations Educational, Scientific and Cultural Organization, EFA Global Monitoring Report and UNESCO Institute for Statistics, 'A Growing Number of Children and Adolescents Are Out of School as Aid Fails to Meet the Mark', Policy Paper 22, Fact Sheet 31, UNESCO and UIS, Paris and Montreal, July 2015.
125. United Nations Children's Fund, *Early Childhood Development: A statistical snapshot – Building better brains and sustainable outcomes for children*, UNICEF, New York, September 2014, p. 7.

126. United Nations Educational, Scientific and Cultural Organization, EFA Global Monitoring Report and UNESCO Institute for Statistics, 'A Growing Number of Children and Adolescents Are Out of School as Aid Fails to Meet the Mark', Policy Paper 22, Fact Sheet 31, UNESCO and UIS, Paris and Montreal, July 2015.

127. Ibid., p. 4.

128. A UNICEF projection based on 2013 enrolment data from UNESCO Institute for Statistics; United Nations Department of Economic and Social Affairs, World Population Prospects: The 2015 revision, UN DESA, Population Division, New York, 2015.

129. United Nations Educational, Scientific and Cultural Organization, EFA Global Monitoring Report, 'How Long Will it Take to Achieve Universal Primary and Secondary Education?', Technical background note for the Framework for Action on the post-2015 education agenda, UNESCO, Paris, May 2015, p. 3.

130. Ibid.

131. Ibid.

132. UNESCO Institute for Statistics and United Nations Children's Fund, Fixing the Broken Promise of Education for All: Findings from the Global Initiative on Out-of-School Children, UIS, Montreal, 2015, p. 101.

133. United Nations Children's Fund, Early Childhood Development: A statistical snapshot – Building better brains and sustainable outcomes for children, UNICEF, New York, September 2014, p. 7.

134. United Nations Children's Fund China, What Matters to UNICEF China, UNICEF, Beijing, 2014, p. 11.

135. United Nations Children's Fund, Early Childhood Development: A statistical snapshot – Building better brains and sustainable outcomes for children, UNICEF, New York, September 2014, p. 7.

136. Dabla-Norris, Era, et al., Causes and Consequences of Income Inequality: A global perspective, International Monetary Fund, Washington, D.C., June 2015, p. 17.

137. UNESCO World Inequality Database on Education (WIDE).

138. United Nations Children's Fund, Progress for Children: Beyond Averages – Learning from the MDGs, No. 11, UNICEF, New York, June 2015, p. 19.

139. United Nations Educational, Scientific and Cultural Organization, EFA Global Monitoring Report 2015: 2000–2015 – Achievements and challenges, UNESCO, Paris, March 2015, p. 83.

140. UNESCO Institute for Statistics database. Note: Government of Pakistan's Academy of Educational Planning and Management, Pakistan Education Statistics 2014–2015, AEPAM, Islamabad, February 2016. Page 1 indicates that there are more than 6 million children of primary school age out of school.

141. Malik, Rabea, and Pauline Rose, Financing Education in Pakistan Opportunities for Action, Country Case Study for the Oslo Summit on Education for Development, 2015, p. 5.

142. United Nations Educational, Scientific and Cultural Organization, EFA Global Monitoring Report 2013/14: Teaching and learning – Achieving quality for all, UNESCO, Paris, 2014, pp. 5, 19.

143. United Nations Children's Fund, Early Childhood Development: A statistical snapshot – Building Better Brains and Sustainable Outcomes for Children, UNICEF, New York, 23 September 2014, p. 7; and UNICEF global databases, 2014, based on MICS and DHS, 2009–2012.

144. United Nations Children's Fund, Early Childhood Development: A statistical snapshot – Building better brains and sustainable outcomes for children, UNICEF, New York, 23 September 2014, p. 7.

145. United Nations Children's Fund, Progress for Children: Beyond Averages – Learning from the MDGs, No. 11, UNICEF, New York, June 2015, p. 53.

146. Rose, Pauline, and Benjamin Alcott, 'How Can Education Systems Become Equitable by 2030?', DFID think pieces – Learning and equity, United Kingdom Department for International Development, London, August 2015, pp. 12–14.

147. Ibid., p. 14.

148. Schady, Norbert, et al., 'Wealth Gradients in Early Childhood Cognitive Development in Five Latin American Countries', Journal of Human Resources, vol. 50, no. 22015, pp. 446–463.

149. Oviedo, Maria, Ariel Fiszbein and Federico Sucre, 'Learning For All: An Urgent Challenge in Latin America, Commission For Quality Education For All Background Paper', The Dialogue Leadership for the Americas, Washington, D.C., July 2015, p. 4.

150. Uwezo Kenya, Are Our Children Learning?: Annual Learning Assessment Report, Uwezo Kenya, Nairobi, 2012, p. 3.

151. Uwezo, Uganda, Are Our Children Learning?: Annual learning assessment report, Uwezo Uganda, Kampala, 2012, p. 14.

152. Ibid., p. 3.

153. Organisation for Economic Co-operation and Development, PISA 2012 Results in Focus: What 15-year-olds know and what they can do with what they know, OECD, Paris, 2014, pp. 4–5.

154. Bos, Maria Soledad, Alejandro J. Ganimian and Emiliana Vegas, América Latina en PISA 2012: ¿Cómo se desempeñan los estudiantes pobres y ricos? Washington, D.C., Inter-American Development Bank, 2013, quoted in Oviedo, M., Ariel Fiszbein and Federico Sucre, 'Learning For All: An Urgent Challenge in Latin America', Commission For Quality Education For All Background Paper, The Dialogue Leadership for the Americas, Washington, D.C., July 2015, p. 4.

155. International Labour Organization, Global Employment Trends for Youth 2015: Scaling up investments in decent jobs for youth, ILO, Geneva, 2015, p.33.

156. Steer, Liesbet, Hafez Ghanem, Maysa Jalbout, et al., Arab Youth: Missing Educational Foundations for a Productive Life?, The Center for Education at the Brookings Institution, Washington, D.C., February 2014, p. 16.

157. Oviedo, Fiszbein and Sucre, 'Learning For All', p. 10.

158. Organisation for Economic Co-operation and Development, Equity and Quality in Education Supporting Disadvantaged Students and Schools, OECD, Paris, 2012, p. 80.

159. Organisation for Economic Co-operation and Development, Education at a Glance 2014: OECD indicators, OECD, Paris, 2014, p. 9.

160. Ibid., p. 14.

161. Email from UNICEF Tunisia, 4 March 2016.

162. United Nations Educational, Scientific and Cultural Organization Institute for Statistics, EFA Global Monitoring Report 2012: Youth and skills – Putting education to work, UNESCO, Paris, March 2012, p. 16.

163. Nicolai, Susan, et al., Education Cannot Wait: Proposing a fund for education in emergencies, Overseas Development Institute, London, May 2016, p. 7.

164. United Nations Educational, Scientific and Cultural Organization, EFA Global Monitoring Report, 'Humanitarian Aid for Education: Why it matters and why more is needed', Policy Paper 21, UNESCO, Paris, June 2015, p. 3.

165. United Nations Children's Fund Regional Office for the Middle East and North Africa, Education under Fire: How conflict in the Middle East is depriving children of their schooling, UNICEF, Amman, September 2015, pp. 4, 12.

166. The Global Coalition to Protect Education from Attack, Education under Attack 2014, The Global Coalition to Protect Education from Attack Secretariat, New York, 2014, p. 8.

167. United Nations, Children and Armed Conflict: Report of the Secretary-General, A/69/926–S/2015/409, United Nations, New York, 5 June 2015, pp. 2, 39 and 40.

168. United Nations Office for the Coordination of Humanitarian Affairs, 2016 Humanitarian Response Plan, Nigeria, OCHA, New York, December 2015, p. 5.

169. United Nations, Children and Armed Conflict, Report of the Secretary-General, A/69/926–S/2015/409, United Nations, New York, 5 June 2015, pp. 2, 6, 9.

170. Multiple Indicator Cluster Surveys 2001 and 2010; Demographic Health Surveys 2007 and 2013–2014.

171. Crawford, Nicholas, et al., Protracted Displacement: Uncertain paths to self-reliance in exile, Overseas Development Institute, London, September 2015, p. 1.

172. United Nations Children's Fund, Unless We Act Now: The impact of climate change on children, UNICEF, New York, November 2015, pp. 25, 32.

173. United Nations Children's Fund, 'Cyclone Pam Humanitarian Situation Report 7', March 2015.

174. United Nations Educational, Scientific and Cultural Organization, Pacific Education for All: 2015 review, UNESCO, Paris, 2015, pp. 53, 64.

175. United Nations Office for the Coordination of Humanitarian Affairs, Financial Tracking Service, <https://fts.unocha.org/pageloader.aspx?page=emerg-globalOverview&year=2016>, accessed 3 June 2016.

176. Nicolai, Susan, and Sébastien Hine, Investment for Education in Emergencies: A review of evidence, Overseas Development Institute, London, February 2015, p. 10.

177. United Nations Division of Economic and Social Affairs, 'Youth Population Trends and Sustainable Development', No. 2015/1, UN DESA, New York, May 2015, p. 1.

178. United Nations Children's Fund, The Investment Case for Education and Equity, UNICEF, New York, January 2015, p. 13.

179. United Nations Division of Economic and Social Affairs, 'Youth Population Trends and Sustainable Development', No. 2015/1, UN DESA, New York, May 2015, p. 1.

180. United Nations Children's Fund, The Investment Case for Education and Equity, UNICEF, New York, January 2015, pp. 8–9.

181. Montenegro, Claudio E., and Harry Anthony Patrinos, 'Comparable Estimates of Returns to Schooling around the World', Policy Research Working Paper 7020, The World Bank, Washington, D.C., 2014, p. 16.

182. United Nations Educational, Scientific and Cultural Organization, *EFA Global Monitoring Report 2013/14: Teaching and Learning – Achieving quality for all*, UNESCO, Paris, 2014, pp. 140–185.

183. Ibid., p. 175.

184. Cunningham, Hugh, and Pier Paolo Viazzo, eds., *Child Labour in Historical Perspective: 1800–1985 – Case studies from Europe, Japan and Colombia*, UNICEF International Child Development Centre and Istituto degli Innocenti, Florence, 1996.

185. Hanushek, Eric A., and Ludger Wößmann, *Education Quality and Economic Growth*, The World Bank, Washington, D.C., 2007, p. 1.; and Hanushek, Eric A., and Ludger Wößmann, 'The Role of Cognitive Skills in Economic Development', *Journal of Economic Literature*, vol. 46, no. 3, 2008, pp. 607–668.

186. Hanushek, Eric A., and Ludger Wößmann *Universal Basic Skills: What countries stand to gain*, OECD Publishing, Paris, 2015, p. 10.

187. Hanushek, Eric A., and Ludger Wößmann, *Education Quality and Economic Growth*, The World Bank, Washington, D.C., 2007, p. 1.; and Hanushek, Eric A., and Ludger Wößmann, 'The Role of Cognitive Skills in Economic Development', *Journal of Economic Literature*, vol. 46, no. 3, 2008, pp. 607–668.

188. United Nations Children's Fund, 'Bilan de Compétences – Enfants à L'entrée au Primaire au Cap Vert', UNICEF, Cabo Verde, 2013, p. 46.

189. Berlinski, Samuel, Sebastian Galiani and Paul Gertler, 'The Effect of Pre-primary Education on Primary School Performance', *Journal of Public Economics*, vol. 93, no.1–2, February 2009, pp. 219–234, section 4.5 and section 6.

190. Rose, Pauline, and Benjamin Alcott, 'How Can Education Systems Become Equitable by 2030?', August 2015.

191. United Nations Children's Fund, *The Investment Case for Education and Equity*, UNICEF, New York, January 2015, p. 27.

192. Bangladesh Institute of Development Studies, *Impact Evaluation Study of Reaching Out-of-School Children (ROSC) Project of the Ministry of Primary and Mass Education*, Bangladesh Institute of Development Studies, Dhaka, June 2014, p. 9.

193. United Nations Children's Fund, *EduTrac: Tracking and monitoring education*, UNICEF, New York, March 2013.

194. United Nations Children's Fund, *The State of the World's Children 2015: Reimagine the future*, UNICEF, New York, 2014.

195. United Nations Children's Fund,' "It's about ability" Campaign Results in 80 Per Cent of Citizens Supporting Inclusive Education', UNICEF, New York, February 2016; and United Nations Children's Fund, *The State of the World's Children 2013: Children with disabilities*, UNICEF, New York, May 2013, p. 13.

196. United Nations Children's Fund, *UNICEF Annual Report 2014: Montenegro*, UNICEF, New York, 2014, p. 5.

197. Rose, Pauline, and Benjamin Alcott, 'How Can Education Systems Become Equitable by 2030?', p. 15.

198. Martin, Gayle, H., and Obert Pimhidzai, *Service Delivery Indicators Kenya: Education and health*, the World Bank, Washington, D.C., July 2013, pp.10–11.

199. Rose, Pauline, and Benjamin Alcott, 'How Can Education Systems Become Equitable by 2030?', pp. 13, 23.

200. United Nations Children's Fund, *The Investment Case for Education and Equity*, UNICEF, New York, January 2015, p. 66.

201. United Nations Children's Fund, 'Advancing WASH in Schools Monitoring', Working Paper, UNICEF, New York, 2015, pp. 17, 20.

202. UNESCO Institute for Statistics, January 2015.

203. Muralidharan, Karthik, 'Priorities for Primary Education Policy in India's 12th Five-year Plan', *India Policy Forum 2013*, vol. 9, National Council of Applied Economic Research and the Brookings Institution, New Delhi, 2013. pp.15–16; and Banerjee, Abhijit, V., et al., 'Remedying Education: Evidence from two randomized experiments in India', *The Quarterly Journal of Economics*, vol. 122, no. 3, pp. 1235–1264.

204. Rose, Pauline, and Benjamin Alcott, 'How Can Education Systems Become Equitable by 2030?', p. 23.

205. United Nations Educational, Scientific and Cultural Organization, *EFA Global Monitoring Report 2013/14: Teaching and Learning – Achieving quality for all*, UNESCO, Paris, 2014, pp. 186, 223.

206. United Nations Educational, Scientific and Cultural Organization, *EFA Global Monitoring Report 2015: 2000–2015 – Achievements and challenges*, UNESCO, Paris, March 2015, p. 242.

207. The World Bank, 'Government expenditure on education as % of GDP (%)', The World Bank, Washington, D.C., February 2016.

208. Government of Pakistan Ministry of Finance, *Pakistan Economic Survey 2014–2015*, Government of Pakistan, Islamabad, March 2016, p. 171. Note: The World Bank puts the figure at 2.5 per cent. The World Bank, 'Government expenditure on education as % of GDP (%)', The World Bank, Washington, D.C., February 2016.

209. Steer, Lisbeth, and Katie Smith, *Financing Education: Opportunities for global action*, Center for Universal Education at the Brookings Institution, Washington, D.C., June 2015, p. 23.

210. United Nations Children's Fund, *The Investment Case for Education and Equity*, UNICEF, New York, January 2015, p. 59.

211. Organisation for Economic Co-operation and Development, *Education Policy Outlook Chile*, OECD, Paris, November 2013, p. 8.

212. United Nations Children's Fund, *The Investment Case for Education and Equity*, UNICEF, New York, January 2015.

213. United Nations Children's Fund, 'Rapport final d'évaluation du Programme Appui d'Urgence à l'Éducation Nationale Malgache (AUENM)', Internal Evaluation Report, UNICEF, June 2015.

214. United Nations Educational, Scientific and Cultural Organization, *EFA Global Monitoring Report*, 'Pricing the Right to Education: The cost of reaching new targets by 2030', Policy Paper 18, UNESCO, Paris, July 2015, p. 4. Figures were in US dollars, in 2012.

215. Ibid.

216. Steer, Lisbeth, and Katie Smith, *Financing Education: Opportunities for global action*, Center for Universal Education at the Brookings Institution, Washington, D.C., June 2015, p. 70;

217. United Nations Educational, Scientific and Cultural Organization and UNESCO Institute for Statistics, 'A Growing Number of Children and Adolescents Are Out of School as Aid Fails to Meet the Mark', Policy Paper 22, Fact Sheet 31, UNESCO and UIS, Paris and Montreal, July 2015.

218. Crawford, Nicholas, et al., *Protracted Displacement: Uncertain paths to self-reliance in exile*, Overseas Development Institute, London, September 2015, pp. 2–3.

219. Nicolai, Susan, et al., Education Cannot Wait: Proposing a fund for education in emergencies, Overseas Development Institute, London, May 2016, pp. 9-10.

220. Organisation for Economic Co-operation and Development, *Equity and Quality in Education Supporting Disadvantaged Students and Schools*, OECD, Paris, 2012, p. 15.

221. Hanushek, Eric A., and Ludger Wößmann, Universal Basic Skills: *What countries stand to gain, OECD Publishing, Paris, 2015*, p. 12.

222. Wales, Joseph, et al., *Improvements in the Quality of Basic Education: Chile's experience*, Overseas Development Institute, London, July 2014, p.8.

223. Ferreira, Francisco H. G., et al., *A Global Count of the Extreme Poor in 2012: Data issues, methodology and initial results*, Policy Research Working Paper 7432, World Bank, Washington, D.C., October 2015.

224. Regional aggregates from the World Bank PovcalNet.

225. Economic and Social Commission for Western Asia, *The Arab Millennium Development Goals Report: Facing challenges and looking beyond 2015*, ESCWA, August 2013, p. 3.

226. Economic and Social Commission for Western Asia, *Conflict in the Syrian Arab Republic: Macroeconomic implications and obstacles to achieving the Millennium Development Goals*, ESCWA, June 2014, p. 27.

227. Verme, Paolo, et al., *The Welfare of Syrian Refugees: Evidence from Jordan and Lebanon*, World Bank and United Nations Refugee Agency, December 2015, p. xvi.

228. United Nations, Department of Economic and Social Affairs, Population Division, *World Population Prospects: The 2015 revision*, UN DESA, New York, 2015.

229. ODI calculations for UNICEF based on data from the World Bank and UN DESA.

230. ODI calculations for UNICEF based on data from the World Bank.

231. The World BankPovcalNet.

232. ODI calculations for UNICEF based on data from The World Bank.

233. The World Bank, *Shifting Gears to Accelerate Shared Prosperity in Latin America and the Caribbean*, World Bank, Washington, D.C., June 2013, p. 9. Note: Extreme poverty is defined in this case as living on less than US$2.50 a day. Vulnerability to poverty is defined as living on US$4.10 a day or less.

234. Stampini, M., et al., 'Poverty, Vulnerability and the Middle Class in Latin America', Working Paper Series No. 591, Inter-American Development Bank, Washington, D.C., May 2015.

235. UNICEF Office of Research, 'Children of the Recession: The impact of the economic crisis on child well-being in rich countries', Innocenti

Report Card 12, UNICEF Office of Research, Florence, September 2014.

236. Ortiz, Isabel, and Matthew Cummins, eds., *A Recovery for All: Rethinking socio-economic policies for children and poor households*, UNICEF, Division of Policy and Practice, New York, 2012.

237. UNICEF Office of Research, 'Children of the Recession: The impact of the economic crisis on child well-being in rich countries', Innocenti Report Card 12, UNICEF Office of Research, Florence, September 2014.

238. Ibid., p. 9.

239. Alkire, Sabina, et al., Global Multidimensional Poverty Index 2015 Summary, Oxford Poverty & Human Development Initiative, Oxford, June 2015, p. 1.

240. de Milliano, Marlous, and Ilze Plavgo, 'Analysing Child Poverty and Deprivation in sub-Saharan Africa', Office of Research Working Paper: WP-2014-19, UNICEF Office of Research, Florence, November 2014, p. 18.

241. ECLAC-UNICEF, *La pobreza infantil en América Latina y el Caribe*, CEPAL, Chile, December 2010.

242. The World Bank, *World Development Report: Conflict, security, and development*, World Bank, Washington, D.C., 2011, p. 62

243. United Nations Children's Fund, *Unless We Act Now: The impact of climate change on children*, UNICEF, New York, November 2015, p. 33.

244. Fotso, Jean-Christophe, 'Child health Inequities in Developing Countries: Differences across urban and rural areas', *International Journal for Equity in Health*, vol. 5, no. 9, 2006, p. 8.

245. United Nations Children's Fund and Informal Settlements Development Facility, Egypt, *Multidimensional Child Poverty in Slums and Unplanned Areas in Egypt*, UNICEF Egypt and ISDF, Cairo, 2013, p. 1.

246. United Nations Children's Fund China, *What Matters to UNICEF China*, UNICEF China, 2014, p. 11.

247. United Nations, Department of Economic and Social Affairs, Population Division, *World Urbanization Prospects: The 2014 revision*, UN DESA, New York, 2014, p. 2.

248. International Labour Organization, 'Decent Work and the Informal Economy: A policy resource guide', ILO, March 2013, p. 329.

249. Ibid., p. 30.

250. Jiang, Yang, Mercedes Ekono and Curtis Skinner, 'Basic Facts About Low-Income Children: Children under 18 years, 2013', Fact Sheet, National Center for Children in Poverty, Mailman School of Public Health, Columbia University, New York, January 2015, pp. 1–4.

251. UNICEF Regional Office for Central and Eastern Europe and the Commonwealth of Independent States (CEE/CIS), Education Section, *The Right of Roma Children to Education: Position paper*, UNICEF Regional Office for CEE/CIS, Geneva, 2011.

252. FRA European Union Agency for Fundamental Rights, *Poverty and Employment: The situation of Roma in 11 EU Member States*, European Union Agency for Fundamental Rights, Vienna, 2014, p. 12.

253. Ibid.

254. Ibid., p. 37.

255. Fanjul, Gonzalo, 'Child poverty and inequality in rich countries', Background Paper for *The State of the World's Children 2016*, UNICEF, 2015, p. 4, citing statistics from Eurostat (not published).

256. Ibid.

257. Internal analysis by UNICEF Social Protection for *2015 Annual Results Report* (not yet published).

258. Fiszbein, Ariel, Ravi Kanbur and Ruslan Yemtsov, *Social Protection, Poverty and the Post-2015 Agenda*, World Bank, Washington, D.C., May 2013, p. 12.

259. Soares, Fabio Veras, et al., *Cash Transfer Programmes in Brazil: Impacts on inequality and poverty*, United Nations Development Programme, June 2006, p. 1.

260. De Neubourg, Chris, Bruno Martarano and Marco Sanfilippo, *The Impact of Social Protection on Children: A review of the literature*, UNICEF Office of Research, Florence, June 2012, p. 12.

261. Plagerson, Sophie and Marianne S. Ulriksen, *Cash Transfer Programmes, Poverty Reduction and Empowerment of Women in South Africa*, Working Paper No. 4 / 2015, International Labour Organization, Gender, Equality and Diversity Branch, Conditions of Work and Equality Department, Geneva, 2015, p. 33.

262. Overseas Development Institute, *Doing Cash Differently: How cash transfers can transform humanitarian aid – Report of the high level panel on humanitarian cash transfers*, ODI, London, September 2015, p. 18.

263. Barakat, Nesreen, et al., *A Window of Hope: UNICEF child cash grant programme in Jordan – Post-distribution monitoring report* (February–June 2015), UNICEF Jordan Country Office, August 2015, p. 29.

264. Merttens, Fred, et al., *Kenya Hunger Safety Net Programme Monitoring and Evaluation Component Impact Evaluation: Impact evaluation final report: 2009 to 2012*, Oxford Policy Management, Oxford, June 2013, p. 22.

265. Handa, Sudhanshu, et al., *Livelihood Empowerment against Poverty Impact Evaluation*, Carolina Population Center, University of North Carolina at Chapel Hill, North Carolina, October 2013.

266. Fiszbein, Ariel, and Norbert Schady, 'Conditional Cash Transfers: Reducing Present and Future Poverty', A World Bank Policy Research Report 47603, World Bank, Washington, D.C., 2009, p. xi.

267. Benhassine, Najy, et al., 'Turning a Shove into a Nudge?: A 'labeled cash transfer' for education', *American Economic Journal: Economic Policy*, vol. 7, no. 3, August 2015, pp. 86–125.

268. Guarcello, Lorenzo, Scott Lyon and Furio Rosati, 'Child Labour and Out-of-School Children: Evidence from 25 developing countries', Background Paper for *Fixing the Broken Promise of Education for All*, UNESCO Institute for Statistics and UNICEF, Montreal, 2015, p. 29; International Labour Organization, *World Report on Child Labour 2015: Paving the way to decent work for young people*, ILO, Geneva, 2015, pp. 66–67.

269. UNESCO Institute for Statistics and United Nations Children's Fund, *Fixing the Broken Promise of Education for All: Findings from the Global Initiative on Out-of-School Children*, UNESCO-UIS, Montreal, 2015, p. 42.

270. Filmer, Deon, and Norbert Schady, 'The Medium-term Effects of Scholarships in a Low-Income Country,' *Journal of Human Resources*, vol. 49, no. 3, summer 2014, pp. 663–694.

271. Kazinga, Harounan, et al., *Seven-Year Impacts of Burkina Faso's BRIGHT Program*, Millennium Challenge Corporation, Washington, D.C., February 2016; and Benhassine, Najy, et al., 'Turning a Shove into a Nudge?: A 'labeled cash transfer' for education', *American Economic Journal: Economic Policy*, vol. 7, no. 3, August 2015, pp. 86–125.

272. Ahmed, Akhter, U., 'Impact of Feeding Children in School: Evidence from Bangladesh', International Food Policy Research Institute, Washington, D.C., November 2004, p. 41, mentioned in Sabates-Wheeler, Rachel, and Jennifer Yablonski, 'Social Protection and Child Poverty: Evidence, practice, and gaps', unpublished UNICEF background paper for this edition of *The State of the World's Children 2016*, p. 19.

273. UNESCO Institute for Statistics and United Nations Children's Fund, *Fixing the Broken Promise of Education for All: Findings from the Global Initiative on Out-of-School Children*, UNESCO-UIS, Montreal, 2015, p. 65.

274. Arráiz, Irani, and Sandra Rozo, 'Same Bureaucracy, Different Outcomes in Human Capital?: How indigenous and rural non-indigenous areas in Panama responded to the CCT', Inter-American Development Bank, Office of Evaluation and Oversight, Working Paper OVE/WP-0311, May 2011.

275. Alam, Andaleeb, et al., 'Does Cash for School Influence Young Women's Behavior in the Longer Term? Evidence from Pakistan', Policy Research Working Paper Series 5669, World Bank, Washington, D.C., May 2011.

276. International Labour Organization, *World Social Protection Report 2014/15: Building economic recovery, inclusive development and social justice*, ILO, Geneva, June 2014, p. 16.

277. Ahmed, Akhter, U., *Impact of Feeding Children in School: Evidence from Bangladesh*, International Food Policy Research Institute, Washington, D.C., November 2004, p. 41, mentioned in Sabates-Wheeler, Rachel, and Jennifer Yablonski, 'Social Protection and Child Poverty: Evidence, practice, and gaps', unpublished UNICEF background paper for *The State of the World's Children 2016*, p. 19.

278. World Health Organization, 'Integrated Health Services – What and why?' Technical Brief No. 1, 2008, p. 6.

279. Refers to countries and areas that are either partially or entirely affected by conflict. UNICEF calculations based on UNICEF global databases.

280. Hutton, G., 'Global Costs and Benefits of Drinking-Water Supply and Sanitation Interventions to Reach the MDG target and Universal Coverage', World Health Organization, 2012

281. United Nations Children's Fund, *The Investment Case for Education and Equity*, UNICEF, New York, Jan. 2015.

282. United Nations Children's Fund and World Food Programme, 'Return on Invesmtment for Emergency Preparedness Study', Final Report, Analysis conducted by the Boston Consulting Group for UNICEF and WFP, n.p., 2015.

283. ALS Association, 'ALS Ice Bucket Challenge Commitments', ALS Association, Washington, D.C., 2016.

Statistical Tables

Economic and social statistics on the countries and areas of the world, with particular reference to children's well-being.

EXPLANATION OF SYMBOLS
The following symbols are common across all tables:

−   Data are not available.

x   Data refer to years or periods other than those specified in the column heading. Such data are not included in the calculation of regional and global averages, unless otherwise noted.

y   Data differ from the standard definition or refer to only part of a country. If they fall within the noted reference period, such data are included in the calculation of regional and global averages.

*   Data refer to the most recent year available during the period specified in the column heading.

** Excludes China.

Sources and years for specific data points are available at <data.unicef.org>. Symbols that appear in specific tables are explained in the footnotes to those tables.

Overview

This reference guide presents the most recent key statistics on child survival, development and protection for the world's countries, areas and regions.

The statistical tables in this volume support UNICEF's focus on progress and results towards internationally agreed-upon goals and compacts relating to children's rights and development.

Efforts have been made to maximize the comparability of statistics across countries and time. Nevertheless, data used at the country level may differ in terms of the methods used to collect data or arrive at estimates, and in terms of the populations covered. Furthermore, data presented here are subject to evolving methodologies, revisions of time series data (e.g., immunization, maternal mortality ratios) and changing regional classifications. Also, data comparable from one year to the next are unavailable for some indicators. It is therefore not advisable to compare data from consecutive editions of *The State of the World's Children*.

The numbers presented in this reference guide are available online at <www.unicef.org/sowc2016> and via the UNICEF global statistical databases at <data.unicef.org>. Please refer to these websites for the latest tables and for any updates or corrigenda subsequent to printing.

General note on the data

Data presented in the following statistical tables are derived from the UNICEF global databases and are accompanied by definitions, sources and, where necessary, additional footnotes. The tables draw on inter-agency estimates and nationally representative household surveys such as Multiple Indicator Cluster Surveys (MICS) and Demographic and Health Surveys (DHS). In addition, data from administrative sources and other United Nations organizations have been used.

Data presented in this year's statistical tables generally reflect information available as of January 2016. More detailed information on methodology and data sources is available at <data.unicef.org>.

This volume includes the latest population estimates and projections from *World Population Prospects: The 2015 revision and World Urbanization Prospects: The 2014 revision* (United Nations Department of Economic and Social Affairs, Population Division). Data quality is likely to be adversely affected for countries that have recently suffered disasters, especially where basic country infrastructure has been fragmented or where major population movements have occurred.

Multiple Indicator Cluster Surveys (MICS): UNICEF assists countries in collecting and analyzing data in order to fill data gaps for monitoring the situation of children and women through its international household survey initiative, the Multiple Indicator Cluster Surveys (MICS). Since 1995, over 280 surveys have been completed in more than 100 countries and areas.

MICS are among the largest sources of data for monitoring progress towards internationally agreed-upon development goals for children, including the MDGs. More information is available at <mics.unicef.org>.

unicef ✿ 70 YEARS FOR EVERY CHILD

Child mortality estimates

Each year, in *The State of the World's Children*, UNICEF reports a series of mortality estimates for children – including the annual neonatal mortality rate, infant mortality rate, the under-five mortality rate (total, male and female) and the number of under-five deaths. These figures represent the best estimates available at the time of printing and are based on the work of the United Nations Inter-agency Group for Child Mortality Estimation (UN IGME), which includes UNICEF, the World Health Organization (WHO), the World Bank and the United Nations Population Division. UN IGME mortality estimates are updated annually through a detailed review of all newly available data points, which often results in adjustments to previously reported estimates. As a result, consecutive editions of *The State of the World's Children* should not be used for analysing mortality trends over time. Comparable global and regional under-five mortality estimates for the period 1970–2015 are presented below. Country-specific mortality indicators for 1970–2015, based on the most recent UN IGME estimates, are presented in Table 10 (for the years 1970, 1990, 2000 and 2015) and are available at <data.unicef.org/child-mortality/under-five> and <www.childmortality.org>.

Under-five mortality rate (per 1,000 live births)

UNICEF Region	1970	1975	1980	1985	1990	1995	2000	2005	2010	2015
Sub-Saharan Africa	244	219	201	188	180	172	154	127	101	83
Eastern and Southern Africa	213	195	189	175	167	159	140	111	84	67
West and Central Africa	276	246	218	206	198	190	172	145	119	99
Middle East and North Africa	200	164	127	91	71	61	50	42	34	29
South Asia	213	195	171	149	129	111	94	77	64	53
East Asia and the Pacific	116	94	76	64	58	51	42	30	23	18
Latin America and the Caribbean	120	103	85	68	54	42	32	25	24	18
CEE/CIS	97	74	69	56	48	47	37	28	21	17
Least developed countries	242	230	212	192	175	158	138	111	90	73
World	**145**	**129**	**116**	**101**	**91**	**85**	**76**	**63**	**52**	**43**

Under-five deaths (millions)

UNICEF Region	1970	1975	1980	1985	1990	1995	2000	2005	2010	2015
Sub-Saharan Africa	3.2	3.2	3.4	3.6	3.9	4.1	4.1	3.7	3.3	2.9
Eastern and Southern Africa	1.3	1.4	1.6	1.6	1.7	1.8	1.8	1.5	1.3	1.1
West and Central Africa	1.7	1.7	1.8	1.9	2.0	2.2	2.2	2.1	1.9	1.8
Middle East and North Africa	1.2	1.1	1.0	0.8	0.7	0.5	0.4	0.4	0.3	0.3
South Asia	5.8	5.8	5.5	5.3	4.7	4.1	3.5	2.9	2.4	1.9
East Asia and the Pacific	5.0	3.5	2.4	2.4	2.5	1.6	1.2	0.9	0.7	0.5
Latin America and the Caribbean	1.2	1.1	1.0	0.8	0.6	0.5	0.4	0.3	0.3	0.2
CEE/CIS	0.6	0.5	0.5	0.4	0.4	0.3	0.2	0.1	0.1	0.1
Least developed countries	3.3	3.5	3.6	3.6	3.6	3.6	3.4	3.0	2.5	2.2
World	**17.2**	**15.6**	**13.9**	**13.4**	**12.7**	**11.0**	**9.8**	**8.3**	**7.0**	**5.9**

UNDER-FIVE MORTALITY RANKINGS

The following list ranks countries and areas in descending order of their estimated 2015 under-five mortality rate (U5MR), a critical indicator of the well-being of children. Countries and areas are listed alphabetically in the tables on the following pages.

HIGHEST UNDER-FIVE MORTALITY RATE

Countries and areas	Under-5 mortality rate (2015) Value	Rank
Angola	157	1
Chad	139	2
Somalia	137	3
Central African Republic	130	4
Sierra Leone	120	5
Mali	115	6
Nigeria	109	7
Benin	100	8
Democratic Republic of the Congo	98	9
Niger	96	10
Equatorial Guinea	94	11
Guinea	94	11
Côte d'Ivoire	93	13
Guinea-Bissau	93	13
South Sudan	93	13
Afghanistan	91	16
Lesotho	90	17
Burkina Faso	89	18
Cameroon	88	19
Mauritania	85	20
Burundi	82	21
Pakistan	81	22
Mozambique	79	23
Togo	78	24
Comoros	74	25
Zimbabwe	71	26
Liberia	70	27
Sudan	70	27
Gambia	69	29
Haiti	69	29
Lao People's Democratic Republic	67	31
Djibouti	65	32

Countries and areas	Under-5 mortality rate (2015) Value	Rank
Malawi	64	33
Zambia	64	33
Ghana	62	35
Swaziland	61	36
Ethiopia	59	37
Papua New Guinea	57	38
Kiribati	56	39
Uganda	55	40
Timor-Leste	53	41
Gabon	51	42
Turkmenistan	51	42
Madagascar	50	44
Myanmar	50	44
Kenya	49	46
United Republic of Tanzania	49	46
India	48	48
Eritrea	47	49
Sao Tome and Principe	47	49
Senegal	47	49
Congo	45	52
Namibia	45	52
Tajikistan	45	52
Botswana	44	55
Rwanda	42	56
Yemen	42	56
South Africa	41	58
Guyana	39	59
Uzbekistan	39	59
Bangladesh	38	61
Bolivia (Plurinational State of)	38	61
Marshall Islands	36	63
Nepal	36	63

Countries and areas	Under-5 mortality rate (2015) Value	Rank
Micronesia (Federated States of)	35	65
Nauru	35	65
Bhutan	33	67
Azerbaijan	32	68
Iraq	32	68
Dominican Republic	31	70
Cambodia	29	71
Guatemala	29	71
Morocco	28	73
Philippines	28	73
Solomon Islands	28	73
Vanuatu	28	73
Indonesia	27	77
Tuvalu	27	77
Algeria	26	79
Cabo Verde	25	80
Democratic People's Republic of Korea	25	80
Egypt	24	82
Niue	23	83
Ecuador	22	84
Fiji	22	84
Mongolia	22	84
Nicaragua	22	84
Viet Nam	22	84
Dominica	21	89
Kyrgyzstan	21	89
Paraguay	21	89
State of Palestine	21	89
Suriname	21	89
Honduras	20	94
Trinidad and Tobago	20	94
Jordan	18	96

unicef ♦   70 YEARS FOR EVERY CHILD

ABOUT 16,000 CHILDREN UNDER 5 YEARS OLD STILL DIE EVERY DAY.

Countries and areas	Under-5 mortality rate (2015) Value	Rank
Saint Vincent and the Grenadines	18	96
Samoa	18	96
Belize	17	99
El Salvador	17	99
Panama	17	99
Peru	17	99
Tonga	17	99
Brazil	16	104
Colombia	16	104
Iran (Islamic Republic of)	16	104
Jamaica	16	104
Palau	16	104
Republic of Moldova	16	104
Saudi Arabia	15	110
Venezuela (Bolivarian Republic of)	15	110
Albania	14	112
Armenia	14	112
Kazakhstan	14	112
Mauritius	14	112
Saint Lucia	14	112
Seychelles	14	112
Tunisia	14	112
Turkey	14	112
Argentina	13	120
Barbados	13	120
Libya	13	120
Mexico	13	120
Syrian Arab Republic	13	120
Bahamas	12	125
Georgia	12	125
Grenada	12	125
Oman	12	125

Countries and areas	Under-5 mortality rate (2015) Value	Rank
Thailand	12	125
China	11	130
Romania	11	130
Saint Kitts and Nevis	11	130
Brunei Darussalam	10	133
Bulgaria	10	133
Costa Rica	10	133
Russian Federation	10	133
Sri Lanka	10	133
Uruguay	10	133
Kuwait	9	139
Maldives	9	139
Ukraine	9	139
Antigua and Barbuda	8	142
Chile	8	142
Cook Islands	8	142
Latvia	8	142
Lebanon	8	142
Qatar	8	142
Malaysia	7	148
Serbia	7	148
Slovakia	7	148
United Arab Emirates	7	148
United States	7	148
Bahrain	6	153
Cuba	6	153
Hungary	6	153
Malta	6	153
New Zealand	6	153
The former Yugoslav Republic of Macedonia	6	153
Belarus	5	159
Bosnia and Herzegovina	5	159
Canada	5	159

Countries and areas	Under-5 mortality rate (2015) Value	Rank
Greece	5	159
Lithuania	5	159
Montenegro	5	159
Poland	5	159
Australia	4	166
Austria	4	166
Belgium	4	166
Croatia	4	166
Denmark	4	166
France	4	166
Germany	4	166
Ireland	4	166
Israel	4	166
Italy	4	166
Monaco	4	166
Netherlands	4	166
Portugal	4	166
Spain	4	166
Switzerland	4	166
United Kingdom	4	166
Andorra	3	182
Cyprus	3	182
Czech Republic	3	182
Estonia	3	182
Japan	3	182
Norway	3	182
Republic of Korea	3	182
San Marino	3	182
Singapore	3	182
Slovenia	3	182
Sweden	3	182
Finland	2	193
Iceland	2	193
Luxembourg	2	193
Holy See	-	-
Liechtenstein	-	-

Regional classification

Averages presented at the end of each of the 14 statistical tables are calculated using data from countries and areas as classified below.

Sub-Saharan Africa
Eastern and Southern Africa; West and Central Africa; Djibouti; Sudan

Eastern and Southern Africa
Angola; Botswana; Burundi; Comoros; Eritrea; Ethiopia; Kenya; Lesotho; Madagascar; Malawi; Mauritius; Mozambique; Namibia; Rwanda; Seychelles; Somalia; South Africa; South Sudan; Swaziland; Uganda; United Republic of Tanzania; Zambia; Zimbabwe

West and Central Africa
Benin; Burkina Faso; Cabo Verde; Cameroon; Central African Republic; Chad; Congo; Côte d'Ivoire; Democratic Republic of the Congo; Equatorial Guinea; Gabon; Gambia; Ghana; Guinea; Guinea-Bissau; Liberia; Mali; Mauritania; Niger; Nigeria; Sao Tome and Principe; Senegal; Sierra Leone; Togo

Middle East and North Africa
Algeria; Bahrain; Djibouti; Egypt; Iran (Islamic Republic of); Iraq; Jordan; Kuwait; Lebanon; Libya; Morocco; Oman; Qatar; Saudi Arabia; State of Palestine; Sudan; Syrian Arab Republic; Tunisia; United Arab Emirates; Yemen

South Asia
Afghanistan; Bangladesh; Bhutan; India; Maldives; Nepal; Pakistan; Sri Lanka

East Asia and Pacific
Brunei Darussalam; Cambodia; China; Cook Islands; Democratic People's Republic of Korea; Fiji; Indonesia; Kiribati; Lao People's Democratic Republic; Malaysia; Marshall Islands; Micronesia (Federated States of); Mongolia; Myanmar; Nauru; Niue; Palau; Papua New Guinea; Philippines; Republic of Korea; Samoa; Singapore; Solomon Islands; Thailand; Timor-Leste; Tonga; Tuvalu; Vanuatu; Viet Nam

Latin America and Caribbean
Antigua and Barbuda; Argentina; Bahamas; Barbados; Belize; Bolivia (Plurinational State of); Brazil; Chile; Colombia; Costa Rica; Cuba; Dominica; Dominican Republic; Ecuador; El Salvador; Grenada; Guatemala; Guyana; Haiti; Honduras; Jamaica; Mexico; Nicaragua; Panama; Paraguay; Peru; Saint Kitts and Nevis; Saint Lucia; Saint Vincent and the Grenadines; Suriname; Trinidad and Tobago; Uruguay; Venezuela (Bolivarian Republic of)

Central and Eastern Europe and the Commonwealth of Independent States (CEE/CIS)
Albania; Armenia; Azerbaijan; Belarus; Bosnia and Herzegovina; Bulgaria; Croatia; Georgia; Kazakhstan; Kyrgyzstan; Montenegro; Republic of Moldova; Romania; Russian Federation; Serbia; Tajikistan; the former Yugoslav Republic of Macedonia; Turkey; Turkmenistan; Ukraine; Uzbekistan

Least developed countries/areas
[Classified as such by the United Nations High Representative for the Least Developed Countries, Landlocked Developing Countries and Small Island Developing States (UN-OHRLLS)].

Afghanistan; Angola; Bangladesh; Benin; Bhutan; Burkina Faso; Burundi; Cambodia; Central African Republic; Chad; Comoros; Democratic Republic of the Congo; Djibouti; Equatorial Guinea; Eritrea; Ethiopia; Gambia; Guinea; Guinea-Bissau; Haiti; Kiribati; Lao People's Democratic Republic; Lesotho; Liberia; Madagascar; Malawi; Mali; Mauritania; Mozambique; Myanmar; Nepal; Niger; Rwanda; Sao Tome and Principe; Senegal; Sierra Leone; Solomon Islands; Somalia; South Sudan; Sudan; Timor-Leste; Togo; Tuvalu; Uganda; United Republic of Tanzania; Vanuatu; Yemen; Zambia

Notes on specific tables

TABLE 2. NUTRITION

Underweight, stunting, wasting and overweight: UNICEF, WHO and the World Bank have continued a process to harmonize anthropometric data used for computation and estimation of regional and global averages and trend analysis. As part of this process, regional and global averages for underweight, stunting, wasting and overweight prevalences are derived from a model described in M. de Onis et al., 'Methodology for Estimating Regional and Global Trends of Child Malnutrition' (*International Journal of Epidemiology*, vol. 33, 2004, pp. 1260–1270). Owing to differences in data sources (i.e., new empirical data are incorporated as made available) and estimation methodology, these regional average prevalence estimates may not be comparable to the averages published in previous editions of *The State of the World's Children*.

Vitamin A supplementation: Emphasizing the importance for children of receiving two annual doses of vitamin A (spaced 4–6 months apart), this report presents only full coverage of vitamin A supplementation. In the absence of a direct method to measure this indicator, full coverage is reported as the lower coverage estimate from semester 1 January–June and semester 2 July–December, in a given year. The regional and global aggregates only contain the 82 countries indicated as priority countries for national level programmes. Hence the aggregates are published where at least 50 per cent of the population coverage for the priority countries in each region have been met. In other words, East Asia and Pacific estimates are presented despite there being no data for China, because China is not a priority country for a national level programme.

Low birthweight: The data have not been updated since November 2014 due to ongoing methodological work to revise the analysis method for estimates from household surveys where a large number of children are not weighed.

Iodized salt: The data have not been updated since November 2014 due to an upcoming change in the definition of the of the indicator that will be reported on in future editions of *The State of the World's Children*.

TABLE 3. HEALTH

Water and sanitation: The drinking water and sanitation coverage estimates in this report come from the WHO/UNICEF Joint Monitoring Programme for Water Supply and Sanitation (JMP). Full details of the JMP methodology can be found at <data.unicef.org> and <www.wssinfo.org>. As the JMP estimates use linear regression applied to data from household sample surveys and censuses, and additional data become available between each issue of estimates, subsequent JMP estimates should not be compared.

Immunization: This report presents WHO and UNICEF estimates of national immunization coverage. Since 2000, the estimates are updated once annually in July, following a consultation process wherein countries are provided draft reports for review and comment. As the system incorporates new empirical data, each annual revision supersedes prior data releases, and coverage levels from earlier revisions are not comparable. A more detailed explanation of the process can be found at <data.unicef.org/child-health/immunization>.

Regional averages for the reported antigens are computed as follows:

- For BCG, regional averages include only those countries where BCG is included in the national routine immunization schedule.

- For DPT, polio, measles, HepB, Hib, PCV and rotavirus vaccines, regional averages include all countries, as these vaccines are universally recommended by WHO.

- For protection at birth (PAB) from tetanus, regional averages include only the countries where maternal and neonatal tetanus is endemic.

Treatment indicators: Until recently, 'Proportion of children under 5 with fever who are treated with appropriate antimalarial drugs' was the standard indicator for monitoring coverage of antimalarial treatment in children under 5. However, it has become increasingly challenging to track trends in this indicator, following a 2010 WHO recommendation that advised universal use of diagnostic testing to confirm malaria infection before applying any treatment. To implement this recommendation, many countries are scaling up the use of diagnostic testing to focus treatment on only those diagnosed with malaria. Given that increasingly higher number of fever cases are not malaria, low levels of antimalarial treatment in febrile children may indicate that antimalarials are being provided only to confirmed cases. For more information on this issue, see the 2013 edition of the Household Survey Indicators for Malaria Control. Given these methodological issues, this indicator is no longer tracked for coverage monitoring and has now been replaced with 'Care seeking for fever' in this publication.

The indicator 'Antibiotic treatment for children with symptoms of pneumonia' has been dropped from this table as well. This indicator refers to antibiotic treatment among children whose caretakers report symptoms that are related to acute respiratory infection. However, these children have not been medically diagnosed with pneumonia, thus leading to substantial validity issues. Studies have shown that high percentage of children with symptoms of acute respiratory infection do not have true pneumonia. Therefore, this indicator is no longer recommended for coverage monitoring.

TABLE 4. HIV/AIDS

In 2015, the Joint United Nations Programme on HIV/AIDS (UNAIDS) released new global, regional and country-level HIV and AIDS estimates for 2014 that reflect key changes in WHO HIV treatment guidelines for adults and children and for the prevention of mother-to-child transmission of HIV, in addition to improvements in assumptions of the probability of HIV transmission from mother to child and net survival rates for infected children. Furthermore, there are also more reliable data available from population-based surveys, expanded national sentinel surveillance systems and programme service statistics in a number of countries. Based on the refined methodology, UNAIDS has retrospectively generated new estimates of HIV prevalence, the number of people living with HIV and those needing treatment, AIDS-related deaths, new HIV infections and the number of children whose parents have died due to all causes including AIDS for past years.

Only new estimates should be used for trend analysis. The new HIV and AIDS estimates included in this table are also published in the UNAIDS How AIDS Changed Everything, 2015. Overall, the global and regional figures published in *The State of the World's Children* are not comparable to estimates previously published. More information on HIV and AIDS estimates, methodology and updates can be found at <www.unaids.org>.

TABLE 7. ECONOMIC INDICATORS

National monetary child poverty has been added to Table 7 in 2016 to reflect Sustainable Development Goal 1, Target 1.2 that includes an explicit commitment to reduce poverty among children. This indicator measures "the percentage of children aged 0–17 years old living in households that have income or consumption level below the government defined national poverty threshold". Data come from official government sources such as Statistical Office tabulations, national household survey and poverty reports and from regional databases such as Eurostat. Note that the methodology used to calculate national poverty prevalence varies by country. For instance, some countries using income and others consumption, some applying an absolute poverty line and others a relative poverty threshold. Therefore, national child poverty rates should be used to monitor progress, but should not be used to compare or rank countries. This indicator is the first of three child poverty indicators and will be supplemented with an international 'extreme child poverty' measure for Target 1 of SDG Goal 1 and national 'multi-dimensional' child poverty for Target 1.2.

TABLE 8. WOMEN

Maternal mortality ratio (adjusted): The table presents the 'adjusted' maternal mortality ratios for the year 2015, as published by the Maternal Mortality Estimation Inter-agency Group (MMEIG), composed of WHO, UNICEF, the United Nations Population Fund (UNFPA), The World Bank, and the United Nations Population Division, together with independent technical experts. To derive these estimates, the inter-agency group used a dual approach: making adjustments to correct misclassification and underreporting in existing estimates of maternal mortality from civil registration systems, and using a model to generate estimates for countries without reliable national-level estimates of maternal mortality. These 'adjusted' estimates should not be compared with previous inter-agency estimates. The full report – with complete country and regional estimates for the years 1990, 1995, 2000, 2005, 2010 and 2015, in addition to details on the methodology – can be found at <data.unicef.org/maternal-health/maternal-mortality>.

Post-natal care indicators: The period immediately following delivery or post-natal period is a critical phase in the lives of mothers and newborn babies as most maternal and infant deaths occur during this time. Given the critical importance of essential newborn care and postnatal care for the baby and the mother, household survey programs such as DHS and MICS have recently included indicators to track their coverage. Thus, two standard indicators related to early post-natal care for mothers and babies have been added to this table: Post-natal health check for newborns within 2 days after delivery and post-natal health check for mothers within 2 days after delivery. These two indicators are now part of the Every Newborn Action Plan (ENAP) global monitoring indicators.

Even though both DHS and MICS strive at providing comparable results for the same indicator, data collection and reporting method for these indicators differs slightly between the two survey programs. Cross-country coverage results and regional aggregates should be analysed with caution. For the specific source for each data point please review the post-natal care database published on

<data.unicef.org> as well as specific country reports available on the respective website of the survey programs (for MICS: see <http://mics.unicef.org>; for DHS see <http://dhsprogram.com>).

TABLE 9. CHILD PROTECTION

Birth registration: Changes in the definition of birth registration were made from the second and third rounds of MICS (MICS2 and MICS3) to the fourth round (MICS4). In order to allow for comparability with later rounds, data from MICS2 and MICS3 on birth registration were recalculated according to the MICS4 indicator definition. Therefore, the recalculated data presented here may differ from estimates included in MICS2 and MICS3 national reports.

Child labour: The prevalence rates of child labour presented in the table vary widely across countries due to significant differences in survey methodology, questionnaire content, national definitions and thresholds used to establish child labour prevalence. Only a limited number of countries have produced child labour prevalence data based on international standards and classifications. Data from the fourth round of MICS (MICS4, 2009–2012) included in the table have been recalculated according to the indicator definition used in MICS3 surveys, to ensure cross-country comparability. In this definition, the activities of fetching water or collecting firewood are classified as household chores rather than as an economic activity. Under this approach, a child aged 5–14 would have to be engaged in fetching water or collecting firewood for at least 28 hours per week to be considered as a child labourer.

Female genital mutilation/cutting (FGM/C): Data on the prevalence of FGM/C among girls aged 0–14 were recalculated for technical reasons and may differ from that presented in original DHS and MICS country reports. For further details, refer to *Female Genital Mutilation/Cutting: A statistical overview and exploration of the dynamics of change*, UNICEF, New York, 2013. Regional estimates on the prevalence of FGM/C and attitudes towards the practice are based on available data from only practising countries and therefore reflect the situation among those living in affected countries within the region, and not the region as a whole, as there are some non-practising countries in the region as well.

Violent discipline: Estimates used in UNICEF publications and in MICS country reports prior to 2010 were calculated using household weights that did not take into account the last-stage selection of children for the administration of the child discipline module in MICS surveys. (A random selection of one child aged 2–14 is undertaken for the administration of the child discipline module.) In January 2010, it was decided that more accurate estimates are produced by using a household weight that takes the last-stage selection into account. MICS3 data were recalculated using this approach.

TABLE 10. THE RATE OF PROGRESS

Under-five mortality is used as the principal indicator of progress in child well-being. In 1970, about 17.2 million children under 5 years old were dying every year. In 2015, by comparison, the estimated number of children who died before their fifth birthday stood at 5.9 million – highlighting a significant long-term decline in the global number of under-five deaths.

U5MR has several advantages as a gauge of child well-being:

- First, U5MR measures an end result of the development process rather than an 'input' such as school enrolment level, per capita calorie availability or number of doctors per thousand population – all of which are means to an end.

- Second, U5MR is known to be the result of a wide variety of inputs: for example, antibiotics to treat pneumonia; insecticide-treated mosquito nets to prevent malaria; the nutritional well-being and health knowledge of mothers; the level of immunization and oral rehydration therapy use; the availability of maternal and child health services, including antenatal care; income and food availability in the family; the availability of safe drinking water and basic sanitation; and the overall safety of the child's environment.

- Third, U5MR is less susceptible to the fallacy of the average than, for example, per capita gross national income (GNI). This is because the natural scale does not allow the children of the rich to be one thousand times more likely to survive, even if the human made scale does permit them to have one thousand times as much income. In other words, it is much more difficult for a wealthy minority to affect a nation's U5MR, and this indicator therefore presents a more accurate, if far from perfect, picture of the health status of the majority of children and of society as a whole. The speed of progress in reducing child mortality can be assessed by calculating its annual rate of reduction (ARR). Unlike the comparison of absolute changes, ARR measures relative changes that reflect differences compared with the starting value.

As lower levels of child mortality are reached, the same absolute reduction represents a greater percentage reduction. ARR therefore shows a higher rate of progress for a 10-point absolute reduction, for example, if that reduction happens at a lower level of child mortality versus a higher level over the same time period. A 10-point decrease in U5MR from 100 in 1990 to 90 in 2015 represents a reduction of 10 per cent, corresponding to an ARR of about 0.4 per cent, whereas the same 10-point decrease from 20 to 10 over the same period represents a reduction of 50 per cent, or an ARR of 2.8 per cent. (A negative value for the percentage reduction indicates an increase in U5MR during the period specified.) When used in conjunction with gross domestic product (GDP) growth rates, child mortality indicators and their rates of reduction can therefore give a picture of the progress being made by any country, area or region, over any period of time, towards the satisfaction of some of the most essential human needs.

As Table 10 shows, there is no fixed relationship between the ARR of U5MR and the annual rate of growth in per capita GDP. Comparing these two indicators helps shed light on the relationship between economic advances and human development.

Finally, the table gives the total fertility rate for each country and area and the corresponding ARR. It is clear that many of the nations that have achieved significant reductions in their U5MR have also achieved significant reductions in fertility.

TABLES 12 AND 13. DISPARITIES BY RESIDENCE AND BY HOUSEHOLD WEALTH

Stunting: Beginning in 2016, *The State of the World's Children* no longer includes the disparities in underweight (weight-for-age) prevalence, and instead provides the breakdown for stunting (height-for-age). This is because stunting has gained precedence as a key global marker of child undernutrition and is now a focus of the SDG agenda, while underweight is no longer among the indicators to be used to track country, regional or global progress on nutrition. Underweight had been the indicator used to track MDG target 1.c. on nutrition of children under the age of 5 years, however, even during the MDG period, UNICEF and other partners had focused on progress in stunting as the marker of success.

TABLE 1. BASIC INDICATORS

Countries and areas	Under-5 mortality rank	Under-5 mortality rate (U5MR) 1990	Under-5 mortality rate (U5MR) 2015	U5MR by sex 2015 male	U5MR by sex 2015 female	Infant mortality rate (under 1) 1990	Infant mortality rate (under 1) 2015	Neonatal mortality rate 2015	Total population (thousands) 2015	Annual number of births (thousands) 2015	Annual number of under-5 deaths (thousands) 2015	GNI per capita (US$) 2015	Life expectancy at birth (years) 2015	Total adult literacy rate (%) 2009–2014*	Primary school net enrolment ratio (%) 2010–2014*
Afghanistan	16	181	91	95	87	123	66	36	32,527	1,081	94	680	61	32	–
Albania	112	41	14	15	13	35	13	6	2,897	40	1	4,450	78	97	96
Algeria	79	47	26	27	24	40	22	16	39,667	936	24	5,490	75	73 x	99
Andorra	182	9	3	3	3	8	2	1	70	–	0	43,270 x	–	–	–
Angola	1	226	157	165	149	134	96	49	25,022	1,128	169	c	53	71	84
Antigua and Barbuda	142	26	8	9	7	24	6	5	92	1	0	13,300	76	99	86
Argentina	120	28	13	14	11	24	11	6	43,417	753	10	13,480	76	98	100
Armenia	112	50	14	16	13	43	13	7	3,018	39	1	4,020	75	100	–
Australia	166	9	4	4	3	8	3	2	23,969	318	1	64,540	83	–	97
Austria	166	10	4	4	3	8	3	2	8,545	82	0	49,670	82	–	–
Azerbaijan	68	95	32	34	29	76	28	18	9,754	193	7	7,590	71	100	95
Bahamas	125	24	12	13	11	20	10	7	388	6	0	20,980	76	–	98
Bahrain	153	23	6	6	6	20	5	1	1,377	20	0	21,060 x	77	95	–
Bangladesh	61	144	38	40	35	100	31	23	160,996	3,134	119	1,080	72	60	95
Barbados	120	18	13	14	12	16	12	8	284	3	0	15,310 x	76	–	91
Belarus	159	17	5	5	4	14	3	2	9,496	112	1	7,340	71	100	94
Belgium	166	10	4	5	4	8	3	2	11,299	130	1	47,260	81	–	99
Belize	99	40	17	18	15	32	14	8	359	8	0	4,350 x	70	–	97
Benin	8	180	100	104	95	108	64	32	10,880	388	37	890	60	29 x	96
Bhutan	67	134	33	36	30	93	27	18	775	13	0	2,370	70	53 x	89
Bolivia (Plurinational State of)	61	124	38	42	35	86	31	20	10,725	253	9	2,870	69	92	88
Bosnia and Herzegovina	159	18	5	6	5	16	5	4	3,810	34	0	4,760	77	98	–
Botswana	55	54	44	47	40	42	35	22	2,262	55	2	7,240	65	87	91
Brazil	104	61	16	18	15	51	15	9	207,848	3,016	52	11,530	75	90	–
Brunei Darussalam	133	12	10	11	9	9	9	4	423	7	0	37,320 x	79	96	–
Bulgaria	133	22	10	12	9	18	9	6	7,150	68	1	7,620	74	98	96
Burkina Faso	18	202	89	94	83	103	61	27	18,106	717	60	700	59	29 x	68
Burundi	21	172	82	88	76	104	54	29	11,179	488	37	270	57	87 x	96
Cabo Verde	80	63	25	27	22	48	21	12	521	11	0	3,450	74	85	98
Cambodia	71	117	29	32	25	85	25	15	15,578	371	10	1,020	69	74	95
Cameroon	19	138	88	94	82	86	57	26	23,344	847	71	1,350	56	71	95
Canada	159	8	5	5	5	7	4	3	35,940	387	2	51,630	82	–	99
Central African Republic	4	177	130	137	123	115	92	43	4,900	164	21	320	51	37	71
Chad	2	215	139	146	131	116	85	39	14,037	630	83	980	52	38	84
Chile	142	19	8	9	7	16	7	5	17,948	234	2	14,910	82	97	93
China	130	54	11	11	10	42	9	6	1,376,049	16,601	182	7,400	76	95	–
Colombia	104	35	16	18	14	29	14	9	48,229	747	12	7,970	74	93	97 x
Comoros	25	125	74	79	68	88	55	34	788	26	2	790	64	77	85
Congo	52	94	45	49	41	61	33	18	4,620	167	7	2,720	63	79	93
Cook Islands	142	24	8	9	7	21	7	4	21	–	0	–	–	–	98
Costa Rica	133	17	10	11	9	14	9	6	4,808	70	1	10,120	80	97	96
Côte d'Ivoire	13	153	93	101	84	105	67	38	22,702	838	75	1,450	52	41	75
Croatia	166	13	4	5	4	11	4	3	4,240	40	0	12,980	77	99	98
Cuba	153	13	6	6	5	11	4	2	11,390	115	1	5,880 x	80	100	93
Cyprus	182	11	3	3	3	10	3	2	1,165	13	0	26,370	80	99	97
Czech Republic	182	15	3	4	3	13	3	2	10,543	107	0	18,370	79	–	–
Democratic People's Republic of Korea	80	43	25	28	22	33	20	14	25,155	360	9	a	71	100 x	97 x
Democratic Republic of the Congo	9	187	98	105	91	120	75	30	77,267	3,217	305	380	59	75	–
Denmark	166	9	4	4	3	7	3	3	5,669	59	0	61,310	80	–	99
Djibouti	32	119	65	71	59	93	54	33	888	22	1	b	62	–	65
Dominica	89	17	21	23	20	14	20	16	73	–	0	6,930	–	–	97 x
Dominican Republic	70	60	31	34	28	47	26	22	10,528	216	7	6,040	74	90	86
Ecuador	84	57	22	24	19	44	18	11	16,144	331	7	6,090	76	92	97
Egypt	82	86	24	25	23	63	20	13	91,508	2,488	66	3,050	71	72	100
El Salvador	99	59	17	19	15	46	14	8	6,127	105	2	3,920	73	84	96
Equatorial Guinea	11	190	94	101	88	128	68	33	845	29	3	10,210	58	95	58
Eritrea	49	151	47	51	41	93	34	18	5,228	175	8	480 x	64	72	41
Estonia	182	20	3	3	3	17	2	2	1,313	14	0	19,030	77	100	100
Ethiopia	37	205	59	65	54	122	41	28	99,391	3,176	184	550	65	39 x	86
Fiji	84	30	22	24	20	25	19	10	892	18	0	4,870	70	–	97
Finland	193	7	2	3	2	6	2	1	5,503	59	0	48,420	81	–	100
France	166	9	4	5	4	7	4	2	64,395	782	3	42,960	82	–	99

TABLE 1. BASIC INDICATORS

Countries and areas	Under-5 mortality rank	Under-5 mortality rate (U5MR) 1990	Under-5 mortality rate (U5MR) 2015	U5MR by sex 2015 male	U5MR by sex 2015 female	Infant mortality rate (under 1) 1990	Infant mortality rate (under 1) 2015	Neonatal mortality rate 2015	Total population (thousands) 2015	Annual number of births (thousands) 2015	Annual number of under-5 deaths (thousands) 2015	GNI per capita (US$) 2015	Life expectancy at birth (years) 2015	Total adult literacy rate (%) 2009–2014*	Primary school net enrolment ratio (%) 2010–2014*
Gabon	42	93	51	55	46	61	36	23	1,725	51	3	9,720	65	82	–
Gambia	29	170	69	74	64	80	48	30	1,991	83	6	500 x	60	53	69
Georgia	125	48	12	13	11	41	11	7	4,000	54	1	3,720	75	100	99
Germany	166	9	4	4	3	7	3	2	80,689	685	3	47,640	81	–	100
Ghana	35	127	62	67	56	80	43	28	27,410	884	54	1,590	62	71	89
Greece	159	13	5	5	4	11	4	3	10,955	92	0	22,680 x	81	97	97
Grenada	125	23	12	13	11	18	11	6	107	2	0	7,910	74	–	98
Guatemala	71	81	29	32	26	60	24	13	16,343	438	13	3,430	72	78	89
Guinea	11	238	94	99	88	141	61	31	12,609	460	42	470	59	25	76
Guinea-Bissau	13	229	93	100	85	136	60	40	1,844	68	6	550	55	58	69
Guyana	59	60	39	44	34	47	32	23	767	15	1	3,940 x	66	85	85
Haiti	29	146	69	75	63	101	52	25	10,711	263	18	820	63	49 x	–
Holy See	–	–	–	–	–	–	–	–	1	–	–	–	–	–	–
Honduras	94	58	20	23	18	45	17	11	8,075	169	3	2,270	73	85	95
Hungary	153	19	6	6	5	17	5	4	9,855	92	1	13,340	75	99	96
Iceland	193	6	2	2	2	5	2	1	329	4	0	46,350 x	83	–	99
India	48	126	48	46	49	88	38	28	1,311,051	25,794	1,201	1,570	68	69	95
Indonesia	77	85	27	30	24	62	23	14	257,564	5,037	147	3,630	69	93	93
Iran (Islamic Republic of)	104	58	16	16	15	45	13	10	79,109	1,350	21	7,120 x	76	84	99
Iraq	68	54	32	35	29	42	27	18	36,423	1,244	39	6,500	70	79	–
Ireland	166	9	4	4	3	8	3	2	4,688	68	0	46,550	81	–	99
Israel	166	12	4	4	4	10	3	2	8,064	167	1	35,320	83	–	97
Italy	166	10	4	4	3	8	3	2	59,798	501	2	34,270	83	99	99
Jamaica	104	31	16	18	14	25	14	12	2,793	48	1	5,150	76	88	–
Japan	182	6	3	3	3	5	2	1	126,573	1,033	3	42,000	84	–	100
Jordan	96	37	18	19	17	30	15	11	7,595	199	4	5,160	74	93	88
Kazakhstan	112	53	14	16	12	45	13	7	17,625	377	6	11,850	70	100	99
Kenya	46	102	49	53	45	66	36	22	46,050	1,571	74	1,290	62	72 x	86
Kiribati	39	96	56	61	51	69	44	24	112	3	0	2,950	66	–	98
Kuwait	139	18	9	9	8	15	7	3	3,892	75	1	49,300	75	96	98
Kyrgyzstan	89	65	21	24	19	54	19	12	5,940	154	4	1,250	71	99	98
Lao People's Democratic Republic	31	162	67	73	61	111	51	30	6,802	179	12	1,660	67	73 x	95
Latvia	142	20	8	9	7	17	7	5	1,971	20	0	15,280	74	100	98
Lebanon	142	33	8	9	8	27	7	5	5,851	86	1	10,030	80	90 x	89
Lesotho	17	88	90	97	83	71	69	33	2,135	61	6	1,330	50	76	81
Liberia	27	255	70	75	65	170	53	24	4,503	156	11	370	61	43 x	38
Libya	120	42	13	15	12	36	11	7	6,278	129	2	7,820	72	90	–
Liechtenstein	–	–	–	–	–	–	–	–	38	–	–	d	–	–	98
Lithuania	159	17	5	6	5	13	3	3	2,878	30	0	15,430	73	100	100
Luxembourg	193	9	2	2	2	7	2	1	567	6	0	75,990	82	–	95
Madagascar	44	161	50	54	45	98	36	20	24,235	831	40	440	66	64	–
Malawi	33	242	64	68	60	143	43	22	17,215	665	40	250	64	61	98 x
Malaysia	148	17	7	8	6	14	6	4	30,331	509	4	11,120	75	93	–
Maldives	139	94	9	9	8	68	7	5	364	8	0	6,410	77	98 x	97 x
Mali	6	254	115	120	108	131	75	38	17,600	758	83	650	58	31	64
Malta	153	11	6	7	6	10	5	4	419	4	0	21,000 x	81	93	97
Marshall Islands	63	50	36	40	32	40	30	17	53	–	0	4,390	–	–	100
Mauritania	20	118	85	96	80	78	65	36	4,068	134	11	1,270	63	46 x	75
Mauritius	112	23	14	15	12	20	12	8	1,273	14	0	9,630	75	89	97
Mexico	120	47	13	14	12	37	11	7	127,017	2,346	31	9,870	77	93	97
Micronesia (Federated States of)	65	56	35	38	31	43	29	19	104	2	0	3,200	69	–	87
Monaco	166	8	4	4	3	6	3	2	38	–	0	d	–	–	–
Mongolia	84	108	22	27	18	77	19	11	2,959	69	2	4,280	70	98	96
Montenegro	159	17	5	5	4	15	4	3	626	7	0	7,320	76	98	94
Morocco	73	80	28	30	25	63	24	18	34,378	699	20	3,070	74	67	99
Mozambique	23	240	79	83	74	160	57	27	27,978	1,087	82	600	55	51	88
Myanmar	44	110	50	55	45	78	40	26	53,897	944	46	1,270	66	93	95
Namibia	52	74	45	49	41	50	33	16	2,459	72	3	5,630	65	76 x	91
Nauru	65	57	35	39	32	44	29	23	10	–	0	–	–	–	87
Nepal	63	141	36	38	34	98	29	22	28,514	577	20	730	70	60	95
Netherlands	166	8	4	4	3	7	3	2	16,925	177	1	51,890	82	–	99
New Zealand	153	11	6	6	5	9	5	3	4,529	60	0	41,070	82	–	98

TABLE 1. BASIC INDICATORS

Countries and areas	Under-5 mortality rank	Under-5 mortality rate (U5MR) 1990	Under-5 mortality rate (U5MR) 2015	U5MR by sex 2015 male	U5MR by sex 2015 female	Infant mortality rate (under 1) 1990	Infant mortality rate (under 1) 2015	Neonatal mortality rate 2015	Total population (thousands) 2015	Annual number of births (thousands) 2015	Annual number of under-5 deaths (thousands) 2015	GNI per capita (US$) 2015	Life expectancy at birth (years) 2015	Total adult literacy rate (%) 2009–2014*	Primary school net enrolment ratio (%) 2010–2014*
Nicaragua	84	67	22	25	20	51	19	10	6,082	121	3	1,870	75	78 x	98
Niger	10	328	96	100	91	138	57	27	19,899	983	88	410	62	15	62
Nigeria	7	213	109	115	102	126	69	34	182,202	7,133	750	2,970	53	51 x	66
Niue	83	14	23	25	20	12	20	13	2	–	0	–	–	–	–
Norway	182	9	3	3	2	7	2	2	5,211	61	0	103,630	82	–	100
Oman	125	39	12	13	10	32	10	5	4,491	81	1	16,870 x	77	87	97
Pakistan	22	139	81	85	77	106	66	46	188,925	5,451	432	1,400	66	55	73
Palau	104	36	16	18	15	31	14	9	21	–	0	11,110	–	100	99
Panama	99	31	17	19	15	26	15	10	3,929	75	1	11,130	78	94	97
Papua New Guinea	38	89	57	62	53	65	45	25	7,619	215	12	2,240	63	63	87
Paraguay	89	47	21	23	18	37	18	11	6,639	141	3	4,400	73	94	89
Peru	99	80	17	18	15	56	13	8	31,377	615	10	6,360	75	94	95
Philippines	73	58	28	31	25	41	22	13	100,699	2,349	66	3,500	68	95 x	97
Poland	159	17	5	6	5	15	5	3	38,612	387	2	13,690	78	100	97
Portugal	166	15	4	4	3	12	3	2	10,350	83	0	21,360	81	94	99
Qatar	142	21	8	9	7	18	7	4	2,235	26	0	92,200	78	96	97
Republic of Korea	182	7	3	4	3	6	3	2	50,293	457	2	27,090	82	–	96
Republic of Moldova	104	33	16	18	14	27	14	12	4,069	43	1	2,560	72	99	91
Romania	130	38	11	12	10	31	10	6	19,511	179	2	9,520	75	99	91
Russian Federation	133	26	10	11	8	22	8	5	143,457	1,823	19	13,220	70	100	98
Rwanda	56	152	42	45	38	93	31	19	11,610	363	14	700	65	66	96
Saint Kitts and Nevis	130	28	11	11	10	23	8	7	56	–	0	14,920	–	–	81
Saint Lucia	112	23	14	16	13	19	13	9	185	3	0	7,260	75	–	91
Saint Vincent and the Grenadines	96	25	18	20	17	20	17	12	109	2	0	6,610	73	–	91
Samoa	96	31	18	19	16	26	15	10	193	5	0	4,060	74	99	97
San Marino	182	11	3	3	3	10	3	1	32	–	0	d	–	–	93
Sao Tome and Principe	49	111	47	52	43	71	35	17	190	6	0	1,670	67	70 x	96
Saudi Arabia	110	44	15	16	14	36	13	8	31,540	619	9	25,140 x	74	94	96
Senegal	49	140	47	54	44	70	42	21	15,129	567	27	1,050	67	52	73
Serbia	148	28	7	7	6	25	6	4	8,851	90	1	5,820	75	98	99
Seychelles	112	17	14	15	12	14	12	9	96	2	0	14,100	73	94	95
Sierra Leone	5	264	120	127	113	157	87	35	6,453	229	26	700	51	46	99
Singapore	182	8	3	3	3	6	2	1	5,604	50	0	55,150	83	96	–
Slovakia	148	18	7	8	7	16	6	4	5,426	57	0	17,750	76	–	–
Slovenia	182	10	3	3	2	9	2	1	2,068	22	0	23,580	81	100	97
Solomon Islands	73	40	28	31	26	32	24	12	584	17	0	1,830	68	–	–
Somalia	3	180	137	143	130	108	85	40	10,787	471	61	a	56	–	–
South Africa	58	60	41	47	37	47	34	11	54,490	1,111	42	6,800	58	93	–
South Sudan	13	253	93	98	87	150	60	39	12,340	446	39	970	56	27 x	41
Spain	166	11	4	4	4	9	4	3	46,122	413	2	29,440	83	98	100
Sri Lanka	133	21	10	11	9	18	8	5	20,715	323	3	3,460	75	91	97
State of Palestine	89	44	21	23	19	36	18	12	4,668	151	3	3,060	73	95	93
Sudan	27	128	70	75	65	80	48	30	40,235	1,319	89	1,710	64	74	55
Suriname	89	48	21	24	19	41	19	12	543	10	0	9,950	71	95	91
Swaziland	36	75	61	65	56	56	45	14	1,287	38	2	3,550	49	83	79
Sweden	182	7	3	3	3	6	2	2	9,779	119	0	61,610	82	–	100
Switzerland	166	8	4	4	4	7	3	3	8,299	86	0	88,120 x	83	–	99
Syrian Arab Republic	120	37	13	14	12	30	11	7	18,502	438	6	b	70	86	71
Tajikistan	52	108	45	50	40	85	39	21	8,482	256	12	1,080	70	100	97
Thailand	125	37	12	14	11	30	11	7	67,959	715	9	5,780	75	96	96 x
The former Yugoslav Republic of Macedonia	153	37	6	6	5	33	5	4	2,078	23	0	5,150	76	98	88
Timor-Leste	41	176	53	57	48	132	45	22	1,185	44	3	2,680	69	58	98
Togo	24	146	78	84	72	90	52	27	7,305	256	20	570	60	60	93
Tonga	99	22	17	15	18	19	14	7	106	3	0	4,260	73	99	96
Trinidad and Tobago	94	31	20	22	18	27	18	13	1,360	19	0	20,070	71	99	99
Tunisia	112	57	14	15	13	44	12	8	11,254	202	3	4,230	75	79	100
Turkey	112	75	14	15	12	56	12	7	78,666	1,289	19	10,830	76	93	93
Turkmenistan	42	91	51	59	44	73	44	23	5,374	112	6	8,020	66	100	–
Tuvalu	77	57	27	30	25	44	23	18	10	–	0	5,720	–	–	96
Uganda	40	187	55	60	49	111	38	19	39,032	1,665	85	670	59	73	94
Ukraine	139	20	9	10	8	17	8	6	44,824	484	4	3,560	71	100	97

TABLE 1. BASIC INDICATORS

Countries and areas	Under-5 mortality rank	Under-5 mortality rate (U5MR) 1990	Under-5 mortality rate (U5MR) 2015	U5MR by sex 2015 male	U5MR by sex 2015 female	Infant mortality rate (under 1) 1990	Infant mortality rate (under 1) 2015	Neonatal mortality rate 2015	Total population (thousands) 2015	Annual number of births (thousands) 2015	Annual number of under-5 deaths (thousands) 2015	GNI per capita (US$) 2015	Life expectancy at birth (years) 2015	Total adult literacy rate (%) 2009–2014*	Primary school net enrolment ratio (%) 2010–2014*
United Arab Emirates	148	17	7	8	6	14	6	4	9,157	98	1	44,600	77	90 x	96
United Kingdom	166	9	4	5	4	8	4	2	64,716	813	3	43,430	81	–	100
United Republic of Tanzania	46	165	49	52	45	100	35	19	53,470	2,064	98	920	66	68	82
United States	148	11	7	7	6	9	6	4	321,774	4,025	25	55,200	79	–	93
Uruguay	133	23	10	11	9	20	9	5	3,432	49	0	16,350	77	98	100
Uzbekistan	59	72	39	44	34	59	34	20	29,893	667	26	2,090	69	100	95
Vanuatu	73	36	28	30	25	29	23	12	265	7	0	3,160	72	84	–
Venezuela (Bolivarian Republic of)	110	30	15	17	13	25	13	9	31,108	599	9	12,500 x	74	95	93
Viet Nam	84	51	22	25	19	37	17	11	93,448	1,582	34	1,890	76	94	98
Yemen	56	126	42	46	38	89	34	22	26,832	856	34	1,300 x	64	68	85
Zambia	33	191	64	69	59	113	43	21	16,212	645	39	1,680	61	61 x	89
Zimbabwe	26	76	71	76	65	51	47	24	15,603	539	38	840	59	84	89
SUMMARY															
Sub-Saharan Africa		180	83	89	77	108	56	29	1,001,417	36,812	2,947	1,661	59	60	79
Eastern and Southern Africa		167	67	72	62	103	46	25	480,144	16,694	1,068	1,610	61	67	84
West and Central Africa		198	99	105	92	116	66	32	480,150	18,778	1,789	1,703	57	53	74
Middle East and North Africa		71	29	31	27	53	23	15	455,880	11,039	324	6,561	72	79	90
South Asia		129	53	52	53	92	42	30	1,743,865	36,381	1,870	1,500	68	67	94
East Asia and Pacific		58	18	19	16	44	15	9	2,097,940	29,541	538	6,845	74	95	96
Latin America and Caribbean		54	18	20	16	43	15	9	628,992	10,772	196	9,634	75	92	94
CEE/CIS		48	17	19	15	39	15	9	413,760	6,084	108	9,216	72	99	95
Least developed countries		175	73	78	68	109	51	27	954,158	30,969	2,181	845	64	60	82
World		**91**	**43**	**44**	**41**	**63**	**32**	**19**	**7,309,846**	**140,244**	**5,945**	**10,647**	**72**	**85**	**91**

For a complete list of countries and areas in the regions, subregions and country categories, see page 112 or visit <data.unicef.org/regionalclassifications>.
It is not advisable to compare data from consecutive editions of *The State of the World's Children*.

DEFINITIONS OF THE INDICATORS

Under-5 mortality rate – Probability of dying between birth and exactly 5 years of age, expressed per 1,000 live births.

Infant mortality rate – Probability of dying between birth and exactly 1 year of age, expressed per 1,000 live births.

Neonatal mortality rate – Probability of dying during the first 28 completed days of life, expressed per 1,000 live births.

GNI per capita – Gross national income (GNI) is the sum of value added by all resident producers, plus any product taxes (less subsidies) not included in the valuation of output, plus net receipts of primary income (compensation of employees and property income) from abroad. Gross national income per capita is GNI divided by midyear population. GNI per capita in US dollars is converted using the World Bank Atlas method.

Life expectancy at birth – Number of years newborn children would live if subject to the mortality risks prevailing for the cross section of population at the time of their birth.

Total adult literacy rate – Percentage of population aged 15 years and over who can both read and write with understanding a short simple statement on his/her everyday life.

Primary school net enrolment ratio – Number of children enrolled in primary or secondary school who are of official primary school age, expressed as a percentage of the total number of children of official primary school age. Because of the inclusion of primary-school-aged children enrolled in secondary school, this indicator can also be referred to as a primary adjusted net enrolment ratio.

MAIN DATA SOURCES

Under-5, infant and neonatal mortality rates – United Nations Inter-agency Group for Child Mortality Estimation (UNICEF, World Health Organization, United Nations Population Division and the World Bank).

Total population and births – United Nations Population Division.

Under-five deaths – United Nations Inter-agency Group for Child Mortality Estimation (UNICEF, World Health Organization, United Nations Population Division and the World Bank).

GNI per capita – The World Bank.

Life expectancy at birth – United Nations Population Division.

Total adult literacy rate and primary school enrolment ratio – UNESCO Institute for Statistics (UIS).

NOTES

a   low-income country (GNI per capita is $1,045 or less).

b   lower-middle-income country (GNI per capita is $1,046 to $4,125).

c   upper-middle-income country (GNI per capita is $4,126 to $12,735).

d   high-income country (GNI per capita is $12,736 or more).

–   Data not available.

x   Data refer to years or periods other than those specified in the column heading. Such data are not included in the calculation of regional and global averages.

*   Data refer to the most recent year available during the period specified in the column heading.

TABLE 2. NUTRITION

Countries and areas	Low birthweight (%) 2009–2013*	Early initiation of breast-feeding (%)	Exclusive breast-feeding <6 months (%)	Introduction to solid, semi-solid or soft foods 6–8 months (%)	Minimum acceptable diet 6–23 months (%)	Breast-feeding at age 2 (%)	Underweight (%) moderate & severe°	Stunting (%) moderate & severe°	Wasting (%) moderate & severe°	Overweight (%) moderate & severe°	Vitamin A supplementation, full coverage△ (%) 2014	Adequately iodized salt consumption (%) 2009–2013*
		2010–2015*					2010–2015*				2014	2009–2013*
Afghanistan	–	54	–	–	–	54 x	25	41	10	5	95 a	20
Albania	–	43 x	39 x	78 x	–	31 x	6 x	23 x	9 x	23 x	–	75
Algeria	6 x	36	26	28	–	27	3	12	4	12	–	61 x
Andorra	–	–	–	–	–	–	–	–	–	–	–	–
Angola	12 x	55 x	–	–	–	–	16 x	29 x	8 x	–	6 a	45 x
Antigua and Barbuda	6	–	–	–	–	–	–	–	–	–	–	–
Argentina	7	53	33	93	–	29	2 x	8 x	1 x	10 x	–	–
Armenia	8	36	35	75	32	23	5	21	4	17	–	97 x
Australia	6	–	–	–	–	–	0 x	2 x	0 x	8 x	–	–
Austria	7	–	–	–	–	–	–	–	–	–	–	–
Azerbaijan	10 x	20	12	77	22	16 x	5	18	3	13	58 a,w	54 x
Bahamas	12	–	–	–	–	–	–	–	–	–	–	–
Bahrain	10	–	34 x	–	–	–	–	–	–	–	–	–
Bangladesh	22 x	57	55	42	23	87	33	36	14	1	0 a	58
Barbados	12	40	20 p	–	–	–	4	8	7	12	–	17
Belarus	5	53	19	64	–	12	1 x	5 x	2 x	10 x	–	85
Belgium	7	–	–	–	–	–	–	–	–	–	–	–
Belize	11	62	15	69	–	35	6	19	3	8	–	–
Benin	15 x	47	41	73	16	46	18	34	5	2	99 a	86
Bhutan	10	78	51	87	–	61	13	34	6	8	– a	– f
Bolivia (Plurinational State of)	6 x	78	64	83 x	–	40 x	4	18	2	–	– a	– f
Bosnia and Herzegovina	5	42	19	71	–	12	2	9	2	17	–	62 x,y
Botswana	13 x	40 x	20 x	–	–	6 x	11 x	31 x	7 x	11 x	70 a	65 x
Brazil	9	43 x	39 x	94 x	–	26 x	2 x	7 x	2 x	7 x	–	96 x
Brunei Darussalam	12	–	–	–	–	–	10 x	20 x	3 x	8 x	–	92
Bulgaria	9	–	–	–	–	–	2 x	9 x	3 x	14 x	–	–
Burkina Faso	14	42	50	59	3	80	24	33	11	–	98 a	34 x,f
Burundi	13	74	69	70	9	79	29	58	6	3	69 a	– f
Cabo Verde	6 x	73 x	60 x	–	–	13 x	–	–	–	–	–	75 x
Cambodia	11	63	65	82	30	37	24	32	10	2	71 a	– f
Cameroon	11 x	31	28	83	–	19	15	32	5	7	96 a	85
Canada	6	–	–	–	–	–	–	–	–	10 x	–	–
Central African Republic	14	44	34	59	–	32	24	41	7	2	34 a	65
Chad	20	29	0	46	5	65	29	40	13	3	96 a	54
Chile	6	–	–	–	–	–	1	2	0	9	–	–
China	–	41 x	28 x	60 x	–	9 x	3	9	2	7	–	97 y
Colombia	10	57	43	86	60	33	3	13	1	5	–	77 x,f
Comoros	25 x	34	12	81	6	57	17	32	11	11	14 a	77 x,f
Congo	13 x	24	33	84	–	11	12	21	8	6	99 a	73 x,f
Cook Islands	–	–	–	–	–	–	–	–	–	–	–	–
Costa Rica	7	60	33	86	–	28	1 x	6 x	1 x	8 x	–	–
Côte d'Ivoire	17 x	31	12	64	5	38	16	30	8	3	99 a	30 x,f
Croatia	5	–	23 x	–	–	–	–	–	–	–	–	–
Cuba	5	48	33	91	56	24	3 x	7 x	2 x	–	–	88 x
Cyprus	12 x	–	–	–	–	–	–	–	–	–	–	–
Czech Republic	8	–	–	–	–	–	2 x	3 x	5 x	4 x	–	–
Democratic People's Republic of Korea	6	28	69	66	–	22	15	28	4	–	99 a	25
Democratic Republic of the Congo	10	52	48	79	8	66	23	43	8	4	99 a	59
Denmark	5	–	–	–	–	–	–	–	–	–	–	–
Djibouti	10 x	55 x	1 x	35 x	–	18 x	30	34	22	8	– a	0 x
Dominica	11	–	–	–	–	–	–	–	–	–	–	–
Dominican Republic	11 x	43	5	81	38	12	4	7	2	8	–	– f
Ecuador	9	55	40 x	74	–	19	6	25	2	8	–	78 x
Egypt	13 x	27	40	77	23	20	7	22	10	16	–	78 x
El Salvador	9	42	47	90	–	57	5	14	2	6	–	62 x
Equatorial Guinea	13 x	21	7	76	11	5	6	26	3	10	– a	– f
Eritrea	14 x	93	69	40 x	–	73	39	50	15	2	49 a	68 x
Estonia	5	–	–	–	–	–	–	–	–	–	–	–
Ethiopia	20 x	52	52	49	4	82	25	40	9	3	71 a	20 x,f
Fiji	10 x	57 x	40 x	–	–	–	5 x	8 x	6 x	5 x	–	–
Finland	4	–	–	–	–	–	–	–	–	–	–	–
France	7	–	–	–	–	–	–	–	–	–	–	–

TABLE 2. NUTRITION

Countries and areas	Low birthweight (%) 2009–2013*	Early initiation of breast-feeding (%)	Exclusive breast-feeding <6 months (%)	Introduction to solid, semi-solid or soft foods 6–8 months (%)	Minimum acceptable diet 6–23 months (%)	Breast-feeding at age 2 (%)	Underweight (%)	Stunting (%)	Wasting (%)	Overweight (%)	Vitamin A supplementation, full coverage (%) 2014	Adequately iodized salt consumption (%) 2009–2013*
				2010–2015*				moderate & severe	2010–2015*			
Gabon	14 x	32	6	82	–	4	7	18	3	8	– a	– f
Gambia	10	52	47	47	8	42	16	25	12	3	27 a	22
Georgia	7	69	55 x	85 x	–	17 x	1 x	11 x	2 x	20 x	–	100
Germany	7	–	–	–	–	–	1 x	1 x	1 x	4 x	–	–
Ghana	11	56	52	73	13	50	11	19	5	3	23 a	35
Greece	10	–	–	–	–	–	–	–	–	–	–	–
Grenada	9	–	39 x	–	–	–	–	–	–	–	–	–
Guatemala	11	56 x	53	–	51	57	13	47	1	5	19 a	– f
Guinea	12 x	17	21	43	4	66	19	31	10	4	– a	– f
Guinea-Bissau	11	34	53	71	–	51	17	28	6	2	98 a	12
Guyana	14	49	23	81	30	41	9	12	6	5	–	10
Haiti	23	47	40	87	14	31	12	22	5	4	30 a	3 x,f
Holy See	–	–	–	–	–	–	–	–	–	–	–	–
Honduras	10	64	31	70	54	43	7	23	1	5	– a	–
Hungary	9	–	–	–	–	–	–	–	–	–	–	–
Iceland	4	–	–	–	–	–	–	–	–	–	–	–
India	28 x	41 x	46 x	56 x	–	77 x,y	29	39	15	–	61 a	71
Indonesia	9 x	49	42	91	37	55	20	36	14	12	84 a	58
Iran (Islamic Republic of)	8	69	53	76	–	51	4	7	4	–	–	– f
Iraq	13	43	20	36	–	23	9	23	7	12	–	29
Ireland	5	–	–	–	–	–	–	–	–	–	–	–
Israel	8	–	–	–	–	–	–	–	–	–	–	–
Italy	7	–	–	–	–	–	–	–	–	–	–	–
Jamaica	11	65	24	55	–	31	3	6	3	8	–	–
Japan	10	–	–	–	–	–	3	7	2	2	–	–
Jordan	13 x	19	23	92	33	13	3	8	2	5	–	– f
Kazakhstan	6	68	32	49	–	26	4	13	4	13	– a	85
Kenya	8	62	61	80	22	53	11	26	4	4	28 a	93
Kiribati	8	–	69 x	–	–	82 x	15 x	–	–	–	– a	–
Kuwait	8	–	12 x	–	–	9 x	3	6	2	9	–	–
Kyrgyzstan	6	83	41	85	36	23	3	13	3	7	– a	76 x
Lao People's Democratic Republic	15	39	40	52	–	40	27	44	6	2	89 a	– f
Latvia	5	–	–	–	–	–	–	–	–	–	–	–
Lebanon	12	41 x	27 x	–	–	11 x	4	17 x	7 x	17 x	–	71
Lesotho	11	53 x	67	68 x	11	30	10	33	3	7	67 a	79
Liberia	14 x	61	55	46	4	44	15	32	6	3	0 a	–
Libya	–	–	–	–	–	–	6 x	21 x	7 x	22 x	–	–
Liechtenstein	–	–	–	–	–	–	–	–	–	–	–	–
Lithuania	5	–	–	–	–	–	–	–	–	–	–	–
Luxembourg	7	–	–	–	–	–	–	–	–	–	–	–
Madagascar	16	66	42	90	–	83	37 x	49 x	15 x	6 x	99 a	50
Malawi	14	75	70	89	14	75	17	42	4	5	41 a	62
Malaysia	11	–	29 x	–	–	–	13 x	17 x	–	–	–	–
Maldives	11	64 x	48 x	91 x	–	68 x	18 x	20 x	10 x	7 x	– a	44 x
Mali	18	46 x	38 x	27 x	–	56 x	28 x	39 x	15 x	5 x	– a	74 x
Malta	7	–	–	–	–	–	–	–	–	–	–	–
Marshall Islands	18 x	73 x	31 x	–	–	53 x	–	–	–	–	– a	–
Mauritania	35	56	27	48	–	36	20	22	12	1	89 a	7
Mauritius	14 x	–	21 x	–	–	–	–	–	–	–	–	–
Mexico	9	39	14	95	–	14	3	14	2	9	– a	91 x
Micronesia (Federated States of)	11	–	60 x	–	–	–	–	–	–	–	– a	–
Monaco	6	–	–	–	–	–	–	–	–	–	–	–
Mongolia	5	71	47	95	–	53	2	11	1	11	79 a	70
Montenegro	5	14	17	95	66	9	1	9	3	22	–	71 x
Morocco	15 x	30	28	86 x	–	15 x	3	15	2	11	– a	21 x
Mozambique	17	69	41	95	11	52	16	43	6	8	99 a	25 f
Myanmar	9	76	24	76	–	65	23	35	8	3	94 a	69
Namibia	16 x	71	49	80	13	21	13	23	7	4	– a	57 x
Nauru	27 x	76 x	67 x	–	–	65 x	5 x	24 x	1 x	3 x	–	–
Nepal	18	49	57	74	32	87	30	37	11	2	85 a	80
Netherlands	6	–	–	–	–	–	–	–	–	–	–	–
New Zealand	6	–	–	–	–	–	–	–	–	–	–	–

TABLE 2. NUTRITION

Countries and areas	Low birthweight (%) 2009–2013*	Early initiation of breast-feeding (%)	Exclusive breast-feeding <6 months (%)	Introduction to solid, semi-solid or soft foods 6–8 months (%)	Minimum acceptable diet 6–23 months (%)	Breast-feeding at age 2 (%)	Underweight (%) moderate & severe°	Stunting (%)	Wasting (%)	Overweight (%)	Vitamin A supplementation, full coverage△ (%) 2014	Adequately iodized salt consumption (%) 2009–2013*
				2010–2015*				2010–2015*				
Nicaragua	8	68	32	–	–	43	6 x	23 x	2 x	6 x	4 α	97 x
Niger	27 x	53	23	–	6	50	38	43	19	3	95 α	19
Nigeria	15	33	17	67	10	35	20	33	8	2	80 α	80
Niue	–	–	–	–	–	–	–	–	–	–	–	–
Norway	5	–	–	–	–	–	–	–	–	–	–	–
Oman	10	71	33	90	–	48	10	14	8	4	–	– f
Pakistan	32 x	18	38	66	15	56	32	45	11	5	96 α	69
Palau	7	–	–	–	–	–	–	–	–	–	–	–
Panama	8	47	22	61	–	34	4 x	19 x	1 x	–	–	–
Papua New Guinea	11 x	–	56 x	–	–	72 x	28	50	14	14	– α	–
Paraguay	6	47 x	24 x	–	–	14 x	3	11	3	12	–	93 y
Peru	7	55	68	82	–	55 y	3	15	1	–	–	88
Philippines	21 x	50	34 x	90 x	–	41	20	30	8	5	83 α	45 x
Poland	6	–	–	–	–	–	–	–	–	–	–	–
Portugal	9	–	–	–	–	–	–	–	–	–	–	–
Qatar	8	34	29	50	–	32	–	–	–	–	–	–
Republic of Korea	4 x	–	–	–	–	–	1	3	1	7	–	–
Republic of Moldova	6	61	36	62	–	12	2	6	2	5	–	44
Romania	8	12 x	16 x	–	–	–	4 x	13 x	4 x	8 x	–	74 x
Russian Federation	6	–	–	–	–	–	–	–	–	–	–	– f
Rwanda	7	71	87	79	17	87	9	38	2	8	95 α	87 x,f
Saint Kitts and Nevis	10	–	–	–	–	–	–	–	–	–	–	– f
Saint Lucia	10	50	–	–	–	–	3	3	4	6	–	46
Saint Vincent and the Grenadines	11	–	–	–	–	–	–	–	–	–	–	–
Samoa	10	88 x	51 x	–	–	74 x	–	–	–	–	–	–
San Marino	10	–	–	–	–	–	–	–	–	–	–	–
Sao Tome and Principe	10	38	74	74	–	24	9	17	4	2	– α	65
Saudi Arabia	9	–	–	–	–	30 x	5 x	9 x	12 x	6 x	–	–
Senegal	19	30	33	63	8	41	13	19	6	1	89 α	43
Serbia	6	51	13	97	72	9	2	6	4	14	–	32 x
Seychelles	–	–	–	–	–	–	–	–	–	–	–	–
Sierra Leone	11	54	32	63	7	48	18	38	9	9	8 α	63
Singapore	10	–	–	–	–	–	3 x	4 x	4 x	3 x	–	–
Slovakia	8	–	–	–	–	–	–	–	–	–	–	–
Slovenia	6	–	–	–	–	–	–	–	–	–	–	–
Solomon Islands	13 x	75 x	74 x	–	–	67 x	12 x	33 x	4 x	3 x	–	–
Somalia	–	23 x	5 x	16 x	–	27 x	23 x	26 x	15 x	3 x	30 α	4 y
South Africa	–	61 x	8 x	–	–	31 x	9 x	24 x	5 x	–	– α	–
South Sudan	–	48	45	21	–	38	28	31	23	6	18 α	45
Spain	8	–	–	–	–	–	–	–	–	–	–	–
Sri Lanka	17 x	80 x	76 x	–	–	84 x	26	15	21	1	72 α	92 x
State of Palestine	9	41	39	90	42	12	1	7	1	8	–	77
Sudan	–	69	55	51	–	49	33	38	16	3	99 α	10
Suriname	14	45	3	47	–	15	6	9	5	4	–	–
Swaziland	9	48	64	90	–	8	6	26	2	9	43 α	52
Sweden	5	–	–	–	–	–	–	–	–	–	–	–
Switzerland	7	–	–	–	–	–	–	–	–	–	–	–
Syrian Arab Republic	10	46 x	43 x	–	–	25 x	10 x	28 x	12 x	18 x	–	79 x
Tajikistan	10 x	50	34	49	20	50	13	27	10	7	99 α	39
Thailand	11	46	12	75	–	18	9	16	7	11	–	71
The former Yugoslav Republic of Macedonia	6	21	23	41	–	13	1	5	2	12	–	94 x,y
Timor-Leste	12 x	93	62	97	18	39	38	50	11	2	– α	60 x
Togo	11	61	58	67	12	61	16	28	7	2	– α	32
Tonga	–	79	52	–	–	30	2	8	5	17	–	–
Trinidad and Tobago	12	41 x	13 x	83 x	–	22 x	4 x	5 x	5 x	5 x	–	28 x
Tunisia	7	40	9	27	–	19	2	10	3	14	–	97 x
Turkey	11 x	50	30	–	–	34	2	10	2	11	–	69 x
Turkmenistan	5	60 x	11 x	–	–	37 x	9 x	19 x	7 x	5 x	– α	75 x,f
Tuvalu	6 x	15 x	35 x	–	–	51 x	2 x	10 x	3 x	6 x	–	–
Uganda	12	53	63	67	6	46	12	34	4	6	66 α	87 x,f
Ukraine	5	66	20	43	–	22	1 x	4 x	0 x	–	–	21
United Arab Emirates	6	–	34 x	–	–	29 x	–	–	–	–	–	–

unicef ● 70 YEARS FOR EVERY CHILD

TABLE 2. NUTRITION

Countries and areas	Low birthweight (%) 2009–2013*	Early initiation of breast-feeding (%)	Exclusive breast-feeding <6 months (%)	Introduction to solid, semi-solid or soft foods 6–8 months (%)	Minimum acceptable diet 6–23 months (%)	Breast-feeding at age 2 (%)	Underweight (%)	Stunting (%)	Wasting (%)	Overweight (%)	Vitamin A supplemen-tation, full coverage△ (%) 2014	Adequately iodized salt consumption (%) 2009–2013*
		2010–2015*					moderate & severe⊖ 2010–2015*					
United Kingdom	7	–	–	–	–	–	–	–	–	–	–	–
United Republic of Tanzania	8	51	41	90	–	48	13	35	4	–	88 α	56
United States	8	–	–	–	–	–	1	2	1	6	–	–
Uruguay	8	77	–	–	–	–	4	11	1	7	–	–
Uzbekistan	5 x	67 x	26 x	47 x	–	38 x	4 x	20 x	5 x	13 x	99 α	53 x
Vanuatu	10 x	85	73	72	–	49	11	29	4	5	–	23 x
Venezuela (Bolivarian Republic of)	9	–	7 x	–	–	–	3 x	13 x	4 x	6 x	–	–
Viet Nam	5	27	24	91	59	22	12	19	6	5	94 α,w	45
Yemen	32	53	10	69	15	45	16	47	16	2	7 α	30 x
Zambia	11 x	66	73	82	11	42	15	40	6	6	– α	64 x
Zimbabwe	11	59	41	87	13	17	11	28	3	4	32 α	– f
SUMMARY												
Sub-Saharan Africa	13	49	40	69	9	52	19	36	8	4	74	59
Eastern and Southern Africa	11	59	54	73	10	60	16	36	6	5	62	–
West and Central Africa	14	40	29	68	9	46	22	35	10	4	83	65
Middle East and North Africa	–	45	35	61	–	33	7	18	8	9	–	–
South Asia	28	39	46	57	–	75	30	37	15	4	62	69
East Asia and Pacific	–	44	31	69	41 **	24	5	11	4	6	86	86
Latin America and Caribbean	9	49	32	88	–	28	3	10	1	7	–	–
CEE/CIS (excluding the Russian Federation)	6	54	27	–	–	29	2	10	2	14	–	–
Least developed countries	14	55	47	66	11	63	–	–	–	–	67	50
World	**16 ****	**44**	**39**	**66**	**–**	**49**	**14**	**24**	**8**	**5**	**69**	**75**

For a complete list of countries and areas in the regions, subregions and country categories, see page 112 or visit <data.unicef.org/regionalclassifications>.
It is not advisable to compare data from consecutive editions of *The State of the World's Children*.

DEFINITIONS OF THE INDICATORS

Low birthweight – Percentage of infants weighing less than 2,500 grams at birth.

Early initiation of breastfeeding – Percentage of infants who are put to the breast within one hour of birth.

Exclusive breastfeeding <6 months – Percentage of children aged 0–5 months who are fed exclusively with breast milk in the 24 hours prior to the survey.

Introduction of solid, semi-solid or soft foods (6–8 months) – Percentage of children aged 6–8 months who received solid, semi-solid or soft foods in the 24 hours prior to the survey.

Minimum acceptable diet (6–23 months) – Percentage of breastfed children 6–23 months of age who had at least the minimum dietary diversity and the minimum meal frequency during the previous day AND percentage of non-breastfed children 6–23 months of age who received at least 2 milk feedings and had at least the minimum dietary diversity not including milk feeds and the minimum meal frequency during the previous day.

Breastfeeding at age 2 – Percentage of children aged 20–23 months who received breast milk in the 24 hours prior to the survey.

Underweight – Moderate and severe: Percentage of children aged 0–59 months who are below minus two standard deviations from median weight-for-age of the World Health Organization (WHO) Child Growth Standards.

Stunting – Moderate and severe: Percentage of children aged 0–59 months who are below minus two standard deviations from median height-for-age of the WHO Child Growth Standards.

Wasting – Moderate and severe: Percentage of children aged 0–59 months who are below minus two standard deviations from median weight-for-height of the WHO Child Growth Standards.

Overweight – Moderate and severe: Percentage of children aged 0–59 months who are above two standard deviations from median weight-for-height of the WHO Child Growth Standards.

Vitamin A supplementation, full coverage – The estimated percentage of children aged 6–59 months reached with 2 doses of vitamin A supplements approximately 4–6 months apart in a given calendar year.

Adequately iodized salt consumption – Percentage of households consuming adequately iodized salt (15 parts per million or more based on rapid test kits).

MAIN DATA SOURCES

Low birthweight – Demographic and Health Surveys (DHS), Multiple Indicator Cluster Surveys (MICS), other national household surveys, data from routine reporting systems, UNICEF and WHO.

Infant and young child feeding – DHS, MICS, other national household surveys and UNICEF.

Underweight, stunting, wasting and overweight – DHS, MICS, other national household surveys, WHO and UNICEF.

Vitamin A supplementation – UNICEF.

Adequately iodized salt consumption – DHS, MICS, other national household surveys and UNICEF.

NOTES

– Data not available.

x Data refer to years or periods other than those specified in the column heading. Such data are not included in the calculation of regional and global averages, with the exception of 2005–2006 and 2007–2008 data from India, and 2008 data from China. Estimates from data years prior to 2000 are not displayed.

y Data differ from the standard definition or refer to only part of a country. If they fall within the noted reference period, such data are included in the calculation of regional and global averages.

p Based on small denominators (typically 25–49 unweighted cases). No data based on fewer than 25 unweighted cases are displayed.

⊖ Regional averages for underweight (moderate and severe), stunting (moderate and severe), wasting (moderate and severe) and overweight (moderate and severe) are estimated using statistical modeling of data from the UNICEF-WHO-World Bank Joint Global Nutrition Database, 2015 revision. For more information see <data.unicef.org/nutrition/malnutrition>.

△ Full coverage with vitamin A supplements is reported as the lower percentage of 2 annual coverage points (i.e., lower point between semester 1 (January–June) and semester 2 (July–December) of 2014). Data are only presented for VAS priority countries; thus aggregates are only based on and representative of these priority countries.

w Identifies countries with national vitamin A supplementation programmes targeted towards a reduced age range. Coverage figure is reported as targeted.

α Identifies countries that are designated 'priority'. Priority countries for national vitamin A supplementation programmes are identified as those having high under-five mortality rates (over 70 per 1,000 live births), and/or evidence of vitamin A deficiency among this age group, and/or a history of vitamin A supplementation programmes.

f The most recent survey for this country uses an indicator definition that is not in line with the international standard. If available, a previous data point that conforms to the standard definition is presented instead.

* Data refer to the most recent year available during the period specified in the column heading.

** Excludes China.

TABLE 3. HEALTH

Countries and areas	Use of improved drinking water sources (%) 2015			Use of improved sanitation facilities (%) 2015			Immunization coverage (%) 2014									Newborns protected against tetanus^	Pneumonia — Care seeking for children with symptoms of pneumonia (%) 2010–2015*	Diarrhoea — Treatment with oral rehydration salts (ORS) (%) 2010–2015*	Malaria — Care seeking for children with fever (%) 2010–2015*	Malaria — Children sleeping under ITNs (%) 2010–2015*	Malaria — Households with at least one ITN (%) 2010–2015*
	total	urban	rural	total	urban	rural	BCG	DTP1	DTP3	polio3	MCV1	HepB3	Hib3	rota	PCV3						
Afghanistan	55	78	47	32	45	27	86	82	75	75	66	75	75	0	40	70	61	53	–	–	–
Albania	95	95	95	93	95	90	99	99	98	98	98	98	98	0	99	92	70 x	54 x	71 x	–	–
Algeria	84	84	82	88	90	82	99	99	95	95	95	95	95	0	0	92	66	25	–	–	–
Andorra	100	100	100	100	100	100	–	99	97	97	96	96	97	0	93	–	–	–	–	–	–
Angola	49	75	28	52	89	22	81	99	80	81	85	80	80	18	61	78	–	–	–	26	35
Antigua and Barbuda	98	–	–	–	–	–	–	99	99	96	98	99	99	0	0	–	–	–	–	–	–
Argentina	99	99	100	96	96	98	99	98	94	92	95	94	94	0	89	–	94	18	–	–	–
Armenia	100	100	100	89	96	78	99	97	93	95	97	93	93	91	0	–	57	33	54	–	–
Australia	100	100	100	100	100	100	–	92	92	92	93	91	91	84	91	–	–	–	–	–	–
Austria	100	100	100	100	100	100	–	93	83	83	76	83	83	61	0	–	–	–	–	–	–
Azerbaijan	87	95	78	89	92	87	98	96	94	97	98	94	94	0	64	–	36 x	11	–	1 x	–
Bahamas	98	–	–	92	–	–	–	96	96	96	92	96	96	0	96	99	–	–	–	–	–
Bahrain	100	–	–	99	99	99	–	99	99	99	99	99	99	97	98	98	–	–	–	–	–
Bangladesh	87	87	87	61	58	62	99	97	95	95	89	95	95	0	0	96	42	77	27	–	–
Barbados	100	–	–	96	96	96	–	98	94	95	95	94	94	0	90	–	–	–	–	–	–
Belarus	100	100	99	94	94	95	98	97	97	97	99	97	20	0	0	–	93	45	–	–	–
Belgium	100	100	100	99	99	99	–	99	99	99	96	98	98	86	93	–	–	–	–	–	–
Belize	100	99	100	91	93	88	98	96	95	95	95	95	95	0	0	91	82	23	–	–	–
Benin	78	85	72	20	36	7	88	84	70	72	63	70	70	0	70	93	23	50	44	73	81
Bhutan	100	100	100	50	78	33	99	99	99	98	97	99	99	0	0	83	74	61	–	–	–
Bolivia (Plurinational State of)	90	97	76	50	61	28	99	98	94	95	95	94	94	99	56	87	62	22	–	–	–
Bosnia and Herzegovina	100	100	100	95	99	92	98	92	86	86	89	89	79	0	0	–	87	36	–	–	–
Botswana	96	99	92	63	79	43	98	98	95	96	97	95	96	82	81	92	14 x	49 x	75 x	–	–
Brazil	98	100	87	83	88	52	99	99	93	96	97	96	95	92	93	93	50 x	–	–	–	–
Brunei Darussalam	–	–	–	–	–	–	99	99	99	99	99	99	96	0	0	95	–	–	–	–	–
Bulgaria	99	100	99	86	87	84	97	90	88	88	93	95	83	0	92	–	–	–	–	–	–
Burkina Faso	82	97	76	20	50	7	98	95	91	91	88	91	91	91	91	89	56	21	61	75	90
Burundi	76	91	74	48	44	49	92	98	95	95	94	95	95	96	95	85	55	38	59	54	63
Cabo Verde	92	94	87	72	82	54	99	99	95	95	93	95	95	0	0	92	–	–	–	–	–
Cambodia	76	100	69	42	88	30	93	99	97	98	94	97	97	0	0	91	69	34	61	4 x	5 x
Cameroon	76	95	53	46	62	27	82	93	87	86	80	87	87	46	87	85	28	17	33	55	71
Canada	100	100	99	100	100	99	–	98	96	96	95	75	96	0	97	–	–	–	–	–	–
Central African Republic	68	90	54	22	44	7	74	69	47	47	49	47	47	0	47	60	30	16	–	36	47
Chad	51	72	45	12	31	6	59	60	46	54	54	46	46	0	0	60	26	20	36	36	77
Chile	99	100	93	99	100	91	98	96	92	92	94	92	92	0	89	–	–	–	–	–	–
China	95	98	93	76	87	64	99	99	99	99	99	99	0	0	0	–	–	–	–	–	–
Colombia	91	97	74	81	85	68	89	91	90	91	91	90	90	89	89	85	64	54	54	–	3 x
Comoros	90	93	89	36	48	31	76	83	80	79	80	80	80	0	0	85	38	38	45	41	59
Congo	76	96	40	15	20	6	95	95	90	90	80	90	90	60	69	85	28	28	51	61	66
Cook Islands	100	–	–	98	98	98	99	99	99	99	98	99	99	0	0	–	–	–	–	–	–
Costa Rica	98	100	92	95	95	92	80	91	91	91	95	91	91	0	83	–	77	40	–	–	–
Côte d'Ivoire	82	93	69	22	33	10	84	78	67	66	63	67	67	0	2	82	38	17	43	37	67
Croatia	100	100	100	97	98	96	98	98	95	95	94	95	95	0	0	–	–	–	–	–	–
Cuba	95	96	90	93	94	89	99	98	96	99	99	96	96	0	0	–	93	61	93	–	–
Cyprus	100	100	100	100	100	100	–	99	99	99	86	96	96	0	0	–	–	–	–	–	–
Czech Republic	100	100	100	99	99	99	–	99	99	99	99	99	99	0	0	–	–	–	–	–	–
Democratic People's Republic of Korea	100	100	99	82	88	73	98	94	93	99	99	93	93	0	0	93	80 x	74 x	–	–	–
Democratic Republic of the Congo	52	81	31	29	29	29	90	81	80	79	77	80	80	0	61	82	42	39	55	56	70
Denmark	100	100	100	100	100	100	–	96	94	94	90	0	94	0	93	–	–	–	–	–	–
Djibouti	90	97	65	47	60	5	86	93	78	78	71	78	78	0	78	80	94	94	–	20 x	32
Dominica	–	96	–	–	–	–	98	99	97	97	94	97	97	0	0	–	–	–	–	–	–
Dominican Republic	85	85	82	84	86	76	99	91	91	90	88	89	87	86	27	90	73	48	65	–	–
Ecuador	87	93	76	85	87	81	89	84	83	84	85	83	83	81	90	85	–	46	–	–	–
Egypt	99	100	99	95	97	93	96	96	94	94	93	94	94	0	0	86	68	28	68	–	–
El Salvador	94	97	87	75	82	60	96	96	93	93	94	93	93	96	92	90	80	58 x	–	–	–
Equatorial Guinea	48	73	31	75	80	71	71	65	24	30	44	24	24	0	0	70	54	40	62	23	38
Eritrea	58	73	53	16	45	7	97	97	94	94	96	94	94	25	0	94	45	43	–	20	71 x
Estonia	100	100	99	97	98	97	95	95	93	93	93	93	93	32	0	–	–	–	–	–	–
Ethiopia	57	93	49	28	27	28	75	86	77	75	70	77	77	63	76	80	27	26	24	30	47
Fiji	96	100	91	91	93	88	99	99	99	99	94	99	99	99	99	94	–	–	–	–	–
Finland	100	100	100	98	99	88	–	99	98	98	97	0	98	93	0	–	–	–	–	–	–

unicef ® 70 YEARS FOR EVERY CHILD

TABLE 3. HEALTH

Countries and areas	Use of improved drinking water sources (%) 2015			Use of improved sanitation facilities (%) 2015			Immunization coverage (%) 2014									Newborns protected against tetanus^	Pneumonia Care seeking for children with symptoms of pneumonia (%) 2010–2015*	Diarrhoea Treatment with oral rehydration salts (ORS) (%) 2010–2015*	Malaria Care seeking for children with fever (%) 2010–2015*	Malaria Children sleeping under ITNs (%) 2010–2015*	Malaria House-holds with at least one ITN (%) 2010–2015*
	total	urban	rural	total	urban	rural	BCG	DTP1β	DTP3β	polio3	MCV1	HepB3	Hib3	rota	PCV3						
France	100	100	100	99	99	99	–	99	99	99	90	82	98	0	89	–	–	–	–	–	–
Gabon	93	97	67	42	43	32	91	77	70	68	61	70	70	0	0	85	68	26	67	39	36
Gambia	90	94	84	59	62	55	96	98	96	97	96	96	96	92	96	92	68	59	65	47	69
Georgia	100	100	100	86	95	76	96	99	91	91	92	91	91	69	0	–	74 x	40 x	–	–	–
Germany	100	100	100	99	99	99	–	98	96	95	97	87	94	0	68	–	–	–	–	–	–
Ghana	89	93	84	15	20	9	99	99	98	98	92	98	98	98	98	88	56	49	77	47	68
Greece	100	100	100	99	99	98	–	99	99	99	97	96	99	0	96	–	–	–	–	–	–
Grenada	97	–	–	98	98	98	–	97	97	81	94	97	97	0	0	–	–	–	–	–	–
Guatemala	93	98	87	64	78	49	91	89	73	65	67	73	73	54	51	85	50	49	49	–	–
Guinea	77	93	67	20	34	12	72	60	51	42	52	51	51	0	0	80	37	34	37	26	47
Guinea-Bissau	79	99	60	21	34	8	94	92	80	78	69	80	80	0	0	80	34	19	51	81	90
Guyana	98	98	98	84	88	82	99	98	98	97	99	98	98	95	97	99	84	43	71	7	5
Haiti	58	65	48	28	34	19	76	72	48	55	53	48	48	40	0	81	38	53	40	12	19
Holy See	–	–	–	–	–	–	–	–	–	–	–	–	–	–	–	–	–	–	–	–	–
Honduras	91	97	84	83	87	78	86	86	85	85	88	85	85	85	85	94	64	60	62	–	–
Hungary	100	100	100	98	98	99	99	99	99	99	99	0	99	0	93	–	–	–	–	–	–
Iceland	100	100	100	99	99	100	–	96	90	90	90	0	90	0	90	–	–	–	–	–	–
India	94	97	93	40	63	28	91	90	83	82	83	70	20	0	0	87	77	26 x	71 x	–	–
Indonesia	87	94	79	61	72	47	93	94	78	79	77	78	21	0	0	85	75	39	74	3 x	3 x
Iran (Islamic Republic of)	96	98	92	90	93	82	99	99	99	99	99	99	0	0	0	95	76	61	–	–	–
Iraq	87	94	70	86	86	84	95	77	64	67	57	62	64	29	0	72	74	23	–	–	–
Ireland	98	98	98	90	89	93	74	98	96	96	93	95	96	0	92	–	–	–	–	–	–
Israel	100	100	100	100	100	100	–	95	94	94	96	97	94	93	93	–	–	–	–	–	–
Italy	100	100	100	100	99	100	–	98	94	94	86	94	94	0	55	–	–	–	–	–	–
Jamaica	94	97	89	82	80	84	–	97	92	94	92	92	92	0	0	80	82	64	–	–	–
Japan	100	100	100	100	100	100	–	99	98	98	98	0	0	0	0	–	–	–	–	–	–
Jordan	97	98	92	99	99	99	95	98	98	98	98	98	98	0	0	90	77	20	69	–	–
Kazakhstan	93	99	86	98	97	98	95	96	95	95	99	95	95	0	58	–	81	62	–	–	–
Kenya	63	82	57	30	31	30	81	88	81	81	79	81	81	19	81	76	66	54	72	54	59
Kiribati	67	87	51	40	51	31	72	83	75	79	91	75	75	0	57	–	81 x	62 x	27 x	–	–
Kuwait	99	99	99	100	100	100	99	97	95	94	94	96	95	0	94	95	–	–	–	–	–
Kyrgyzstan	90	97	86	93	89	96	97	96	96	95	96	96	96	0	0	–	60	33	56	–	–
Lao People's Democratic Republic	76	86	69	71	94	56	82	94	88	88	87	88	88	0	72	90	54	42	–	43	50
Latvia	99	100	98	88	91	82	92	93	92	92	95	92	92	0	87	–	–	–	–	–	–
Lebanon	99	–	–	81	81	81	–	84	81	75	79	81	81	0	0	–	74 x	44 x	–	–	–
Lesotho	82	95	77	30	37	28	87	97	96	95	92	96	96	0	0	83	63	53	61	–	–
Liberia	76	89	63	17	28	6	73	74	50	49	58	50	50	0	45	89	51	60	71	38	55
Libya	–	–	–	97	97	96	99	96	94	94	93	94	94	86	39	–	–	–	–	–	–
Liechtenstein	–	–	–	–	–	–	–	–	–	–	–	–	–	–	–	–	–	–	–	–	–
Lithuania	97	100	90	92	97	83	98	97	93	93	93	94	93	0	0	–	–	–	–	–	–
Luxembourg	100	100	100	98	98	99	–	99	99	99	99	94	99	89	95	–	–	–	–	–	–
Madagascar	52	82	35	12	18	9	75	83	73	73	64	73	73	50	72	78	41	15	48	62	68
Malawi	90	96	89	41	47	40	97	97	91	87	85	91	91	83	87	89	68	64	75	66	78
Malaysia	98	100	93	96	96	96	–	99	97	97	94	96	97	0	0	90	–	–	–	–	–
Maldives	99	100	98	98	97	98	99	99	99	99	99	99	99	0	0	95	22 x	57 x	84 x	–	–
Mali	77	97	64	25	38	16	79	80	77	84	80	77	77	13	84	85	38 x	14 x	59	27 x	85
Malta	100	100	100	100	100	100	–	99	99	99	90	90	99	0	0	–	–	–	–	–	–
Marshall Islands	95	94	98	77	84	56	89	97	78	77	79	79	65	44	29	–	–	38 x	63 x	–	–
Mauritania	58	58	57	40	58	14	98	88	84	84	84	84	84	5	84	80	43	19	–	18	46
Mauritius	100	100	100	93	94	93	97	97	97	98	98	97	97	0	0	95	–	–	–	–	–
Mexico	96	97	92	85	88	74	96	90	87	87	97	84	87	85	94	88	–	52	–	–	–
Micronesia (Federated States of)	89	95	87	57	85	49	70	98	81	81	91	83	68	33	61	–	–	–	–	–	–
Monaco	100	100	–	100	100	–	89	99	99	99	99	99	99	0	0	–	–	–	–	–	–
Mongolia	64	66	59	60	66	43	99	99	99	99	98	99	99	0	0	–	70	31	–	–	–
Montenegro	100	100	99	96	98	92	91	97	91	91	88	87	91	0	0	–	89 x	16 x	74	–	–
Morocco	85	99	65	77	84	66	99	99	99	99	99	99	99	90	80	88	70	22	–	–	–
Mozambique	51	81	37	21	42	10	93	93	78	78	85	78	78	0	73	83	50	55	56	36	51
Myanmar	81	93	74	80	84	77	86	90	75	76	86	75	75	0	0	87	69	61	–	11	–
Namibia	91	98	85	34	54	17	97	92	88	88	83	88	88	0	0	85	68	72	63	6	24
Nauru	97	97	–	66	66	–	99	99	95	95	98	95	95	0	0	–	69 x	23 x	51 x	–	–
Nepal	92	91	92	46	56	43	99	94	92	92	88	92	92	0	0	82	50	44	46	–	–

TABLE 3. HEALTH

Countries and areas	Use of improved drinking water sources (%) 2015			Use of improved sanitation facilities (%) 2015			Immunization coverage (%) 2014									Newborns protected against tetanus^	Pneumonia Care seeking for children with symptoms of pneumonia (%) 2010–2015*	Diarrhoea Treatment with oral rehydration salts (ORS) (%) 2010–2015*	Malaria Care seeking for children with fever (%) 2010–2015*	Children sleeping under ITNs (%) 2010–2015*	Households with at least one ITN (%) 2010–2015*
	total	urban	rural	total	urban	rural	BCG	DTP1β	DTP3β	polio3	MCV1	HepB3	Hib3	rota	PCV3						
Netherlands	100	100	100	98	97	100	–	98	96	96	96	95	96	0	95	–	–	–	–	–	–
New Zealand	100	100	100	–	–	–	–	93	93	93	93	93	93	0	93	–	–	–	–	–	–
Nicaragua	87	99	69	68	76	56	98	99	98	99	99	98	98	98	98	81	58 x	65	–	–	–
Niger	58	100	49	11	38	5	76	89	68	67	72	68	68	19	13	81	59	41	75	96	87
Nigeria	69	81	57	29	33	25	74	75	66	66	51	66	66	0	0	55	35	34	32	17	50
Niue	99	–	–	100	100	100	99	99	99	99	99	99	99	0	99	–	–	–	–	–	–
Norway	100	100	100	98	98	98	–	99	93	93	94	0	94	0	91	–	–	–	–	–	–
Oman	93	95	86	97	97	95	99	99	99	99	99	98	99	0	98	98	56	59	–	–	–
Pakistan	91	94	90	64	83	51	85	79	73	72	63	73	73	0	68	75	64	38	65	0 x	1
Palau	–	97	–	100	100	100	–	99	95	95	83	99	99	99	93	–	–	–	–	–	–
Panama	95	98	89	75	84	58	99	96	80	80	90	80	80	87	48	–	82	52	–	–	–
Papua New Guinea	40	88	33	19	56	13	81	87	62	53	65	62	62	0	0	70	63 x	–	–	–	–
Paraguay	98	100	95	89	95	78	95	98	87	83	90	87	87	85	88	85	–	–	–	–	–
Peru	87	91	69	76	82	53	94	98	88	79	89	88	88	86	86	85	60	28	60	–	–
Philippines	92	94	90	74	78	71	87	86	79	84	88	79	79	1	0	87	64	49	50	–	–
Poland	98	99	97	97	98	97	93	99	99	95	98	96	99	0	0	–	–	–	–	–	–
Portugal	100	100	100	100	100	100	99	99	98	98	98	98	98	0	0	–	–	–	–	–	–
Qatar	100	–	–	98	98	98	90	99	99	99	99	99	99	90	93	–	–	–	–	–	–
Republic of Korea	–	100	–	100	100	100	99	99	99	99	99	99	97	0	0	–	–	–	–	–	–
Republic of Moldova	88	97	81	76	88	67	97	94	90	92	90	92	89	69	28	–	79	42	–	–	–
Romania	100	100	100	79	92	63	98	98	94	94	89	94	92	0	0	–	–	–	–	–	–
Russian Federation	97	99	91	72	77	59	96	97	97	97	98	97	31	0	0	–	–	–	–	–	–
Rwanda	76	87	72	62	59	63	99	99	99	99	98	99	99	98	99	90	54	28	49	68	81
Saint Kitts and Nevis	98	–	–	–	–	–	99	99	97	93	93	98	98	0	0	–	–	–	–	–	–
Saint Lucia	96	100	96	91	85	92	89	99	99	99	99	99	99	0	0	–	–	–	–	–	–
Saint Vincent and the Grenadines	95	–	–	–	–	–	96	99	98	97	99	98	98	0	0	–	–	–	–	–	–
Samoa	99	97	99	91	93	91	95	99	91	91	91	91	91	0	0	–	78	63	59	–	–
San Marino	–	–	–	–	–	–	–	82	80	80	57	80	79	0	0	–	–	–	–	–	–
Sao Tome and Principe	97	99	94	35	41	23	95	98	95	95	92	95	95	0	95	–	69	49	66	61	78
Saudi Arabia	97	–	–	100	100	100	98	99	98	98	98	98	98	94	98	–	–	–	–	–	–
Senegal	79	93	67	48	65	34	95	94	89	85	80	89	89	0	81	91	42	23	56	43	74
Serbia	99	99	99	96	98	94	98	97	93	93	86	92	94	0	0	–	90	36	–	–	–
Seychelles	96	–	–	98	98	98	98	99	99	99	99	99	99	0	0	–	–	–	–	–	–
Sierra Leone	63	85	48	13	23	7	90	88	83	83	78	83	83	53	83	85	72	85	72	49	64
Singapore	100	100	–	100	100	–	99	98	97	97	95	97	0	0	0	–	–	–	–	–	–
Slovakia	100	100	100	99	99	98	–	99	97	97	97	97	97	0	96	–	–	–	–	–	–
Slovenia	100	100	99	99	99	99	–	98	95	95	94	0	95	0	0	–	–	–	–	–	–
Solomon Islands	81	93	77	30	81	15	99	95	88	94	93	88	88	0	0	85	73 x	38 x	68 x	40 x	49 x
Somalia	–	–	–	–	–	–	37	52	42	47	46	42	42	0	0	64	13 x	13 x	–	11 x	12 x
South Africa	93	100	81	66	70	61	77	73	70	71	70	74	70	72	65	80	65 x	40 x	65 x	–	–
South Sudan	59	67	57	7	16	4	46	49	39	44	22	0	0	0	0	–	48	39	57	46	66
Spain	100	100	100	100	100	100	–	99	97	97	96	96	96	0	0	–	–	–	–	–	–
Sri Lanka	96	99	95	95	88	97	99	99	99	99	99	99	99	0	0	95	58 x	50 x	85 x	3 x	5 x
State of Palestine	58	51	81	92	93	90	99	99	99	99	99	99	99	0	97	–	77	32	–	–	–
Sudan	–	–	–	–	–	–	95	99	94	94	86	94	94	86	97	74	48	22	–	30 x	25
Suriname	95	98	88	79	88	61	–	91	85	85	85	85	85	0	0	93	76	42	–	43	61
Swaziland	74	94	69	57	63	56	99	99	98	98	98	98	98	0	67	88	60	57	–	2	10
Sweden	100	100	100	99	99	100	26	99	98	98	97	42	98	0	98	–	–	–	–	–	–
Switzerland	100	100	100	100	100	100	–	98	96	96	93	0	95	0	80	–	–	–	–	–	–
Syrian Arab Republic	90	92	87	96	96	95	81	65	43	52	54	71	43	0	0	92	77 x	50 x	–	–	–
Tajikistan	74	93	67	95	94	95	98	98	97	94	98	97	97	0	0	–	63	60	57	1 x	2 x
Thailand	98	98	98	93	90	96	99	99	99	99	99	99	0	0	0	95	83	58	–	–	–
The former Yugoslav Republic of Macedonia	99	100	99	91	97	83	99	98	95	96	93	97	94	0	0	–	93 x	62	–	–	–
Timor-Leste	72	95	61	41	69	27	79	81	77	76	74	77	77	0	0	81	71	71	73	41	41
Togo	63	91	44	12	25	3	97	91	87	85	82	87	87	35	34	81	49	19	58	43	65
Tonga	100	100	100	91	98	89	89	86	82	82	67	82	82	0	0	–	–	64	–	–	–
Trinidad and Tobago	95	95	95	92	92	92	–	93	92	94	96	92	92	0	95	–	74 x	–	–	–	–
Tunisia	98	100	93	92	97	80	95	99	98	98	98	98	98	0	0	96	60	65	–	–	–
Turkey	100	100	100	95	98	86	95	97	96	96	94	96	96	0	96	–	–	–	–	–	–
Turkmenistan	–	–	–	–	–	–	99	99	98	98	98	97	97	0	0	–	51 x	40 x	–	–	–
Tuvalu	98	98	97	–	86	–	99	99	90	90	96	90	90	0	0	–	–	44 x	79 x	–	–

TABLE 3. HEALTH

Countries and areas	Use of improved drinking water sources (%) 2015 total	urban	rural	Use of improved sanitation facilities (%) 2015 total	urban	rural	BCG	DTP1β	DTP3β	polio3	MCV1	HepB3	Hib3	rota	PCV3	Newborns protected against tetanus^λ	Pneumonia Care seeking for children with symptoms of pneumonia (%) 2010–2015*	Diarrhoea Treatment with oral rehydration salts (ORS) (%) 2010–2015*	Malaria Care seeking for children with fever (%) 2010–2015*	Children sleeping under ITNs (%) 2010–2015*	House-holds with at least one ITN (%) 2010–2015*
										Immunization coverage (%) 2014											
Uganda	79	96	76	19	29	17	93	89	78	82	82	78	78	0	50	85	79	44	82	74	90
Ukraine	96	96	98	96	97	93	95	90	76	74	79	46	83	0	0	–	92	59	–	–	–
United Arab Emirates	100	100	100	98	98	95	90	94	94	94	94	94	94	56	94	–	–	–	–	–	–
United Kingdom	100	100	100	99	99	100	–	98	95	95	93	0	95	0	93	–	–	–	–	–	–
United Republic of Tanzania	56	77	46	16	31	8	99	99	97	97	99	97	97	97	93	88	71	44	77	72	91
United States	99	99	98	100	100	100	–	98	94	93	91	90	93	69	92	–	–	–	–	–	–
Uruguay	100	100	94	96	97	93	99	99	95	95	96	95	95	0	95	–	91	–	–	–	–
Uzbekistan	–	98	–	100	100	100	99	99	99	99	99	99	99	52	0	–	68 x	28 x	–	–	–
Vanuatu	94	99	93	58	65	55	73	75	64	65	53	64	64	0	0	75	72	48	57	51	83
Venezuela (Bolivarian Republic of)	93	95	78	94	97	70	95	88	78	79	89	78	78	76	0	75	72 x	38 x	–	–	–
Viet Nam	98	99	97	78	94	70	96	95	95	96	97	95	95	0	0	91	81	51	–	9	10
Yemen	–	–	–	–	–	–	73	94	88	88	75	88	88	72	88	70	34	25	33	–	–
Zambia	65	86	51	44	56	36	95	96	86	78	85	86	86	73	77	85	70	64	75	41	68
Zimbabwe	77	97	67	37	49	31	99	98	91	92	92	91	91	48	91	75	59	43	47	27	42
SUMMARY																					
Sub-Saharan Africa	68	87	56	30	40	23	83	85	77	77	72	77	77	32	53	76	46	36	51	44	61
Eastern and Southern Africa	66	88	57	33	47	26	84	88	80	80	79	80	79	48	70	82	55	41	57	49	63
West and Central Africa	69	86	55	27	35	20	81	80	73	73	65	73	73	14	33	72	40	34	46	39	63
Middle East and North Africa	93	95	89	91	93	87	94	94	89	90	87	91	75	33	33	84	65	32	–	–	–
South Asia	92	95	91	45	65	35	91	89	83	82	81	73	37	0	10	85	71	52 ‡	50 ‡	–	–
East Asia and Pacific	94	97	90	76	86	64	96	97	93	94	94	93	23	0	0	87 **	73 **	46 **	66 **	–	–
Latin America and Caribbean	95	97	84	83	88	64	95	94	88	88	92	88	88	75	79	88	–	45	–	–	–
CEE/CIS	97	99	93	86	89	81	96	97	95	94	95	92	74	7	28	–	–	–	–	–	–
Least developed countries	69	86	62	38	47	33	87	89	81	81	79	81	81	31	53	83	49	43	51	50	64
World	**91**	**96**	**84**	**68**	**82**	**51**	**91**	**91**	**86**	**86**	**85**	**82**	**56**	**19**	**31**	**83 ****	**63 ****	**41 ‡****	**54 ‡****	**–**	**–**

For a complete list of countries and areas in the regions, subregions and country categories, see page 112 or visit <data.unicef.org/regionalclassifications>.
It is not advisable to compare data from consecutive editions of *The State of the World's Children*.

DEFINITIONS OF THE INDICATORS

Use of improved drinking water sources – Percentage of the population using any of the following as their main drinking water source: drinking water supply piped into dwelling, plot, yard or neighbor's yard; public tap or standpipe; tube well or borehole; protected dug well; protected spring; rainwater; bottled water plus one of the previous sources as their secondary source.

Use of improved sanitation facilities – Percentage of the population using any of the following sanitation facilities, not shared with other households: flush or pour-flush latrine connected to a piped sewerage system, septic tank or pit latrine; ventilated improved pit latrine; pit latrine with a slab; composting toilet.

EPI – Expanded Programme on Immunization: The first diseases targeted by the EPI were diphtheria, pertussis (whooping cough) and tetanus (DPT); measles; poliomyelitis; and tuberculosis (TB). Additional vaccines have been added to the original six recommended in 1974 and include vaccines to protect against hepatitis B (HepB), and Haemophilus influenzae type b (Hib). Pneumococcal conjugate vaccine (PCV) and rotavirus vaccine, also recommended by the WHO, are increasingly being added to national schedules.

BCG – Percentage of live births who received bacille Calmette-Guérin (vaccine against tuberculosis).

DTP1 – Percentage of surviving infants who received their first dose of diphtheria, pertussis and tetanus vaccine.

DTP3 – Percentage of surviving infants who received three doses of diphtheria, pertussis and tetanus vaccine.

Polio3 – Percentage of surviving infants who received three doses of the polio vaccine.

MCV1 – Percentage of surviving infants who received the first dose of the measles-containing vaccine.

HepB3 – Percentage of surviving infants who received three doses of hepatitis B vaccine.

Hib3 – Percentage of surviving infants who received three doses of Haemophilus influenzae type b vaccine.

rota – Percentage of surviving infants who received the last dose of rotavirus vaccine as recommended.

PCV3 – Percentage of surviving infants who received three doses of pneumococcal conjugate vaccine.

Newborns protected against tetanus – Percentage of newborns protected at birth against tetanus.

Care seeking for children with symptoms of pneumonia – Percentage of children under age 5 with symptoms of pneumonia (cough and fast or difficult breathing due to a problem in the chest) in the two weeks preceding the survey for whom advice or treatment was sought from a health facility or provider.

Diarrhoea treatment with oral rehydration salts (ORS) – Percentage of children under age 5 who had diarrhoea in the two weeks preceding the survey and who received oral rehydration salts (ORS packets or pre-packaged ORS fluids).

Care seeking for children with fever – Percentage of children under age 5 with fever for whom advice or treatment was sought from a health facility or provider. Excludes drug vendor, stores, shops and traditional healer. In some countries, particularly non-malaria endemic countries, pharmacies have also been excluded from the calculation.

Children sleeping under ITNs – Percentage of children under age 5 who slept under an insecticide-treated mosquito net the night prior to the survey.

Households with at least one ITN – Percentage of households with at least one insecticide-treated mosquito net.

MAIN DATA SOURCES

Use of improved drinking water sources and improved sanitation facilities – WHO/UNICEF Joint Monitoring Programme for Water Supply and Sanitation (JMP).

Immunization – UNICEF and WHO.

Care seeking for children with symptoms of pneumonia – Demographic and Health Surveys (DHS), Multiple Indicator Cluster Surveys (MICS) and other national household surveys.

Diarrhoea treatment with oral rehydration salts (ORS) – DHS, MICS and other national household surveys.

Malaria treatment – DHS, MICS, Malaria Indicator Surveys (MIS) and other national household surveys.

NOTES

– Data not available.

x Data refer to years or periods other than those specified in the column heading. Such data are not included in the calculation of regional and global averages. Estimates from data years prior to 2000 are not displayed.

β Coverage for DPT1 should be at least as high as DPT3. Discrepancies where DPT1 coverage is less than DPT3 reflect deficiencies in the data collection and reporting process. UNICEF and WHO are working with national and territorial systems to eliminate these discrepancies.

λ WHO and UNICEF have employed a model to calculate the percentage of births that can be considered as protected against tetanus because pregnant women were given two doses or more of tetanus toxoid (TT) vaccine. The model aims to improve the accuracy of this indicator by capturing or including other potential scenarios where women might be protected (e.g., women who receive doses of TT in supplemental immunization activities). A fuller explanation of the methodology can be found at <data.unicef.org>.

* Data refer to the most recent year available during the period specified in the column heading.

** Excludes China.

‡ Excludes India.

TABLE 4. HIV/AIDS

Countries and areas	Adult HIV prevalence (%) 2014 estimate	People of all ages living with HIV (thousands) 2014 estimate	low	high	Women living with HIV (thousands) 2014 estimate	Children living with HIV (thousands) 2014 estimate	HIV prevalence among young people (%) 2014 total	male	female	Comprehensive knowledge of HIV (%) 2010–2014* male	female	Condom use among young people with multiple partners (%) 2010–2014* male	female	Young people who were tested for HIV in the last 12 months and received results (%) 2010–2014* male	female	Children orphaned by AIDS (thousands) 2014 estimate	Children orphaned due to all causes (thousands) 2014 estimate	Orphan school attendance ratio (%) 2010–2014*
Afghanistan	<0.1	7	4	13	3	<0.5	<0.1	<0.1	<0.1	–	2	–	–	–	–	–	–	–
Albania	–	–	–	–	–	–	–	–	–	22 x	36 x	55 x	–	1 x	0 x	–	–	–
Algeria	<0.1	11	3	26	5	–	<0.1	<0.1	<0.1	–	9	–	–	–	2	–	–	–
Andorra	–	–	–	–	–	–	–	–	–	–	–	–	–	–	–	–	–	–
Angola	2.4	300	220	430	160	32	0.8	0.6	1.1	32 x	25 x	–	–	–	–	120	1,300	85 x
Antigua and Barbuda	–	–	–	–	–	–	–	–	–	53	46	–	–	–	–	–	–	–
Argentina	0.5	130	78	170	38	–	0.2	0.2	0.1	–	40	–	–	–	–	–	–	–
Armenia	0.2	4	3	6	<1	–	0.1	0.2	<0.1	9	16	86	–	0	3	–	–	–
Australia	–	–	–	–	–	–	–	–	–	–	–	–	–	–	–	–	–	–
Austria	–	–	–	–	–	–	–	–	–	–	–	–	–	–	–	–	–	–
Azerbaijan	0.1	8	6	12	3	<0.2	<0.1	0.1	<0.1	5 x	5 x	29 x	–	–	–	–	–	–
Bahamas	–	–	–	–	–	–	–	–	–	–	–	–	–	–	–	–	–	–
Bahrain	–	–	–	–	–	–	–	–	–	–	–	–	–	–	–	–	–	–
Bangladesh	<0.1	9	8	10	3	<0.5	<0.1	<0.1	<0.1	–	9	–	–	–	–	–	–	88
Barbados	–	–	–	–	–	–	–	–	–	–	68	–	–	–	24	–	–	–
Belarus	0.5	29	24	36	10	–	0.2	0.1	0.2	51	56	73	64 p	19	24	–	–	–
Belgium	–	–	–	–	–	–	–	–	–	–	–	–	–	–	–	–	–	–
Belize	1.2	3	2	8	1	<0.2	0.4	0.3	0.4	–	43	–	26 x,p	–	25	–	–	92
Benin	1.1	78	68	90	41	8	0.3	0.2	0.4	31	22	44	35	5	14	28	440	78
Bhutan	–	–	–	–	–	–	–	–	–	–	21	–	–	–	8	–	–	–
Bolivia (Plurinational State of)	0.3	18	13	29	5	<1	0.2	0.2	0.1	28 x	22 x	41 x	–	2 x	–	–	–	–
Bosnia and Herzegovina	–	–	–	–	–	–	–	–	–	47	48	67	–	1	0	–	–	–
Botswana	25.2	390	370	410	210	16	7.2	5.7	8.9	–	–	–	–	–	–	67	100	–
Brazil	–	–	–	–	–	–	–	–	–	–	–	–	–	–	–	–	–	–
Brunei Darussalam	–	–	–	–	–	–	–	–	–	–	–	–	–	–	–	–	–	–
Bulgaria	–	–	–	–	–	–	–	–	–	–	–	–	–	–	–	–	–	–
Burkina Faso	0.9	110	92	130	57	13	0.5	0.4	0.5	36	31	75	65	7	12	75	830	101
Burundi	1.1	85	72	110	42	14	0.4	0.3	0.4	47	45	–	–	11	18	77	580	82
Cabo Verde	1.1	3	3	4	<1	–	0.5	0.8	0.3	–	–	–	–	–	–	–	–	–
Cambodia	0.6	75	47	140	36	6	0.2	0.1	0.2	46	38	–	–	7	12	–	–	88
Cameroon	4.8	660	610	790	350	58	1.7	1.2	2.1	41	32	67	47	13	21	310	1,200	86
Canada	–	–	–	–	–	–	–	–	–	–	–	–	–	–	–	–	–	–
Central African Republic	4.3	140	120	150	70	15	1.7	1.4	2.0	25	17	47	34	13	19	91	300	88
Chad	2.5	210	170	270	110	29	0.8	0.6	1.0	–	10	–	57 p	–	4	130	970	117
Chile	0.3	39	32	47	4	–	0.1	0.2	<0.1	–	–	–	–	–	–	–	–	–
China	–	–	–	–	–	–	–	–	–	–	–	–	–	–	–	–	–	–
Colombia	0.4	120	96	160	38	2	0.2	0.2	0.1	–	24	–	39	–	11	–	–	–
Comoros	–	–	–	–	–	–	–	–	–	24	19	52	–	4	3	–	–	108
Congo	2.8	81	72	88	43	11	1.2	0.9	1.4	28	14	51	45	6	12	46	210	100
Cook Islands	–	–	–	–	–	–	–	–	–	–	–	–	–	–	–	–	–	–
Costa Rica	0.3	9	6	12	2	<0.2	0.1	0.1	<0.1	–	33	–	55	–	14	–	–	–
Côte d'Ivoire	3.5	460	420	510	250	42	1.1	0.9	1.4	25	16	57	34	8	14	230	1,200	66
Croatia	–	–	–	–	–	–	–	–	–	–	–	–	–	–	–	–	–	–
Cuba	0.3	17	15	21	4	–	0.2	0.2	<0.1	59	61	–	70	25	27	–	–	–
Cyprus	–	–	–	–	–	–	–	–	–	–	–	–	–	–	–	–	–	–
Czech Republic	–	–	–	–	–	–	–	–	–	–	–	–	–	–	–	–	–	–
Democratic People's Republic of Korea	–	–	–	–	–	–	–	–	–	–	8 x	–	–	–	–	–	–	–
Democratic Republic of the Congo	1.0	450	400	490	230	59	0.4	0.3	0.5	25	19	22	11	4	7	290	4,000	80
Denmark	0.2	6	4	8	2	–	<0.1	<0.1	<0.1	–	–	–	–	–	–	–	–	–
Djibouti	1.6	10	8	14	5	1	0.6	0.5	0.8	–	18 x	–	–	–	–	6	32	–
Dominica	–	–	–	–	–	–	–	–	–	48	56	–	–	–	–	–	–	–
Dominican Republic	1.0	69	52	100	31	3	0.4	0.4	0.4	41	45	57	40	10	16	–	–	97
Ecuador	0.3	33	25	46	8	–	0.1	0.2	<0.1	–	–	–	–	–	–	–	–	–
Egypt	<0.1	9	6	14	2	<0.5	<0.1	<0.1	<0.1	–	4 y	–	–	–	–	–	–	–
El Salvador	0.5	21	13	29	7	<1	0.2	0.2	0.2	–	31	–	–	–	–	–	–	–
Equatorial Guinea	6.2	32	29	34	16	3	1.9	1.3	2.5	18	19	36	19	16	35	6	43	–
Eritrea	0.7	16	12	24	9	2	0.3	0.2	0.3	34	25	–	–	–	–	11	140	–
Estonia	–	–	–	–	–	–	–	–	–	–	–	–	–	–	–	–	–	–
Ethiopia	1.2	730	600	970	390	110	0.5	0.5	0.6	34	24	47	–	20	21	450	3,500	90
Fiji	0.1	<1	<0.5	1	<0.5	–	<0.1	<0.1	<0.1	–	–	–	–	–	–	–	–	–
Finland	–	–	–	–	–	–	–	–	–	–	–	–	–	–	–	–	–	–
France	–	–	–	–	–	–	–	–	–	–	–	–	–	–	–	–	–	–

TABLE 4. HIV/AIDS

Countries and areas	Adult HIV prevalence (%) 2014 estimate	People of all ages living with HIV (thousands) 2014 estimate	low	high	Mother-to-child transmission Women living with HIV (thousands) 2014 estimate	Paediatric infections Children living with HIV (thousands) 2014 estimate	HIV prevalence among young people (%) 2014 total	male	female	Comprehensive knowledge of HIV (%) 2010–2014* male	female	Condom use among young people with multiple partners (%) 2010–2014* male	female	HIV testing Young people who were tested for HIV in the last 12 months and received results (%) 2010–2014* male	female	Children orphaned by AIDS (thousands) 2014 estimate	Children orphaned due to all causes (thousands) 2014 estimate	Orphan school attendance ratio (%) 2010–2014*
Gabon	3.9	48	41	55	29	4	0.9	0.6	1.3	36	30	77	56	12	30	18	68	101
Gambia	1.8	20	16	25	11	2	0.5	0.4	0.7	32	26	51 p	–	4	10	10	87	90
Georgia	0.3	7	5	8	1	–	0.2	0.3	<0.1	–	–	–	–	–	5	–	–	–
Germany	–	–	–	–	–	–	–	–	–	–	–	–	–	–	–	–	–	–
Ghana	1.5	250	190	330	140	21	0.5	0.4	0.6	27	20	34	15	3	10	120	950	94
Greece	–	–	–	–	–	–	–	–	–	–	–	–	–	–	–	–	–	–
Grenada	–	–	–	–	–	–	–	–	–	60	65	–	–	–	–	–	–	–
Guatemala	0.5	49	34	69	18	3	0.2	0.2	0.2	24 x	22 x	74 x	27 x,p	–	–	–	–	–
Guinea	1.6	120	100	140	65	–	0.6	0.4	0.7	34	23	54	37	3	5	–	–	71
Guinea-Bissau	3.7	42	38	47	22	5	1.2	0.8	1.5	–	15	–	50	–	7	13	120	108
Guyana	1.8	10	7	15	5	<0.5	0.9	0.7	1.2	47 x	54 x	76 x	–	18 x	29 x	–	–	–
Haiti	1.9	140	130	160	79	8	0.7	0.5	0.8	28	35	62	52	9	17	64	300	96
Holy See	–	–	–	–	–	–	–	–	–	–	–	–	–	–	–	–	–	–
Honduras	0.4	23	19	27	9	2	0.2	0.2	0.2	35	33	59	38	7	13	–	–	91
Hungary	–	–	–	–	–	–	–	–	–	–	–	–	–	–	–	–	–	–
Iceland	–	–	–	–	–	–	–	–	–	–	–	–	–	–	–	–	–	–
India	0.3	2,100	1,600	2,800	760	130	–	–	–	36 x	20 x	32 x	17 x,p	1 x	1 x	530	29,600	72 x
Indonesia	0.5	660	600	720	230	19	0.4	0.4	0.4	10 y	11 y	–	–	–	–	–	–	–
Iran (Islamic Republic of)	0.1	74	51	110	9	<1	<0.1	<0.1	<0.1	–	20 y	–	–	–	–	–	–	–
Iraq	–	–	–	–	–	–	–	–	–	–	4	–	–	–	0	–	–	94
Ireland	0.3	8	6	10	2	–	0.1	0.1	<0.1	–	–	–	–	–	–	–	–	–
Israel	–	–	–	–	–	–	–	–	–	–	–	–	–	–	–	–	–	–
Italy	–	–	–	–	–	–	–	–	–	–	–	–	–	–	–	–	–	–
Jamaica	1.6	29	25	38	11	<1	0.7	0.8	0.6	36 y	43 y	76	49	49	69	–	–	–
Japan	–	–	–	–	–	–	–	–	–	–	–	–	–	–	–	–	–	–
Jordan	–	–	–	–	–	–	–	–	–	–	9	–	–	–	–	–	–	80
Kazakhstan	0.2	20	18	25	7	–	<0.1	<0.1	<0.1	34	36	76	74	15	21	–	–	–
Kenya	5.3	1,400	1,200	1,600	700	160	2.8	2.2	3.5	64	57	69	38	39	50	650	2,000	99
Kiribati	–	–	–	–	–	–	–	–	–	49 x	44 x	30 x	2 x,p	–	–	–	–	82 x
Kuwait	–	–	–	–	–	–	–	–	–	–	–	–	–	–	–	–	–	–
Kyrgyzstan	0.3	9	7	12	4	<0.5	<0.1	<0.1	<0.1	24	20	76	–	1	12	–	–	–
Lao People's Democratic Republic	0.3	11	10	12	5	<1	0.1	0.1	0.2	28	24	–	–	2	2	–	–	80
Latvia	–	–	–	–	–	–	–	–	–	–	–	–	–	–	–	–	–	–
Lebanon	<0.1	2	<0.2	4	<0.2	–	<0.1	<0.1	<0.1	–	–	–	–	–	–	–	–	–
Lesotho	23.4	310	290	340	170	19	8.0	5.9	10.2	29 x	39 x	60 x	45 x	17 x	40 x	74	120	98 x
Liberia	1.2	33	29	38	17	4	0.3	0.3	0.4	29	36	32	26	6	18	25	190	75
Libya	–	–	–	–	–	–	–	–	–	–	–	–	–	–	–	–	–	–
Liechtenstein	–	–	–	–	–	–	–	–	–	–	–	–	–	–	–	–	–	–
Lithuania	–	–	–	–	–	–	–	–	–	–	–	–	–	–	–	–	–	–
Luxembourg	–	–	–	–	–	–	–	–	–	–	–	–	–	–	–	–	–	–
Madagascar	0.3	39	34	45	16	5	0.1	0.2	0.1	26	23	7	9	2	3	–	–	74 x
Malawi	10.0	1,100	990	1,100	560	130	3.2	2.4	4.1	51	44	53	38	34	42	530	990	96
Malaysia	0.5	100	91	110	20	<1	<0.1	0.1	<0.1	–	–	–	–	–	–	–	–	–
Maldives	–	–	–	–	–	–	–	–	–	–	35 x,y	–	–	–	–	–	–	–
Mali	1.4	130	110	170	68	18	0.6	0.5	0.7	33	24	38	8 p	4	6	59	810	81
Malta	–	–	–	–	–	–	–	–	–	–	–	–	–	–	–	–	–	–
Marshall Islands	–	–	–	–	–	–	–	–	–	39 x	27 x	23 x,p	9 x,p	–	–	–	–	–
Mauritania	0.7	16	13	20	8	2	0.3	0.2	0.4	–	6	–	–	–	–	–	–	100 p
Mauritius	0.9	8	7	9	2	–	0.2	0.2	0.2	–	–	–	–	–	–	–	–	–
Mexico	0.2	190	140	270	40	3	<0.1	0.1	<0.1	–	–	–	–	–	–	–	–	–
Micronesia (Federated States of)	–	–	–	–	–	–	–	–	–	–	–	–	–	–	–	–	–	–
Monaco	–	–	–	–	–	–	–	–	–	–	–	–	–	–	–	–	–	–
Mongolia	–	–	–	–	–	–	–	–	–	21	23	69	–	13	17	–	–	102
Montenegro	–	–	–	–	–	–	–	–	–	37	48	65	–	1	0	–	–	–
Morocco	0.1	29	20	37	9	<1	<0.1	<0.1	<0.1	–	–	–	–	–	–	–	–	–
Mozambique	10.6	1,500	1,300	2,100	830	160	4.5	2.4	6.6	52	30	41	38	11	26	610	1,800	91
Myanmar	0.7	210	190	230	70	11	0.3	0.4	0.3	–	32	–	–	–	–	–	–	–
Namibia	16.0	260	240	280	130	16	4.0	2.9	5.0	51	62	79	68	26	43	53	100	102
Nauru	–	–	–	–	–	–	–	–	–	10 x	13 x	17 x,p	8 x,p	4 x	4 x	–	–	–
Nepal	0.2	39	35	43	13	2	<0.1	<0.1	<0.1	–	36	45	–	–	3	–	–	–
Netherlands	–	–	–	–	–	–	–	–	–	–	–	–	–	–	–	–	–	–
New Zealand	–	–	–	–	–	–	–	–	–	–	–	–	–	–	–	–	–	–

TABLE 4. HIV/AIDS

Countries and areas	Adult HIV prevalence (%) 2014 estimate	People of all ages living with HIV (thousands) 2014 estimate	low	high	Mother-to-child transmission Women living with HIV (thousands) 2014 estimate	Paediatric infections Children living with HIV (thousands) 2014 estimate	HIV prevalence among young people (%) 2014 total	male	female	Comprehensive knowledge of HIV (%) 2010–2014* male	female	Condom use among young people with multiple partners (%) 2010–2014* male	female	HIV testing Young people who were tested for HIV in the last 12 months and received results (%) 2010–2014* male	female	Orphans Children orphaned by AIDS (thousands) 2014 estimate	Children orphaned due to all causes (thousands) 2014 estimate	Orphan school attendance ratio (%) 2010–2014*
Nicaragua	0.3	10	8	15	3	<0.5	0.1	0.2	<0.1	–	–	–	–	–	–	–	–	–
Niger	0.5	52	46	59	25	–	0.1	<0.1	0.2	25	14	42 x,p	–	2	7	–	–	109
Nigeria	3.2	3,400	3,100	3,700	1,700	380	1.0	0.7	1.3	34	24	51	41	5	8	1,600	9,900	123
Niue	–	–	–	–	–	–	–	–	–	–	–	–	–	–	–	–	–	–
Norway	0.2	6	4	9	2	–	<0.1	<0.1	<0.1	–	–	–	–	–	–	–	–	–
Oman	0.2	2	2	3	<1	–	<0.1	<0.1	<0.1	–	–	–	–	–	–	–	–	101
Pakistan	<0.1	94	58	180	26	2	<0.1	<0.1	<0.1	5 y	4 y	–	–	–	–	–	–	79 p
Palau	–	–	–	–	–	–	–	–	–	–	–	–	–	–	–	–	–	–
Panama	0.6	17	13	24	4	<0.5	0.2	0.2	0.1	–	37	–	–	–	–	–	–	–
Papua New Guinea	0.7	37	34	41	19	4	0.2	0.2	0.2	–	–	–	–	–	–	13	300	–
Paraguay	0.4	17	12	32	6	<0.5	0.3	0.3	0.2	–	–	–	51 x	–	–	–	–	–
Peru	0.4	72	61	100	21	2	0.1	0.1	0.1	–	22 x	–	34	–	–	–	–	100
Philippines	<0.1	36	21	100	4	<0.5	<0.1	<0.1	<0.1	–	21 x	–	–	–	0	–	–	–
Poland	<0.1	–	–	–	–	–	<0.1	<0.1	<0.1	–	–	–	–	–	–	–	–	–
Portugal	–	–	–	–	–	–	–	–	–	–	–	–	–	–	–	–	–	–
Qatar	–	–	–	–	–	–	–	–	–	25	16	–	–	–	–	–	–	–
Republic of Korea	–	–	–	–	–	–	–	–	–	–	–	–	–	–	–	–	–	–
Republic of Moldova	0.6	18	15	21	8	<0.2	0.2	0.1	0.3	28	36	68	49	9	17	–	–	–
Romania	–	–	–	–	–	–	–	–	–	–	–	–	–	–	–	–	–	–
Russian Federation	–	–	–	–	–	–	–	–	–	–	–	–	–	–	–	–	–	–
Rwanda	2.8	210	190	230	120	22	1.2	1.0	1.3	47	53	58 p	29 p	32	37	85	500	91
Saint Kitts and Nevis	–	–	–	–	–	–	–	–	–	50	53	–	–	–	–	–	–	–
Saint Lucia	–	–	–	–	–	–	–	–	–	–	62	–	42 p	–	22	–	–	–
Saint Vincent and the Grenadines	–	–	–	–	–	–	–	–	–	–	–	–	–	–	–	–	–	–
Samoa	–	–	–	–	–	–	–	–	–	6 x	3 x	–	–	1 x	0 x	–	–	–
San Marino	–	–	–	–	–	–	–	–	–	–	–	–	–	–	–	–	–	–
Sao Tome and Principe	0.8	1	<1	2	<0.5	–	0.2	0.2	0.2	43	42	59 x	–	14 x	29 x	–	–	–
Saudi Arabia	–	–	–	–	–	–	–	–	–	–	–	–	–	–	–	–	–	–
Senegal	0.5	44	37	53	17	4	0.1	0.1	<0.1	31	29	49	–	7	13	–	–	97
Serbia	–	–	–	–	–	–	–	–	–	48	54	63	65	2	2	–	–	–
Seychelles	–	–	–	–	–	–	–	–	–	–	–	–	–	–	–	–	–	–
Sierra Leone	1.4	54	47	61	29	4	0.3	0.2	0.4	30	29	21	6	5	14	19	310	81
Singapore	–	–	–	–	–	–	–	–	–	–	–	–	–	–	–	–	–	–
Slovakia	<0.1	–	–	–	–	–	<0.1	<0.1	<0.1	–	–	–	–	–	–	–	–	–
Slovenia	<0.1	<1	<1	1	<0.1	–	<0.1	<0.1	<0.1	–	–	–	–	–	–	–	–	–
Solomon Islands	–	–	–	–	–	–	–	–	–	35 x	29 x	39 x	18 x	–	–	–	–	–
Somalia	0.5	35	27	45	15	5	0.2	0.2	0.2	–	4 x	–	–	–	–	27	630	78 x
South Africa	18.9	6,800	6,500	7,500	3,900	340	6.1	4.0	8.1	23	25	–	–	–	–	2,300	2,800	98 x
South Sudan	2.7	190	130	270	100	19	1.0	0.7	1.3	–	10	–	7	–	–	91	570	78
Spain	–	–	–	–	–	–	–	–	–	–	–	–	–	–	–	–	–	–
Sri Lanka	<0.1	3	2	6	1	<0.1	<0.1	<0.1	<0.1	–	–	–	–	–	–	–	–	–
State of Palestine	–	–	–	–	–	–	–	–	–	–	6	–	–	–	–	–	–	–
Sudan	0.2	53	41	69	23	4	0.1	0.1	0.2	–	9	–	–	–	0	–	–	82
Suriname	1.0	4	3	4	2	–	0.4	0.3	0.5	–	42	–	39	–	21	–	–	–
Swaziland	27.7	210	210	220	120	19	11.3	7.2	15.5	51	49	85	69	23	37	56	87	100
Sweden	0.2	–	–	–	–	–	<0.1	<0.1	<0.1	–	–	–	–	–	–	–	–	–
Switzerland	–	–	–	–	–	–	–	–	–	–	–	–	–	–	–	–	–	–
Syrian Arab Republic	<0.1	<1	<0.1	2	<0.2	–	<0.1	<0.1	<0.1	–	7 x	–	–	–	–	–	–	–
Tajikistan	0.4	16	12	21	6	1	0.1	0.1	0.1	–	9	–	–	–	5	–	–	81
Thailand	1.1	450	400	490	190	7	0.3	0.3	0.2	–	56	–	–	–	10	–	–	94 p
The former Yugoslav Republic of Macedonia	–	–	–	–	–	–	–	–	–	–	27 x	–	–	–	–	–	–	–
Timor-Leste	–	–	–	–	–	–	–	–	–	20	12	–	–	–	–	–	–	75
Togo	2.4	110	95	140	60	12	0.7	0.5	0.8	32	23	63	59 p	9	16	54	330	97
Tonga	–	–	–	–	–	–	–	–	–	14	12	–	–	1	2	–	–	–
Trinidad and Tobago	–	–	–	–	–	–	–	–	–	–	54 x	–	67 x	–	–	–	–	–
Tunisia	<0.1	3	2	4	<1	–	<0.1	<0.1	<0.1	–	20	–	–	–	0	–	–	–
Turkey	–	–	–	–	–	–	–	–	–	–	–	–	–	–	–	–	–	–
Turkmenistan	–	–	–	–	–	–	–	–	–	–	5 x	–	–	–	–	–	–	–
Tuvalu	–	–	–	–	–	–	–	–	–	61 x	39 x	–	–	8 x	4 x	–	–	–
Uganda	7.3	1,500	1,400	1,800	770	150	3.0	2.3	3.7	39	39	31	24	24	40	650	1,900	87
Ukraine	–	–	–	–	–	–	–	–	–	46	50	84	67	12	13	–	–	–
United Arab Emirates	–	–	–	–	–	–	–	–	–	–	–	–	–	–	–	–	–	–

TABLE 4. HIV/AIDS

Countries and areas	Adult HIV prevalence (%) 2014 estimate	People of all ages living with HIV (thousands) 2014 estimate	low	high	Mother-to-child transmission — Women living with HIV (thousands) 2014 estimate	Paediatric infections — Children living with HIV (thousands) 2014 estimate	HIV prevalence among young people (%) 2014 total	male	female	Comprehensive knowledge of HIV (%) 2010–2014* male	female	Condom use among young people with multiple partners (%) 2010–2014* male	female	Young people who were tested for HIV in the last 12 months and received results (%) 2010–2014* male	female	Children orphaned by AIDS (thousands) 2014 estimate	Children orphaned due to all causes (thousands) 2014 estimate	Orphan school attendance ratio (%) 2010–2014*
United Kingdom	–	–	–	–	–	–	–	–	–	–	–	–	–	–	–	–	–	–
United Republic of Tanzania	5.3	1,500	1,300	1,900	800	140	1.8	1.4	2.1	47	40	41	34	21	29	810	2,600	95
United States	–	–	–	–	–	–	–	–	–	–	–	–	–	–	–	–	–	–
Uruguay	0.7	14	12	17	2	–	0.3	0.4	0.1	–	35	–	–	–	–	–	–	–
Uzbekistan	0.2	32	26	40	13	–	<0.1	<0.1	<0.1	–	31 x	–	–	–	–	–	–	–
Vanuatu	–	–	–	–	–	–	–	–	–	–	15 x	–	–	–	–	–	–	–
Venezuela (Bolivarian Republic of)	0.6	110	43	180	36	3	0.2	0.2	0.2	–	–	–	–	–	–	–	–	–
Viet Nam	0.5	250	220	280	77	5	0.3	0.3	0.2	–	49	–	–	–	9	–	–	–
Yemen	<0.1	7	5	11	2	<0.5	<0.1	<0.1	<0.1	–	2 x,y	–	–	–	–	–	–	–
Zambia	12.4	1,200	1,100	1,200	540	100	3.7	3.3	4.2	47	42	40	34	29	43	380	950	86
Zimbabwe	16.7	1,600	1,500	1,600	830	150	5.9	4.8	7.0	52	56	65	43	32	46	570	810	94
SUMMARY																		
Sub-Saharan Africa	4.7	25,800	24,000	28,700	13,800	2,300	1.6	1.2	2.0	36	28	46	33	13	18	11,000	46,600	96
Eastern and Southern Africa	7.3	19,200	18,100	21,900	10,300	1,600	2.5	1.8	3.2	41	35	45	31	23	30	7,600	21,700	91
West and Central Africa	2.3	6,600	5,900	7,500	3,400	730	0.8	0.6	0.9	31	22	46	33	6	10	3,400	24,700	101
Middle East and North Africa	0.1	220	130	300	66	11	<0.1	<0.1	<0.1	–	9	–	–	–	–	71	6,500	–
South Asia	0.2	2,200	950	3,700	800	140	<0.1	<0.1	<0.1	–	8 ‡	–	–	–	–	580	37,800	83 ‡
East Asia and Pacific	0.2	2,700	2,400	3,000	900	62	0.1	0.1	0.1	–	27 **	–	–	–	–	770	23,000	–
Latin America and Caribbean	0.5	2,000	1,700	2,300	670	46	0.2	0.2	0.2	–	–	–	–	–	–	550	10,200	–
CEE/CIS	0.6	1,500	1,300	1,800	610	17	0.2	0.1	0.2	–	–	–	–	–	–	250	7,700	–
Least developed countries	1.9	10,900	9,900	13,100	5,600	1,100	0.8	0.6	1.0	36	23	40	–	14	17	5,200	35,500	89
World	**0.8**	**36,900**	**34,300**	**41,400**	**17,400**	**2,600**	**0.3**	**0.3**	**0.4**	–	**23 ‡****	–	–	–	–	**13,300**	**140,000**	–

For a complete list of countries and areas in the regions, subregions and country categories, see page 112 or visit <data.unicef.org/regionalclassifications>.
It is not advisable to compare data from consecutive editions of *The State of the World's Children*.

DEFINITIONS OF THE INDICATORS

Adult HIV prevalence – Estimated percentage of adults (aged 15–49) living with HIV as of 2014.

People of all ages living with HIV – Estimated number of people (all ages) living with HIV as of 2014.

Women living with HIV – Estimated number of women (aged 15+) living with HIV as of 2014.

Children living with HIV – Estimated number of children (aged 0–14) living with HIV as of 2014.

HIV prevalence among young people – Estimated percentage of young men and women (aged 15–24) living with HIV as of 2014.

Comprehensive knowledge of HIV – Percentage of young men and women (aged 15–24) with comprehensive, correct knowledge of HIV. Comprehensive, correct knowledge about HIV and AIDS is defined as correctly identifying the two major ways of preventing the sexual transmission of HIV (using condoms and limiting sex to one faithful, uninfected partner), rejecting the two most common local misconceptions about HIV transmission and knowing that a healthy-looking person can transmit HIV.

Condom use among young people with multiple partners– Among young men and women (aged 15–24) who reported having had more than one sexual partner in the last 12 months, the percentage who reported the use of a condom the last time they had sex with any partner.

Tested for HIV in the last 12 months and received results – Percentage of young men and women (aged 15–24) who were tested for HIV in the last 12 months and received the result of the most recent test.

Children orphaned by AIDS – Estimated number of children (aged 0–17) who have lost one or both parents to AIDS as of 2014.

Children orphaned due to all causes – Estimated number of children (aged 0–17) who have lost one or both parents due to any cause as of 2014.

Orphan school attendance ratio – Percentage of children (aged 10–14) who have lost both biological parents and who are currently attending school as a percentage of the non-orphaned children of the same age who live with at least one parent who are attending school.

MAIN DATA SOURCES

Estimated adult HIV prevalence – UNAIDS 2014 HIV and AIDS estimates, based on 2015 Spectrum modelling, July 2015.

Estimated number of people living with HIV – UNAIDS 2014 HIV and AIDS estimates, based on 2015 Spectrum modelling, July 2015.

Estimated number of women living with HIV – UNAIDS 2014 HIV and AIDS estimates, based on 2015 Spectrum modelling, July 2015.

Estimated number of children living with HIV – UNAIDS 2014 HIV and AIDS estimates, based on 2015 Spectrum modelling, July 2015.

HIV prevalence among young people – UNAIDS 2014 HIV and AIDS estimates, based on 2015 Spectrum modelling, July 2015.

Comprehensive knowledge of HIV – AIDS Indicator Surveys (AIS), Demographic and Health Surveys (DHS), Multiple Indicator Cluster Surveys (MICS) and other national household surveys; DHS STATcompiler, <www.statcompiler.com>.

Condom use among young people with multiple partners – AIS, DHS, MICS and other national household surveys; DHS STATcompiler, <www.statcompiler.com>.

Tested for HIV in the last 12 months and received results – AIS, DHS, MICS and other national household surveys; DHS STATcompiler, <www.statcompiler.com>.

Children orphaned by AIDS – UNAIDS 2014 HIV and AIDS estimates, based on 2015 Spectrum modelling, July 2015.

Children orphaned by all causes – UNAIDS 2014 HIV and AIDS estimates, based on 2015 Spectrum modelling, July 2015.

Orphan school attendance ratio – AIS, DHS, MICS and other national household surveys; DHS STATcompiler, www.statcompiler.com.

NOTES

– Data not available.

x Data refer to years or periods other than those specified in the column heading. Such data are not included in the calculation of regional and global averages. Estimates from years prior to 2006 are not displayed.

y Data differ from the standard definition or refer to only part of a country. If they fall within the noted reference period, such data are included in the calculation of regional and global averages.

p Based on small denominators (typically 25–49 unweighted cases). No data based on fewer than 25 unweighted cases are displayed.

* Data refer to the most recent year available during the period specified in the column heading.

** Excludes China.

‡ Excludes India.

TABLE 5. EDUCATION

Countries and areas	Youth (15–24 years) literacy rate (%) 2009–2014* male	female	Mobile phones / Internet users per 100 population 2014 mobile phones	internet users	Pre-primary school participation — Gross enrolment ratio (%) 2010–2014* male	female	Primary — Gross enrolment ratio (%) 2010–2014* male	female	Net enrolment ratio (%) 2010–2014* male	female	Net attendance ratio (%) 2009–2014* male	female	Out-of-school children of primary school age 2010–2014* rate (%)	number (000)	Survival rate to last primary grade (%) 2010–2014* admin. data	2009–2014* survey data	Secondary — Net enrolment ratio (%) 2010–2014* male	female	Net attendance ratio (%) 2009–2014* male	female
Afghanistan	62	32	75	6	–	–	131	92	–	–	62 y	46 y	–	–	–	84	62	35	47 y	27 y
Albania	99	99	105	60	90	87	114	111	–	–	92	93	4	7	99	100	86	85	78	79
Algeria	94 x	89 x	93	18	79	79	122	115	–	–	98	97	1	36	93	98 x	–	–	77	81
Andorra	–	–	83	96	–	–	–	–	–	–	–	–	–	–	71	–	–	–	–	–
Angola	79	67	63	21	64	94	157	100	95	73	77	75	16	624	32 x	83 x	14	11	21	17
Antigua and Barbuda	–	–	132	64	78	72	101	93	87	85	–	–	14	1	95	97	78	81	–	–
Argentina	99	99	159	65	71	72	111	110	–	–	98	99	0	6	90	100 x	82 x	97 x	92	93
Armenia	100	100	116	46	46	60	96 x	111 x	–	–	100	99	–	–	–	–	86	88	–	–
Australia	–	–	131	85	110	108	107	106	97	98	–	–	3	51	–	–	86	88	–	–
Austria	–	–	152	81	102	101	103	102	–	–	–	–	–	–	99	–	–	–	–	–
Azerbaijan	100	100	111	61	23	24	107	105	96	94	69 y	67 y	5	23	97	100 x	89	87	87 y	85 y
Bahamas	–	–	82	77	–	–	107	109	–	–	–	–	2	1	89 x	–	80	86	–	–
Bahrain	99	98	173	91	55	55	–	–	–	–	86 x	87 x	–	–	98	99 x	–	–	77 x	85 x
Bangladesh	79	83	80	10	32	32	109	115	93	97	71	76	5	907	66 x	96 x	50	55	40	52
Barbados	–	–	129	77	83	86	93	94	91	92	100	99	9	2	93	–	99	100	93	91
Belarus	100	100	123	59	107	103	99	99	94	94	93	90	6	22	98	100	99	100	96	98
Belgium	–	–	114	85	119	118	105	105	99	99	–	–	1	6	97	–	94	95	–	–
Belize	–	–	51	39	50	51	114	109	98	95	94	95	3	2	95	97	67	71	50	61
Benin	55 x	31 x	100	5	20	21	131	120	–	–	77	73	4	70	53	88 x	50	34	50	38
Bhutan	80 x	68 x	82	34	16	18	101	103	88	90	96	95	11	11	79	94	59	67	54	56
Bolivia (Plurinational State of)	99	99	96	39	64	63	99	96	88	87	97 x	97 x	12	169	97	96 x	75	76	78 x	75 x
Bosnia and Herzegovina	100	100	91	61	–	–	–	–	–	–	97	95	–	–	87	100	–	–	93	95
Botswana	96	99	167	19	18	18	110	107	91	92	86 x,y	88 x,y	9	27	94	–	59	67	36 x	44 x
Brazil	97	98	139	58	–	–	–	–	–	–	97	97	–	–	–	88 x	–	–	76	78
Brunei Darussalam	99	100	110	69	73	74	107	108	–	–	–	–	–	–	96	–	87	88	–	–
Bulgaria	98	98	138	55	83	83	99	99	96	97	–	–	4	10	98	–	89	87	–	–
Burkina Faso	47 x	33 x	72	9	4	4	89	85	70	66	54	50	32	957	69	89 x	23	20	22	17
Burundi	90 x	88 x	30	1	7	7	127	128	95	97	85	84	4	69	53	82 x	25	25	20	14
Cabo Verde	98	98	122	40	70	70	116	110	98	98	–	–	2	1	91	–	65	74	–	–
Cambodia	88	86	133	9	18	18	120	113	96	94	84 y	86 y	5	97	47	92 x	40 x	37 x	46	45
Cameroon	85	76	76	11	34	35	120	107	100	90	87	84	5	193	70	93	46	40	55	50
Canada	–	–	81	87	73	73	99	100	–	–	–	–	–	–	1	11	–	–	–	–
Central African Republic	49	27	25	4	6	6	107	80	79	62	78	68	29	207	47	81	18	9	23	15
Chad	54	46	40	3	1	1	115	88	95	74	55	48	16	357	51	89	–	–	22	12
Chile	99	100	133	72	125	121	102	98	93	92	90 y	92 y	7	110	99	–	87	90	80 y	84 y
China	100	100	92	49	117	118	109	109	–	–	97 y	97 y	–	–	–	–	–	–	87 y	88 y
Colombia	98	99	113	53	55	55	130 x	129 x	97 x	97 x	95	96	3 x	129 x	83	95	74 x	80 x	76	83
Comoros	87	87	51	7	22	24	108	102	88	83	85	85	15	17	–	19 x	42	45	51	56
Congo	86	77	108	7	14	14	107	115	89	97	96	97	7	47	–	96	–	–	67	67
Cook Islands	–	–	–	–	75	81	108	104	–	–	–	–	2	0.03	77	–	82	85	–	–
Costa Rica	99	99	144	49	79	79	111	110	96	96	96	96	4	16	90	93	76	80	69	74
Côte d'Ivoire	58	39	106	15	7	7	96	84	80	71	72	66	25	879	74	90 x	–	–	32	23
Croatia	100	100	104	69	63	62	96	96	97	100	–	–	2	3	99	–	94	96	–	–
Cuba	100	100	22	30	98	99	100	96	93	94	–	–	7	53	96	–	88	91	–	–
Cyprus	100	100	96	69	77	77	99	100	97	98	–	–	3	2	91	–	94	96	–	–
Czech Republic	–	–	130	80	106	103	99	99	–	–	–	–	–	–	99	–	–	–	–	–
Democratic People's Republic of Korea	100 x	100 x	11	0	84 x	85 x	100 x	100 x	97 x	97 x	99	99	3 x	47 x	–	100	98	99 x	98	98
Democratic Republic of the Congo	91	77	53	3	4	4	112	102	–	–	88	85	–	–	55	75	–	–	54	41
Denmark	–	–	126	96	99	96	102	101	98	99	–	–	1	6	98	–	89	92	–	–
Djibouti	–	–	32	11	5	4	73	63	69	60	71 y	68 y	35	33	84	92 x	29 x	21 x	45 x	37 x
Dominica	–	–	127	63	88	82	118	118	96 x	99 x	–	–	3 x	0.2 x	85	–	76	82	–	–
Dominican Republic	96	98	79	50	43	45	105	96	86	85	95	96	14	179	79	90	61	70	66	79
Ecuador	98	99	104	43	185	189	113	113	96	98	97 y	97 y	3	63	89	–	81	84	81 y	83 y
Egypt	91	84	114	32	25	24	106	105	–	–	97	97	0	12	96 x	99 x	77	77	81	79
El Salvador	96	96	144	30	68	70	118	112	96	96	91 y	91 y	4	30	84	–	69	70	–	–
Equatorial Guinea	98	99	66	19	68	68	85	84	58	58	61 x	60 x	42	46	72	–	–	–	23 x	22 x
Eritrea	94	90	6	1	15	15	55	47	43	38	57 y	56 y	59	405	78	–	31	26	23 x	21 x
Estonia	100	100	161	84	90	87	101	100	100	99	–	–	0	0.3	97	–	92	93	–	–
Ethiopia	63 x	47 x	32	3	31	30	104	96	89	84	64 y	67 y	14	2,124	37	84 x	–	–	13 y	18 y
Fiji	–	–	99	42	17 x	19 x	105	106	96	98	–	–	3	3	97	–	79	88	–	–

unicef 70 YEARS FOR EVERY CHILD

TABLE 5. EDUCATION

Countries and areas	Youth (15–24 years) literacy rate (%) 2009–2014*		Mobile phones / Internet users per 100 population 2014		Pre-primary school participation — Gross enrolment ratio (%) 2010–2014*		Primary school participation — Gross enrolment ratio (%) 2010–2014*		Net enrolment ratio (%) 2010–2014*		Net attendance ratio (%) 2009–2014*		Out-of-school children of primary school age 2009–2014*		Survival rate to last primary grade (%)		Secondary school participation — Net enrolment ratio (%) 2010–2014*		Net attendance ratio (%) 2009–2014*	
	male	female	mobile phones	internet users	male	female	male	female	male	female	male	female	rate (%)	number (000)	admin. data 2010–2014*	survey data 2009–2014*	male	female	male	female
Finland	–	–	140	92	81	81	101	101	99	100	–	–	0	1	99	–	94	94	–	–
France	–	–	101	84	108	108	106	105	99	100	–	–	1	26	–	–	99	100	–	–
Gabon	87	89	171	10	36	38	144	140	–	–	94	96	–	–	–	–	–	–	48	57
Gambia	74	67	120	16	33	35	84	88	66	72	61	64	31	99	77	95	–	–	34	34
Georgia	100	100	125	49	–	–	116	118	–	–	95	96	1	2	99	98 x	92	92	85	88
Germany	–	–	120	86	110	109	103	103	–	–	–	–	0	4	96	–	–	–	–	–
Ghana	88	83	115	19	114	117	107	106	89	89	70	70	11	413	84	100	55	54	38	37
Greece	99	99	110	63	77	76	99	98	98	97	–	–	3	18	91	–	96	95	–	–
Grenada	–	–	110	37	95	93	105	101	98	98	–	–	2	0.2	–	–	80	81	–	–
Guatemala	95	92	107	23	65	66	106	102	89	89	–	–	11	258	72	–	48	45	–	–
Guinea	38	22	72	2	15	15	95	84	80	72	63	53	24	449	53	96 x	38	25	38	25
Guinea-Bissau	80	71	63	3	6	7	118	110	71	68	62	62	31	76	–	73	–	–	27	20
Guyana	92	94	71	37	95	93	87	84	86	84	97	97	15	17	92	96	82	83	81	88
Haiti	74 x	70 x	65	11	78	84	176	175	–	–	83	84	–	–	–	88	–	–	33	39
Holy See	–	–	–	–	–	–	–	–	–	–	–	–	–	–	–	–	–	–	–	–
Honduras	94	96	94	19	47	48	110	108	95	95	91 y	92 y	5	54	75	84	46	53	46	55
Hungary	99	99	118	76	87	86	101	99	96	96	–	–	4	15	98	–	93	92	–	–
Iceland	–	–	111	98	98	97	98	99	98	99	–	–	1	0.4	98	–	88	88	–	–
India	90	82	74	18	54	57	105	117	92	99	85 x	82 x	5	6,402	–	95 x	61	62	59 x	49 x
Indonesia	99	99	129	17	51	58	106	106	93	94	98	99	7	1,900	82	–	76	74	72	75
Iran (Islamic Republic of)	98	98	88	39	43	42	107	112	–	–	96	97	1	45	82	97	80	81	–	–
Iraq	83	81	95	11	–	–	–	–	–	–	93	87	–	–	–	96	–	–	53	45
Ireland	–	–	105	80	107	110	103	103	99	100	–	–	1	4	–	–	–	–	–	–
Israel	–	–	121	71	113	112	104	105	97	98	–	–	3	22	99	–	97	99	–	–
Italy	100	100	154	62	101	99	102	101	100	99	–	–	1	15	99	–	95	95	–	–
Jamaica	94	99	107	41	102	108	–	–	–	–	97	99	–	–	95	99	70	77	91	92
Japan	–	–	120	91	–	–	102	101	100	100	–	–	0	3	100	–	99	100	–	–
Jordan	99	99	148	44	33	31	89	88	88	87	98	98	12	119	98	–	83	88	74	77
Kazakhstan	100	100	172	55	57	57	111	111	99	100	99	99	1	5	99	100	95	97	96	96
Kenya	83 x	82 x	74	43	75	73	111	112	84	88	84	87	14	956	–	96	57	56	57	61
Kiribati	–	–	17	12	–	–	111	115	–	–	83	87	2	0.3	–	–	–	–	54	65
Kuwait	99	99	218	79	82	80	103	105	97	99	–	–	2	4	96	–	81	85	–	–
Kyrgyzstan	100	100	134	28	25	25	108	107	98	98	99	99	2	8	99	100	80	80	85	86
Lao People's Democratic Republic	89 x	79 x	67	14	30	31	119	113	96	94	85	85	5	36	78	95	52	50	45	45
Latvia	100	100	117	76	93	92	103	102	98	99	–	–	2	2	92	–	89	91	–	–
Lebanon	98 x	99 x	88	75	87	82	102	93	92	86	98	98	11	54	93	93 x	65	65	77	85
Lesotho	74	92	85	11	30	32	108	106	79	82	92	96	19	66	67	84 x	27	42	34	47
Liberia	63 x	37 x	73	5	–	–	100	92	39	37	42	43	62	442	68 x	76 x	18	15	27	24
Libya	100	100	161	18	–	–	–	–	–	–	–	–	–	–	–	–	–	–	–	–
Liechtenstein	–	–	109	95	102	97	103	105	–	–	–	–	2	0.03	79 x	–	97	87	–	–
Lithuania	100	100	147	72	85	84	101	101	100	100	–	–	0	0.3	97	–	94	94	–	–
Luxembourg	–	–	149	95	93	94	96	97	94	96	–	–	5	2	85	–	84	87	–	–
Madagascar	66	64	41	4	13	14	147	147	–	–	68 y	71 y	–	–	40	89	31	32	27	28
Malawi	74	70	33	6	–	–	145	148	–	–	93	94	2 x	48 x	49	88	33	33	32	34
Malaysia	98	98	149	68	–	–	–	–	–	–	–	–	–	–	–	–	–	–	–	–
Maldives	99 x	99 x	189	49	–	–	104 x	101 x	97 x	96 x	94	95	3 x	2 x	82	99	–	–	63	70
Mali	56	34	149	7	4	4	81	73	67	60	60	55	36	1,030	62	94	39	30	36	23
Malta	98	99	127	73	112	119	100	95	99	94	–	–	3	1	97	–	85	76	–	–
Marshall Islands	–	–	29	17	46	49	106	105	–	–	–	–	0	0.02	83 x	–	–	–	–	–
Mauritania	66 x	48 x	94	11	3	4	95	101	73	77	60	62	25	151	64	78	23	20	26	22
Mauritius	98	99	132	41	101	104	102	104	96	98	–	–	3	4	98	–	–	–	–	–
Mexico	98	98	82	44	101	104	105	104	97	98	97 x	97 x	3	357	95	–	66	69	–	–
Micronesia (Federated States of)	–	–	–	30	–	–	98	97	86	88	–	–	13	2	–	–	–	–	–	–
Monaco	–	–	88	92	–	–	–	–	–	–	–	–	–	–	–	–	–	–	–	–
Mongolia	98	99	105	27	85	86	103	101	96	95	95	97	4	10	–	99	85	88	91	96
Montenegro	99	99	163	61	57	54	95	93	94	93	98	98	6	3	80	100 x	–	–	94	95
Morocco	89	74	132	57	65	53	119	113	99	99	91 x	88 x	1	37	89	–	59	53	39 x	36 x
Mozambique	80	57	70	6	–	–	109	100	90	85	76	76	12	678	31	60 x	18	18	25	23
Myanmar	96	96	54	2	23	24	101	98	98	91	90	91	5	284	75 x	93	48	49	58	59
Namibia	83 x	91 x	114	15	21	22	113	110	89	92	92	93	9	36	91	89 x	48	60	55	65

TABLE 5. EDUCATION

Countries and areas	Youth (15–24 years) literacy rate (%) 2009–2014*		Mobile phones / Internet users per 100 population 2014		Pre-primary school participation — Gross enrolment ratio (%) 2010–2014*		Primary school participation — Gross enrolment ratio (%) 2010–2014*		Net enrolment ratio (%) 2010–2014*		Net attendance ratio (%) 2009–2014*		Out-of-school children of primary school age 2010–2014*		Survival rate to last primary grade (%) 2010–2014* admin. data	2009–2014* survey data	Secondary school participation — Net enrolment ratio (%) 2010–2014*		Net attendance ratio (%) 2009–2014*	
	male	female	mobile phones	internet users	male	female	male	female	male	female	male	female	rate (%)	number (000)			male	female	male	female
Nauru	–	–	–	–	85	96	110	100	89	84	97 y	98 y	13	0.2	–	–	70	75	65 y	72 y
Nepal	90	80	82	15	88	84	130	141	95	94	76	76	5	174	70	–	58	62	62	62
Netherlands	–	–	116	93	94	95	107	106	99	99	–	–	1	11	–	–	92	93	–	–
New Zealand	–	–	112	86	97	99	98	99	98	99	–	–	2	6	–	–	96	97	–	–
Nicaragua	85 x	89 x	115	18	57	59	124	123	97	100	71 y	70 y	2	12	–	56 x	45	53	38 x	48 x
Niger	35	15	44	2	7	7	76	65	66	57	55	46	38	1,233	79 x	92	19	13	21	13
Nigeria	76 x	58 x	78	43	13	13	88	81	71	60	70	66	34	8,735	79 x	97	–	–	56	49
Niue	–	–	–	92	113	125	127	125	–	–	100	100	–	–	–	–	–	–	–	–
Norway	–	–	116	96	99	99	100	100	100	100	–	–	0	1	99	–	95	95	–	–
Oman	97	98	158	70	53	55	106	115	97	97	97	98	3	6	99	99	87	90	91	92
Pakistan	80	62	73	14	74	66	101	86	79	67	67	60	27	5,612	80	–	46	36	45	38
Palau	100	100	91	–	71	77	116	112	–	–	–	–	1	0.01	–	–	90	99	–	–
Panama	98	97	158	45	71	72	107	104	97	96	97	97	3	14	93	–	75	81	77	84
Papua New Guinea	67	77	45	9	102 x	99 x	120	109	90	84	–	–	13	160	–	–	–	–	–	–
Paraguay	99	99	106	43	38	38	108	104	89	89	87 x	89 x	11	85	84	–	67	66	81 x	80 x
Peru	99	99	104	40	87	88	101	101	95	96	92 y	93 y	5	162	91	87	77	79	80 y	82 y
Philippines	97 x	98 x	111	40	53 x	56 x	117	117	95	99	88 x	89 x	3	402	76 x	90 x	62	74	55 x	70 x
Poland	100	100	149	67	78	77	101	101	97	97	–	–	3	62	99	–	91	93	–	–
Portugal	99	99	112	65	92	89	112	108	99	99	–	–	1	7	–	–	92	94	–	–
Qatar	96	98	146	91	58	58	104	99	97	95	96	97	3	3	98	100	100	89	94	93
Republic of Korea	–	–	116	84	92	92	99	99	97	96	–	–	4	101	100	–	97	96	–	–
Republic of Moldova	100	100	108	47	83	81	94	94	91	91	99	98	9	14	95	100 x	77	78	84	88
Romania	99	99	106	54	92	93	96	95	92	91	–	–	9	72	94	–	87	87	–	–
Russian Federation	100	100	155	71	92	91	100	101	97	98	–	–	2	141	97	–	–	–	–	–
Rwanda	77	78	64	11	14	15	136	139	95	97	87 y	89 y	4	68	35	76 x	–	–	21 y	25 y
Saint Kitts and Nevis	–	–	119	65	97	92	83	84	80	83	–	–	19	1	93	–	81	85	–	–
Saint Lucia	–	–	103	51	63	67	–	–	–	–	100	99	–	–	90	100	80	81	91	92
Saint Vincent and the Grenadines	–	–	105	56	68	70	106	103	92	91	–	–	9	1	69	–	84	87	–	–
Samoa	99	99	56	21	35	39	106	106	97	98	88 y	89 y	3	1	90	–	75	84	51 y	70 y
San Marino	–	–	119	–	106	108	94	93	93	93	–	–	7	0.1	96	–	–	–	–	–
Sao Tome and Principe	83 x	77 x	65	24	–	–	114	109	96	95	94	94	4	1	80	92	44	51	55	65
Saudi Arabia	99	99	180	64	14	18	109	108	98	95	–	–	4	121	99	–	97	79	–	–
Senegal	74	59	99	18	14	16	78	84	70	76	63	66	27	634	61	90	–	–	39	37
Serbia	99	99	122	54	59	59	101	101	98	99	99	99	1	4	98	100	91	93	92	95
Seychelles	99	99	162	54	93	93	104	105	94	95	–	–	5	0.5	–	–	74	75	–	–
Sierra Leone	73	56	77	2	9	10	130	130	100	99	74	78	1	7	48	93	40	35	48	42
Singapore	100	100	147	82	–	–	–	–	–	–	–	–	–	–	99 x	–	–	–	–	–
Slovakia	–	–	117	80	93	91	103	101	–	–	–	–	–	–	98	–	–	–	–	–
Slovenia	100	100	112	72	95	93	99	99	97	98	–	–	3	3	100	–	95	95	–	–
Solomon Islands	–	–	66	9	98	98	116	112	–	–	63 x,y	69 x,y	–	–	71	–	42	42	29 x,y	30 x,y
Somalia	–	–	51	2	–	–	–	–	–	–	24 x	19 x	–	–	–	88 x	–	–	7 x	4 x
South Africa	98	99	149	49	77	78	102	97	–	–	97	97	–	–	–	–	–	–	88	88
South Sudan	44 x	30 x	25	16	6	6	101	67	47	34	26	21	59	1,022	–	71	–	–	10	6
Spain	100	100	108	76	99	99	105	106	99	100	–	–	0	14	97	–	96	97	–	–
Sri Lanka	98	99	103	26	95	95	102	100	98	96	–	–	3	47	98	100 x	84	87	–	–
State of Palestine	99	99	72	54	50	51	95	95	93	93	99	99	7	33	98	100	77	84	85	94
Sudan	91	86	72	25	38	36	73	65	53	56	72	68	45	2,713	80	90	–	–	46	45
Suriname	98	99	171	40	92	96	122	118	91	92	95	96	9	5	86	96	44	50	53	66
Swaziland	92	95	72	27	25	26	118	108	79	78	96	97	21	45	75	93	31	38	42	52
Sweden	–	–	128	93	95	95	117	124	100	100	–	–	0	2	100	–	95	94	–	–
Switzerland	–	–	137	87	99	99	103	103	99	100	–	–	1	4	–	–	82	80	–	–
Syrian Arab Republic	97	95	64	28	6	6	81	79	72	70	97 x	96 x	29	563	93	100 x	47	46	64 x	65 x
Tajikistan	100	100	95	17	11	10	98	97	97	97	98	97	3	19	99	100 x	88	79	92	82
Thailand	97	97	144	35	117	116	99	97	97 x	96 x	96	96	4 x	202 x	–	100	77	82	75	83
The former Yugoslav Republic of Macedonia	99	98	106	68	28	29	86	85	89	88	98	98	12	15	–	100	–	–	90	88
Timor-Leste	80	79	119	1	17	17	138	136	96	99	71	73	2	4	81	91	48	56	43	48
Togo	87	73	65	6	15	15	129	121	96	90	90	87	7	79	53	90	–	–	52	41
Tonga	99	100	64	40	36	35	110	110	95	97	93 y	93 y	4	1	–	–	74	79	82 y	84 y
Trinidad and Tobago	100	100	147	65	–	–	108	104	99	98	98 x	98 x	1	2	89 x	98 x	–	–	84 x	90 x

unicef ✪ 70 YEARS FOR EVERY CHILD

TABLE 5. EDUCATION

Countries and areas	Youth (15–24 years) literacy rate (%) 2009–2014* male	female	Mobile phones / Internet users per 100 population 2014 mobile phones	internet users	Pre-primary school participation Gross enrolment ratio (%) 2010–2014* male	female	Primary school participation Gross enrolment ratio (%) 2010–2014* male	female	Net enrolment ratio (%) 2010–2014* male	female	Net attendance ratio (%) 2009–2014* male	female	Out-of-school children of primary school age 2010–2014* rate (%)	number (000)	Survival rate to last primary grade (%) 2010–2014* admin. data	2009–2014* survey data	Secondary school participation Net enrolment ratio (%) 2010–2014* male	female	Net attendance ratio (%) 2009–2014* male	female
Tunisia	98	96	128	46	40	43	113	109	–	–	98	98	0	4	94	97	–	–	69	77
Turkey	99	97	95	51	28	27	107	107	94	93	94 x,y	92 x,y	7	357	90	95 x	90	86	75 x	64 x
Turkmenistan	100	100	136	12	64	62	90	89	–	–	99 x	99 x	–	–	–	–	–	–	95 x	95 x
Tuvalu	–	–	38	–	93	93	101	102	95	98	97 x,y	99 x,y	4	0.1	–	–	62	78	35 x	47 x
Uganda	90	85	52	18	11	11	109	111	92	95	86	87	6	477	25	72 x	24	22	20	21
Ukraine	100	100	144	43	105	103	103	105	96	98	100	100	3	56	99	100	88	89	93	93
United Arab Emirates	94 x	97 x	178	90	92	92	106	107	96	96	–	–	4	15	92	–	–	–	–	–
United Kingdom	–	–	124	92	80	76	109	109	–	–	–	–	0	7	–	–	94	95	–	–
United Republic of Tanzania	76	73	63	5	32	33	86	87	81	82	75 y	78 y	18	1,715	67	91 x	–	–	26	25
United States	–	–	110	87	71	71	100	99	93	93	–	–	7	1,774	–	–	87	89	–	–
Uruguay	98	99	161	61	89	89	114	110	–	–	97	98	0	0.5	95 x	–	68	76	72	78
Uzbekistan	100	100	78	44	25	25	98	96	96	94	95 x	95 x	5	101	98	100 x	–	–	91 x	90 x
Vanuatu	95	95	60	19	64	64	125	122	–	–	76 y	78 y	–	–	71 x	88 x	51	53	22 y	26 y
Venezuela (Bolivarian Republic of)	97	98	99	57	73	73	102	100	93	93	91 x	93 x	7	243	87	82 x	71	79	–	–
Viet Nam	97	97	147	48	83	80	110	109	–	–	98	98	2	127	90	99	–	–	89	92
Yemen	97	80	68	23	1	1	106	89	92	78	80	72	15	583	69	73 x	50	33	81	58
Zambia	70 x	58 x	67	17	–	–	103	104	88	90	86	88	11	325	55	87 x	–	–	47	43
Zimbabwe	90	92	81	20	27	27	103	102	88	90	93	94	11	283	–	91	43	43	46	50
SUMMARY																				
Sub-Saharan Africa	76	66	71	19	18	19	103	96	81	76	75	74	21	32,960	57	91	36	32	40	36
Eastern and Southern Africa	79	72	64	17	21	22	108	102	85	84	78	79	16	11,826	47	–	34	33	32	33
West and Central Africa	73	57	78	21	15	15	100	91	78	70	72	68	26	18,403	67	91	37	30	46	38
Middle East and North Africa	94	90	107	37	28	28	108	102	91	88	91	89	10	4,852	83	–	70	66	71	67
South Asia	87	79	75	17	55	56	111	112	94	94	81	77	6	10,259	63	94	55	48	56	48
East Asia and Pacific	99	99	101	43	69	70	118	117	96	96	96	97	4	6,500	92	–	77	78	82	84
Latin America and Caribbean	98	98	115	50	76	77	106	103	93	94	95	96	6	4,020	83	90	73	78	75	78
CEE/CIS	100	100	128	56	61	60	101	101	95	95	–	–	5	954	95	–	89	88	–	–
Least developed countries	77	69	64	9	15	15	109	101	84	80	73	73	18	24,360	54	–	36	33	37	36
World	**93**	**89**	**97**	**40**	**54**	**54**	**109**	**107**	**92**	**90**	**85**	**83**	**9**	**59,204**	**75**	**93 ****	**67**	**65**	**62**	**58**

For a complete list of countries and areas in the regions, subregions and country categories, see page 112 or visit <data.unicef.org/regionalclassifications>.
It is not advisable to compare data from consecutive editions of *The State of the World's Children*.

DEFINITIONS OF THE INDICATORS

Youth literacy rate – Number of literate persons aged 15–24 years, expressed as a percentage of the total population in that group.
Mobile phones – The number of active subscriptions to a public mobile telephone service, including the number of prepaid SIM cards active during the past three months.
Internet users – The estimated number of Internet users out of the total population. This includes those using the Internet from any device (including mobile phones) in the last 12 months.
Pre-primary school gross enrolment ratio – Number of children enrolled in pre-primary school, regardless of age, expressed as a percentage of the total number of children of official pre-primary school age.
Primary school gross enrolment ratio – Number of children enrolled in primary school, regardless of age, expressed as a percentage of the total number of children of official primary school age.
Primary school net enrolment ratio – Number of children enrolled in primary or secondary school who are of official primary school age, expressed as a percentage of the total number of children of official primary school age. Because of the inclusion of primary-school-aged children enrolled in secondary school, this indicator can also be referred to as a primary adjusted net enrolment ratio.
Primary school net attendance ratio – Number of children attending primary or secondary school who are of official primary school age, expressed as a percentage of the total number of children of official primary school age. Because of the inclusion of primary-school-aged children attending secondary school, this indicator can also be referred to as a primary adjusted net attendance ratio.
Rate of out-of-school children of primary school age – Number of children of official primary school age who are not enrolled in primary or secondary school, expressed as a percentage of the population of official primary school age.
Out-of-school children of primary school age – Children in the official primary school age range who are not enrolled in either primary or secondary schools. Children enrolled in pre-primary education are excluded and considered out of school.
Survival rate to last primary grade – Percentage of children entering the first grade of primary school who eventually reach the last grade of primary school.
Secondary school net enrolment ratio – Number of children enrolled in secondary school who are of official secondary school age, expressed as a percentage of the total number of children of official secondary school age. Secondary net enrolment ratio does not include secondary-school-aged children enrolled in tertiary education owing to challenges in age reporting and recording at that level.
Secondary school net attendance ratio – Number of children attending secondary or tertiary school who are of official secondary school age, expressed as a percentage of the total number of children of official secondary school age. Because of the inclusion of secondary-school-aged children attending tertiary school, this indicator can also be referred to as a secondary adjusted net attendance ratio.
All data refer to official International Standard Classifications of Education (ISCED) for the primary and secondary education levels and thus may not directly correspond to a country-specific school system.

MAIN DATA SOURCES

Youth literacy – UNESCO Institute for Statistics (UIS).
Mobile phone and Internet use – International Telecommunications Union, Geneva.
Pre-primary, primary and secondary enrolment and rate and number of out-of-school children – UIS. Estimates based on administrative data from national Education Management Information Systems (EMIS) with UN population estimates.
Primary and secondary school attendance – Demographic and Health Surveys (DHS), Multiple Indicator Cluster Surveys (MICS) and other national household surveys.
Survival rate to last primary grade – Administrative data: UIS; survey data: DHS, MICS and other national household surveys.

NOTES

– Data not available.
x Data refer to years or periods other than those specified in the column heading. Such data are not included in the calculation of regional and global averages, with the exception of 2005–2006 data from India and 2006 survival rate data from Brazil. Estimates from data years prior to 2000 are not displayed.
y Data differ from the standard definition or refer to only part of a country. If they fall within the noted reference period, such data are included in the calculation of regional and global averages.
* Data refer to the most recent year available during the period specified in the column heading.
** Excludes China.

TABLE 6. DEMOGRAPHIC INDICATORS

Countries and areas	Population (thousands) 2015			Population annual growth rate (%)		Crude death rate			Crude birth rate			Life expectancy			Total fertility rate	Urbanized population (%)	Average annual growth rate of urban population (%)	
	total	under 18	under 5	1990–2015	2015–2030◊	1970	1990	2015	1970	1990	2015	1970	1990	2015	2015	2015	1990–2015	2015–2030◊
Afghanistan	32,527	16,716	4,950	4.0	2.0	28	16	8	52	49	33	37	50	61	4.7	27	5.5	3.7
Albania	2,897	687	185	-0.5	0.1	8	6	7	32	25	14	67	72	78	1.8	57	1.5	1.4
Algeria	39,667	13,067	4,590	1.7	1.3	17	6	5	47	32	24	50	67	75	2.8	71	3.0	1.8
Andorra	70	12	3	1.0	0.1	–	–	–	–	–	–	–	–	–	–	85	1.2	0.2
Angola	25,022	13,598	4,718	3.2	3.0	27	23	13	53	53	45	37	41	53	6.0	44	5.3	4.2
Antigua and Barbuda	92	27	7	1.6	0.9	7	7	6	30	19	16	66	71	76	2.1	24	0.0	0.2
Argentina	43,417	13,006	3,718	1.1	0.9	9	8	8	23	22	17	66	72	76	2.3	92	1.2	0.8
Armenia	3,018	654	207	-0.6	-0.1	6	8	9	23	22	13	70	68	75	1.5	63	-1.0	0.0
Australia	23,969	5,354	1,546	1.4	1.1	9	7	7	20	15	13	71	77	83	1.9	89	1.5	1.3
Austria	8,545	1,481	404	0.4	0.2	13	11	9	16	11	10	70	75	82	1.5	66	0.5	0.6
Azerbaijan	9,754	2,538	930	1.2	0.6	9	8	7	29	27	20	65	65	71	2.3	55	1.2	1.2
Bahamas	388	99	29	1.7	0.9	6	5	6	26	24	15	66	71	76	1.9	83	1.8	1.1
Bahrain	1,377	347	109	4.1	1.2	7	3	2	38	29	14	63	72	77	2.0	89	4.1	1.4
Bangladesh	160,996	57,168	15,331	1.7	1.0	19	10	5	48	35	19	48	58	72	2.1	34	3.8	2.8
Barbados	284	66	17	0.4	0.1	10	10	11	22	16	12	66	71	76	1.8	31	0.3	0.6
Belarus	9,496	1,774	586	-0.3	-0.4	9	11	14	16	14	12	71	71	71	1.6	77	0.2	-0.2
Belgium	11,299	2,280	653	0.5	0.4	12	11	10	14	12	12	71	76	81	1.8	98	0.5	0.3
Belize	359	140	39	2.6	1.8	8	5	6	42	36	23	66	71	70	2.5	44	2.2	2.0
Benin	10,880	5,312	1,708	3.1	2.4	24	14	9	47	46	36	42	54	60	4.7	44	4.1	3.4
Bhutan	775	252	66	1.5	0.9	26	13	6	49	38	17	37	52	70	2.0	39	4.9	2.4
Bolivia (Plurinational State of)	10,725	4,138	1,186	1.8	1.4	20	13	7	42	35	24	46	55	69	2.9	69	2.8	1.9
Bosnia and Herzegovina	3,810	643	172	-0.7	-0.4	7	8	11	24	15	9	66	71	77	1.3	40	-0.6	0.6
Botswana	2,262	856	266	2.0	1.5	13	7	8	46	35	25	55	63	65	2.8	57	2.8	1.4
Brazil	207,848	58,433	15,032	1.3	0.6	10	7	6	35	24	15	59	65	75	1.8	86	1.8	0.8
Brunei Darussalam	423	119	34	2.0	1.1	6	4	3	36	32	16	67	73	79	1.9	77	2.7	1.3
Bulgaria	7,150	1,199	337	-0.8	-0.8	9	13	15	16	12	9	71	71	74	1.6	74	-0.4	-0.5
Burkina Faso	18,106	9,475	3,144	2.9	2.7	25	17	9	47	47	40	39	49	59	5.4	30	5.9	4.7
Burundi	11,179	5,685	2,062	2.8	2.9	21	18	11	47	50	43	44	48	57	5.9	12	5.2	5.2
Cabo Verde	521	186	54	1.7	1.1	14	8	5	42	40	21	54	66	74	2.3	66	3.1	1.6
Cambodia	15,578	5,850	1,772	2.2	1.3	20	13	6	43	42	24	42	54	69	2.6	21	3.3	2.7
Cameroon	23,344	11,472	3,738	2.6	2.3	19	14	11	45	45	36	46	54	56	4.6	54	3.9	3.2
Canada	35,940	6,961	1,942	1.0	0.8	7	7	7	17	14	11	72	77	82	1.6	82	1.3	1.0
Central African Republic	4,900	2,242	708	2.0	1.9	23	17	14	43	41	33	42	49	51	4.2	40	2.3	2.8
Chad	14,037	7,671	2,632	3.4	3.0	23	19	14	47	51	45	41	47	52	6.1	22	3.6	4.0
Chile	17,948	4,398	1,170	1.2	0.8	10	6	5	30	22	13	63	73	82	1.7	90	1.5	0.8
China	1,376,049	282,260	83,186	0.7	0.2	11	7	7	37	23	12	59	69	76	1.6	56	3.7	1.7
Colombia	48,229	14,144	3,738	1.4	0.7	9	6	6	38	26	15	61	68	74	1.9	76	2.0	1.3
Comoros	788	368	119	2.6	2.1	19	11	7	46	43	33	46	57	64	4.4	28	2.6	2.8
Congo	4,620	2,259	759	2.6	2.6	14	12	8	43	38	36	53	55	63	4.8	65	3.4	3.0
Cook Islands	21	7	2	0.7	0.5	–	–	–	–	–	–	–	–	–	–	75	1.7	0.7
Costa Rica	4,808	1,308	350	1.8	0.8	7	4	5	33	27	15	66	76	80	1.8	77	3.7	1.6
Côte d'Ivoire	22,702	11,193	3,667	2.5	2.3	21	14	13	53	43	37	44	52	52	4.9	54	3.5	3.1
Croatia	4,240	775	207	-0.5	-0.4	11	11	13	15	11	9	68	72	77	1.5	59	-0.1	0.2
Cuba	11,390	2,269	588	0.3	-0.1	7	7	8	29	17	10	70	75	80	1.6	77	0.4	-0.1
Cyprus	1,165	236	66	1.7	0.7	7	7	7	19	19	11	73	77	80	1.4	67	1.7	0.8
Czech Republic	10,543	1,846	538	0.1	-0.1	12	12	10	16	12	10	70	72	79	1.5	73	0.1	0.3
Democratic People's Republic of Korea	25,155	6,486	1,747	0.9	0.4	10	6	9	37	21	14	60	70	71	2.0	61	1.0	0.8
Democratic Republic of the Congo	77,267	40,639	13,876	3.2	3.0	20	17	10	47	48	42	44	49	59	5.9	42	4.2	3.6
Denmark	5,669	1,167	295	0.4	0.4	10	12	10	15	12	10	73	75	80	1.7	88	0.5	0.6
Djibouti	888	344	102	1.6	1.1	15	11	9	45	40	25	49	57	62	3.1	77	1.8	1.3
Dominica	73	22	6	0.1	0.3	–	–	–	–	–	–	–	–	–	–	70	0.5	0.7
Dominican Republic	10,528	3,744	1,062	1.5	0.9	11	6	6	42	30	21	58	68	74	2.5	79	3.0	1.6
Ecuador	16,144	5,588	1,610	1.8	1.3	12	6	5	41	30	20	58	69	76	2.5	64	2.5	1.7
Egypt	91,508	35,095	12,116	1.9	1.6	16	9	6	40	33	27	52	65	71	3.3	43	1.6	1.8
El Salvador	6,127	2,039	520	0.6	0.3	13	8	7	43	31	17	55	64	73	1.9	67	2.0	1.0
Equatorial Guinea	845	383	128	3.2	2.5	25	19	11	39	47	35	40	48	58	4.7	40	3.6	3.0
Eritrea	5,228	2,562	815	2.0	2.2	22	15	6	47	43	33	41	48	64	4.2	23	4.3	4.4
Estonia	1,313	243	72	-0.7	-0.4	11	13	12	15	14	11	70	69	77	1.6	68	-1.0	-0.3
Ethiopia	99,391	48,448	14,602	2.9	2.2	21	18	7	48	48	32	43	47	65	4.3	19	4.6	4.3
Fiji	892	302	88	0.8	0.3	8	6	7	34	29	20	60	66	70	2.5	54	1.8	1.0
Finland	5,503	1,077	304	0.4	0.2	10	10	10	14	13	11	70	75	81	1.8	84	0.6	0.4
France	64,395	14,211	3,927	0.5	0.4	11	9	9	17	13	12	72	77	82	2.0	80	0.8	0.7
Gabon	1,725	748	239	2.4	2.0	20	11	8	37	37	30	47	61	65	3.8	87	3.4	2.2

TABLE 6. DEMOGRAPHIC INDICATORS

Countries and areas	Population (thousands) 2015 total	under 18	under 5	Population annual growth rate (%) 1990–2015	2015–2030°	Crude death rate 1970	1990	2015	Crude birth rate 1970	1990	2015	Life expectancy 1970	1990	2015	Total fertility rate 2015	Urbanized population (%) 2015	Average annual growth rate of urban population (%) 1990–2015	2015–2030°
Gambia	1,991	1,051	366	3.1	3.0	26	14	9	50	47	42	38	52	60	5.7	60	4.8	3.6
Georgia	4,000	832	275	-1.2	-0.2	10	9	12	19	17	13	67	70	75	1.8	54	-1.1	-0.1
Germany	80,689	12,769	3,384	0.1	-0.1	12	12	11	14	10	9	71	75	81	1.4	75	0.2	0.0
Ghana	27,410	12,330	4,056	2.5	2.0	16	11	9	47	39	32	49	57	62	4.1	54	4.0	2.8
Greece	10,955	1,899	533	0.3	-0.3	10	9	11	17	10	8	71	77	81	1.3	78	0.7	0.3
Grenada	107	34	10	0.4	0.3	9	9	7	28	28	19	64	69	74	2.1	36	0.7	0.4
Guatemala	16,343	7,085	2,089	2.3	1.8	15	9	5	44	38	27	52	62	72	3.2	52	3.3	3.0
Guinea	12,609	6,196	2,046	2.9	2.5	27	17	10	45	47	36	37	50	59	4.9	37	4.0	3.6
Guinea-Bissau	1,844	871	289	2.2	2.1	22	18	12	43	45	37	42	49	55	4.8	49	4.5	3.3
Guyana	767	279	67	0.3	0.5	9	9	8	35	33	19	62	63	66	2.5	29	0.3	1.1
Haiti	10,711	4,294	1,238	1.6	1.1	18	13	9	39	37	25	47	55	63	3.0	59	4.5	2.3
Holy See	1	0	0	0.2	0.0	–	–	–	–	–	–	–	–	–	–	100	0.2	0.0
Honduras	8,075	3,109	816	2.0	1.2	15	7	5	47	38	21	53	67	73	2.3	55	3.4	2.6
Hungary	9,855	1,724	463	-0.2	-0.4	11	14	13	15	12	9	70	69	75	1.4	71	0.1	0.2
Iceland	329	80	23	1.0	0.7	7	7	6	21	17	13	74	78	83	1.9	94	1.3	0.9
India	1,311,051	451,990	123,711	1.6	1.0	17	11	7	39	31	20	48	58	68	2.4	33	2.6	2.2
Indonesia	257,564	85,276	24,864	1.4	0.9	13	8	7	40	26	20	55	63	69	2.4	54	3.7	2.0
Iran (Islamic Republic of)	79,109	21,847	6,855	1.4	0.7	16	7	5	42	33	17	51	64	76	1.7	73	2.4	1.5
Iraq	36,423	17,270	5,727	2.9	2.6	12	7	5	46	38	34	58	66	70	4.5	69	2.8	2.6
Ireland	4,688	1,187	353	1.1	0.7	11	9	6	22	14	14	71	75	81	2.0	63	1.6	1.3
Israel	8,064	2,626	832	2.3	1.4	7	6	5	26	22	21	72	76	83	3.0	92	2.3	1.4
Italy	59,798	9,870	2,570	0.2	-0.1	10	10	10	17	10	8	71	77	83	1.5	69	0.4	0.3
Jamaica	2,793	821	204	0.6	0.2	8	7	7	36	26	17	68	72	76	2.0	55	1.1	0.9
Japan	126,573	19,827	5,269	0.1	-0.3	7	7	10	19	10	8	72	79	84	1.4	93	0.9	-0.1
Jordan	7,595	3,160	980	3.3	1.2	10	5	4	51	34	27	60	70	74	3.4	84	3.8	1.5
Kazakhstan	17,625	5,356	1,948	0.3	0.9	9	9	9	25	24	21	63	67	70	2.6	53	-0.1	1.0
Kenya	46,050	22,234	7,166	2.7	2.3	15	10	8	51	42	34	52	59	62	4.3	26	4.5	4.0
Kiribati	112	46	15	1.8	1.5	13	10	7	35	37	29	54	60	66	3.7	44	2.5	1.9
Kuwait	3,892	997	348	2.5	1.7	6	3	3	49	21	20	66	72	75	2.1	98	2.2	2.0
Kyrgyzstan	5,940	2,170	780	1.2	1.2	11	8	6	31	31	26	60	66	71	3.1	36	0.8	2.0
Lao People's Democratic Republic	6,802	2,813	839	1.9	1.5	18	14	7	43	43	26	46	54	67	2.9	39	5.7	3.3
Latvia	1,971	339	95	-1.2	-0.6	11	13	15	14	14	10	70	69	74	1.5	67	-1.2	-0.5
Lebanon	5,851	1,733	461	3.1	-0.7	8	7	5	32	25	15	66	70	80	1.7	88	2.7	0.3
Lesotho	2,135	921	278	1.2	1.0	17	10	15	43	35	28	49	59	50	3.1	27	3.8	2.6
Liberia	4,503	2,203	701	3.0	2.4	24	18	9	49	45	35	39	47	61	4.6	50	2.6	3.2
Libya	6,278	2,187	649	1.4	1.1	13	5	5	51	29	20	56	69	72	2.4	79	1.7	1.4
Liechtenstein	38	7	2	1.1	0.6	–	–	–	–	–	–	–	–	–	–	14	0.4	1.1
Lithuania	2,878	508	152	-1.0	-0.5	9	11	16	17	15	10	71	71	73	1.6	67	-0.9	-0.2
Luxembourg	567	113	32	1.6	1.2	12	10	7	13	12	11	70	75	82	1.6	90	1.8	1.3
Madagascar	24,235	11,776	3,770	3.0	2.6	21	15	7	48	45	34	45	51	66	4.4	35	4.6	4.2
Malawi	17,215	8,949	2,954	2.4	2.9	25	20	7	54	50	39	41	44	64	5.0	16	3.8	4.2
Malaysia	30,331	9,080	2,477	2.0	1.2	7	5	5	33	28	17	64	71	75	1.9	75	3.7	1.8
Maldives	364	119	37	2.0	1.2	21	9	4	50	41	21	44	61	77	2.1	46	4.3	2.7
Mali	17,600	9,526	3,271	2.9	2.9	32	20	10	50	49	43	32	46	58	6.1	40	5.0	4.7
Malta	419	76	19	0.7	0.1	8	7	9	16	16	9	71	76	81	1.5	95	0.8	0.2
Marshall Islands	53	19	5	0.5	0.3	–	–	–	–	–	–	–	–	–	–	73	0.9	0.9
Mauritania	4,068	1,890	601	2.8	2.2	16	11	8	46	41	33	49	58	63	4.5	60	4.3	2.9
Mauritius	1,273	304	71	0.7	0.2	7	6	8	29	21	11	63	69	75	1.5	40	0.3	0.2
Mexico	127,017	42,245	11,617	1.6	1.0	10	5	5	44	29	18	61	71	77	2.2	79	1.9	1.2
Micronesia (Federated States of)	104	43	12	0.3	0.8	9	7	6	41	34	24	62	66	69	3.2	22	-0.2	1.5
Monaco	38	7	2	1.0	0.4	–	–	–	–	–	–	–	–	–	–	100	1.1	0.9
Mongolia	2,959	968	338	1.2	1.2	15	10	6	44	32	23	55	60	70	2.6	72	2.1	1.7
Montenegro	626	142	37	0.1	-0.1	7	7	10	22	16	11	70	75	76	1.7	64	1.2	0.2
Morocco	34,378	11,121	3,421	1.3	1.0	14	7	6	43	29	20	53	65	74	2.5	60	2.2	1.7
Mozambique	27,978	14,589	4,816	3.0	2.6	25	21	11	48	46	39	39	43	55	5.3	32	3.8	3.5
Myanmar	53,897	17,885	4,565	1.0	0.7	15	10	8	40	27	17	51	59	66	2.2	34	2.3	2.0
Namibia	2,459	1,063	338	2.2	1.9	15	9	7	43	38	29	53	61	65	3.5	47	4.2	3.1
Nauru	10	4	1	0.4	0.3	–	–	–	–	–	–	–	–	–	–	100	0.4	0.5
Nepal	28,514	11,316	2,807	1.7	1.0	23	13	6	43	39	20	41	54	70	2.2	19	4.8	2.9
Netherlands	16,925	3,390	885	0.5	0.3	8	9	9	17	13	10	74	77	82	1.8	90	1.6	0.5
New Zealand	4,529	1,097	309	1.1	0.8	8	8	7	22	17	13	71	75	82	2.0	86	1.3	0.9
Nicaragua	6,082	2,189	606	1.5	1.0	13	7	5	46	36	20	54	64	75	2.2	59	2.1	1.7
Niger	19,899	11,332	4,145	3.7	3.9	28	23	9	56	55	49	36	44	62	7.6	19	4.4	5.7

unicef 70 YEARS FOR EVERY CHILD

TABLE 6. DEMOGRAPHIC INDICATORS

Countries and areas	Population (thousands) 2015			Population annual growth rate (%)		Crude death rate			Crude birth rate			Life expectancy			Total fertility rate	Urbanized population (%)	Average annual growth rate of urban population (%)	
	total	under 18	under 5	1990–2015	2015–2030	1970	1990	2015	1970	1990	2015	1970	1990	2015	2015	2015	1990–2015	2015–2030
Nigeria	182,202	91,855	31,109	2.6	2.4	23	18	13	46	44	39	41	46	53	5.6	48	4.5	4.0
Niue	2	1	0	-1.5	0.2	–	–	–	–	–	–	–	–	–	–	43	-1.1	0.2
Norway	5,211	1,129	315	0.8	0.9	10	11	8	16	14	12	74	76	82	1.8	80	1.2	1.1
Oman	4,491	1,051	385	3.6	1.0	16	5	3	48	38	19	50	67	77	2.7	78	4.0	1.6
Pakistan	188,925	77,779	24,664	2.3	1.7	15	11	7	43	40	29	53	60	66	3.6	39	3.1	2.6
Palau	21	8	2	1.4	1.0	–	–	–	–	–	–	–	–	–	–	87	2.3	1.4
Panama	3,929	1,275	368	1.9	1.3	8	5	5	38	26	19	66	73	78	2.4	67	2.7	1.8
Papua New Guinea	7,619	3,330	996	2.4	1.9	17	10	8	44	35	28	46	56	63	3.7	13	1.9	2.8
Paraguay	6,639	2,412	674	1.8	1.1	7	6	6	37	34	21	65	68	73	2.5	60	2.8	1.9
Peru	31,377	10,417	3,020	1.5	1.1	14	7	6	42	30	20	53	66	75	2.4	79	2.0	1.4
Philippines	100,699	38,277	11,255	1.9	1.4	9	7	7	39	33	23	61	65	68	2.9	44	1.6	1.8
Poland	38,612	6,911	1,994	0.0	-0.2	8	10	10	17	15	10	70	71	78	1.3	61	0.0	0.1
Portugal	10,350	1,782	439	0.2	-0.3	11	10	10	21	11	8	67	74	81	1.3	63	1.4	0.6
Qatar	2,235	406	132	6.2	1.5	5	2	1	36	23	12	68	75	78	2.0	99	6.7	1.1
Republic of Korea	50,293	8,925	2,287	0.6	0.3	9	6	6	32	16	9	61	72	82	1.3	82	1.0	0.5
Republic of Moldova	4,069	777	223	-0.3	-0.4	10	10	11	20	19	11	65	68	72	1.2	45	-1.1	-0.2
Romania	19,511	3,670	924	-0.7	-0.7	10	11	13	21	14	9	68	70	75	1.5	55	-0.2	0.1
Russian Federation	143,457	27,684	9,166	-0.1	-0.2	9	12	14	15	14	13	69	68	70	1.7	74	-0.1	-0.2
Rwanda	11,610	5,532	1,695	1.9	2.0	20	33	7	50	48	31	44	33	65	3.8	29	8.9	4.8
Saint Kitts and Nevis	56	17	5	1.2	0.8	–	–	–	–	–	–	–	–	–	–	32	0.9	1.5
Saint Lucia	185	52	14	1.2	0.6	9	6	7	39	28	15	63	71	75	1.9	19	-0.7	1.1
Saint Vincent and the Grenadines	109	33	9	0.1	0.2	9	7	7	40	25	16	65	70	73	2.0	51	0.9	0.7
Samoa	193	85	24	0.7	0.6	11	7	5	41	33	25	55	65	74	4.0	19	0.3	0.5
San Marino	32	6	1	1.1	0.3	–	–	–	–	–	–	–	–	–	–	94	1.3	0.3
Sao Tome and Principe	190	94	30	2.1	2.0	13	10	7	41	40	34	56	62	67	4.5	65	3.8	2.7
Saudi Arabia	31,540	10,560	3,161	2.6	1.4	15	5	3	47	36	20	53	69	74	2.7	83	2.8	1.4
Senegal	15,129	7,596	2,601	2.8	2.7	25	11	6	50	44	38	39	57	67	5.0	44	3.2	3.5
Serbia	8,851	1,774	451	-0.3	-0.4	9	10	13	19	15	10	68	71	75	1.6	56	0.3	-0.2
Seychelles	96	27	8	1.2	0.3	9	7	8	35	23	17	66	71	73	2.3	54	1.6	0.9
Sierra Leone	6,453	3,166	1,004	2.0	1.9	29	27	13	46	46	35	35	37	51	4.5	40	2.5	2.7
Singapore	5,604	1,081	269	2.5	0.9	5	4	5	23	18	9	68	76	83	1.2	100	2.5	1.1
Slovakia	5,426	984	283	0.1	-0.1	9	10	10	18	15	11	70	71	76	1.4	54	-0.1	0.1
Slovenia	2,068	361	111	0.1	0.0	10	10	10	17	11	10	69	73	81	1.6	50	0.1	0.3
Solomon Islands	584	269	82	2.5	1.7	13	11	6	45	40	29	54	57	68	3.9	22	4.5	3.4
Somalia	10,787	5,787	1,971	2.1	2.8	23	20	12	46	48	43	41	45	56	6.4	40	3.4	4.0
South Africa	54,490	19,084	5,370	1.6	0.6	14	8	12	38	29	20	53	62	58	2.3	65	2.4	1.2
South Sudan	12,340	6,028	1,956	3.0	2.4	28	21	11	51	47	36	36	44	56	4.9	19	4.4	3.9
Spain	46,122	8,119	2,144	0.7	0.0	9	8	9	20	10	9	72	77	83	1.3	80	1.0	0.4
Sri Lanka	20,715	6,051	1,643	0.7	0.3	8	6	7	31	21	16	64	70	75	2.1	18	0.8	1.4
State of Palestine	4,668	2,200	703	3.2	2.5	13	5	4	50	46	32	56	68	73	4.1	75	3.5	2.6
Sudan	40,235	18,954	5,952	2.8	2.3	15	12	8	47	42	33	52	56	64	4.3	34	3.4	3.1
Suriname	543	175	48	1.1	0.7	9	7	7	37	28	18	63	67	71	2.3	66	1.2	0.7
Swaziland	1,287	569	173	1.6	1.1	18	10	14	49	43	29	48	59	49	3.2	21	1.3	1.6
Sweden	9,779	1,977	590	0.5	0.6	10	11	9	14	14	12	74	78	82	1.9	86	0.6	0.8
Switzerland	8,299	1,479	423	0.9	0.7	9	9	8	16	12	10	73	78	83	1.5	74	0.9	1.1
Syrian Arab Republic	18,502	8,206	2,192	1.6	2.9	11	5	6	46	36	23	59	70	70	2.9	58	3.0	2.7
Tajikistan	8,482	3,475	1,176	1.9	1.8	12	10	6	41	40	30	60	63	70	3.5	27	1.3	2.7
Thailand	67,959	14,656	3,799	0.7	0.0	10	6	8	38	19	11	59	70	75	1.5	50	2.9	1.6
The former Yugoslav Republic of Macedonia	2,078	433	115	0.2	0.0	7	7	9	25	18	11	66	71	76	1.5	57	0.1	0.3
Timor-Leste	1,185	581	204	1.9	1.9	23	16	7	42	43	37	40	48	69	5.6	33	3.6	3.4
Togo	7,305	3,553	1,160	2.6	2.4	19	12	9	48	43	35	47	56	60	4.5	40	3.9	3.4
Tonga	106	46	13	0.4	0.9	7	6	6	36	31	24	65	70	73	3.7	24	0.6	1.5
Trinidad and Tobago	1,360	334	96	0.4	0.1	7	8	10	27	21	14	65	68	71	1.8	8	0.3	-0.4
Tunisia	11,254	3,115	982	1.3	0.8	16	6	7	41	26	18	51	69	75	2.1	67	1.9	1.1
Turkey	78,666	24,240	6,821	1.5	0.7	15	8	6	40	26	16	52	64	76	2.1	73	2.3	1.3
Turkmenistan	5,374	1,791	528	1.5	0.9	12	9	8	37	35	21	58	63	66	2.3	50	1.9	1.7
Tuvalu	10	4	1	0.4	0.5	–	–	–	–	–	–	–	–	–	–	60	1.9	1.6
Uganda	39,032	21,473	7,278	3.2	3.1	17	19	9	49	50	43	49	45	59	5.7	16	4.8	5.1
Ukraine	44,824	7,897	2,461	-0.5	-0.6	9	13	15	15	12	11	71	70	71	1.5	70	-0.4	-0.4
United Arab Emirates	9,157	1,510	491	6.5	1.2	7	3	2	37	26	11	62	71	77	1.8	86	7.0	1.9
United Kingdom	64,716	13,715	4,058	0.5	0.5	12	11	9	15	14	13	72	76	81	1.9	83	0.7	0.7
United Republic of Tanzania	53,470	27,611	9,398	3.0	2.9	18	15	7	48	44	39	47	50	66	5.1	32	4.9	4.7

TABLE 6. DEMOGRAPHIC INDICATORS

Countries and areas	Population (thousands) 2015			Population annual growth rate (%)		Crude death rate			Crude birth rate			Life expectancy			Total fertility rate	Urbanized population (%)	Average annual growth rate of urban population (%)	
	total	under 18	under 5	1990–2015	2015–2030ᵃ	1970	1990	2015	1970	1990	2015	1970	1990	2015	2015	2015	1990–2015	2015–2030ᵃ
United States	321,774	73,169	19,701	1.0	0.7	10	9	8	17	16	12	71	75	79	1.9	82	1.3	0.9
Uruguay	3,432	889	241	0.4	0.3	10	10	9	21	18	14	69	73	77	2.0	95	0.7	0.4
Uzbekistan	29,893	10,081	3,195	1.5	0.9	10	7	7	33	34	22	63	67	69	2.4	36	1.1	1.7
Vanuatu	265	113	35	2.4	1.9	14	8	5	42	36	26	52	63	72	3.3	26	3.7	3.0
Venezuela (Bolivarian Republic of)	31,108	10,418	2,960	1.8	1.1	7	5	6	37	29	19	65	70	74	2.3	89	2.1	1.2
Viet Nam	93,448	25,578	7,741	1.3	0.8	12	6	6	36	29	17	60	71	76	2.0	34	3.2	2.2
Yemen	26,832	12,629	3,925	3.2	2.0	25	12	7	53	52	32	41	58	64	4.0	35	5.1	3.4
Zambia	16,212	8,535	2,851	2.8	3.0	17	19	9	50	46	40	49	44	61	5.3	41	2.9	4.3
Zimbabwe	15,603	7,504	2,505	1.6	2.1	13	9	9	48	37	35	55	60	59	3.9	32	1.9	2.3
SUMMARY																		
Sub-Saharan Africa	1,001,417	496,043	163,267	2.7	2.5	21	16	10	47	44	37	44	50	59	4.9	37	4.0	3.6
Eastern and Southern Africa	480,144	233,503	75,181	2.6	2.4	19	16	9	47	43	35	46	50	61	4.5	31	3.7	3.6
West and Central Africa	480,150	243,243	82,032	2.8	2.6	22	17	11	47	45	39	42	49	57	5.4	44	4.2	3.7
Middle East and North Africa	455,880	165,800	53,283	2.1	1.6	15	8	5	44	34	24	53	65	72	2.9	60	2.7	1.9
South Asia	1,743,865	621,390	173,210	1.7	1.1	17	11	7	40	33	21	48	58	68	2.5	32	2.8	2.3
East Asia and Pacific	2,097,940	504,114	146,650	0.9	0.4	11	7	7	37	24	14	58	68	74	1.8	54	3.3	1.7
Latin America and Caribbean	628,992	195,496	53,155	1.4	0.9	10	7	6	37	27	17	60	68	75	2.1	79	1.9	1.1
CEE/CIS	413,760	98,592	30,726	0.2	0.1	10	11	11	20	18	15	66	68	72	1.9	65	0.3	0.4
Least developed countries	954,158	444,297	139,575	2.5	2.2	21	15	8	47	42	32	44	52	64	4.1	31	4.0	3.6
World	**7,309,846**	**2,262,157**	**668,970**	**1.3**	**1.0**	**13**	**9**	**8**	**33**	**26**	**19**	**59**	**65**	**72**	**2.5**	**54**	**2.2**	**1.6**

For a complete list of countries and areas in the regions, subregions and country categories, see page 112 or visit <data.unicef.org/regionalclassifications>.
It is not advisable to compare data from consecutive editions of *The State of the World's Children*.

DEFINITIONS OF THE INDICATORS

Crude death rate – Annual number of deaths per 1,000 population.

Crude birth rate – Annual number of births per 1,000 population.

Life expectancy– Number of years newborn children would live if subject to the mortality risks prevailing for the cross section of population at the time of their birth.

Total fertility rate – Number of children who would be born per woman if she lived to the end of her childbearing years and bore children at each age in accordance with prevailing age-specific fertility rates.

Urbanized population – Percentage of population living in urban areas as defined according to the national definition used in the most recent population census.

MAIN DATA SOURCES

Population – United Nations Population Division. Growth rates calculated by UNICEF based on data from United Nations Population Division.

Crude death and birth rates – United Nations Population Division.

Life expectancy – United Nations Population Division.

Total fertility rate – United Nations Population Division.

NOTES

– Data not available.

ɑ Based on medium-fertility variant projections.

TABLE 7. ECONOMIC INDICATORS

Countries and areas	GNI per capita (US$) US$ 2014	GNI per capita (US$) PPP US$ 2014	GDP per capita average annual growth rate (%) 1970–1990	GDP per capita average annual growth rate (%) 1990–2014	Average annual rate of inflation (%) 1990–2014	Population below international poverty line of US$1.90 per day (%) 2009–2013*	National monetary child poverty (%) 2010–2014*	Public spending as a % of GDP (2009–2013*) allocated to: health	education	military	ODA inflow in millions US$ 2014	ODA inflow as a % of recipient GNI 2014	Debt service as a % of exports of goods and services 2013	Share of household income (%, 2009–2013*) poorest 40%	richest 20%
Afghanistan	680	2,000 e	–	5.6 x	8 x	–	–	2	5	1	4,823	23	0	–	–
Albania	4,450	10,180	-0.6 x	5.7	11	1	–	3	–	1	280	2	6	22	38
Algeria	5,490	13,880	1.8	1.7	11	–	–	5	–	5	158	0	1	–	–
Andorra	43,270 x	–	-1.3	1.2 x	4 x	–	–	6	2	–	–	–	–	–	–
Angola	c	6,340 x	–	-0.4 x	–	30 x	–	2	3	4	231	–	7	15 x	49 x
Antigua and Barbuda	13,300	21,370	7.9 x	1.2	3	–	–	3	3	–	2	0	–	–	–
Argentina	13,480	–	-0.8	2.3	11	2	–	5	5	1	49	0	–	15	47
Armenia	4,020	8,450	–	6.2	37	2	37	2	2	4	265	2	32	21	40
Australia	64,540	42,760	1.6	2.0	3	–	–	6	5	2	–	–	–	19	42
Austria	49,670	45,930	2.5	1.6	2	–	–	8	6	1	–	–	–	21	38
Azerbaijan	7,590	16,910	–	6.4	40	0 x	5	1	2	5	215	0	6	30 x	30 x
Bahamas	20,980	22,290	1.9	0.1	3	–	–	3	–	–	–	–	–	–	–
Bahrain	21,060 x	37,680 x	-1.0 x	0.1	5	–	–	3	3	4	–	–	–	–	–
Bangladesh	1,080	3,330	0.7	3.6	6	44	–	1	2	1	2,418	1	3	21	41
Barbados	15,310 x	15,190 x	1.4 x	1.2	3	–	–	4	6	–	–	–	–	–	–
Belarus	7,340	17,610	–	5.0	94	0	9	4	5	1	120	0	6	24	36
Belgium	47,260	43,220	2.2	1.4	2	–	–	8	6	1	–	–	–	23	36
Belize	4,350 x	7,590 x	3.1	1.7	1	–	–	4	7	1	36	–	12	–	–
Benin	890	2,020	0.4	1.1	5	53	–	2	5	1	600	6	–	16	51
Bhutan	2,370	7,280	7.0 x	5.3	6	2	–	3	6	–	130	7	11	18	46
Bolivia (Plurinational State of)	2,870	6,290	-1.0	2.0	7	8	–	4	6	1	672	2	4	12	52
Bosnia and Herzegovina	4,760	10,010	–	7.4 x	5 x	0 x	–	7	–	1	632	3	10	20 x	41 x
Botswana	7,240	16,030	8.1	2.7	9	18	26 y	4	9	3	100	1	2	9	65
Brazil	11,530	15,590	2.2	1.8	39	5	–	5	6	1	912	0	28	11	57
Brunei Darussalam	37,320 x	72,190 x	-2.2 x	-0.4	5	–	–	2	3	2	–	–	–	–	–
Bulgaria	7,620	16,260	3.4 x	3.5	30	2	28	4	4	1	–	–	13	18	43
Burkina Faso	700	1,600	1.4	2.9	3	55	–	4	4	1	1,120	9	–	17	47
Burundi	270	770	1.2	-1.5	14	78 x	55 y	4	5	2	502	16	8	21 x	43 x
Cabo Verde	3,450	6,200	3.5 x	6.3	1	18 x	–	3	5	1	230	13	4	14 x	53 x
Cambodia	1,020	3,080	–	5.9 x	4 x	6	–	1	3	2	799	5	1	22	40
Cameroon	1,350	2,950	3.4	0.6	4	29 x	–	2	3	1	852	3	3	15 x	49 x
Canada	51,630	43,360	2.0	1.6	2	–	–	8	5	1	–	–	–	20	41
Central African Republic	320	600	-1.3	-0.6	3	66 x	–	2	1	3	610	35	–	10 x	61 x
Chad	980	2,070	-0.9	3.3	6	38	–	2	2	5	388	3	–	15	49
Chile	14,910	21,580	1.5	3.3	6	1	23	3	5	2	241	0	–	13	57
China	7,400	13,170	6.6	9.2	5	11	–	3	–	2	-960	0	1	14	47
Colombia	7,970	12,910	1.9	2.1	12	6	–	5	5	3	1,221	0	13	11	58
Comoros	790	1,430	-0.2 x	-0.2	3	14 x	–	2	–	–	74	12	–	11 x	61 x
Congo	2,720	5,200	3.3	0.6	8	29	54 x	1	6	2	106	1	–	16	46
Cook Islands	–	–	–	–	–	–	–	–	–	–	–	–	–	–	–
Costa Rica	10,120	14,420	0.8	2.9	11	2	–	7	7	–	54	0	20	12	54
Côte d'Ivoire	1,450	3,130	-1.7	-0.5	5	29 x	–	2	–	2	922	3	9	15 x	49 x
Croatia	12,980	20,500	–	2.6 x	4 x	1	21	6	4	2	–	–	–	20	39
Cuba	5,880 x	18,630 x	3.9	3.3 x	4 x	–	–	10	13	3	262	–	–	–	–
Cyprus	26,370	29,800	5.9 x	1.5	3	–	–	4	7	2	–	–	–	20	43
Czech Republic	18,370	28,020	–	2.5	5	0	–	6	4	1	–	–	–	24	36
Democratic People's Republic of Korea	a	–	–	–	–	–	–	–	–	–	153	–	–	–	–
Democratic Republic of the Congo	380	650	-2.1	-1.9	165	77	–	2	2	1	2,398	8	3	16	48
Denmark	61,310	46,210	2.0	1.2	2	–	–	9	9	1	–	–	–	23	38
Djibouti	b	–	–	0.4	3	18	–	5	4	–	163	–	8	14	50
Dominica	6,930	10,480	5.2 x	2.0	3	–	–	4	–	–	16	3	8	–	–
Dominican Republic	6,040	12,600	2.1	3.7	10	2	–	3	4	1	167	0	12	14	53
Ecuador	6,090	11,190	1.7	1.5	5	4	–	3	4	3	160	0	10	13	53
Egypt	3,050	10,260	4.1	2.6	8	–	29	2	–	2	3,532	1	5	22 x	40 x
El Salvador	3,920	8,000	-1.9	2.2	4	3	44	4	3	1	98	0	10	15	50
Equatorial Guinea	10,210	17,660	-2.4 x	19.0	7	–	–	4	–	4	1	0	–	–	–
Eritrea	480 x	1,400 x,e	–	-0.2 x	13 x	–	–	1	–	–	83	–	–	–	–
Estonia	19,030	26,330	–	4.7 x	6 x	1	–	5	5	2	–	–	–	20	41
Ethiopia	550	1,500	–	3.8	8	34	–	3	5	1	3,585	6	–	21	42
Fiji	4,870	8,410	0.6	1.1	4	4 x	–	3	4	2	92	2	2	16 x	50 x
Finland	48,420	39,940	2.9	2.1	2	–	–	7	7	1	–	–	–	23	37
France	42,960	39,610	2.2	1.2	2	–	–	9	6	2	–	–	–	20	41

TABLE 7. ECONOMIC INDICATORS

Countries and areas	GNI per capita (US$) US$ 2014	GNI per capita (US$) PPP US$ 2014	GDP per capita average annual growth rate (%) 1970–1990	GDP per capita average annual growth rate (%) 1990–2014	Average annual rate of inflation (%) 1990–2014	Population below international poverty line of US$1.90 per day (%) 2009–2013*	National monetary child poverty (%) 2010–2014*	Public spending as a % of GDP (2009–2013*) allocated to: health	education	military	ODA inflow in millions US$ 2014	ODA inflow as a % of recipient GNI 2014	Debt service as a % of exports of goods and services 2013	Share of household income (%, 2009–2013*) poorest 40%	richest 20%
Gabon	9,720	17,200	0.6	-0.7	6	8 x	–	2	–	1	111	1	–	16 x	49 x
Gambia	500 x	1,600 x	0.7	0.3 x	6 x	45 x	–	4	4	1	100	–	–	14 x	53 x
Georgia	3,720	7,510	3.1	3.3	52	12	27 y	2	2	3	563	3	13	16	46
Germany	47,640	46,850	2.3	1.3	1	–	–	9	5	1	–	–	–	22	39
Ghana	1,590	3,900	-2.0	2.9	25	25 x	–	4	8	1	1,126	3	5	15 x	49 x
Greece	22,680 x	25,660 x	1.3	1.4	4	–	–	7	–	3	–	–	–	17	42
Grenada	7,910	11,720	4.2 x	2.4	4	–	–	3	–	–	39	5	14	–	–
Guatemala	3,430	7,250	0.1	1.3	6	12	68	2	3	0	277	0	16	12	57
Guinea	470	1,130	–	0.6	11	35	–	2	4	3	561	9	4	20	42
Guinea-Bissau	550	1,380	0.8	-0.9	14	67	–	2	–	2	109	11	–	13	57
Guyana	3,940 x	6,940 x,e	-1.5	2.9 x	10 x	–	–	4	3	1	159	5	2	–	–
Haiti	820	1,730	–	-0.6 x	12 x	54	–	1	–	–	1,084	12	0	8	64
Holy See	–	–	–	–	–	–	–	–	–	–	–	–	–	–	–
Honduras	2,270	4,570	0.8	1.7	11	19	–	4	6	1	604	3	10	10	58
Hungary	13,340	23,630	–	2.5 x	9 x	0	–	5	5	1	–	–	–	21	39
Iceland	46,350 x	41,090 x	3.2	2.1	5	–	–	7	7	0	–	–	–	23	36
India	1,570	5,630	2.0	5.0	6	21	–	1	4	3	2,984	0	7	20	44
Indonesia	3,630	10,190	4.5	2.9	14	16	17 x	1	4	1	-388	0	19	19	44
Iran (Islamic Republic of)	7,120 x	16,590 x	-4.3	2.4	21	0	–	3	4	2	81	–	–	18	45
Iraq	6,500	15,030	4.2	3.7	30	–	–	3	–	3	1,370	1	–	22	39
Ireland	46,550	42,270	2.8	3.8	3	–	–	6	6	1	–	–	–	20	41
Israel	35,320	32,830	1.9	2.4	4	–	–	4	6	6	–	–	–	14	47
Italy	34,270	34,700	2.8	0.6	3	–	–	7	4	2	–	–	–	19	42
Jamaica	5,150	8,640	-1.3	0.4	14	2 x	–	3	6	1	92	1	14	15 x	52 x
Japan	42,000	37,920	3.4	0.7	-1	–	–	8	4	1	–	–	–	20 x	40 x
Jordan	5,160	11,910	2.5 x	2.6	4	0	19	5	–	4	2,699	8	4	20	42
Kazakhstan	11,850	21,710	–	4.3	45	0	–	3	3	1	88	0	34	24	36
Kenya	1,290	2,940	1.2	0.8	10	34 x	–	2	6	2	2,665	4	5	13 x	54 x
Kiribati	2,950	3,340 e	-5.0	1.0	3	14 x	–	8	–	–	79	26	–	18 x	44 x
Kuwait	49,300	79,850	-6.7 x	0.0 x	6 x	–	–	2	–	3	–	–	–	–	–
Kyrgyzstan	1,250	3,220	–	1.1	30	3	46 y	4	7	3	624	9	7	24	37
Lao People's Democratic Republic	1,660	5,060	–	4.9	18	30	–	1	3	0	472	4	11	18	46
Latvia	15,280	22,690	–	5.7 x	6 x	1	–	4	5	1	–	–	–	19	42
Lebanon	10,030	17,590 e	–	2.1	6	–	–	4	3	4	820	2	12	–	–
Lesotho	1,330	3,150	3.0	2.7	8	60	–	9	–	2	104	4	3	10	58
Liberia	370	700	-4.1	2.4	4	69 x	–	3	3	1	744	44	0	18 x	44 x
Libya	7,820	16,000 e	–	-1.4 x	11 x	–	–	3	–	4	210	0	–	–	–
Liechtenstein	d	–	2.2	2.9 x	1 x	–	–	–	3	–	–	–	–	–	–
Lithuania	15,430	25,490	–	5.8 x	3 x	1	–	5	5	3	–	–	–	19	42
Luxembourg	75,990	65,040	2.6	2.2	3	–	–	6	–	0	–	–	–	19	42
Madagascar	440	1,400	-2.4	-0.3	12	82	–	3	2	1	583	6	2	17	48
Malawi	250	790	0.0	1.4	24	71	–	4	8	2	930	23	–	15	52
Malaysia	11,120	24,770	4.0	3.2	4	0	–	2	6	2	12	0	4	13	51
Maldives	6,410	10,920	–	4.1 x	6 x	6	–	6	6	–	25	1	2	18	44
Mali	650	1,510	1.4	1.5	5	49	–	2	4	1	1,234	11	2	20	41
Malta	21,000 x	27,020 x	6.0	2.2 x	3 x	–	–	6	7	1	–	–	–	–	–
Marshall Islands	4,390	4,700 e	–	0.7	2	–	–	14	–	–	56	24	–	–	–
Mauritania	1,270	3,710	-1.1	1.2	9	11 x	–	2	4	3	257	5	5	17 x	44 x
Mauritius	9,630	18,150	3.1 x	3.6	6	1	–	2	4	0	49	0	41	19	44
Mexico	9,870	16,640	1.7	1.1	10	3	54	3	5	1	807	0	8	14	54
Micronesia (Federated States of)	3,200	3,590 e	–	0.6	2	50 x	–	11	–	–	116	34	–	7 x	64 x
Monaco	d	–	1.5	1.7 x	2 x	–	–	4	1	–	–	–	–	–	–
Mongolia	4,280	11,120	–	4.1	23	0	–	4	5	1	315	3	24	20	42
Montenegro	7,320	14,530	–	2.8 x	6 x	2	13 y	4	–	1	102	2	16	20	41
Morocco	3,070	7,290	2.6	2.8	2	3 x	11 x	2	6	4	2,247	2	13	17 x	48 x
Mozambique	600	1,120	-1.1 x	5.1	13	69 x	–	3	7	1	2,103	13	2	15 x	51 x
Myanmar	1,270	–	1.4	11.8 x	15 x	–	–	0	–	4	1,380	2	1	–	–
Namibia	5,630	9,810	-2.1 x	2.2	8	23	34 y	5	8	4	227	2	–	9	66
Nauru	–	–	–	–	–	–	–	–	–	–	–	–	–	–	–
Nepal	730	2,410	1.2	2.6	8	15	–	3	4	2	880	4	3	20	41
Netherlands	51,890	48,260	1.5	1.7	2	–	–	10	6	1	–	–	–	23	37
New Zealand	41,070	34,970	1.5 x	1.7	2	–	–	8	7	1	–	–	–	–	–

unicef 70 YEARS FOR EVERY CHILD

TABLE 7. ECONOMIC INDICATORS

Countries and areas	GNI per capita (US$) US$ 2014	GNI per capita (US$) PPP US$ 2014	GDP per capita average annual growth rate (%) 1970–1990	GDP per capita average annual growth rate (%) 1990–2014	Average annual rate of inflation (%) 1990–2014	Population below international poverty line of US$1.90 per day (%) 2009–2013*	National monetary child poverty (%) 2010–2014*	Public spending as a % of GDP (2009–2013*) allocated to: health	education	military	ODA inflow in millions US$ 2014	ODA inflow as a % of recipient GNI 2014	Debt service as a % of exports of goods and services 2013	Share of household income (%, 2009–2013*) poorest 40%	richest 20%
Nicaragua	1,870	4,790	-3.7	2.1	16	11	–	4	4	1	430	4	11	14	51
Niger	410	910	-1.9	0.0	4	50	63 x	2	5	1	918	12	–	22	41
Nigeria	2,970	5,710	-2.3	3.4	19	54	–	1	–	0	2,476	0	–	15	49
Niue	–	–	–	–	–	–	–	–	–	–	–	–	–	–	–
Norway	103,630	66,330	3.3	1.6	4	–	–	8	7	1	–	–	–	24	35
Oman	16,870 x	33,690 x	3.2	0.6	6	–	–	2	4	9	–	–	–	–	–
Pakistan	1,400	5,090	2.7	1.7	11	8	–	1	2	3	3,612	1	9	23	40
Palau	11,110	14,280 e	–	-0.4 x	4 x	–	–	8	–	–	23	10	–	–	–
Panama	11,130	19,930	0.2	3.8	3	3	–	5	3	–	-196	0	6	11	56
Papua New Guinea	2,240	2,790 e	-1.0	0.9	7	39	–	4	–	1	577	3	–	14	49
Paraguay	4,400	8,470	3.8	0.9	10	2	–	4	5	1	60	0	12	13	53
Peru	6,360	11,440	-0.5	3.4	8	4	–	3	3	1	325	0	13	14	50
Philippines	3,500	8,450	0.6	2.3	6	13	–	2	3	1	676	0	6	15	50
Poland	13,690	23,930	–	4.2	8	0	–	5	5	2	–	–	–	20	41
Portugal	21,360	28,010	2.5	1.2	3	–	–	7	5	2	–	–	–	19	43
Qatar	92,200	134,420	–	1.5 x	8 x	–	–	2	–	1	–	–	–	–	–
Republic of Korea	27,090	34,620	7.5	4.3	3	–	–	4	5	3	–	–	–	–	–
Republic of Moldova	2,560	5,500	1.8 x	0.8	32	0	13 y	5	8	0	517	6	12	23	38
Romania	9,520	19,020	–	3.4	36	0	32	4	3	1	–	–	27	23	36
Russian Federation	13,220	24,710	–	2.5	43	0	–	3	–	4	–	–	–	16	48
Rwanda	700	1,630	1.1	3.3	9	60	47 y	7	5	1	1,034	13	3	13	58
Saint Kitts and Nevis	14,920	22,600	6.5 x	1.8	3	–	–	2	–	–	–	–	–	–	–
Saint Lucia	7,260	10,540	5.1 x	1.2	3	–	–	5	5	–	18	1	5	–	–
Saint Vincent and the Grenadines	6,610	10,730	3.3	2.9	2	–	–	4	5	–	9	1	14	–	–
Samoa	4,060	5,610 e	–	2.5	5	1 x	–	7	–	–	93	12	4	16 x	50 x
San Marino	d	–	1.8	3.4 x	3 x	–	–	5	2	–	–	–	–	–	–
Sao Tome and Principe	1,670	3,140	–	3.0 x	14 x	34	–	3	9	–	39	12	7	21	40
Saudi Arabia	25,140 x	51,320 x	-2.1	1.4	5	–	–	2	–	9	–	–	–	–	–
Senegal	1,050	2,300	-0.6	1.1	3	38	49	2	6	2	1,107	7	–	17	47
Serbia	5,820	12,150	–	3.7 x	20 x	0	30	6	4	2	371	1	33	22	38
Seychelles	14,100	24,780	2.9	2.1	7	0 x	–	3	4	1	10	1	–	16 x	49 x
Sierra Leone	700	1,770	-0.6	1.4	18	52	–	2	3	1	911	21	1	20	42
Singapore	55,150	80,270	5.9	3.5	1	–	–	2	3	3	–	–	–	–	–
Slovakia	17,750	26,820	–	4.2 x	4 x	0	–	6	4	1	–	–	–	23	35
Slovenia	23,580	29,920	–	2.5 x	4 x	0	–	7	6	1	–	–	–	24	35
Solomon Islands	1,830	2,020 e	–	-0.4	7	46 x	–	7	10	–	199	18	7	14 x	52 x
Somalia	a	–	-0.8	–	–	–	–	–	–	0	1,109	21	–	–	–
South Africa	6,800	12,700	0.1	1.2	8	17	56	4	6	1	1,070	0	7	7	69
South Sudan	970	1,800 e	–	–	–	–	–	1	–	7	1,964	17	–	–	–
Spain	29,440	33,080	1.9	1.5	3	–	–	7	4	1	–	–	–	18	42
Sri Lanka	3,460	10,370	3.0	4.4	10	2	–	1	2	2	488	1	7	18	47
State of Palestine	3,060	5,000	–	1.8 x	3 x	0	–	–	–	–	2,487	18	–	20	43
Sudan	1,710	3,920	-0.1	3.5	24	15	–	2	2	–	872	1	4	19	42
Suriname	9,950	17,040	-2.3 x	2.2	37	–	–	3	–	–	13	0	–	–	–
Swaziland	3,550	7,880	3.1	1.0	9	42	–	5	8	2	86	2	1	12	57
Sweden	61,610	46,750	1.8	2.0	2	–	–	8	6	1	–	–	–	23	36
Switzerland	88,120 x	57,960 x	1.7 x	1.0	1	–	–	8	5	1	–	–	–	21	40
Syrian Arab Republic	b	–	2.1	1.8 x	7 x	–	–	2	5	–	4,198	–	–	19 x	44 x
Tajikistan	1,080	2,660	–	0.9	59	5	–	2	4	1	356	4	8	21	39
Thailand	5,780	14,870	4.8	3.1	3	0	–	4	5	1	351	0	4	17	46
The former Yugoslav Republic of Macedonia	5,150	12,800	–	1.8	18	1 x	32	4	–	1	211	2	17	15 x	50 x
Timor-Leste	2,680	5,080 e	–	3.4 x	5 x	47 x	–	1	9	2	247	8	–	22 x	41 x
Togo	570	1,290	-0.5	0.1	4	54	–	4	4	2	208	5	–	14	52
Tonga	4,260	5,270 e	–	1.3	6	1	–	4	–	–	80	18	–	18	45
Trinidad and Tobago	20,070	31,970	-0.5	5.1	5	–	–	3	–	1	–	–	–	–	–
Tunisia	4,230	11,020	2.5	3.0	4	2	–	4	6	2	921	2	10	18	43
Turkey	10,830	18,980	1.9	2.5	37	0	33	4	–	2	3,442	0	26	16	47
Turkmenistan	8,020	14,520 e	–	3.5	74	–	–	1	3	–	34	0	–	–	–
Tuvalu	5,720	5,410 e	–	1.6	4	–	–	20	–	–	34	63	–	–	–
Uganda	670	1,720	–	3.6	8	33	22	4	2	1	1,633	6	1	16	49
Ukraine	3,560	8,560	–	1.0	54	0	–	4	7	2	1,404	1	34	25	35
United Arab Emirates	44,600	67,720	-4.3 x	-2.9	5	–	–	2	–	6	–	–	–	–	–

unicef ⊛ 70 YEARS FOR EVERY CHILD

TABLE 7. ECONOMIC INDICATORS

Countries and areas	GNI per capita (US$) US$ 2014	GNI per capita (US$) PPP US$ 2014	GDP per capita average annual growth rate (%) 1970–1990	GDP per capita average annual growth rate (%) 1990–2014	Average annual rate of inflation (%) 1990–2014	Population below international poverty line of US$1.90 per day (%) 2009–2013*	National monetary child poverty (%) 2010–2014*	Public spending as a % of GDP (2009–2013*) allocated to: health	Public spending education	Public spending military	ODA inflow in millions US$ 2014	ODA inflow as a % of recipient GNI 2014	Debt service as a % of exports of goods and services 2013	Share of household income (%, 2009–2013*) poorest 40%	Share of household income (%, 2009–2013*) richest 20%
United Kingdom	43,430	39,040	2.2	1.8	2	–	–	8	6	2	–	–	–	20	40
United Republic of Tanzania	920	2,510	–	2.5	14	47	–	3	5	1	2,648	6	2	19	46
United States	55,200	55,860	2.2	1.6	2	–	–	8	5	5	–	–	–	15	46
Uruguay	16,350	20,220	0.9	2.5	14	0	–	5	4	2	89	0	–	15	48
Uzbekistan	2,090	5,830 e	–	3.2	64	67 x	–	3	–	–	324	0	–	19 x	43 x
Vanuatu	3,160	3,030 e	1.1 x	0.6	3	15	–	3	5	–	98	12	1	18	44
Venezuela (Bolivarian Republic of)	12,500 x	17,700 x	-1.2	0.6	31 x	9 x	–	2	7	1	41	–	–	12 x	51 x
Viet Nam	1,890	5,350	–	5.5	11	3	–	3	6	2	4,218	2	3	17	46
Yemen	1,300 x	3,650 x	–	0.7 x	15 x	–	–	1	–	5	1,164	–	2	20 x	44 x
Zambia	1,680	3,690	-2.4	2.4	24	64	65 y	3	–	1	995	4	3	11	61
Zimbabwe	840	1,650	-0.4	-2.8	3	–	78	–	2	1	758	6	–	–	–

SUMMARY

Countries and areas	GNI per capita US$ 2014	GNI per capita PPP US$ 2014	GDP 1970–1990	GDP 1990–2014	Inflation 1990–2014	Poverty 2009–2013*	Child poverty 2010–2014*	health	education	military	ODA US$ 2014	ODA % GNI 2014	Debt service 2013	poorest 40%	richest 20%
Sub-Saharan Africa	1,661	3,416	-0.1	2.4	17	47	–	3	5	2	40,706	2	6	16	49
Eastern and Southern Africa	1,610	3,383	0.3	1.7	10	41	–	3	5	2	22,543	3	7	16	51
West and Central Africa	1,703	3,405	-0.7	2.8	22	56	–	–	–	–	17,129	2	–	16	48
Middle East and North Africa	6,561	14,047	0.8	1.4	11	–	–	–	–	–	20,921	1	6	–	–
South Asia	1,500	5,297	2.0	4.6	7	22	–	1	4	2	15,360	1	7	20	43
East Asia and Pacific	6,845	12,983	6.0	7.7	5	11	–	3 **	4 **	2 **	8,723	0	3	15	47
Latin America and Caribbean	9,634	14,247	1.4	1.8	22	5	–	4	6	1	7,739	0	15	12	55
CEE/CIS	9,216	17,627	–	2.8	43	0	–	–	–	–	9,549	1	24	19	44
Least developed countries	845	2,133	0.0	3.1	19	45	–	2	3	2	43,726	5	4	18	45
World	**10,647**	**14,633**	**2.5**	**2.9**	**7**	**18**	**–**	**7 ****	**5 ****	**2 ****	**101,963**	**0**	**8**	**17**	**46**

For a complete list of countries and areas in the regions, subregions and country categories, see page 112 or visit <data.unicef.org/regionalclassifications>.
It is not advisable to compare data from consecutive editions of *The State of the World's Children*.

DEFINITIONS OF THE INDICATORS

GNI per capita – Gross national income (GNI) is the sum of value added by all resident producers plus any product taxes (less subsidies) not included in the valuation of output plus net receipts of primary income (compensation of employees and property income) from abroad. Gross national income per capita is GNI divided by midyear population. GNI per capita in US dollars is converted using the World Bank Atlas method.

GNI per capita (PPP US$) – GNI per capita converted to international dollars taking into account differences in price levels (purchasing power) between countries. Based on data from the International Comparison Programme.

GDP per capita – Gross domestic product (GDP) is the sum of value added by all resident producers plus any product taxes (less subsidies) not included in the valuation of output. Gross domestic product per capita is GDP divided by midyear population. Growth is calculated from constant price GDP data in local currency.

Population below international poverty line of US$1.90 per day – Poverty headcount ratio at $1.90 a day is the percentage of the population living on less than $1.90 a day at 2011 international prices. As a result of revisions in PPP exchange rates, poverty rates for individual countries cannot be compared with poverty rates reported in earlier editions.

National monetary child poverty – Percentage of children aged 0–17 years old living in households with income or consumption below the government defined national monetary poverty threshold.

ODA – Net official development assistance.

Debt service – Sum of interest payments and repayments of principal on external public and publicly guaranteed long-term debts.

Share of household income – Percentage of income received by the 20 per cent of households with the highest income and by the 40 per cent of households with the lowest income.

MAIN DATA SOURCES

GNI per capita – The World Bank.

GDP per capita – The World Bank.

Rate of inflation – The World Bank.

Population below international poverty line of US$1.90 per day – The World Bank.

National monetary child poverty – Data are compiled from official national government sources such as Statistical Office tabulations and national household survey and poverty reports, and from official regional databases such as those compiled by Eurostat. National estimates are based on representative household income or expenditure surveys.

Spending on health, education and military – The World Bank.

ODA – Organisation for Economic Co-operation and Development.

Debt service – The World Bank.

Share of household income – The World Bank.

NOTES

a low-income country (GNI per capita is $1,045 or less).

b lower-middle-income country (GNI per capita is $1,046 to $4,125).

c upper-middle-income country (GNI per capita is $4,126 to $12,735).

d high-income country (GNI per capita is $12,736 or more).

– Data not available.

x Data refer to years or periods other than those specified in the column heading. Such data are not included in the calculation of regional and global averages.

y Data differ from the standard definition or refer to only part of a country. If they fall within the reference period, such data are included in the calculation of regional and global averages.

e Estimate is based on regression; other PPP figures are extrapolated from the 2011 International Comparison Programme benchmark estimates.

* Data refer to the most recent year available during the period specified in the column heading.

** Excludes China.

TABLE 8. WOMEN

Countries and areas	Life expectancy: females as a % of males 2015	Adult literacy rate: females as a % of males 2009–2014*	Enrolment ratios: females as a % of males — Primary GER 2010–2014*	Secondary GER 2010–2014*	Survival rate to the last grade of primary: females as a % of males 2010–2014*	Contraceptive prevalence (%) 2010–2015*	Antenatal care (%) — At least one visit 2010–2015*	At least four visits 2010–2015*	Delivery care (%) — Skilled attendant at birth 2010–2015*	Institutional delivery 2010–2015*	C-section 2010–2015*	Post-natal health check (%) — For new-borns 2010–2015*	For mothers 2010–2015*	Maternal mortality ratio — Reported 2010–2015*	Adjusted 2015	Lifetime risk of maternal death (1 in:) 2015
Afghanistan	104	39	70	56	–	21	63	23	45	43	4	–	23	330	396	52
Albania	107	98	98	93	101	69 x	97 x	67 x	99 x	97 x	19 x	–	–	6	29	1,900
Algeria	106	79 x	94	104	102	57	93	67	97	97	16	–	–	–	140	240
Andorra	–	–	–	–	99	–	–	–	–	–	–	–	–	–	–	–
Angola	106	72	64	65	73 x	–	80 x	–	47 x	46 x	–	–	–	–	477	32
Antigua and Barbuda	107	101	92	101	–	–	100 x	100	100	–	–	–	–	0 x	–	–
Argentina	110	100	99	108	102	77	98	90	97	99	28 x	–	–	37	52	790
Armenia	111	100	116 x	117 x	100	55	99	93	100	99	13	50	92	22	25	2,300
Australia	105	–	99	95	–	72 x	98 x	92 x	–	99	31 x	–	–	–	6	8,700
Austria	106	–	99	95	101	70 x	–	–	–	99	24 x	–	–	–	4	18,200
Azerbaijan	109	100	99	99	105	55	92	66	97	93	20	–	83	15	25	1,600
Bahamas	108	–	102	105	96 x	45 x	98	85	98	–	–	–	–	37	80	660
Bahrain	102	95	–	–	97	–	100 x	100	100	–	–	–	–	17 x	15	3,000
Bangladesh	104	89	106	108	114 x	62	64	31	42	37	23	32	34	190	176	240
Barbados	107	–	101	103	–	59	93	88	98	100	21	98	97	52	27	2,100
Belarus	118	100	100	98	100	63	100	100	100	100	25	100	100	0	4	13,800
Belgium	106	–	100	114	103	70	–	–	–	–	18 x	–	–	–	7	8,000
Belize	108	–	95	104	98	55	96	83	96	94	28	97	95	45	28	1,300
Benin	105	45 x	91	68	96	18	83	59	77	87	5	80	78	350	405	51
Bhutan	101	59 x	101	107	101	66	98	85	75	74	12	30	41	86	148	310
Bolivia (Plurinational State of)	107	91	97	99	101	61 x	90	75	85	71	27	–	–	310 x	206	160
Bosnia and Herzegovina	107	98	–	–	100	46	87	84	100	100	14	–	–	0	11	6,800
Botswana	107	101	97	106	103	53 x	94 x	73 x	95 x	100	–	–	–	160	129	270
Brazil	111	101	–	–	–	81 x	98 x	89	98	99	56	–	–	58	44	1,200
Brunei Darussalam	105	97	100	100	97	–	99 x	93	100	100 x	–	–	–	–	23	2,300
Bulgaria	110	99	99	97	101	69 x	–	–	100	94	36	–	–	12	11	6,200
Burkina Faso	105	59 x	96	87	115	16	94	34	66	66	2	26	72	340	371	48
Burundi	107	95 x	101	85	127	22	99	33	60	60	4	8	30	500	712	23
Cabo Verde	105	89	95	114	104	61 x	98 x	72 x	92	76 x	11 x	–	–	10	42	900
Cambodia	106	80	95	85 x	134	56	95	76	89	83	6	79	90	170	161	210
Cameroon	104	83	89	85	102	34	83	59	65	61	2	69	65	780	596	35
Canada	105	–	101	100	–	74 x	100 x	99 x	100	98	26 x	–	–	11	7	8,800
Central African Republic	108	48	74	51	96	15	68	38	54	53	5	–	–	540 x	882	27
Chad	104	61	77	46	85	6	53	31	24	22	2	–	15	860	856	18
Chile	107	100	97	102	101	58 x	–	–	100	100	50	–	–	17	22	2,600
China	104	95	100	102	–	85 x	96	–	100	100	36	–	–	22	27	2,400
Colombia	110	100	100 x	110 x	106	79	97	89	99	99	46	7	1	71	64	800
Comoros	105	89	94	104	–	19	92	49	82	76	10	14	49	170	335	66
Congo	105	84	107	87	–	30	93	79	94	92	5	86	80	440	442	45
Cook Islands	–	–	97	110	94	31	100 x	–	100 x	100 x	–	–	–	0	–	–
Costa Rica	106	100	99	105	102	76	98	90	97	99	22	–	–	23	25	2,100
Côte d'Ivoire	103	59	87	71	89	18	91	44	59	57	3	34	70	610	645	32
Croatia	109	99	100	104	101	–	–	93	100	–	20	–	–	3	8	7,900
Cuba	105	100	96	103	101	74	99	98	99	99	40	98	99	35	39	1,800
Cyprus	106	99	101	100	102	–	99 x	–	–	100	–	–	–	–	7	9,400
Czech Republic	108	–	100	101	100	86 x	–	–	100	100	20 x	–	–	1	4	14,800
Democratic People's Republic of Korea	110	100 x	100 x	100 x	–	71	100 x	94 x	100 x	95 x	13 x	–	–	77 x	82	660
Democratic Republic of the Congo	105	72	91	62	99	20	88	48	80	80	5	8	44	850	693	24
Denmark	105	–	99	102	101	–	–	–	–	98	21 x	–	–	–	6	9,500
Djibouti	105	–	87	81	–	19	88	23	87	87	11	–	–	380	229	140
Dominica	–	–	100	107	–	–	100 x	–	100	–	–	–	–	110	–	–
Dominican Republic	109	100	91	111	105	70	98	93	98	98	58	95	95	110	92	400
Ecuador	107	97	100	104	99	80	84 x	58 x	94	92	41	–	–	46	64	580
Egypt	106	79	99	98	101 x	59	90	83	92	87	52	14	82	52	33	810
El Salvador	113	94	95	99	106	72	96	90	98	98	32	97	94	38	54	890
Equatorial Guinea	105	95	98	–	100	13	91	67	68	67	7	–	–	310	342	61
Eritrea	107	77	85	80	99	8	89	57	34	34	3	–	–	490	501	43
Estonia	113	100	99	99	100	63 x	–	97	100 x	99	–	–	–	7	9	6,300
Ethiopia	106	59 x	92	91	116	42	41	32	16	16	2	0	13	680	353	64
Fiji	109	–	101	111	98	44	100 x	94	100	99	–	–	–	59	30	1,200
Finland	107	–	100	109	100	–	100 x	–	–	100	16 x	–	–	–	3	21,700

THE STATE OF THE WORLD'S CHILDREN 2016

unicef 70 YEARS FOR EVERY CHILD

TABLE 8. WOMEN

Countries and areas	Life expectancy: females as a % of males	Adult literacy rate: females as a % of males	Enrolment ratios: females as a % of males — Primary GER	Secondary GER	Survival rate to the last grade of primary: females as a % of males	Contraceptive prevalence (%)	Antenatal care (%) — At least one visit	At least four visits	Delivery care (%) — Skilled attendant at birth	Institutional delivery	C-section	Post-natal health check (%)[+] — For new-borns	For mothers	Maternal mortality ratio[†] — Reported	Adjusted	Lifetime risk of maternal death (1 in:)
	2015	2009–2014*	2010–2014*		2010–2014*	2010–2015*	2010–2015*		2010–2015*			2010–2015*		2010–2015*	2015	
France	107	–	99	101	–	76 x	100 x	99	–	98	21 x	–	–	–	8	6,100
Gabon	102	94	97	–	–	31	95	78	89	90	10	25	60	320	291	85
Gambia	105	72	105	95	107	9	86	78	57	63	2	6	76	430	706	24
Georgia	110	100	101	100	100	53	98	87	100	100	39	–	–	32	36	1,500
Germany	106	–	99	95	100	66 x	100 x	99	–	99	29 x	–	–	–	6	11,700
Ghana	103	83	100	94	97	27	91	87	71	73	13	23	81	450 x	319	74
Greece	107	98	99	96	101	76 x	–	–	–	–	–	–	–	–	3	23,700
Grenada	107	–	96	98	–	54 x	100 x	–	99	–	–	–	–	23	27	1,500
Guatemala	110	85	96	94	99	61	91	86	66	65	26	–	75	140	88	330
Guinea	102	33	88	66	152	6	85	57	45	40	2	25	37	720	679	29
Guinea-Bissau	107	64	93	–	–	16	92	65	45	44	4	55	48	900	549	38
Guyana	107	106	97	99	105	34	91	87	92	93	17	95	93	86 x	229	170
Haiti	107	84 x	99	–	–	35	90	67	37	36	6	19	32	380	359	90
Holy See	–	–	–	–	–	–	–	–	–	–	–	–	–	–	–	–
Honduras	107	100	98	117	103	73	97	89	83	83	19	81	85	73	129	300
Hungary	110	100	99	100	100	–	–	–	99	–	31 x	–	–	15	17	4,400
Iceland	104	–	100	99	102	–	–	–	–	–	17 x	–	–	–	3	14,600
India	104	75	112	101	–	55 x	74 x	45	52 x	79	9 x	–	–	170	174	220
Indonesia	106	94	100	97	–	60	95	84	87	70	12	48	80	360	126	320
Iran (Islamic Republic of)	103	88	104	99	84	77	97	94 x	96	95	46	–	–	25 x	25	2,000
Iraq	107	85	–	–	–	53	78	50	91	77	22	–	–	35	50	420
Ireland	105	–	101	102	–	65 x	100 x	–	100 x	100	25 x	–	–	–	8	6,100
Israel	104	–	100	102	99	–	–	–	–	–	–	–	–	–	5	6,200
Italy	106	100	99	98	101	–	99	68 x	–	100	40 x	–	–	–	4	19,700
Jamaica	107	111	–	108	103	72 x	98	86	99	99	21	–	–	80	89	520
Japan	108	–	100	100	100	54 x	–	–	–	100	–	–	–	–	5	13,400
Jordan	105	93	99	105	102	61	99	95	100	99	28	75	82	19 x	58	490
Kazakhstan	115	100	100	103	100	51	99	87	100	100	15	–	–	13	12	3,000
Kenya	106	86 x	100	93	–	58	96	58	62	61	9	36	53	360	510	42
Kiribati	110	–	104	110 x	–	22 x	88 x	71 x	80 x	66 x	10 x	–	–	33	90	300
Kuwait	103	99	102	108	101	–	100 x	–	100 x	100	–	–	–	2	4	10,300
Kyrgyzstan	112	99	99	101	102	42	98	95	98	98	7	99	98	36	76	390
Lao People's Democratic Republic	104	77 x	95	91	104	50	54	37	42	38	4	41	39	360	197	150
Latvia	114	100	99	97	100	–	92 x	–	100 x	98	–	–	–	24	18	3,500
Lebanon	105	92 x	91	101	106	54 x	96 x	–	98 x	–	–	–	–	–	15	3,700
Lesotho	100	130	98	137	134	60	95	74	78	77	7 x	–	61	1,200 x	487	61
Liberia	103	44 x	92	78	85 x	20	96	78	61	56	4	35	71	1,100	725	28
Libya	108	88	–	–	–	42 x	93 x	–	100 x	100	–	–	–	–	9	4,200
Liechtenstein	–	–	102	85	96 x	–	–	–	–	–	–	–	–	–	–	–
Lithuania	116	100	100	96	100	63 x	100 x	–	100 x	–	–	–	–	7	10	6,300
Luxembourg	106	–	101	103	105	–	–	97	100 x	100 x	29 x	–	–	–	10	6,500
Madagascar	105	91	100	98	106	40	82	51	44	38	2	–	–	480	353	60
Malawi	103	71	102	91	94	59	96	45	87	89	5	82	75	570	634	29
Malaysia	106	95	–	–	–	49 x	97	–	99	99	–	–	–	23	40	1,200
Maldives	103	100 x	97 x	–	106	35	99 x	85 x	96	95 x	32 x	–	–	140 x	68	600
Mali	99	47	90	76	94	8 x	70 x	35 x	49 x	45 x	2 x	–	–	460 x	587	27
Malta	104	103	95	89	102	–	100 x	–	–	100	–	–	–	–	9	8,300
Marshall Islands	–	–	99	103 x	91 x	45 x	81 x	77 x	90	85 x	9 x	–	–	110	–	–
Mauritania	105	62 x	106	91	98	11	84	48	65	65	10	–	9	630	602	36
Mauritius	110	94	102	102	101	76 x	–	–	100	98 x	–	–	–	22 x	53	1,300
Mexico	106	97	99	107	102	52	97	91	96	96	46	–	–	38	38	1,100
Micronesia (Federated States of)	103	–	99	–	–	55 x	80 x	–	100 x	87 x	11 x	–	–	160	100	310
Monaco	–	–	–	–	–	–	–	–	–	–	–	–	–	–	–	–
Mongolia	113	100	98	103	–	55	99	90	99	98	23	99	95	51	44	800
Montenegro	106	98	98	100	102	23	92	87	99	99	20	99	95	0 x	7	8,300
Morocco	103	76	95	85	99	67	77	55	74	73	16	–	–	110	121	320
Mozambique	105	54	92	92	96	12	91	51	54	55	4	–	–	410	489	40
Myanmar	106	95	97	103	107 x	46	83	73 x	71	36	–	–	–	280	178	260
Namibia	108	105 x	97	–	104	56	97	63	88	87	14	20	69	390	265	100
Nauru	–	–	92	102	–	36 x	95 x	40 x	97 x	99 x	8 x	–	–	0	–	–
Nepal	104	68	108	106	105	50	68	60	56	55	9	58	58	280 x	258	150

TABLE 8. WOMEN

Countries and areas	Life expectancy: females as a % of males	Adult literacy rate: females as a % of males	Enrolment ratios: females as a % of males Primary GER	Enrolment ratios: females as a % of males Secondary GER	Survival rate to the last grade of primary: females as a % of males	Contraceptive prevalence (%)	Antenatal care (%) At least one visit	Antenatal care (%) At least four visits	Delivery care (%) Skilled attendant at birth	Delivery care (%) Institutional delivery	Delivery care (%) C-section	Post-natal health check (%) For new-borns	Post-natal health check (%) For mothers	Maternal mortality ratio Reported	Maternal mortality ratio Adjusted	Lifetime risk of maternal death (1 in:)
	2015	2009–2014*	2010–2014*	2010–2014*	2010–2014*	2010–2015*	2010–2015*	2010–2015*	2010–2015*	2010–2015*	2010–2015*	2010–2015*	2010–2015*	2010–2015*	2015	2015
Netherlands	105	–	99	99	–	69 x	–	–	–	100 x	14 x	–	–	–	7	8,700
New Zealand	104	–	100	106	–	–	–	–	–	97	23 x	–	–	–	11	4,500
Nicaragua	108	100 x	99	113	–	80	95	88	88	71	30	–	–	51	150	270
Niger	103	38	86	70	104	13	83	38	40	59	1	13	37	520	553	23
Nigeria	101	68 x	92	89	107 x	15	61	51	38	36	2	14	40	550	814	22
Niue	–	–	98	–	–	23 x	100 x	–	100	–	–	–	–	0	–	–
Norway	105	–	100	97	–	88 x	–	–	–	97	16 x	–	–	–	5	11,500
Oman	105	91	109	101	99	30	99	94	99	99	19	98	95	12	17	1,900
Pakistan	103	60	85	79	90	35	73	37	52	48	14	43	60	280 x	178	140
Palau	–	100	96	106	–	22	90	81	100	100	–	–	–	0	–	–
Panama	108	99	97	106	–	63	93	88	91	91	28	93	92	81	94	420
Papua New Guinea	107	93	91	76	–	32 x	79 x	55 x	53 x	43	–	–	–	730 x	215	120
Paraguay	106	98	97	107	104	79 x	96 x	91 x	96	96	33 x	–	–	96	132	270
Peru	107	94	100	100	103	75	97	95	90	90	29	92	93	93	68	570
Philippines	111	101 x	100	110	111 x	55	95	84	73	61	9	53	72	220	114	280
Poland	111	100	100	96	101	–	–	–	100 x	100	21 x	–	–	2	3	22,100
Portugal	107	96	96	98	–	67 x	100 x	–	100 x	99	31 x	–	–	–	10	8,200
Qatar	103	99	95	89	97	38	91	85	100	99	20	–	–	13	13	3,500
Republic of Korea	108	–	99	99	100	80 x	–	97	–	100	32 x	–	–	–	11	7,200
Republic of Moldova	112	99	100	101	99	60	99	95	99	99	16	–	–	30	23	3,200
Romania	110	99	98	98	100	70 x	94 x	76 x	99	98 x	19 x	–	–	15	31	2,300
Russian Federation	117	100	101	99	–	68	–	–	100	–	–	–	–	11	25	2,300
Rwanda	109	87	102	107	125	53	99	44	91	91	15	5	18	210	290	85
Saint Kitts and Nevis	–	–	102	103	–	54 x	100 x	–	100	–	–	–	–	310	–	–
Saint Lucia	107	–	–	99	100	56	97	90	99	100	19	100	90	34	48	1,100
Saint Vincent and the Grenadines	106	–	97	97	127	48 x	100 x	100 x	99	–	–	–	–	45	45	1,100
Samoa	109	100	100	112	98	27	93	73	83	82	5	–	63	29 x	51	500
San Marino	–	–	99	103	103	–	–	–	–	–	–	–	–	–	–	–
Sao Tome and Principe	106	75 x	96	–	–	41	98	84	93	91	6	91	87	–	156	140
Saudi Arabia	104	95	99	76	–	24 x	97 x	–	98	–	–	–	–	–	12	3,100
Senegal	106	61	109	91	108	22	96	48	59	77	4	45	67	430	315	61
Serbia	108	97	100	102	101	58	98	94	98	98	29	–	–	14	17	3,900
Seychelles	113	101	101	102	–	–	–	–	–	–	–	–	–	57 x	–	–
Sierra Leone	102	62	100	85	101	17	97	76	60	54	3	39	73	1,200	1,360	17
Singapore	108	96	–	–	100 x	–	–	–	–	100	–	–	–	–	10	8,200
Slovakia	110	–	98	102	100	–	97 x	–	99	–	24 x	–	–	0	6	12,100
Slovenia	108	100	100	100	100	–	100 x	–	100	100	–	–	–	0	9	7,000
Solomon Islands	104	–	97	94	93	35 x	74 x	65 x	86 x	85 x	6 x	–	–	150 x	114	220
Somalia	106	–	–	–	–	15 x	26 x	6 x	33 x	9 x	–	–	–	1,000 x	732	22
South Africa	107	97	95	126	–	60 x	97 x	87 x	94 x	95 x	21 x	–	–	580	138	300
South Sudan	104	55 x	66	–	–	4	62	17	19	12	1	–	–	2,100 x	789	26
Spain	107	98	101	100	99	66 x	–	–	–	–	26 x	–	–	–	5	14,700
Sri Lanka	109	97	98	105	100	68 x	99 x	93 x	99	98 x	24 x	–	–	31	30	1,600
State of Palestine	106	94	99	110	–	57	99	96	100	99	20	94	91	–	45	490
Sudan	105	81	89	91	98	12	79	51	23	28	9	28	27	220	311	72
Suriname	109	99	97	131	122	48	91	67	91	92	19	–	–	130	155	270
Swaziland	97	98	92	98	107	66	99	76	88	88	12	90	87	590 x	389	76
Sweden	104	–	106	113	100	–	100 x	–	–	–	–	–	–	–	4	12,900
Switzerland	105	–	100	97	–	–	–	–	–	–	30 x	–	–	–	5	12,400
Syrian Arab Republic	120	88	97	100	101	54 x	88 x	64 x	96 x	78 x	26 x	–	–	65 x	68	440
Tajikistan	111	100	100	90	101	28	79	53	87	77	4	54	80	29	32	790
Thailand	109	100	98	107	–	79	98	93	100	100	32	–	–	12 x	20	3,600
The former Yugoslav Republic of Macedonia	106	98	98	98	–	40	99	94	100	98	25	–	–	4	8	8,500
Timor-Leste	105	83	99	108	109	22	84	55	29	22	2	–	–	570	215	82
Togo	103	65	94	–	95	20	73	57	59	73	7	35	71	400	368	58
Tonga	108	100	100	103	–	34	99	70	98	98	17	–	–	36	124	230
Trinidad and Tobago	110	99	97	–	106 x	43 x	96 x	100	100	97 x	–	–	–	84	63	860
Tunisia	106	81	97	–	98	63	98	85	99	99	27	98	92	–	62	710
Turkey	109	91	99	97	98	73	97	89	97	97	48	72	88	29 x	16	3,000
Turkmenistan	114	100	98	96	–	48 x	99 x	83 x	100 x	98 x	3 x	–	–	7	42	940
Tuvalu	–	–	101	125	–	31 x	97 x	67 x	98 x	93 x	7 x	–	–	0 x	–	–

unicef 70 YEARS FOR EVERY CHILD

TABLE 8. WOMEN

Countries and areas	Life expectancy: females as a % of males	Adult literacy rate: females as a % of males	Enrolment ratios: females as a % of males		Survival rate to the last grade of primary: females as a % of males	Contraceptive prevalence (%)	Antenatal care (%)		Delivery care (%)			Post-natal health check (%)[+]		Maternal mortality ratio[†]		
			Primary GER	Secondary GER			At least one visit	At least four visits	Skilled attendant at birth	Institutional delivery	C-section	For newborns	For mothers	Reported	Adjusted	Lifetime risk of maternal death (1 in:)
	2015	2009–2014*	2010–2014*		2010–2014*	2010–2015*	2010–2015*		2010–2015*			2010–2015*		2010–2015*	2015	
Uganda	107	78	102	87	97	30	93	48	57	57	5	11	33	440	343	47
Ukraine	115	100	102	98	101	65	99	87	99	99	12	99	96	14	24	2,600
United Arab Emirates	103	102 x	101	–	103	–	100 x	–	100	100	–	–	–	0 x	6	7,900
United Kingdom	105	–	100	104	–	84 x	–	–	–	–	26 x	–	–	–	9	5,800
United Republic of Tanzania	104	81	101	91	115	34	88	43	49	50	5	2	31	430	398	45
United States	106	–	99	101	–	76	–	97	99	–	31 x	–	–	28	14	3,800
Uruguay	110	101	97	114	103 x	78 x	97	77	98	100	30	–	–	10	15	3,300
Uzbekistan	110	100	98	99	101	65 x	99 x	–	100 x	97 x	–	–	–	20	36	1,000
Vanuatu	106	97	98	100	94 x	49	76	52	89	89	12	–	–	86 x	78	360
Venezuela (Bolivarian Republic of)	112	101	98	108	91	–	94 x	61	100	95	–	–	–	72	95	420
Viet Nam	113	95	99	–	115	76	96	74	94	94	28	89	90	67	54	870
Yemen	104	62	84	69	93	34	60	25	45	30	5	11	20	150	385	60
Zambia	107	72 x	101	–	94	49	96	56	64	67	4	16	63	400	224	79
Zimbabwe	105	91	99	97	–	67	94	70	80	80	6	85	77	–	443	52
SUMMARY																
Sub-Saharan Africa	105	76	93	86	102	27	78	49	50	51	4	21	43	–	546	36
Eastern and Southern Africa	106	82	94	93	105	40	80	45	49	49	5	18	36	–	417	51
West and Central Africa	103	69	91	79	100	18	76	52	54	54	3	22	49	–	679	27
Middle East and North Africa	105	83	95	94	101	57	85	63	80	75	29	–	–	–	110	280
South Asia	104	75	100	94	106	47 ‡	69 ‡	42	49 ‡	69	15 ‡	40 ‡	48 ‡	–	182	200
East Asia and Pacific	105	95	99	101	102	63 **	95	82 **	93	88	28	57 **	80 **	–	62	880
Latin America and Caribbean	109	99	98	106	104	65	96	87	94	93	44	–	–	–	68	670
CEE/CIS	113	99	100	98	101	65	96	85	98	96	28	–	–	–	25	2,000
Least developed countries	105	77	93	88	103	37	77	42	50	49	6	20	37	–	436	52
World	**106**	**91**	**98**	**97**	**103**	**53 ‡***	**85 ‡**	**58 ***	**75 ‡**	**73**	**20 ‡**	**34 ‡***	**54 ‡***	–	**216**	**180**

For a complete list of countries and areas in the regions, subregions and country categories, see page 112 or visit <data.unicef.org/regionalclassifications>.
It is not advisable to compare data from consecutive editions of *The State of the World's Children*.

DEFINITIONS OF THE INDICATORS

Life expectancy – Number of years newborn children would live if subject to the mortality risks prevailing for the cross section of population at the time of their birth.

Adult literacy rate – Percentage of the population aged 15 years and over who can both read and write with understanding a short, simple statement on his/her everyday life.

Primary gross enrolment ratio (GER) – Total enrolment in primary school, regardless of age, expressed as a percentage of the official primary-school-aged population.

Secondary gross enrolment ratio (GER) – Total enrolment in secondary school, regardless of age, expressed as a percentage of the official secondary-school-aged population.

Survival rate to last grade of primary – Percentage of children entering the first grade of primary school who eventually reach the last grade (administrative data).

Contraceptive prevalence – Percentage of women (aged 15–49) in union currently using any contraceptive method.

Antenatal care – Percentage of women (aged 15–49) attended at least once during pregnancy by skilled health personnel (doctor, nurse or midwife) and the percentage attended by any provider at least four times.

Skilled attendant at birth – Percentage of births attended by skilled heath personnel (doctor, nurse or midwife).

Institutional delivery – Percentage of women (aged 15–49) who gave birth in a health facility.

C-section – Percentage of births delivered by Caesarean section. NB: C-section rates between 5 per cent and 15 per cent expected with adequate levels of emergency obstetric care.

Post-natal health check for newborns – Percentage of last live births in the last 2 years who received a health check within 2 days after delivery. NB: For MICS, health check refers to a health check while in facility or at home following delivery or a post-natal visit.

Post-natal health check for mothers – Percentage of women aged 15–49 years who received a health check within 2 days after delivery of their most recent live birth in the last 2 years. NB: For MICS, health check refers to a health check while in facility or at home following delivery or a post-natal visit.

Maternal mortality ratio – Number of deaths of women from pregnancy-related causes per 100,000 live births during the same time period. The 'reported' column shows country-reported figures that are not adjusted for under-reporting and misclassification. For the 'adjusted' column, see note below (†). Maternal mortality ratio values have been rounded according to the following scheme: Reported: <100, no rounding; 100–999, rounded to nearest 10; and >1,000, rounded to nearest 100. Adjusted: <1,000, rounded to nearest 1; and ≥1,000, rounded to nearest 10.

Lifetime risk of maternal death – Lifetime risk of maternal death takes into account both the probability of becoming pregnant and the probability of dying as a result of that pregnancy, accumulated across a woman's reproductive years. Lifetime risk values have been rounded according to the following scheme: <1,000, rounded to nearest 1; and ≥1,000, rounded to nearest 10.

MAIN DATA SOURCES

Life expectancy – United Nations Population Division.

Adult literacy – UNESCO Institute for Statistics (UIS).

Primary and secondary school enrolment – UIS.

Survival rate to last grade of primary – UIS.

Contraceptive prevalence – DHS, MICS and other nationally representative sources; United Nations Population Division.

Antenatal care, skilled attendant at birth, institutional delivery and C-section: – DHS, MICS and other nationally representative sources.

Post-natal health check for newborns and mothers – DHS and MICS.

Maternal mortality ratio (reported) – Nationally representative sources, including household surveys and vital registration.

Maternal mortality ratio (adjusted) – United Nations Maternal Mortality Estimation Inter-agency Group (WHO, UNICEF, UNFPA, The World Bank and the United Nations Population Division).

Lifetime risk of maternal death – United Nations Maternal Mortality Estimation Inter-agency Group (WHO, UNICEF, UNFPA, The World Bank and the United Nations Population Division).

NOTES

– Data not available.

x Data refer to years or periods other than those specified in the column heading. Such data are not included in the calculation of regional and global averages. Estimates from data years prior to 2000 are not displayed.

* Data refer to the most recent year available during the period specified in the column heading.

** Excludes China.

† The maternal mortality data in the column headed 'reported' refer to data reported by national authorities. The data in the column headed 'adjusted' refer to the 2015 United Nations inter-agency maternal mortality estimates. Periodically, the United Nations Maternal Mortality Estimation Inter-agency Group (WHO, UNICEF, UNFPA The World Bank and the United Nations Population Division) produces internationally comparable sets of maternal mortality data that account for the well-documented problems of under-reporting and misclassification of maternal deaths, including also estimates for countries with no data. Please note that owing to an evolving methodology, these values are not comparable with previously reported maternal mortality ratio 'adjusted' values. Comparable time series on maternal mortality ratios for the years 1990, 1995, 2000, 2005 and 2015 are available at <http://data.unicef.org/maternal-health/maternal-mortality.html>.

+ Data collection method for this indicator varies across surveys and may affect comparability of the coverage estimates. For detailed explanation see General Note on the Data, page 108.

TABLE 9. CHILD PROTECTION

Countries and areas	Child labour (%)* 2009–2015*			Child marriage (%) 2008–2014*		Birth registration (%)** 2010–2015*	Female genital mutilation/cutting (%)* 2004–2015*			Justification of wife-beating (%) 2010–2015*		Violent discipline (%)* 2010–2015*		
	total	male	female	married by 15	married by 18	total	prevalence women[a]	girls[b]	attitudes support for the practice[c]	male	female	total	male	female
Afghanistan	29 y	34 y	24 y	–	33	37	–	–	–	–	90	74	75	74
Albania	5 y	6 y	4 y	0	10	99 x	–	–	–	36 x	30 x	77 x	81 x	73 x
Algeria	5	6	5	0	3	100	–	–	–	–	59 y	86	88	85
Andorra	–	–	–	–	–	100 v	–	–	–	–	–	–	–	–
Angola	24 x	22 x	25 x	–	–	36 x	–	–	–	–	–	–	–	–
Antigua and Barbuda	–	–	–	–	–	–	–	–	–	–	–	–	–	–
Argentina	4	5	4	–	–	100 y	–	–	–	–	2	72	74	71
Armenia	4	5	3	0	7	100	–	–	–	20	9	70	72	67
Australia	–	–	–	–	–	100 v	–	–	–	–	–	–	–	–
Austria	–	–	–	–	–	100 v	–	–	–	–	–	–	–	–
Azerbaijan	7 x,y	8 x,y	5 x,y	2	11	94 x	–	–	–	–	28	77 x	80 x	74 x
Bahamas	–	–	–	–	–	–	–	–	–	–	–	–	–	–
Bahrain	5 x	6 x	3 x	–	–	–	–	–	–	–	–	–	–	–
Bangladesh	4 y	5 y	4 y	18	52	37	–	–	–	–	33 y	82 y	83 y	82 y
Barbados	2	3	1	1	11	99	–	–	–	–	3	75	78	72
Belarus	1	1	2	0	3	100 y	–	–	–	4	4	65 y	67 y	62 y
Belgium	–	–	–	–	–	100 v	–	–	–	–	–	–	–	–
Belize	3 y	5 y	1 y	3	26	95	–	–	–	–	9	71	71	70
Benin	15	15	16	11	32	85	9	0	3	17	36	91 y	–	–
Bhutan	3	3	3	6	26	100	–	–	–	–	68	–	–	–
Bolivia (Plurinational State of)	26 x,y	28 x,y	24 x,y	3	22	76 x,y	–	–	–	–	16 x	–	–	–
Bosnia and Herzegovina	5 x	7 x	4 x	0	4	100 x	–	–	–	6	5	55	60	50
Botswana	9 x,y	11 x,y	7 x,y	–	–	72 x	–	–	–	–	–	–	–	–
Brazil	8 y	10 y	6 y	11 x	36 x	96	–	–	–	–	–	–	–	–
Brunei Darussalam	–	–	–	–	–	–	–	–	–	–	–	–	–	–
Bulgaria	–	–	–	–	–	100 v	–	–	–	–	–	–	–	–
Burkina Faso	39	42	36	10	52	77	76	13	9	34	44	83 x	84 x	82 x
Burundi	26	26	27	3	20	75	–	–	–	44	73	–	–	–
Cabo Verde	6 y	–	–	3 x	18 x	91	–	–	–	16 x,y	17 x,y	–	–	–
Cambodia	19 y	20 y	19 y	2	19	73	–	–	–	27 y	50 y	–	–	–
Cameroon	47 y	–	–	13	38	66	1	1 y	7	39	36	85 y	–	–
Canada	–	–	–	–	–	100 v	–	–	–	–	–	–	–	–
Central African Republic	29	27	30	29	68	61	24	1	11	75	80	92	92	92
Chad	26	25	28	29	68	12	44	18 y	38	–	62	84	85	84
Chile	7 y	–	–	–	–	99 y	–	–	–	–	–	–	–	–
China	–	–	–	–	–	–	–	–	–	–	–	–	–	–
Colombia	10 y	13 y	7 y	6	23	97	–	–	–	–	–	–	–	–
Comoros	22	20	24	10	32	87	–	–	–	17	39	–	–	–
Congo	23 y	–	–	6	33	96	–	–	–	40	54	83 y	–	–
Cook Islands	–	–	–	–	–	–	–	–	–	–	–	–	–	–
Costa Rica	4	4	5	7	21	100 y	–	–	–	–	4	46	52	39
Côte d'Ivoire	26	25	28	10	33	65	38	10	14	42	48	91 x	91 x	91 x
Croatia	–	–	–	–	–	–	–	–	–	–	–	–	–	–
Cuba	–	–	–	5	26	100	–	–	–	7 y	4 y	36 y	37 y	35 y
Cyprus	–	–	–	–	–	100 v	–	–	–	–	–	–	–	–
Czech Republic	–	–	–	–	–	100 v	–	–	–	–	–	–	–	–
Democratic People's Republic of Korea	–	–	–	–	–	100 x	–	–	–	–	–	–	–	–
Democratic Republic of the Congo	38 y	36 y	41 y	10	37	25	–	–	–	61	75	82 y	82 y	81 y
Denmark	–	–	–	–	–	100 v	–	–	–	–	–	–	–	–
Djibouti	8 x	8 x	8 x	2 x	5 x	92 x	93	49 y	37	–	–	72 x	73 x	71 x
Dominica	–	–	–	–	–	–	–	–	–	–	–	–	–	–
Dominican Republic	13 y	–	–	10	37	88	–	–	–	–	2	63 y	–	–
Ecuador	3 y	4 y	2 y	4 x	22 x	92	–	–	–	–	–	–	–	–
Egypt	7 y	8 y	6 y	2	17	99	87	14 y	54	–	36 y	93 y	93 y	93 y
El Salvador	19 y	–	–	5	25	99	–	–	–	–	8	52 y	–	–
Equatorial Guinea	28 x	28 x	28 x	9	30	54	–	–	–	52	53	–	–	–
Eritrea	–	–	–	13	41	–	83	33	12	45	51	–	–	–
Estonia	–	–	–	–	–	100 v	–	–	–	–	–	–	–	–
Ethiopia	27	31	24	16	41	7 x	74	24	31	45	68	–	–	–
Fiji	–	–	–	–	–	–	–	–	–	–	–	72 x,y	–	–
Finland	–	–	–	–	–	100 v	–	–	–	–	–	–	–	–
France	–	–	–	–	–	100 v	–	–	–	–	–	–	–	–
Gabon	13	15	12	6	22	90	–	–	–	40	50	–	–	–

TABLE 9. CHILD PROTECTION

Countries and areas	Child labour (%)[*] 2009–2015*			Child marriage (%) 2008–2014*		Birth registration (%)[*+] 2010–2015*	Female genital mutilation/cutting (%)[*] 2004–2015*			Justification of wife-beating (%) 2010–2015*		Violent discipline (%)[*] 2010–2015*		
							prevalence		attitudes					
	total	male	female	married by 15	married by 18	total	women[a]	girls[b]	support for the practice[c]	male	female	total	male	female
Gambia	19	21	18	9	30	72	75	56	65	33	58	90	90	91
Georgia	18 x	20 x	17 x	1	14	100	–	–	–	–	7 x	67 x	70 x	63 x
Germany	–	–	–	–	–	100 v	–	–	–	–	–	–	–	–
Ghana	22 y	23 y	21 y	5	21	71	4	1	2	13	28	94	94	94
Greece	–	–	–	–	–	100 v	–	–	–	–	–	–	–	–
Grenada	–	–	–	–	–	–	–	–	–	–	–	–	–	–
Guatemala	26 y	35 y	16 y	7	30	97 x	–	–	–	–	–	–	–	–
Guinea	28	29	27	21	52	58	97	46	76	66	92	–	–	–
Guinea-Bissau	38	40	36	7	22	24	45	30	13	29	42	82 y	–	–
Guyana	18 y	–	–	6	23	89	–	–	–	10	10	70 y	–	–
Haiti	24	25	24	3	18	80	–	–	–	15	17	85	85	84
Holy See	–	–	–	–	–	–	–	–	–	–	–	–	–	–
Honduras	15 y	22 y	8 y	8	34	94	–	–	–	10	12	–	–	–
Hungary	–	–	–	–	–	100 v	–	–	–	–	–	–	–	–
Iceland	–	–	–	–	–	100 v	–	–	–	–	–	–	–	–
India	12 x	12 x	12 x	18 x	47 x	72	–	–	–	42 x	47 x	–	–	–
Indonesia	7	8	6	–	14	69 y	–	49 y	–	18 y	35	–	–	–
Iran (Islamic Republic of)	11 y	13 y	10 y	3	17	99 y	–	–	–	–	–	–	–	–
Iraq	5	5	4	5	24	99	8	3 y	5	–	51	79	81	77
Ireland	–	–	–	–	–	100 v	–	–	–	–	–	–	–	–
Israel	–	–	–	–	–	100 v	–	–	–	–	–	–	–	–
Italy	–	–	–	–	–	100 v	–	–	–	–	–	–	–	–
Jamaica	3	4	3	1	8	100	–	–	–	–	5	85	87	82
Japan	–	–	–	–	–	100 v	–	–	–	–	–	–	–	–
Jordan	2 x,y	3 x,y	0 x,y	0	8	99	–	–	–	–	70 y	90	91	89
Kazakhstan	2 x	2 x	2 x	0	6	100	–	–	–	17	12	49	54	45
Kenya	26 x	27 x	25 x	4	23	67	21	3	6	36	42	–	–	–
Kiribati	–	–	–	3	20	94 x	–	–	–	60 x	76 x	81 x,y	–	–
Kuwait	–	–	–	–	–	–	–	–	–	–	–	–	–	–
Kyrgyzstan	26 y	30 y	22 y	1	12	98	–	–	–	–	33	57 y	60 y	54 y
Lao People's Democratic Republic	10 y	9 y	11 y	9	35	75	–	–	–	49	58	76	77	74
Latvia	–	–	–	–	–	100 v	–	–	–	–	–	–	–	–
Lebanon	2	3	1	1	6	100 x	–	–	–	–	10 x,y	82 x	82 x	82 x
Lesotho	23 x	25 x	21 x	2	19	45 x	–	–	–	48 x	37 x	–	–	–
Liberia	21 x	21 x	21 x	9	36	25 y	50	–	39	24	43	90 x	90 x	90 x
Libya	–	–	–	–	–	–	–	–	–	–	–	–	–	–
Liechtenstein	–	–	–	–	–	100 v	–	–	–	–	–	–	–	–
Lithuania	–	–	–	–	–	100 v	–	–	–	–	–	–	–	–
Luxembourg	–	–	–	–	–	100 v	–	–	–	–	–	–	–	–
Madagascar	23 y	23 y	23 y	12	41	83	–	–	–	46 y	45	–	–	–
Malawi	39 y	42 y	37 y	9	46	6 y	–	–	–	8	13	72 y	73 y	72 y
Malaysia	–	–	–	–	–	–	–	–	–	–	–	–	–	–
Maldives	–	–	–	0	4	93 x	–	–	–	14 x,y	31 x,y	–	–	–
Mali	21	22	21	15	55	81	89	74 y	73	–	87	–	–	–
Malta	–	–	–	–	–	100 v	–	–	–	–	–	–	–	–
Marshall Islands	–	–	–	6 x	26 x	96 x	–	–	–	58 x	56 x	–	–	–
Mauritania	15	14	15	14	34	59	69	54	41	–	38	87	87	87
Mauritius	–	–	–	–	–	–	–	–	–	–	–	–	–	–
Mexico	4	–	–	5	23	93	–	–	–	–	–	–	–	–
Micronesia (Federated States of)	–	–	–	–	–	–	–	–	–	–	–	–	–	–
Monaco	–	–	–	–	–	100 v	–	–	–	–	–	–	–	–
Mongolia	15 y	–	–	0	5	99	–	–	–	9 y	10	47 y	–	–
Montenegro	13 y	15 y	10 y	1	5	99	–	–	–	5	3	69 y	73 y	66 y
Morocco	8 x	9 x	8 x	3 x	16 x	94 y	–	–	–	–	64 x	91 x	92 x	90 x
Mozambique	22 x	21 x	24 x	14	48	48	–	–	–	20	23	–	–	–
Myanmar	–	–	–	–	–	72	–	–	–	–	–	–	–	–
Namibia	–	–	–	2	7	87 y	–	–	–	22	28	–	–	–
Nauru	–	–	–	2 x	27 x	83 x	–	–	–	–	–	–	–	–
Nepal	37 y	37 y	38 y	10	37	58	–	–	–	–	43	82 y	83 y	81 y
Netherlands	–	–	–	–	–	100 v	–	–	–	–	–	–	–	–
New Zealand	–	–	–	–	–	100 v	–	–	–	–	–	–	–	–
Nicaragua	15 x	18 x	11 x	10 x	41 x	85	–	–	–	–	14 x,y	–	–	–
Niger	31	31	30	28	76	64	2	2 y	6	27	60	82	82	81
Nigeria	25	24	25	17	43	30 y	25	17	23	25	35	91	91	90

TABLE 9. CHILD PROTECTION

Countries and areas	Child labour (%)* 2009–2015* total	male	female	Child marriage (%) 2008–2014* married by 15	married by 18	Birth registration (%)++ 2010–2015* total	Female genital mutilation/cutting (%)* 2004–2015* prevalence women[a]	girls[b]	attitudes support for the practice[c]	Justification of wife-beating (%) 2010–2015* male	female	Violent discipline (%)* 2010–2015* total	male	female
Niue	–	–	–	–	–	–	–	–	–	–	–	–	–	–
Norway	–	–	–	–	–	100 v	–	–	–	–	–	–	–	–
Oman	–	–	–	–	–	–	–	–	–	–	8	–	–	–
Pakistan	–	–	–	3	21	34	–	–	–	32 y	42 y	–	–	–
Palau	–	–	–	–	–	–	–	–	–	–	–	–	–	–
Panama	6 y	8 y	3 y	7	26	96	–	–	–	–	6	45 y	47 y	43 y
Papua New Guinea	–	–	–	2 x	21 x	–	–	–	–	–	–	–	–	–
Paraguay	28 y	32 y	24 y	–	18 x	85 y	–	–	–	–	–	–	–	–
Peru	34 x,y	31 x,y	36 x,y	3	19	97 y	–	–	–	–	–	–	–	–
Philippines	11 y	14 y	8 y	2	15	90	–	–	–	–	13	–	–	–
Poland	–	–	–	–	–	100 v	–	–	–	–	–	–	–	–
Portugal	3 x,y	4 x,y	3 x,y	–	–	100 v	–	–	–	–	–	–	–	–
Qatar	–	–	–	0	4	–	–	–	–	16	7	50 y	53 y	46 y
Republic of Korea	–	–	–	–	–	–	–	–	–	–	–	–	–	–
Republic of Moldova	16	20	12	0	12	100	–	–	–	13	11	76	77	74
Romania	1 x	1 x	1 x	–	–	–	–	–	–	–	–	–	–	–
Russian Federation	–	–	–	–	–	100 v	–	–	–	–	–	–	–	–
Rwanda	29	27	30	1	8	63	–	–	–	25	56	–	–	–
Saint Kitts and Nevis	–	–	–	–	–	–	–	–	–	–	–	–	–	–
Saint Lucia	4	5	3	1	8	92	–	–	–	–	7	68	71	64
Saint Vincent and the Grenadines	–	–	–	–	–	–	–	–	–	–	–	–	–	–
Samoa	–	–	–	1	11	59	–	–	–	30	37	–	–	–
San Marino	–	–	–	–	–	100 v	–	–	–	–	–	–	–	–
Sao Tome and Principe	26 y	–	–	5	34	95	–	–	–	14	19	80 y	–	–
Saudi Arabia	–	–	–	–	–	–	–	–	–	–	–	–	–	–
Senegal	15	19	10	9	32	73	25	13	16	27	57	–	–	–
Serbia	10 y	12 y	7 y	0	3	99	–	–	–	–	4	43 y	44 y	42 y
Seychelles	–	–	–	–	–	–	–	–	–	–	–	–	–	–
Sierra Leone	37	38	37	13	39	77	90	31 y	69	34	63	82	81	82
Singapore	–	–	–	–	–	–	–	–	–	–	–	–	–	–
Slovakia	–	–	–	–	–	100 v	–	–	–	–	–	–	–	–
Slovenia	–	–	–	–	–	100 v	–	–	–	–	–	–	–	–
Solomon Islands	–	–	–	3 x	22 x	–	–	–	–	65 x	69 x	72 x,y	–	–
Somalia	49 x	45 x	54 x	8 x	45 x	3 x	98	46 y	65	–	76 x,y	–	–	–
South Africa	–	–	–	1 x	6 x	85 y	–	–	–	–	–	–	–	–
South Sudan	–	–	–	9	52	35	–	–	–	–	79	–	–	–
Spain	–	–	–	–	–	100 v	–	–	–	–	–	–	–	–
Sri Lanka	3 y	3 y	2 y	2 x	12 x	97 x	–	–	–	–	53 x,y	–	–	–
State of Palestine	6	7	4	1	15	99	–	–	–	–	–	92 y	93 y	92 y
Sudan	25 y	–	–	7	33	67	87	32	41	–	34	64 y	–	–
Suriname	4	4	4	5	19	99	–	–	–	–	13	86	87	85
Swaziland	7	8	7	1	7	54	–	–	–	17	20	88 y	–	–
Sweden	–	–	–	–	–	100 v	–	–	–	–	–	–	–	–
Switzerland	–	–	–	–	–	100 v	–	–	–	–	–	–	–	–
Syrian Arab Republic	4 x	5 x	3 x	3 x	13 x	96 x	–	–	–	–	–	89 x	90 x	88 x
Tajikistan	10 x	9 x	11 x	0	12	88	–	–	–	–	60	78 x	80 x	75 x
Thailand	8 x	8 x	8 x	4	22	99 x	–	–	–	–	13	–	–	–
The former Yugoslav Republic of Macedonia	13	12	13	1	7	100	–	–	–	–	15	69	71	67
Timor-Leste	4 x	4 x	4 x	3	19	55	–	–	–	81	86	–	–	–
Togo	28 y	29 y	27 y	6	22	78	5	0	1	18	29	81 y	81 y	80 y
Tonga	–	–	–	0	6	93	–	–	–	21	29	–	–	–
Trinidad and Tobago	1 x	1 x	1 x	2 x	8 x	97 x	–	–	–	–	8 x	77 x	78 x	77 x
Tunisia	2	3	2	0	2	99	–	–	–	–	30	93	94	92
Turkey	6 y	8 y	4 y	1	15	99 y	–	–	–	–	13	–	–	–
Turkmenistan	–	–	–	1 x	7 x	96 x	–	–	–	–	38 x,y	–	–	–
Tuvalu	–	–	–	0 x	10 x	50 x	–	–	–	73 x	70 x	–	–	–
Uganda	16 y	17 y	16 y	10	40	30	1	1	9	44	58	–	–	–
Ukraine	2	3	2	0	9	100	–	–	–	9	3	61	68	55
United Arab Emirates	–	–	–	–	–	100 y	–	–	–	–	–	–	–	–
United Kingdom	–	–	–	–	–	100 v	–	–	–	–	–	–	–	–
United Republic of Tanzania	29 y	29 y	28 y	7	37	15 y	15	3 y	6	38	54	–	–	–
United States	–	–	–	–	–	100 v	–	–	–	–	–	–	–	–

TABLE 9. CHILD PROTECTION

Countries and areas	Child labour (%)[+] 2009–2015*			Child marriage (%) 2008–2014*		Birth registration (%)[++] 2010–2015*	Female genital mutilation/cutting (%)[+] 2004–2015*			Justification of wife-beating (%) 2010–2015*		Violent discipline (%)[+] 2010–2015*		
							prevalence		attitudes					
	total	male	female	married by 15	married by 18	total	women[a]	girls[b]	support for the practice[c]	male	female	total	male	female
Uruguay	8 x,y	8 x,y	8 x,y	1	25	100	–	–	–	–	2	55	58	51
Uzbekistan	–	–	–	0 x	7 x	100 x	–	–	–	61 x	70 x	–	–	–
Vanuatu	15 y	15 y	16 y	3	21	43 y	–	–	–	60	60	84	83	84
Venezuela (Bolivarian Republic of)	8 x	9 x	6 x	–	–	81 y	–	–	–	–	–	–	–	–
Viet Nam	16 y	17 y	16 y	1	11	96	–	–	–	–	28	68 y	72 y	65 y
Yemen	23 x	21 x	24 x	9	32	31	19	16 y	19	–	49	79 y	81 y	77 y
Zambia	41 x,y	42 x,y	40 x,y	6	31	11	–	–	–	32	47	–	–	–
Zimbabwe	–	–	–	4	34	32	–	–	–	24	37	63 y	63 y	62 y
SUMMARY														
Sub-Saharan Africa	28	27	27	12	39	46	39	16	22	35	50	–	–	–
Eastern and Southern Africa	26	28	24	10	36	45	43	13	19	37	52	–	–	–
West and Central Africa	28	27	28	14	42	45	31	17	23	34	49	87	88	87
Middle East and North Africa	10	8	6	3	18	89	–	16	–	–	43	83	88	86
South Asia	–	–	–	–	–	62	–	–	–	–	–	–	–	–
East Asia and Pacific	10 **	11 **	9 **	–	15 **	80 **	–	–	–	–	28 **	–	–	–
Latin America and Caribbean	9	12	7	5	23	94	–	–	–	–	–	–	–	–
CEE/CIS	–	–	–	1	11	99	–	–	–	–	–	–	–	–
Least developed countries	24	25	23	13	41	45	–	–	–	40	52	–	–	–
World	–	–	–	–	–	**71 ****	–	–	–	–	–	–	–	–

For a complete list of countries and areas in the regions, subregions and country categories, see page 112 or visit <data.unicef.org/regionalclassifications>.
It is not advisable to compare data from consecutive editions of *The State of the World's Children*.

DEFINITIONS OF THE INDICATORS

Child labour – Percentage of children 5–14 years old involved in child labour at the moment of the survey. A child is considered to be involved in child labour under the following conditions: (a) children 5–11 years old who, during the reference week, did at least 1 hour of economic activity or at least 28 hours of household chores, or (b) children 12–14 years old who, during the reference week, did at least 14 hours of economic activity or at least 28 hours of household chores.

Child marriage – Percentage of women 20–24 years old who were first married or in union before they were 15 years old and percentage of women 20–24 years old who were first married or in union before they were 18 years old.

Birth registration – Percentage of children less than 5 years old who were registered at the moment of the survey. The numerator of this indicator includes children reported to have a birth certificate, regardless of whether or not it was seen by the interviewer, and those without a birth certificate whose mother or caregiver says the birth has been registered.

Female genital mutilation/cutting (FGM/C) – (a) Women: percentage of women 15–49 years old who have undergone FGM/C; (b) girls: percentage of girls 0–14 years old who have undergone FGM/C (as reported by their mothers); (c) support for the practice: percentage of women 15–49 years old who have heard about FGM/C and think the practice should continue.

Justification of wife-beating – Percentage of women and men 15–49 years old who consider a husband to be justified in hitting or beating his wife for at least one of the specified reasons, i.e., if his wife burns the food, argues with him, goes out without telling him, neglects the children or refuses sexual relations.

Violent discipline – Percentage of children 2–14 years old who experience any violent discipline (psychological aggression and/or physical punishment).

MAIN DATA SOURCES

Child labour – Demographic and Health Surveys (DHS), Multiple Indicator Cluster Surveys (MICS) and other national surveys.

Child marriage – DHS, MICS and other national surveys.

Birth registration – DHS, MICS, other national surveys, censuses and vital registration systems.

Female genital mutilation/cutting – DHS, MICS and other national surveys.

Justification of wife-beating – DHS, MICS and other national surveys.

Violent discipline – DHS, MICS and other national surveys.

Italicized data are from older sources than the data presented for a country for other indicators on the same topic.

NOTES

– Data not available.

v Estimates of 100% were assumed given that civil registration systems in these countries are complete and all vital events (including births) are registered. Source: United Nations, Department of Economic and Social Affairs, Statistics Division, *Population and Vital Statistics Report*, Series A Vol. LXV, New York, 2013.

x Data refer to years or periods other than those specified in the column heading. Such data are not included in the calculation of regional and global averages.

y Data differ from the standard definition or refer to only part of a country. If they fall within the noted reference period, such data are included in the calculation of regional and global averages.

+ A more detailed explanation of the methodology and the changes in calculating these estimates can be found in the General Note on the Data, page 108.

++ Changes in the definition of birth registration were made from the second and third rounds of MICS (MICS2 and MICS3) to the fourth round (MICS4). In order to allow for comparability with later rounds, data from MICS2 and MICS3 on birth registration were recalculated according to the MICS4 indicator definition. Therefore, the recalculated data presented here may differ from estimates included in MICS2 and MICS3 national reports.

* Data refer to the most recent year available during the period specified in the column heading.

** Excludes China.

TABLE 10. THE RATE OF PROGRESS

Countries and areas	Under-5 mortality rank	Under-5 mortality rate				Annual rate of reduction (%) Under-5 mortality rate				Reduction since 1990 (%)	Reduction since 2000 (%)	GDP per capita average annual growth rate (%)		Total fertility rate			Average annual rate of reduction (%) Total fertility rate	
		1970	1990	2000	2015	1970–1990	1990–2000	2000–2015	1990–2015			1970–1990	1990–2014	1970	1990	2015	1970–1990	1990–2015
Afghanistan	16	308	181	137	91	2.7	2.8	2.7	2.7	50	34	–	5.6 x	7.5	7.5	4.7	0.0	1.9
Albania	112	–	41	26	14	–	4.4	4.2	4.3	66	47	-0.6 x	5.7	4.9	3.0	1.8	2.5	2.0
Algeria	79	242	47	40	26	8.2	1.6	3.0	2.4	46	36	1.8	1.7	7.6	4.7	2.8	2.4	2.1
Andorra	182	–	9	5	3	–	6.1	3.3	4.4	67	39	-1.3	1.2 x	–	–	–	–	–
Angola	1	–	226	217	157	–	0.4	2.2	1.5	31	28	–	-0.4 x	7.4	7.2	6.0	0.1	0.7
Antigua and Barbuda	142	–	26	16	8	–	5.0	4.3	4.6	68	48	7.9 x	1.2	3.7	2.1	2.1	2.9	0.0
Argentina	120	72	28	20	13	4.8	3.1	3.2	3.2	55	38	-0.8	2.3	3.1	3.0	2.3	0.1	1.0
Armenia	112	–	50	30	14	–	5.0	5.1	5.0	72	53	–	6.2	3.2	2.5	1.5	1.2	2.1
Australia	166	21	9	6	4	4.2	3.9	3.3	3.5	59	39	1.6	2.0	2.7	1.9	1.9	1.9	-0.1
Austria	166	29	10	6	4	5.6	5.5	3.0	4.0	63	36	2.5	1.6	2.3	1.5	1.5	2.3	-0.1
Azerbaijan	68	–	95	74	32	–	2.5	5.7	4.4	67	57	–	6.4	4.6	3.0	2.3	2.2	1.1
Bahamas	125	31	24	16	12	1.3	4.0	1.7	2.7	49	23	1.9	0.1	3.5	2.6	1.9	1.5	1.4
Bahrain	153	77	23	13	6	6.0	6.0	4.7	5.2	73	51	-1.0 x	0.1	6.5	3.7	2.0	2.8	2.4
Bangladesh	61	224	144	88	38	2.2	4.9	5.7	5.4	74	57	0.7	3.6	6.9	4.5	2.1	2.2	3.0
Barbados	120	48	18	16	13	4.9	0.9	1.5	1.3	27	20	1.4 x	1.2	3.1	1.7	1.8	2.9	-0.1
Belarus	159	–	17	14	5	–	1.5	7.6	5.1	72	68	–	5.0	2.3	1.9	1.6	1.1	0.5
Belgium	166	24	10	6	4	4.4	5.4	2.3	3.6	59	29	2.2	1.4	2.2	1.6	1.8	1.7	-0.6
Belize	99	97	40	25	17	4.5	4.6	2.8	3.5	58	34	3.1	1.7	6.3	4.5	2.5	1.7	2.3
Benin	8	266	180	145	100	2.0	2.2	2.5	2.4	45	31	0.4	1.1	6.7	6.7	4.7	0.0	1.5
Bhutan	67	272	134	80	33	3.5	5.2	5.9	5.6	75	59	7.0 x	5.3	6.7	5.6	2.0	0.8	4.2
Bolivia (Plurinational State of)	61	231	124	80	38	3.1	4.4	4.9	4.7	69	52	-1.0	2.0	6.3	4.9	2.9	1.2	2.1
Bosnia and Herzegovina	159	–	18	9	5	–	6.9	3.6	4.9	70	41	–	7.4 x	2.9	1.8	1.3	2.5	1.4
Botswana	55	121	54	83	44	4.0	-4.2	4.3	0.9	20	47	8.1	2.7	6.6	4.7	2.8	1.7	2.1
Brazil	104	134	61	32	16	3.9	6.4	4.5	5.2	73	49	2.2	1.8	5.0	2.8	1.8	2.9	1.8
Brunei Darussalam	133	–	12	9	10	–	2.6	-0.5	0.7	16	-9	-2.2 x	-0.4	5.8	3.5	1.9	2.4	2.6
Bulgaria	133	39	22	21	10	2.8	0.5	4.7	3.0	53	50	3.4 x	3.5	2.1	1.8	1.6	0.9	0.5
Burkina Faso	18	319	202	186	89	2.3	0.9	4.9	3.3	56	52	1.4	2.9	6.6	7.0	5.4	-0.3	1.0
Burundi	21	248	172	152	82	1.8	1.2	4.1	3.0	52	46	1.2	-1.5	7.3	7.5	5.9	-0.2	1.0
Cabo Verde	80	165	63	36	25	4.8	5.7	2.5	3.8	61	31	3.5 x	6.3	6.9	5.3	2.3	1.3	3.4
Cambodia	71	–	117	108	29	–	0.8	8.9	5.6	76	73	–	5.9 x	6.5	5.6	2.6	0.7	3.1
Cameroon	19	213	138	150	88	2.2	-0.9	3.6	1.8	36	42	3.4	0.6	6.2	6.4	4.6	-0.2	1.3
Canada	159	22	8	6	5	4.9	2.9	1.6	2.1	41	21	2.0	1.6	2.2	1.7	1.6	1.5	0.2
Central African Republic	4	223	177	175	130	1.2	0.1	2.0	1.2	26	26	-1.3	-0.6	6.0	5.8	4.2	0.1	1.3
Chad	2	–	215	190	139	–	1.2	2.1	1.7	35	27	-0.9	3.3	6.5	7.3	6.1	-0.6	0.8
Chile	142	80	19	11	8	7.1	5.6	2.0	3.4	58	26	1.5	3.3	4.0	2.5	1.7	2.4	1.4
China	130	113	54	37	11	3.7	3.8	8.3	6.5	80	71	6.6	9.2	5.7	2.4	1.6	4.3	1.7
Colombia	104	98	35	25	16	5.1	3.4	3.0	3.2	55	37	1.9	2.1	5.5	3.0	1.9	3.1	1.9
Comoros	25	227	125	101	74	3.0	2.1	2.1	2.1	41	27	-0.2 x	-0.2	7.1	6.4	4.4	0.5	1.5
Congo	52	143	94	122	45	2.1	-2.6	6.6	2.9	52	63	3.3	0.6	6.3	5.3	4.8	0.8	0.4
Cook Islands	142	52	24	17	8	3.8	3.7	4.9	4.4	67	52	–	–	–	–	–	–	–
Costa Rica	133	76	17	13	10	7.5	2.6	2.0	2.2	43	25	0.8	2.9	4.6	3.2	1.8	1.9	2.3
Côte d'Ivoire	13	241	153	146	93	2.3	0.5	3.0	2.0	39	36	-1.7	-0.5	7.9	6.6	4.9	0.9	1.2
Croatia	166	–	13	8	4	–	4.4	4.4	4.4	67	48	–	2.6 x	2.0	1.6	1.5	1.1	0.3
Cuba	153	44	13	8	6	5.9	4.6	2.8	3.5	59	35	3.9	3.3 x	4.0	1.8	1.6	4.2	0.3
Cyprus	182	–	11	7	3	–	5.2	6.0	5.7	76	59	5.9 x	1.5	2.6	2.4	1.4	0.4	2.1
Czech Republic	182	–	15	7	3	–	7.9	4.4	5.8	77	48	–	2.5	2.1	1.8	1.5	0.7	0.8
Democratic People's Republic of Korea	80	–	43	60	25	–	-3.2	5.9	2.2	43	59	–	–	4.3	2.3	2.0	3.2	0.6
Democratic Republic of the Congo	9	248	187	161	98	1.4	1.5	3.3	2.6	47	39	-2.1	-1.9	6.2	7.1	5.9	-0.6	0.7
Denmark	166	17	9	6	4	3.1	4.6	3.1	3.7	61	38	2.0	1.2	2.1	1.7	1.7	1.2	-0.2
Djibouti	32	–	119	101	65	–	1.7	2.9	2.4	45	35	–	0.4	6.8	6.1	3.1	0.6	2.7
Dominica	89	64	17	15	21	6.6	1.1	-2.2	-0.9	-24	-39	5.2 x	2.0	–	–	–	–	–
Dominican Republic	70	122	60	41	31	3.5	3.8	1.9	2.7	49	25	2.1	3.7	6.2	3.5	2.5	2.9	1.4
Ecuador	84	138	57	34	22	4.4	5.0	3.1	3.9	62	37	1.7	1.5	6.1	3.8	2.5	2.4	1.6
Egypt	82	243	86	47	24	5.2	6.1	4.4	5.1	72	48	4.1	2.6	5.9	4.7	3.3	1.2	1.4
El Salvador	99	155	59	32	17	4.8	6.1	4.4	5.1	72	48	-1.9	2.2	6.2	3.9	1.9	2.3	2.9
Equatorial Guinea	11	–	190	152	94	–	2.2	3.2	2.8	50	38	-2.4 x	19.0	5.7	5.9	4.7	-0.2	0.9
Eritrea	49	–	151	89	47	–	5.3	4.3	4.7	69	48	–	-0.2 x	6.7	6.4	4.2	0.2	1.7
Estonia	182	–	20	11	3	–	6.1	8.9	7.8	86	74	–	4.7 x	2.1	1.9	1.6	0.4	0.7
Ethiopia	37	241	205	145	59	0.8	3.4	6.0	5.0	71	59	–	3.8	7.0	7.2	4.3	-0.2	2.1
Fiji	84	55	30	25	22	3.1	2.0	0.6	1.1	25	9	0.6	1.1	4.5	3.4	2.5	1.5	1.2
Finland	193	16	7	4	2	4.4	4.4	4.2	4.3	66	47	2.9	2.1	1.9	1.7	1.8	0.3	0.0
France	166	18	9	5	4	3.5	5.1	1.5	3.0	52	20	2.2	1.2	2.5	1.8	2.0	1.8	-0.5
Gabon	42	–	93	85	51	–	0.9	3.5	2.4	45	40	0.6	-0.7	5.1	5.4	3.8	-0.3	1.4

unicef 70 YEARS FOR EVERY CHILD

TABLE 10. THE RATE OF PROGRESS

Countries and areas	Under-5 mortality rank	Under-5 mortality rate				Annual rate of reduction (%)ᵉ Under-5 mortality rate				Reduction since 1990 (%)ᵉ	Reduction since 2000 (%)ᵉ	GDP per capita average annual growth rate (%)		Total fertility rate			Average annual rate of reduction (%) Total fertility rate	
		1970	1990	2000	2015	1970–1990	1990–2000	2000–2015	1990–2015			1970–1990	1990–2014	1970	1990	2015	1970–1990	1990–2015
Gambia	29	303	170	119	69	2.9	3.6	3.6	3.6	60	42	0.7	0.3 x	6.1	6.1	5.7	0.0	0.3
Georgia	125	–	48	36	12	–	2.9	7.3	5.6	75	67	3.1	3.3	2.6	2.2	1.8	0.9	0.7
Germany	166	26	9	5	4	5.5	4.5	2.5	3.3	56	31	2.3	1.3	2.0	1.4	1.4	2.0	-0.2
Ghana	35	202	127	101	62	2.3	2.4	3.3	2.9	52	39	-2.0	2.9	7.0	5.6	4.1	1.1	1.2
Greece	159	38	13	8	5	5.5	4.8	3.5	4.0	63	41	1.3	1.4	2.4	1.4	1.3	2.5	0.3
Grenada	125	–	23	16	12	–	3.8	2.0	2.7	49	26	4.2 x	2.4	4.6	3.8	2.1	0.9	2.4
Guatemala	71	174	81	51	29	3.8	4.7	3.7	4.1	64	42	0.1	1.3	6.2	5.3	3.2	0.8	2.1
Guinea	11	327	238	170	94	1.6	3.4	4.0	3.7	61	45	–	0.6	6.2	6.6	4.9	-0.3	1.2
Guinea-Bissau	13	–	229	178	93	–	2.6	4.3	3.6	60	48	0.8	-0.9	6.0	6.6	4.8	-0.5	1.3
Guyana	59	74	60	47	39	1.0	2.6	1.1	1.7	35	16	-1.5	2.9 x	5.2	3.6	2.5	1.8	1.4
Haiti	29	245	146	105	69	2.6	3.3	2.8	3.0	53	34	–	-0.6 x	5.8	5.4	3.0	0.3	2.4
Holy See	–	–	–	–	–	–	–	–	–	–	–	–	–	–	–	–	–	–
Honduras	94	148	58	37	20	4.7	4.4	4.0	4.2	65	45	0.8	1.7	7.3	5.1	2.3	1.7	3.2
Hungary	153	43	19	11	6	4.0	5.3	4.3	4.7	69	47	–	2.5 x	2.0	1.8	1.4	0.5	1.2
Iceland	193	16	6	4	2	4.5	4.7	4.6	4.7	69	50	3.2	2.1	3.0	2.2	1.9	1.7	0.5
India	48	213	126	91	48	2.6	3.2	4.3	3.9	62	48	2.0	5.0	5.6	4.0	2.4	1.6	2.1
Indonesia	77	166	85	52	27	3.4	4.8	4.4	4.5	68	48	4.5	2.9	5.5	3.1	2.4	2.8	1.0
Iran (Islamic Republic of)	104	–	58	35	16	–	5.1	5.4	5.2	73	55	-4.3	2.4	6.4	4.8	1.7	1.5	4.2
Iraq	68	115	54	45	32	3.8	1.9	2.2	2.1	41	28	4.2	3.7	7.4	5.9	4.5	1.1	1.1
Ireland	166	22	9	7	4	4.4	2.6	4.5	3.8	61	49	2.8	3.8	3.8	2.0	2.0	3.2	0.0
Israel	166	–	12	7	4	–	5.2	3.6	4.3	66	42	1.9	2.4	3.8	3.0	3.0	1.2	0.0
Italy	166	34	10	6	4	6.2	5.7	3.0	4.1	64	36	2.8	0.6	2.4	1.3	1.5	3.2	-0.5
Jamaica	104	58	31	22	16	3.2	3.3	2.2	2.7	49	29	-1.3	0.4	5.5	2.9	2.0	3.1	1.5
Japan	182	18	6	5	3	5.1	3.4	3.4	3.4	57	40	3.4	0.7	2.1	1.6	1.4	1.5	0.4
Jordan	96	90	37	28	18	4.5	2.8	2.9	2.9	51	35	2.5 x	2.6	7.9	5.5	3.4	1.8	2.0
Kazakhstan	112	–	53	44	14	–	1.9	7.5	5.3	73	68	–	4.3	3.5	2.8	2.6	1.1	0.3
Kenya	46	148	102	108	49	1.9	-0.5	5.2	2.9	52	54	1.2	0.8	8.1	6.0	4.3	1.5	1.4
Kiribati	39	140	96	71	56	1.9	3.1	1.6	2.2	42	21	-5.0	1.0	5.5	4.7	3.7	0.8	1.0
Kuwait	139	71	18	13	9	6.9	3.4	2.6	2.9	52	32	-6.7 x	0.0 x	7.3	2.6	2.1	5.1	0.9
Kyrgyzstan	89	–	65	49	21	–	2.9	5.5	4.5	67	56	–	1.1	4.9	3.9	3.1	1.2	0.9
Lao People's Democratic Republic	31	–	162	118	67	–	3.2	3.8	3.6	59	43	–	4.9	6.0	6.2	2.9	-0.1	3.0
Latvia	142	–	20	17	8	–	1.7	5.2	3.8	61	54	–	5.7 x	1.9	1.9	1.5	0.0	1.0
Lebanon	142	63	33	20	8	3.3	4.9	5.9	5.5	74	59	–	2.1	4.9	3.0	1.7	2.5	2.2
Lesotho	17	175	88	117	90	3.4	-2.8	1.7	-0.1	-2	23	3.0	2.7	5.8	4.9	3.1	0.8	1.8
Liberia	27	286	255	182	70	0.6	3.4	6.4	5.2	73	62	-4.1	2.4	6.7	6.5	4.6	0.1	1.3
Libya	120	138	42	28	13	6.0	3.9	4.9	4.5	68	52	–	-1.4 x	8.1	5.0	2.4	2.5	2.9
Liechtenstein	–	–	–	–	–	–	–	–	–	–	–	2.2	2.9 x	–	–	–	–	–
Lithuania	159	25	17	12	5	2.1	3.4	5.5	4.6	68	56	–	5.8 x	2.3	2.0	1.6	0.8	0.8
Luxembourg	193	22	9	5	2	4.7	6.1	6.2	6.1	78	60	2.6	2.2	2.0	1.6	1.6	1.1	-0.1
Madagascar	44	152	161	109	50	-0.3	3.9	5.3	4.7	69	55	-2.4	-0.3	7.3	6.3	4.4	0.8	1.5
Malawi	33	347	242	174	64	1.8	3.3	6.7	5.3	74	63	0.0	1.4	7.3	7.0	5.0	0.2	1.3
Malaysia	148	56	17	10	7	6.1	4.9	2.5	3.5	58	31	4.0	3.2	4.9	3.5	1.9	1.6	2.4
Maldives	139	261	94	44	9	5.1	7.5	10.9	9.6	91	81	–	4.1 x	7.2	6.0	2.1	0.9	4.2
Mali	6	400	254	220	115	2.3	1.5	4.3	3.2	55	48	1.4	1.5	7.1	7.2	6.1	0.0	0.6
Malta	153	28	11	8	6	4.5	3.7	1.3	2.3	43	18	6.0	2.2 x	2.0	2.0	1.5	-0.1	1.3
Marshall Islands	63	88	50	41	36	2.8	1.9	0.9	1.3	28	13	–	0.7	–	–	–	–	–
Mauritania	20	194	118	114	85	2.5	0.4	2.0	1.3	28	25	-1.1	1.2	6.8	6.0	4.5	0.6	1.1
Mauritius	112	83	23	19	14	6.4	2.2	2.1	2.1	42	27	3.1 x	3.6	4.0	2.3	1.5	2.7	1.8
Mexico	120	109	47	26	13	4.2	6.0	4.4	5.0	72	48	1.7	1.1	6.8	3.5	2.2	3.4	1.8
Micronesia (Federated States of)	65	–	56	54	35	–	0.3	2.9	1.9	38	36	–	0.6	6.9	5.0	3.2	1.7	1.8
Monaco	166	–	8	5	4	–	4.1	2.6	3.2	55	33	1.5	1.7 x	–	–	–	–	–
Mongolia	84	–	108	63	22	–	5.4	6.9	6.3	79	64	–	4.1	7.6	4.1	2.6	3.1	1.7
Montenegro	159	–	17	14	5	–	1.8	7.2	5.0	72	66	–	2.8 x	2.7	2.1	1.7	1.4	0.9
Morocco	73	189	80	50	28	4.3	4.7	4.0	4.3	66	45	2.6	2.8	6.7	4.1	2.5	2.5	2.0
Mozambique	23	273	240	171	79	0.6	3.4	5.2	4.5	67	54	-1.1 x	5.1	6.6	6.2	5.3	0.3	0.7
Myanmar	44	179	110	82	50	2.4	2.9	3.3	3.2	55	39	1.4	11.8 x	6.0	3.5	2.2	2.7	1.8
Namibia	52	97	74	76	45	1.4	-0.3	3.4	1.9	38	40	-2.1 x	2.2	6.5	5.2	3.5	1.1	1.6
Nauru	65	–	57	41	35	–	3.2	1.0	1.9	38	14	–	–	–	–	–	–	–
Nepal	63	268	141	81	36	3.2	5.6	5.4	5.5	75	56	1.2	2.6	5.9	5.2	2.2	0.7	3.5
Netherlands	166	16	8	6	4	3.2	2.9	3.3	3.1	54	39	1.5	1.7	2.4	1.6	1.8	2.2	-0.5
New Zealand	153	21	11	7	6	3.1	4.1	1.7	2.7	49	23	1.5 x	1.7	3.1	2.1	2.0	2.0	0.1
Nicaragua	84	171	67	40	22	4.7	5.1	4.0	4.4	67	45	-3.7	2.1	6.9	4.6	2.2	2.0	2.9
Niger	10	327	328	227	96	0.0	3.7	5.8	4.9	71	58	-1.9	0.0	7.4	7.7	7.6	-0.2	0.1

TABLE 10. THE RATE OF PROGRESS

Countries and areas	Under-5 mortality rank	Under-5 mortality rate				Annual rate of reduction (%)◦ Under-5 mortality rate				Reduction since 1990 (%)◦	Reduction since 2000 (%)◦	GDP per capita average annual growth rate (%)		Total fertility rate			Average annual rate of reduction (%) Total fertility rate	
		1970	1990	2000	2015	1970–1990	1990–2000	2000–2015	1990–2015			1970–1990	1990–2014	1970	1990	2015	1970–1990	1990–2015
Nigeria	7	285	213	187	109	1.5	1.3	3.6	2.7	49	42	-2.3	3.4	6.5	6.5	5.6	0.0	0.6
Niue	83	–	14	23	23	–	-5.2	0.1	-2.0	-67	1	–	–	–	–	–	–	–
Norway	182	16	9	5	3	3.1	5.7	4.2	4.8	70	47	3.3	1.6	2.5	1.9	1.8	1.5	0.1
Oman	125	228	39	17	12	8.8	8.6	2.4	4.9	71	30	3.2	0.6	7.3	7.2	2.7	0.1	3.9
Pakistan	22	189	139	112	81	1.5	2.1	2.2	2.1	41	28	2.7	1.7	6.6	6.0	3.6	0.5	2.1
Palau	104	–	36	27	16	–	3.0	3.3	3.2	55	39	–	-0.4 x	–	–	–	–	–
Panama	99	68	31	26	17	3.9	1.7	2.8	2.4	45	35	0.2	3.8	5.2	3.1	2.4	2.6	0.9
Papua New Guinea	38	144	89	79	57	2.4	1.3	2.1	1.8	36	27	-1.0	0.9	6.2	4.8	3.7	1.2	1.0
Paraguay	89	78	47	34	21	2.6	3.3	3.3	3.3	56	39	3.8	0.9	5.7	4.5	2.5	1.2	2.4
Peru	99	164	80	39	17	3.6	7.3	5.5	6.2	79	56	-0.5	3.4	6.4	3.8	2.4	2.6	1.8
Philippines	73	84	58	40	28	1.8	3.8	2.3	2.9	52	29	0.6	2.3	6.3	4.3	2.9	1.9	1.5
Poland	159	36	17	9	5	3.7	6.2	3.9	4.8	70	44	–	4.2	2.3	2.1	1.3	0.4	1.7
Portugal	166	68	15	7	4	7.7	7.1	4.6	5.6	76	50	2.5	1.2	3.0	1.5	1.3	3.4	0.8
Qatar	142	66	21	12	8	5.8	5.2	2.9	3.8	62	35	–	1.5 x	6.9	4.0	2.0	2.7	2.8
Republic of Korea	182	53	7	6	3	10.0	1.5	3.9	2.9	52	44	7.5	4.3	4.5	1.6	1.3	5.2	0.9
Republic of Moldova	104	–	33	31	16	–	0.6	4.6	3.0	52	50	1.8 x	0.8	2.6	2.4	1.2	0.3	2.6
Romania	130	66	38	27	11	2.8	3.4	5.9	4.9	71	59	–	3.4	2.8	1.9	1.5	2.1	0.9
Russian Federation	133	44	26	23	10	2.7	1.1	5.9	4.0	63	59	–	2.5	2.0	1.9	1.7	0.3	0.4
Rwanda	56	219	152	184	42	1.8	-1.9	9.9	5.2	73	77	1.1	3.3	8.2	7.3	3.8	0.6	2.6
Saint Kitts and Nevis	130	69	28	19	11	4.5	4.2	3.8	4.0	63	44	6.5 x	1.8	–	–	–	–	–
Saint Lucia	112	76	23	18	14	6.0	2.4	1.5	1.8	37	20	5.1 x	1.2	6.1	3.4	1.9	2.9	2.4
Saint Vincent and the Grenadines	96	80	25	22	18	5.9	1.0	1.3	1.2	25	18	3.3	2.9	6.0	3.0	2.0	3.6	1.7
Samoa	96	–	31	22	18	–	3.6	1.4	2.3	44	19	–	2.5	7.2	5.1	4.0	1.7	1.0
San Marino	182	–	11	6	3	–	6.8	4.3	5.3	73	47	1.8	3.4 x	–	–	–	–	–
Sao Tome and Principe	49	87	111	89	47	-1.2	2.1	4.2	3.4	57	47	–	3.0 x	6.5	5.8	4.5	0.5	1.0
Saudi Arabia	110	–	44	23	15	–	6.6	3.0	4.5	67	37	-2.1	1.4	7.3	5.9	2.7	1.0	3.1
Senegal	49	291	140	135	47	3.6	0.4	7.0	4.4	66	65	-0.6	1.1	7.3	6.6	5.0	0.5	1.1
Serbia	148	–	28	13	7	–	8.1	4.2	5.8	76	47	–	3.7 x	2.4	2.1	1.6	0.7	1.1
Seychelles	112	72	17	14	14	7.4	1.4	0.3	0.8	18	5	2.9	2.1	5.8	2.7	2.3	3.7	0.7
Sierra Leone	5	335	264	236	120	1.2	1.1	4.5	3.1	54	49	-0.6	1.4	6.0	6.7	4.5	-0.5	1.6
Singapore	182	27	8	4	3	6.3	6.5	2.6	4.2	65	32	5.9	3.5	3.2	1.7	1.2	3.1	1.3
Slovakia	148	–	18	12	7	–	4.1	3.1	3.5	59	38	–	4.2 x	2.5	2.0	1.4	1.0	1.5
Slovenia	182	–	10	6	3	–	6.4	5.0	5.5	75	53	–	2.5 x	2.2	1.5	1.6	2.1	-0.4
Solomon Islands	73	107	40	33	28	5.0	1.8	1.1	1.4	29	15	–	-0.4	6.9	5.9	3.9	0.8	1.6
Somalia	3	–	180	174	137	–	0.3	1.6	1.1	24	22	-0.8	–	7.2	7.4	6.4	-0.1	0.6
South Africa	58	–	60	75	41	–	-2.3	4.1	1.6	32	46	0.1	1.2	5.6	3.7	2.3	2.1	1.8
South Sudan	13	–	253	182	93	–	3.3	4.5	4.0	63	49	–	–	6.9	6.8	4.9	0.1	1.3
Spain	166	29	11	7	4	4.9	5.3	3.1	3.9	63	37	1.9	1.5	2.9	1.3	1.3	3.8	0.0
Sri Lanka	133	71	21	16	10	6.1	2.6	3.4	3.1	54	40	3.0	4.4	4.3	2.5	2.1	2.8	0.7
State of Palestine	89	–	44	30	21	–	4.0	2.3	3.0	52	29	–	1.8 x	7.9	6.7	4.1	0.8	2.0
Sudan	27	155	128	106	70	1.0	1.9	2.8	2.4	45	34	-0.1	3.5	6.9	6.2	4.3	0.6	1.4
Suriname	89	–	48	34	21	–	3.2	3.2	3.2	55	38	-2.3 x	2.2	5.7	3.3	2.3	2.7	1.4
Swaziland	36	176	75	128	61	4.3	-5.4	5.0	0.8	19	53	3.1	1.0	6.9	5.7	3.2	0.9	2.3
Sweden	182	13	7	4	3	3.3	5.2	2.1	3.3	57	27	1.8	2.0	2.0	2.0	1.9	0.1	0.2
Switzerland	166	18	8	6	4	4.0	3.8	2.4	3.0	52	30	1.7 x	1.0	2.1	1.5	1.5	1.6	0.0
Syrian Arab Republic	120	105	37	23	13	5.2	4.6	4.0	4.2	65	45	2.1	1.8 x	7.6	5.3	2.9	1.8	2.4
Tajikistan	52	–	108	93	45	–	1.5	4.9	3.5	59	52	–	0.9	6.9	5.2	3.5	1.4	1.6
Thailand	125	100	37	23	12	5.0	5.0	4.0	4.4	67	45	4.8	3.1	5.6	2.1	1.5	4.9	1.4
The former Yugoslav Republic of Macedonia	153	–	37	16	6	–	8.3	7.1	7.6	85	66	–	1.8	3.2	2.2	1.5	1.8	1.5
Timor-Leste	41	–	176	110	53	–	4.7	4.9	4.8	70	52	–	3.4 x	5.9	5.3	5.6	0.5	-0.2
Togo	24	225	146	121	78	2.1	1.9	2.9	2.5	46	35	-0.5	0.1	7.1	6.3	4.5	0.6	1.3
Tonga	99	50	22	18	17	4.1	2.2	0.3	1.1	24	5	–	1.3	5.9	4.6	3.7	1.2	0.9
Trinidad and Tobago	94	52	31	29	20	2.6	0.6	2.3	1.6	33	29	-0.5	5.1	3.6	2.5	1.8	1.9	1.3
Tunisia	112	181	57	32	14	5.8	5.9	5.4	5.6	75	56	2.5	3.0	6.7	3.5	2.1	3.3	2.0
Turkey	112	187	75	40	14	4.6	6.3	7.2	6.8	82	66	1.9	2.5	5.6	3.1	2.1	3.0	1.6
Turkmenistan	42	–	91	82	51	–	1.0	3.1	2.3	43	37	–	3.5	6.3	4.3	2.3	1.9	2.6
Tuvalu	77	–	57	43	27	–	2.9	3.0	3.0	53	36	–	1.6	–	–	–	–	–
Uganda	40	190	187	148	55	0.1	2.3	6.7	4.9	71	63	–	3.6	7.1	7.1	5.7	0.0	0.9
Ukraine	139	–	20	19	9	–	0.5	4.8	3.1	54	51	–	1.0	2.0	1.8	1.5	0.7	0.6
United Arab Emirates	148	98	17	11	7	8.9	4.0	3.3	3.5	59	39	-4.3 x	-2.9	6.6	4.4	1.8	2.0	3.6
United Kingdom	166	21	9	7	4	4.1	3.4	3.0	3.2	55	36	2.2	1.8	2.3	1.8	1.9	1.2	-0.2
United Republic of Tanzania	46	216	165	131	49	1.3	2.4	6.6	4.9	71	63	–	2.5	6.8	6.2	5.1	0.4	0.8

TABLE 10. THE RATE OF PROGRESS

Countries and areas	Under-5 mortality rank	Under-5 mortality rate 1970	Under-5 mortality rate 1990	Under-5 mortality rate 2000	Under-5 mortality rate 2015	Annual rate of reduction (%)ᶿ Under-5 mortality rate 1970–1990	Annual rate of reduction (%)ᶿ Under-5 mortality rate 1990–2000	Annual rate of reduction (%)ᶿ Under-5 mortality rate 2000–2015	Annual rate of reduction (%)ᶿ Under-5 mortality rate 1990–2015	Reduction since 1990 (%)ᶿ	Reduction since 2000 (%)ᶿ	GDP per capita average annual growth rate (%) 1970–1990	GDP per capita average annual growth rate (%) 1990–2014	Total fertility rate 1970	Total fertility rate 1990	Total fertility rate 2015	Average annual rate of reduction (%) Total fertility rate 1970–1990	Average annual rate of reduction (%) Total fertility rate 1990–2015
United States	148	23	11	8	7	3.7	2.9	1.7	2.2	42	23	2.2	1.6	2.3	2.0	1.9	0.6	0.2
Uruguay	133	54	23	17	10	4.3	3.2	3.4	3.3	56	40	0.9	2.5	2.9	2.5	2.0	0.7	0.9
Uzbekistan	59	–	72	63	39	–	1.2	3.2	2.4	45	38	–	3.2	5.7	4.1	2.4	1.6	2.1
Vanuatu	73	109	36	29	28	5.6	2.2	0.2	1.0	23	4	1.1 x	0.6	6.3	4.9	3.3	1.2	1.6
Venezuela (Bolivarian Republic of)	110	63	30	22	15	3.7	3.1	2.5	2.7	50	31	-1.2	0.6	5.4	3.4	2.3	2.2	1.6
Viet Nam	84	86	51	34	22	2.6	4.1	3.0	3.4	57	36	–	5.5	6.5	3.6	2.0	3.0	2.4
Yemen	56	329	126	95	42	4.8	2.8	5.5	4.4	67	56	–	0.7 x	7.8	8.6	4.0	-0.5	3.0
Zambia	33	182	191	163	64	-0.2	1.6	6.2	4.4	66	61	-2.4	2.4	7.4	6.5	5.3	0.7	0.8
Zimbabwe	26	114	76	106	71	2.0	-3.3	2.7	0.3	7	33	-0.4	-2.8	7.4	5.2	3.9	1.8	1.2
SUMMARY																		
Sub-Saharan Africa		244	180	154	83	1.5	1.6	4.1	3.1	54	46	-0.1	2.4	6.7	6.4	4.9	0.3	1.0
Eastern and Southern Africa		213	167	140	67	1.2	1.8	4.9	3.7	60	52	0.3	1.7	6.9	6.1	4.5	0.6	1.3
West and Central Africa		276	198	172	99	1.6	1.4	3.7	2.8	50	43	-0.7	2.8	6.6	6.6	5.4	0.0	0.8
Middle East and North Africa		200	71	50	29	5.2	3.4	3.7	3.6	59	43	0.8	1.4	6.7	5.1	2.9	1.4	2.2
South Asia		213	129	94	53	2.5	3.2	3.9	3.6	59	44	2.0	4.6	5.8	4.3	2.5	1.5	2.1
East Asia and Pacific		116	58	42	18	3.5	3.4	5.6	4.7	69	57	6.0	7.7	5.7	2.6	1.8	3.8	1.5
Latin America and Caribbean		120	54	32	18	4.0	5.2	3.9	4.4	67	44	1.4	1.8	5.3	3.2	2.1	2.5	1.7
CEE/CIS		97	48	37	17	3.5	2.5	5.1	4.1	64	54	–	2.8	2.8	2.3	1.9	0.9	0.8
Least developed countries		242	175	138	73	1.6	2.4	4.2	3.5	58	47	0.0	3.1	6.8	6.0	4.1	0.6	1.5
World		**145**	**91**	**76**	**43**	**2.3**	**1.8**	**3.9**	**3.0**	**53**	**44**	**2.5**	**2.9**	**4.8**	**3.3**	**2.5**	**1.9**	**1.1**

For a complete list of countries and areas in the regions, subregions and country categories, see page 112 or visit <data.unicef.org/regionalclassifications>.
It is not advisable to compare data from consecutive editions of *The State of the World's Children*.

DEFINITIONS OF THE INDICATORS

Under-5 mortality rate – Probability of dying between birth and exactly 5 years of age, expressed per 1,000 live births.

GDP per capita – Gross domestic product (GDP) is the sum of value added by all resident producers plus any product taxes (less subsidies) not included in the valuation of output. GDP per capita is gross domestic product divided by midyear population. Growth is calculated from constant price GDP data in local currency.

Total fertility rate – Number of children who would be born per woman if she lived to the end of her childbearing years and bore children at each age in accordance with prevailing age-specific fertility rates.

MAIN DATA SOURCES

Under-5 mortality rate – United Nations Inter-agency Group for Child Mortality Estimation (UNICEF, World Health Organization, United Nations Population Division and the World Bank).

GDP per capita – The World Bank.

Total fertility rate – United Nations Population Division.

NOTES

– Data not available.

ᶿ A negative value indicates an increase in the under-five mortality rate.

x Data refer to years or periods other than those specified in the column heading. Such data are not included in the calculation of regional and global averages.

TABLE 11. ADOLESCENTS

Countries and areas	Adolescent population Aged 10–19 (thousands) 2015	Proportion of total population (%) 2015	Adolescents currently married/ in union (%) 2010–2015* male	female	Births by age 18 (%) 2010–2015*	Adolescent birth rate 2009–2014*	Justification of wife-beating among adolescents (%) 2010–2014* male	female	Use of mass media among adolescents (%) 2010–2014* male	female	Lower secondary school gross enrolment ratio 2010–2014*	Upper secondary school gross enrolment ratio 2010–2014*	Comprehensive knowledge of HIV among adolescents (%) 2010–2014* male	female
Afghanistan	8,305	26	–	20	26	90 x	–	84	–	–	66	44	–	2
Albania	454	16	1 x	8 x	3 x	18	37 x	24 x	97 x	99 x	99	94	21 x	36 x
Algeria	5,924	15	–	3	1	12	–	55 y	–	–	132	63	–	7
Andorra	–	–	–	–	–	5	–	–	–	–	–	–	–	–
Angola	5,954	24	–	–	–	191	–	–	–	–	36	21	26 x	24 x
Antigua and Barbuda	16	17	–	–	–	67 x	–	–	–	–	116	82	55	40
Argentina	7,020	16	–	–	12	70	–	2	–	–	128	84	–	36
Armenia	338	11	1	8	2	23	21	8	94	92	97 x	99	4	10
Australia	2,900	12	–	–	–	14	–	–	–	–	115	181	–	–
Austria	874	10	–	–	–	8	–	–	–	–	99	99	–	–
Azerbaijan	1,295	13	–	9	4	47	–	24	–	98	89	135	2 x	3 x
Bahamas	55	14	–	–	–	40 x	–	–	–	–	98	87	–	–
Bahrain	177	13	–	–	–	15	–	–	–	–	–	85	–	–
Bangladesh	32,530	20	–	34	24	83	–	33 y	–	63	76	45	–	10
Barbados	37	13	–	1	7	49 x	–	5	–	98	107	113	–	66
Belarus	879	9	1	7	3 x	22	3	3	–	–	104	113	53	51
Belgium	1,231	11	–	–	–	8	–	–	–	–	181	155	–	–
Belize	78	22	–	15	17	64	–	11	–	–	91	59	–	39
Benin	2,528	23	1	17	20	98	16	15	67	59	68	35	27	26
Bhutan	144	19	–	15	15	28	–	70	–	–	92	69	–	22
Bolivia (Plurinational State of)	2,216	21	4 x	13 x	20 x	89 x	–	17 x	100 x	97 x	100	77	24 x	20 x
Bosnia and Herzegovina	386	10	0	1	–	11	5	1	100	100	–	–	41	42
Botswana	441	19	–	–	–	39	–	–	–	–	91	73	–	–
Brazil	34,887	17	1	4	–	65	–	–	–	–	–	–	–	–
Brunei Darussalam	69	16	–	–	–	17 x	–	–	–	–	108	96	–	–
Bulgaria	635	9	–	2 y	5	43	–	–	–	–	93	108	–	–
Burkina Faso	4,319	24	2	32	28	136 x	40	39	61	55	42	13	31	29
Burundi	2,403	21	1	9	11	65 x	56	74	83	69	50	21	45	43
Cabo Verde	104	20	2 x	8 x	22 x	92 x	24 x	23 x	88 x	88 x	114	72	–	–
Cambodia	3,064	20	3	16	7	57	26 y	46 y	77	74	61	29 x	42	33
Cameroon	5,405	23	1	22	28	128 x	43	50	77	66	67	42	30	26
Canada	3,966	11	–	–	–	13	–	–	–	–	100	119	–	–
Central African Republic	1,120	23	11	55	45	229	83	79	–	–	23	9	26	17
Chad	3,428	24	–	48	47	203	–	59	55 x	24 x	26	18	–	10
Chile	2,568	14	–	–	–	50	–	–	–	–	103	99	–	–
China	154,222	11	–	2	–	6	–	–	–	–	107	87	–	–
Colombia	8,139	17	–	14	20	85 x	–	–	–	–	110 x	82	–	21
Comoros	175	22	8	16	17	71	17	43	79	67	66	50	21	18
Congo	1,020	22	2	16	26	147	76 y	73 y	56	68	65	38	25	16
Cook Islands	–	–	–	–	–	56	–	–	–	–	97	72	–	–
Costa Rica	759	16	2	10	13	67	–	3	–	–	133	102	–	29
Côte d'Ivoire	5,329	23	1	21	31	125	51	51	73	62	50	26	21	15
Croatia	448	11	–	–	–	12	–	–	–	–	102	98	–	–
Cuba	1,348	12	7	16	6	50	5 y	4 y	–	–	101	99	48	59
Cyprus	139	12	–	–	–	4	–	–	–	–	101	98	–	–
Czech Republic	932	9	–	–	–	11	–	–	–	–	104	105	–	–
Democratic People's Republic of Korea	3,820	15	–	–	–	1 x	–	–	–	–	102 x	102 x	–	7 x
Democratic Republic of the Congo	18,121	23	1	21	27	135	69	75	49	38	56	37	20	17
Denmark	688	12	–	–	–	2	–	–	–	–	117	142	–	–
Djibouti	181	20	–	3	–	21	–	–	–	–	51	40	–	16 x
Dominica	–	–	–	–	–	47 x	–	–	–	–	106	81	39	49
Dominican Republic	2,007	19	–	28	21	90	–	7	91	96	87	74	39	39
Ecuador	3,005	19	–	16 x	–	100 x	–	–	–	–	116	92	–	–
Egypt	16,511	18	–	14	7	56	–	46 y	100	100	100	72	–	3 y
El Salvador	1,230	20	–	21	18	63	–	–	–	–	101	55	–	–
Equatorial Guinea	178	21	5	22	42	177 x	56	57	91	91	–	–	12	17
Eritrea	1,178	23	1	17	19	–	60	51	70	54	45	28	32	22
Estonia	118	9	–	–	–	16	–	–	–	–	110	107	–	–
Ethiopia	24,725	25	–	20	22	71	51	64	42	38	42	13	32	24
Fiji	157	18	–	–	–	28 x	–	–	–	–	105	76	–	–
Finland	592	11	–	–	–	7	–	–	–	–	101	182	–	–

unicef 70 YEARS FOR EVERY CHILD

TABLE 11. ADOLESCENTS

Countries and areas	Adolescent population – Aged 10–19 (thousands) 2015	Adolescent population – Proportion of total population (%) 2015	Adolescents currently married/ in union (%) 2010–2015* male	Adolescents currently married/ in union (%) 2010–2015* female	Births by age 18 (%) 2010–2015*	Adolescent birth rate 2009–2014*	Justification of wife-beating among adolescents (%) 2010–2014* male	Justification of wife-beating among adolescents (%) 2010–2014* female	Use of mass media among adolescents (%) 2010–2014* male	Use of mass media among adolescents (%) 2010–2014* female	Lower secondary school gross enrolment ratio 2010–2014*	Upper secondary school gross enrolment ratio 2010–2014*	Comprehensive knowledge of HIV among adolescents (%) 2010–2014* male	Comprehensive knowledge of HIV among adolescents (%) 2010–2014* female
France	7,792	12	–	–	–	9	–	–	–	–	108	115	–	–
Gabon	366	21	1	14	28	115	47	58	95	94	–	–	35	29
Gambia	464	23	0	24	19	88	42	58	82	70	64	48	27	22
Georgia	434	11	–	11	6	40	–	5 x	–	–	109	91	–	–
Germany	7,644	9	–	–	–	8	–	–	–	–	102	104	–	–
Ghana	5,860	21	1	6	17	65	20	35	81	67	85	48	25	18
Greece	1,040	9	–	–	–	9	–	–	–	–	104	113	–	–
Grenada	19	17	–	–	–	53 x	–	–	–	–	104	97	67	59
Guatemala	3,721	23	–	20 x	22 x	92	–	–	–	–	69	55	24 x	20 x
Guinea	2,899	23	1	33	40	154	63	89	55	53	44	31	29	20
Guinea-Bissau	410	22	0	12	28	137	–	39 y	–	–	–	–	–	12
Guyana	185	24	13	13	16	97 x	25 x	18 x	94 x	94 x	93	83	45 x	53 x
Haiti	2,285	21	2	12	13	65	22	24	85	80	57	–	25	32
Holy See	–	–	–	–	–	–	–	–	–	–	–	–	–	–
Honduras	1,793	22	5	23	22	99	18	15	98	94	73	61	33	29
Hungary	979	10	–	–	–	20	–	–	–	–	101	114	–	–
Iceland	43	13	–	–	–	7	–	–	–	–	97	121	–	–
India	250,098	19	5 x	30 x	22 x	39	47 x	45 x	88 x	72 x	85	56	35 x	19 x
Indonesia	46,476	18	–	11	7	47	48 y	45	88 y	91	90	74	4 y,p	9
Iran (Islamic Republic of)	10,905	14	–	16 x	5	35	–	–	–	–	100	83	–	–
Iraq	8,040	22	–	21	12	68 x	–	50	–	–	–	–	–	3
Ireland	582	12	–	–	–	9	–	–	–	–	115	145	–	–
Israel	1,296	16	–	–	–	10	–	–	–	–	103	100	–	–
Italy	5,611	9	–	–	–	6	–	–	–	–	109	99	–	–
Jamaica	510	18	–	3	15	72 x	–	8	–	–	86	79	34 y	39 y
Japan	11,564	9	–	–	–	4	–	–	–	–	101	102	–	–
Jordan	1,577	21	–	6	4	27	–	84 y	–	100 y	87	78	–	6
Kazakhstan	2,274	13	1	5	2	31 x	14	9	99	99	109	98	30	30
Kenya	10,392	23	1	12	23	101	37	45	84	75	97	52	58	52
Kiribati	23	20	5 x	16 x	9 x	49	65 x	77 x	58 x	57 x	103	74 x	46 x	41 x
Kuwait	445	11	–	–	–	8	–	–	–	–	99	85	–	–
Kyrgyzstan	1,003	17	–	14	4	42	–	22	–	100	95	82	18	14
Lao People's Democratic Republic	1,484	22	9	25	18	94	50	56	92	93	71	39	25	23
Latvia	172	9	–	–	–	15	–	–	–	–	111	110	–	–
Lebanon	1,061	18	–	3 x	–	18 x	–	22 x,y	–	–	79	58	–	–
Lesotho	493	23	1 x	16 x	13 x	94	54 x	48 x	64 x	69 x	62	37	28 x	35 x
Liberia	1,044	23	2	14	37	147	29	45	59	47	45	30	19	35
Libya	1,089	17	–	–	–	4 x	–	–	–	–	–	–	–	–
Liechtenstein	–	–	–	–	–	2	–	–	–	–	104	118	–	–
Lithuania	292	10	–	–	–	14	–	–	–	–	104	110	–	–
Luxembourg	65	12	–	–	–	6	–	–	–	–	114	94	–	–
Madagascar	5,714	24	7	28	36	147 x	44	47	62	59	50	22	24	21
Malawi	4,111	24	3	28	31	143	15	16	70	51	47	22	50	43
Malaysia	5,400	18	5	6	–	13	–	–	–	–	92	56	–	–
Maldives	62	17	–	5 x	1 x	14	–	41 x,y	–	100 x	101	–	–	22 x,y
Mali	4,151	24	–	40	46 x	178	–	83	81 x	79 x	55	30	31	23
Malta	48	12	–	–	–	16	–	–	–	–	90	82	–	–
Marshall Islands	–	–	5 x	21 x	21 x	85	71 x	47 x	86 x	85 x	125	97 x	35 x	27 x
Mauritania	909	22	–	25	24	71	–	36	55 x	44 x	36	21	–	5
Mauritius	193	15	–	–	–	31	–	–	–	–	112	87	–	–
Mexico	23,754	19	6	15	39	84	–	–	–	–	111	63	–	–
Micronesia (Federated States of)	25	24	–	–	–	33	–	–	–	–	86	–	–	–
Monaco	–	–	–	–	–	–	–	–	–	–	–	–	–	–
Mongolia	448	15	1	5	3	40	9	14	99	98	95	85	24	28
Montenegro	83	13	0	2	3	12	5	2	–	–	95	86	35	42
Morocco	5,827	17	1	11	8 x	32 x	–	64 x	–	90 x	95	55	–	–
Mozambique	6,731	24	8	37	40	166	20	24	73	57	31	14	49	27
Myanmar	10,278	19	4	12	13 x	17 x	–	–	–	–	59	34	–	31
Namibia	538	22	1	5	15	78	30	28	65 y	69	–	–	51	56
Nauru	–	–	9 x	18 x	22 x	106	–	–	89 x	86 x	77	94	8 x	8 x
Nepal	6,623	23	–	25	16	87 x	–	35	–	77	89	50	–	38
Netherlands	1,985	12	–	–	–	5	–	–	–	–	135	126	–	–

TABLE 11. ADOLESCENTS

Countries and areas	Adolescent population — Aged 10–19 (thousands) 2015	Adolescent population — Proportion of total population (%) 2015	Adolescents currently married/ in union (%) 2010–2015* male	Adolescents currently married/ in union (%) 2010–2015* female	Births by age 18 (%) 2010–2015*	Adolescent birth rate 2009–2014*	Justification of wife-beating among adolescents (%) 2010–2014* male	Justification of wife-beating among adolescents (%) 2010–2014* female	Use of mass media among adolescents (%) 2010–2014* male	Use of mass media among adolescents (%) 2010–2014* female	Lower secondary school gross enrolment ratio 2010–2014*	Upper secondary school gross enrolment ratio 2010–2014*	Comprehensive knowledge of HIV among adolescents (%) 2010–2014* male	Comprehensive knowledge of HIV among adolescents (%) 2010–2014* female
New Zealand	604	13	–	–	–	22	–	–	–	–	103	135	–	–
Nicaragua	1,207	20	–	24 x	28 x	92	–	19 x,y	–	95 x	85	58	–	–
Niger	4,654	23	3	61	48	210	41	54	35	44	24	10	21	12
Nigeria	41,386	23	1	29	29	123	25	33	54	50	46	41	29	22
Niue	–	–	–	–	–	16	–	–	–	–	91	–	–	–
Norway	632	12	–	–	–	6	–	–	–	–	99	126	–	–
Oman	476	11	–	3	2	12	–	–	–	–	108	97	–	–
Pakistan	38,797	21	2	14	8	48	33 y	53 y	59 y	49 y	56	31	5 y,p	1 y
Palau	–	–	–	–	–	27	–	–	–	–	104	119	–	–
Panama	686	17	–	14	–	89	–	9	–	96	94	57	–	–
Papua New Guinea	1,698	22	3 x	15 x	14 x	65 x	–	–	–	–	73	22	–	–
Paraguay	1,342	20	–	11 x	–	63 x	–	–	–	–	84	69	–	–
Peru	5,606	18	–	11	15	68	–	–	–	90	100	88	–	21 x
Philippines	20,389	20	–	10	8	59	–	14	–	90	92	77	–	19 x
Poland	3,751	10	–	–	–	14	–	–	–	–	100	116	–	–
Portugal	1,072	10	–	–	–	12	–	–	–	–	120	119	–	–
Qatar	213	10	1	4	–	16	22	6 y	98	98	102	98	23	10
Republic of Korea	5,740	11	–	–	–	2	–	–	–	–	102	94	–	–
Republic of Moldova	444	11	1	10	4	25	14	13	96	96	87	92	26	35
Romania	2,108	11	–	–	–	36	–	–	–	–	95	101	–	–
Russian Federation	13,252	9	–	–	–	27	–	–	–	–	97	102	–	–
Rwanda	2,654	23	–	4	5	41 x	35	56	88	73	48	31	44	49
Saint Kitts and Nevis	–	–	–	–	–	75 x	–	–	–	–	95	86	55	54
Saint Lucia	31	17	–	4	–	50 x	–	15	–	99	88	84	–	58
Saint Vincent and the Grenadines	19	17	–	–	–	70	–	–	–	–	118	85	–	–
Samoa	43	22	1	8	6	39	28	34	99	97	102	80	5 x	2 x
San Marino	–	–	–	–	–	1	–	–	–	–	94	95	–	–
Sao Tome and Principe	45	24	2	19	27	110 x	25 x	23 x	96 x	95 x	105	45	39 x	39 x
Saudi Arabia	5,285	17	–	–	–	7 x	–	–	–	–	108	108	–	–
Senegal	3,430	23	0	23	18	80	38	58	96	96	39 x	16 x	28	26
Serbia	1,078	12	–	4	1	22	–	2	99	100	99	90	43	53
Seychelles	13	14	–	–	–	62	–	–	–	–	110	49	–	–
Sierra Leone	1,507	23	1	19	36	131	32	55	55	49	63	27	29	28
Singapore	674	12	–	–	–	3	–	–	–	–	–	–	–	–
Slovakia	543	10	–	–	–	21	–	–	–	–	97	86	–	–
Slovenia	185	9	–	–	–	5	–	–	–	–	99	120	–	–
Solomon Islands	133	23	0 x	13 x	15 x	62 x	73 x	72 x	71 x	54 x	75	29	26 x	29 x
Somalia	2,599	24	–	25 x	–	123 x	–	75 x,y	–	–	–	–	–	3 x
South Africa	10,328	19	2 x	4 x	15 x	54 x	–	–	–	–	95	95	–	–
South Sudan	2,874	23	–	40	28	158 x	–	72	–	–	17	–	–	8
Spain	4,373	9	–	–	–	9	–	–	–	–	132	130	–	–
Sri Lanka	3,284	16	–	9 x	4 x	24 x	–	54 x,y	–	88 x,y	100	99	–	–
State of Palestine	1,086	23	–	9	22	67	–	–	–	–	87	68	–	5
Sudan	9,240	23	–	21	22	102	–	52	–	–	50	33	10	4
Suriname	96	18	–	12	–	66 x	–	19	–	99	100	52	–	40
Swaziland	295	23	0	4	17	89	34	42	94 x	89 x	73	49	52	56
Sweden	1,025	10	–	–	–	3	–	–	–	–	112	142	–	–
Switzerland	833	10	–	–	–	3	–	–	–	–	110	86	–	–
Syrian Arab Republic	4,469	24	–	10 x	9 x	75 x	–	–	–	–	61	32	–	6 x
Tajikistan	1,707	20	–	13	2	47	–	47	–	89	97	68	–	7
Thailand	8,604	13	–	16	13	60	–	10	–	–	94	78	–	57
The former Yugoslav Republic of Macedonia	261	13	–	4	2	19	–	14	–	–	85	79	–	23 x
Timor-Leste	277	23	0	8	9	54 x	72	81	61	62	81	64	15	11
Togo	1,650	23	1	13	15	77	19	26	67	63	68	36	28	23
Tonga	24	23	4	5	2	30	29	27	92	95	–	–	13	10
Trinidad and Tobago	177	13	–	6 x	–	36 x	–	10 x	–	–	98 x	–	–	49 x
Tunisia	1,618	14	–	1	1	7	–	27	–	98	107	78	–	15
Turkey	13,397	17	–	7	6	29	–	10	–	–	140	95	–	–
Turkmenistan	959	18	–	5 x	2 x	21 x	–	37 x,y	–	96 x	87	82	–	4 x
Tuvalu	–	–	2 x	8 x	3 x	42 x	83 x	69 x	89 x	95 x	99	56	57 x	31 x
Uganda	9,603	25	2	20	33	140	52	62	88	82	31 x	14 x	36	36

unicef 70 YEARS FOR EVERY CHILD

TABLE 11. ADOLESCENTS

Countries and areas	Adolescent population — Aged 10–19 (thousands) 2015	Proportion of total population (%) 2015	Adolescents currently married/ in union (%) 2010–2015* male	female	Births by age 18 (%) 2010–2015*	Adolescent birth rate 2009–2014*	Justification of wife-beating among adolescents (%) 2010–2014* male	female	Use of mass media among adolescents (%) 2010–2014* male	female	Lower secondary school gross enrolment ratio 2010–2014*	Upper secondary school gross enrolment ratio 2010–2014*	Comprehensive knowledge of HIV among adolescents (%) 2010–2014* male	female
Ukraine	3,954	9	0	7	4	27	2	2	97	96	102	93	37	43
United Arab Emirates	781	9	–	–	–	34	–	–	–	–	–	–	–	–
United Kingdom	7,252	11	–	–	–	21	–	–	–	–	111	133	–	–
United Republic of Tanzania	12,291	23	8	17	28	128 x	39	52	79	70	43	9	42	37
United States	41,364	13	–	–	–	27	–	–	–	–	101	91	–	–
Uruguay	508	15	–	7	–	60	–	3	–	–	110	71	–	36
Uzbekistan	5,148	17	–	5 x	2 x	26 x	63 x	63 x	–	–	99	136	–	27 x
Vanuatu	54	21	4	11	13	78	63	56	58	58	69	47	–	14 x
Venezuela (Bolivarian Republic of)	5,640	18	–	16	–	101	–	–	–	–	99	80	–	–
Viet Nam	13,588	15	–	10	5	36	–	28	–	97	94	–	–	51
Yemen	6,283	23	–	17	17	67	–	49	–	85	58	39	–	2 x,y
Zambia	3,863	24	1	17	31	145	41	49	75	69	63	–	42	39
Zimbabwe	3,504	22	2	25	22	120	37	50	66	64	67	36	49	51
SUMMARY														
Sub-Saharan Africa	230,815	23	2	24	27	122	40	51	63	56	50	35	32	26
Eastern and Southern Africa	111,070	23	4	21	26	114	42	52	67	60	50	34	40	34
West and Central Africa	110,324	23	1	27	29	130	39	49	59	53	49	36	27	21
Middle East and North Africa	81,187	18	–	14	9	52	–	50	–	–	89	63	–	4
South Asia	339,843	19	–	–	16 ‡	44	–	–	–	–	81	54	–	7 ‡
East Asia and Pacific	276,692	13	–	6	7 **	22	–	33 **	–	91 **	95	76	–	25 **
Latin America and Caribbean	110,944	18	3	11	26	74	–	–	–	–	104	80	–	–
CEE/CIS	50,538	12	–	7	4	29	–	12	–	–	98	99	–	–
Least developed countries	217,127	23	–	25	26	112	46	52	63	60	51	31	31	22
World	**1,192,785**	**16**	–	**14**	**18‡****	**50**	–	–	–	–	**85**	**66**	-	**21 ‡****

For a complete list of countries and areas in the regions, subregions and country categories, see page 112 or visit <data.unicef.org/regionalclassifications>.
It is not advisable to compare data from consecutive editions of *The State of the World's Children*.

DEFINITIONS OF THE INDICATORS

Adolescents currently married/ in union – Percentage of boys and girls aged 15–19 who are currently married or in union. This indicator is meant to provide a snapshot of the current marital status of boys and girls in this age group. However, it is worth noting that those not married at the time of the survey are still exposed to the risk of marrying before they exit adolescence.

Births by age 18 – Percentage of women aged 20–24 who gave birth before age 18. This standardized indicator from population-based surveys captures levels of fertility among adolescents up to the age of 18. Note that the data are based on the answers of women aged 20–24, whose risk of giving birth before the age of 18 is behind them.

Adolescent birth rate – Number of births per 1,000 adolescent girls aged 15–19.

Justification of wife-beating among adolescents – The percentage of boys and girls aged 15–19 who consider a husband to be justified in hitting or beating his wife for at least one of the specified reasons: if his wife burns the food, argues with him, goes out without telling him, neglects the children or refuses sexual relations.

Use of mass media among adolescents – The percentage of boys and girls aged 15–19 who make use of at least one of the following types of information media at least once a week: newspaper, magazine, television or radio.

Lower secondary school gross enrolment ratio – Number of children enrolled in lower secondary school, regardless of age, expressed as a percentage of the total number of children of official lower secondary school age.

Upper secondary school gross enrolment ratio – Number of children enrolled in upper secondary school, regardless of age, expressed as a percentage of the total number of children of official upper secondary school age.

Comprehensive knowledge of HIV among adolescents – Percentage of young men and women aged 15–19 who correctly identify the two major ways of preventing the sexual transmission of HIV (using condoms and limiting sex to one faithful, uninfected partner), who reject the two most common local misconceptions about HIV transmission and who know that a healthy-looking person can be HIV-positive.

MAIN DATA SOURCES

Adolescent population – United Nations Population Division.

Adolescents currently married/ in union – Demographic and Health Surveys (DHS), Multiple Indicator Cluster Surveys (MICS), other national surveys and censuses.

Births by age 18 – DHS, MICS and other national surveys.

Adolescent birth rate – United Nations Population Division.

Justification of wife-beating among adolescents – DHS, MICS and other national surveys.

Use of mass media among adolescents –DHS, MICS and other national surveys

Gross enrolment ratio – UNESCO Institute for Statistics (UIS).

Comprehensive knowledge of HIV among adolescents – AIS, DHS, MICS and other national household surveys; DHS STATcompiler, <www.statcompiler.com>.

Italicized data are from different sources than the data presented for the same indicators in other tables of the report.

NOTES

– Data not available.

x Data refer to years or periods other than those specified in the column heading. Such data are not included in the calculation of regional and global averages. Estimates from data years prior to 2000 are not displayed.

y Data differ from the standard definition or refer to only part of a country. If they fall within the noted reference period, such data are included in the calculation of regional and global averages.

p Based on small denominators (typically 25–49 unweighted cases). No data based on fewer than 25 unweighted cases are displayed.

* Data refer to the most recent year available during the period specified in the column heading.

** Excludes China.

‡ Excludes India.

TABLE 12. DISPARITIES BY RESIDENCE

Countries and areas	Birth registration (%)++ 2010–2015*			Skilled attendant at birth (%) 2010–2015*			Stunting prevalence in children under 5 (%) 2009–2015*			Oral rehydration salts (ORS) treatment for children with diarrhoea (%) 2010–2015*			Primary school net attendance ratio 2009–2014*			Comprehensive knowledge of HIV/AIDS (%) Females 15–24 2010–2014*			Use of improved sanitation facilities (%) 2015		
	urban	rural	ratio of urban to rural	urban	rural	ratio of urban to rural	urban	rural	ratio of rural to urban	urban	rural	ratio of urban to rural	urban	rural	ratio of urban to rural	urban	rural	ratio of urban to rural	urban	rural	ratio of urban to rural
Afghanistan	60	33	1.8	82	37 ●	2.2	–	–	–	48	54	0.9	77 y	51 y	1.5 y	5	1	4.9	45	27	1.7
Albania	99 x	98 x	1.0 x	100 x	99 x	1.0 x	20	19	1.0	–	–	–	93	92	1.0	51 x	26 x	2.0 x	95	90	1.1
Algeria	100	100	1.0	98	95	1.0	11	12	1.1	25	26	1.0	98	97	1.0	11	7	1.7	90	82	1.1
Andorra	–	–	–	–	–	–	–	–	–	–	–	–	–	–	–	–	–	–	100	100	1.0
Angola	40 x	26 x	1.5 x	71 x	26 x	2.8 x	30 x	33 x	1.1 x	–	–	–	85	67	1.3	–	–	–	89	22	3.9
Antigua and Barbuda	–	–	–	–	–	–	–	–	–	–	–	–	–	–	–	–	–	–	–	–	–
Argentina	–	–	–	–	–	–	–	–	–	–	–	–	–	–	–	–	–	–	96	98	1.0
Armenia	99	100	1.0	100	99	1.0	17	22	1.3	–	–	–	100	99	1.0	16	16	1.0	96	78	1.2
Australia	–	–	–	–	–	–	–	–	–	–	–	–	–	–	–	–	–	–	100	100	1.0
Austria	–	–	–	–	–	–	–	–	–	–	–	–	–	–	–	–	–	–	100	100	1.0
Azerbaijan	96 x	92 x	1.0 x	99	95	1.0	15	21	1.4	11	11	1.0	68 y	67 y	1.0 y	7 x	2 x	3.3 x	92	87	1.1
Bahamas	–	–	–	–	–	–	–	–	–	–	–	–	–	–	–	–	–	–	–	–	–
Bahrain	–	–	–	–	–	–	–	–	–	–	–	–	–	–	–	–	–	–	99	99	1.0
Bangladesh	43	36	1.2	61	36	1.7	31	38	1.2	83	75	1.1	77	72	1.1	14	8	1.8	58	62	0.9
Barbados	98	100	1.0	98	100	1.0	8	7	0.9	–	–	–	99	99	1.0	67	69	1.0	96	96	1.0
Belarus	–	–	–	100	100	1.0	3 x	8 x	2.6 x	–	–	–	91	93	1.0	56	57	1.0	94	95	1.0
Belgium	–	–	–	–	–	–	–	–	–	–	–	–	–	–	–	–	–	–	99	99	1.0
Belize	95	96	1.0	98	95	1.0	16	21	1.4	54	47	1.1	98	92	1.1	55	33	1.7	93	88	1.1
Benin	87	76	1.1	90	75	1.2	36 x	47 x	1.3 x	54	47	1.1	84	72	1.2	29	20	1.5	36	7	4.9
Bhutan	100	100	1.0	96	67	1.4	28	36	1.3	64	60	1.1	98	94	1.0	32	15	2.1	78	33	2.4
Bolivia (Plurinational State of)	79 x,y	72 x,y	1.1 x,y	94	68	1.4	14	25	1.8	23	20	1.2	98 x	96 x	1.0 x	32 x	9 x	3.5 x	61	28	2.2
Bosnia and Herzegovina	99 x	100 x	1.0 x	100	100	1.0	11	8	0.7	–	–	–	95	97	1.0	50	47	1.1	99	92	1.1
Botswana	78 x	67 x	1.2 x	99 x	90 x	1.1 x	30 x	29 x	1.0 x	47 x	51 x	0.9 x	–	–	–	–	–	–	79	43	1.8
Brazil	–	–	–	–	–	–	7 x	8 x	1.1 x	–	–	–	–	–	–	–	–	–	88	52	1.7
Brunei Darussalam	–	–	–	–	–	–	–	–	–	–	–	–	–	–	–	–	–	–	–	–	–
Bulgaria	–	–	–	–	–	–	6 x	15 x	2.5 x	–	–	–	–	–	–	–	–	–	87	84	1.0
Burkina Faso	93	74	1.3	93	61	1.5	21	37	1.8	31	19	1.6	83	45	1.8	46	24	1.9	50	7	7.5
Burundi	87	74	1.2	88	58	1.5	38	60	1.6	33	38	0.9	91	84	1.1	59	43	1.4	44	49	0.9
Cabo Verde	–	–	–	–	–	–	–	–	–	–	–	–	–	–	–	–	–	–	82	54	1.5
Cambodia	84	72	1.2	98	88	1.1	24	34	1.4	33	34	1.0	96	93	1.0	55	33	1.7	88	30	2.9
Cameroon	81	48	1.7	87	47	1.9	22	41	1.8	27	12	2.2	94	78	1.2	37	18	2.1	62	27	2.3
Canada	–	–	–	–	–	–	–	–	–	–	–	–	–	–	–	–	–	–	100	99	1.0
Central African Republic	78	52	1.5	83	38	2.2	38	42	1.1	23	12	2.0	86	66	1.3	19	16	1.2	44	7	6.0
Chad	36	6	5.6	60	12	5.1	32	42	1.3	28	18	1.5	71	47	1.5	18	7	2.6	31	6	4.9
Chile	–	–	–	–	–	–	–	–	–	–	–	–	91 y	92 y	1.0 y	–	–	–	100	91	1.1
China	–	–	–	100	100	1.0	3	12	3.6	–	–	–	97 y	96 y	1.0 y	–	–	–	87	64	1.4
Colombia	97	95	1.0	98	86	1.1	12	17	1.5	57	49	1.2	96	95	1.0	26	17	1.5	85	68	1.3
Comoros	90	87	1.0	92	79	1.2	25	32	1.3	40	37	1.1	90	82	1.1	24	17	1.4	48	31	1.6
Congo	95	85	1.1	98	84	1.2	20	30	1.5	31	22	1.4	99	96	1.0	16	10	1.5	20	6	3.6
Cook Islands	–	–	–	–	–	–	–	–	–	–	–	–	–	–	–	–	–	–	98	98	1.0
Costa Rica	100	99	1.0	99	97	1.0	–	–	–	43	35	1.2	97	95	1.0	37	27	1.4	95	92	1.0
Côte d'Ivoire	85	54	1.6	84	45	1.9	21	35	1.7	22	14	1.5	78	64	1.2	22	8	2.7	33	10	3.2
Croatia	–	–	–	–	–	–	–	–	–	–	–	–	–	–	–	–	–	–	98	96	1.0
Cuba	100	100	1.0	99	100	1.0	–	–	–	62	59	1.0	–	–	–	61	63	1.0	94	89	1.1
Cyprus	–	–	–	–	–	–	–	–	–	–	–	–	–	–	–	–	–	–	100	100	1.0
Czech Republic	–	–	–	–	–	–	–	–	–	–	–	–	–	–	–	–	–	–	99	99	1.0
Democratic People's Republic of Korea	100 x	100 x	1.0 x	100 x	100 x	1.0 x	23	45	1.9	75 x	73 x	1.0 x	100	99	1.0	11 x	4 x	2.8 x	88	73	1.2
Democratic Republic of the Congo	30	22	1.3	94	74	1.3	33	47	1.4	44	37	1.2	93	84	1.1	24	15	1.6	29	29	1.0
Denmark	–	–	–	–	–	–	–	–	–	–	–	–	–	–	–	–	–	–	100	100	1.0
Djibouti	92 x	84 x	1.1 x	98	55	1.8	30	42	1.4	–	–	–	–	–	–	18 x	9 x	2.0 x	60	5	11.7
Dominica	–	–	–	–	–	–	–	–	–	–	–	–	–	–	–	–	–	–	–	–	–
Dominican Republic	85	80	1.1	99	97	1.0	7	6	0.9	48	48	1.0	95	97	1.0	45	44	1.0	86	76	1.1
Ecuador	92	93	1.0	98	84	1.2	22	32	1.5	52	35	1.5	97 y	97 y	1.0 y	–	–	–	87	81	1.1
Egypt	100	99	1.0	97	89	1.1	23	21	0.9	26	29	0.9	97	97	1.0	7 x	3 x	2.3 x	97	93	1.0
El Salvador	99 x	99 x	1.0 x	–	–	–	14 x	24 x	1.8 x	60 x	56 x	1.1 x	92 y	90 y	1.0 y	–	–	–	82	60	1.4
Equatorial Guinea	60	47	1.3	86	53	1.6	20	32	1.6	55	27	2.0	–	–	–	27	9	2.9	80	71	1.1
Eritrea	–	–	–	74	17	4.4	38	56	1.4	51	41	1.2	79 y	47 y	1.7 y	32	20	1.7	45	7	6.1
Estonia	–	–	–	–	–	–	–	–	–	–	–	–	–	–	–	–	–	–	98	97	1.0
Ethiopia	29 x	5 x	5.9 x	58	9	6.4	27	42	1.6	45	24	1.9	80 y	63 y	1.3 y	38	19	2.0	27	28	1.0
Fiji	–	–	–	–	–	–	5 x	9 x	1.7 x	–	–	–	–	–	–	–	–	–	93	88	1.1
Finland	–	–	–	–	–	–	–	–	–	–	–	–	–	–	–	–	–	–	99	88	1.1

unicef ◎ | 70 YEARS FOR EVERY CHILD

TABLE 12. DISPARITIES BY RESIDENCE

Countries and areas	Birth registration (%)++ 2010–2015* urban	rural	ratio of urban to rural	Skilled attendant at birth (%) 2010–2015* urban	rural	ratio of urban to rural	Stunting prevalence in children under 5 (%) 2009–2015* urban	rural	ratio of rural to urban	Oral rehydration salts (ORS) treatment for children with diarrhoea (%) 2010–2015* urban	rural	ratio of urban to rural	Primary school net attendance ratio 2009–2014* urban	rural	ratio of urban to rural	Comprehensive knowledge of HIV/AIDS (%) Females 15–24 2010–2014* urban	rural	ratio of urban to rural	Use of improved sanitation facilities (%) 2015 urban	rural	ratio of urban to rural
France	–	–	–	–	–	–	–	–	–	–	–	–	–	–	–	–	–	–	99	99	1.0
Gabon	89	91	1.0	93	69	1.3	14	29	2.0	27	21	1.3	95	95	1.0	32	15	2.2	43	32	1.4
Gambia	72	72	1.0	75	41	1.9	19	29	1.5	62	57	1.1	75	54	1.4	32	18	1.8	62	55	1.1
Georgia	100	100	1.0	–	–	–	10	12	1.2	44 x	36 x	1.2 x	97	95	1.0	–	–	–	95	76	1.3
Germany	–	–	–	–	–	–	–	–	–	–	–	–	–	–	–	–	–	–	99	99	1.0
Ghana	79	63	1.3	87	57	1.5	15	22	1.5	48	49	1.0	75	66	1.1	23	17	1.4	20	9	2.3
Greece	–	–	–	–	–	–	–	–	–	–	–	–	–	–	–	–	–	–	99	98	1.0
Grenada	–	–	–	–	–	–	–	–	–	–	–	–	–	–	–	–	–	–	98	98	1.0
Guatemala	96 x	97 x	1.0 x	84	55	1.5	35	53	1.5	51	48	1.1	–	–	–	32 x	14 x	2.2 x	78	49	1.6
Guinea	83	49	1.7	84	32	2.7	18	36	2.1	46	30	1.5	84	47	1.8	32	16	2.0	34	12	2.9
Guinea-Bissau	30	21	1.4	69	29	2.4	23	37	1.6	28	13	2.1	74	53	1.4	22	8	2.8	34	8	3.9
Guyana	91 x	87 x	1.0 x	–	–	–	11	20	1.8	–	–	–	97	97	1.0	72 x	47 x	1.5 x	88	82	1.1
Haiti	85	77	1.1	59	25	2.4	16	25	1.6	56	51	1.1	90	81	1.1	41	29	1.4	34	19	1.8
Holy See	–	–	–	–	–	–	–	–	–	–	–	–	–	–	–	–	–	–	–	–	–
Honduras	95	93	1.0	94	73	1.3	15	29	2.0	59	61	1.0	92 y	92 y	1.0 y	42	23	1.9	87	78	1.1
Hungary	–	–	–	–	–	–	–	–	–	–	–	–	–	–	–	–	–	–	98	99	1.0
Iceland	–	–	–	–	–	–	–	–	–	–	–	–	–	–	–	–	–	–	99	100	1.0
India	83	67	1.2	76 x	43 x	1.7 x	32	42	1.3	33 x	24 x	1.4 x	88 x	82 x	1.1 x	33 x	14 x	2.4 x	63	28	2.2
Indonesia	78 y	60 y	1.3 y	94	81	1.2	33	42	1.3	41	37	1.1	99	98	1.0	14 y	9 y	1.6 y	72	47	1.5
Iran (Islamic Republic of)	99 y	98 y	1.0 y	98	93	1.1	5	9	1.7	64	58	1.1	97	95	1.0	–	–	–	93	82	1.1
Iraq	99	99	1.0	94	85	1.1	22	24	1.1	25	19	1.3	94	84	1.1	4	1	3.7	86	84	1.0
Ireland	–	–	–	–	–	–	–	–	–	–	–	–	–	–	–	–	–	–	89	93	1.0
Israel	–	–	–	–	–	–	–	–	–	–	–	–	–	–	–	–	–	–	100	100	1.0
Italy	–	–	–	–	–	–	–	–	–	–	–	–	–	–	–	–	–	–	99	100	1.0
Jamaica	100	99	1.0	100	98	1.0	–	–	–	–	–	–	98	98	1.0	–	–	–	80	84	1.0
Japan	–	–	–	–	–	–	–	–	–	–	–	–	–	–	–	–	–	–	100	100	1.0
Jordan	99	100	1.0	100	100	1.0	7	9	1.2	20	23	0.9	98	98	1.0	8	11	0.7	99	99	1.0
Kazakhstan	100	100	1.0	100	100	1.0	13	13	1.0	–	–	–	99	99	1.0	40	31	1.3	97	98	1.0
Kenya	79	61	1.3	82	50	1.6	20	29	1.5	58	52	1.1	89	84	1.1	63	52	1.2	31	30	1.1
Kiribati	95 x	93 x	1.0 x	–	–	–	–	–	–	–	–	–	–	–	–	45 x	43 x	1.1 x	51	31	1.7
Kuwait	–	–	–	–	–	–	–	–	–	–	–	–	–	–	–	–	–	–	100	100	1.0
Kyrgyzstan	99	97	1.0	99	98	1.0	12	13	1.1	34	33	1.0	99	100	1.0	26	16	1.7	89	96	0.9
Lao People's Democratic Republic	88	71	1.2	80	31	2.6	27	49	1.8	65	40	1.6	95	83	1.1	39	18	2.2	94	56	1.7
Latvia	–	–	–	–	–	–	–	–	–	–	–	–	–	–	–	–	–	–	91	82	1.1
Lebanon	–	–	–	–	–	–	–	–	–	–	–	–	–	–	–	–	–	–	81	81	1.0
Lesotho	43 x	46 x	1.0 x	90	73	1.2	27	35	1.3	53	54	1.0	98	93	1.0	44 x	36 x	1.2 x	37	28	1.4
Liberia	29 y	20 y	1.5 y	73	50	1.5	30	33	1.1	57	63	0.9	52	31	1.7	40	27	1.5	28	6	4.7
Libya	–	–	–	–	–	–	–	–	–	–	–	–	–	–	–	–	–	–	97	96	1.0
Liechtenstein	–	–	–	–	–	–	–	–	–	–	–	–	–	–	–	–	–	–	–	–	–
Lithuania	–	–	–	–	–	–	–	–	–	–	–	–	–	–	–	–	–	–	97	83	1.2
Luxembourg	–	–	–	–	–	–	–	–	–	–	–	–	–	–	–	–	–	–	98	99	1.0
Madagascar	97	81	1.2	78	39	2.0	43	51	1.2	16	14	1.1	86 y	66 y	1.3 y	44	18	2.5	18	9	2.1
Malawi	11 y	5 y	2.4 y	94	87	1.1	36	43	1.2	65	63	1.0	98	93	1.1	50	43	1.2	47	40	1.2
Malaysia	–	–	–	–	–	–	–	–	–	–	–	–	–	–	–	–	–	–	96	96	1.0
Maldives	93 x	92 x	1.0 x	–	–	–	16	20	1.3	–	–	–	94	94	1.0	43 x,y	32 x,y	1.4 x,y	97	98	1.0
Mali	92	77	1.2	80 x	38 x	2.1 x	26 x	42 x	1.6 x	26 x	11 x	2.3 x	80	50	1.6	36	19	1.9	38	16	2.3
Malta	–	–	–	–	–	–	–	–	–	–	–	–	–	–	–	–	–	–	100	100	1.0
Marshall Islands	96 x	96 x	1.0 x	–	–	–	–	–	–	39 x	37 x	1.1 x	–	–	–	33 x	12 x	2.7 x	84	56	1.5
Mauritania	75	49	1.5	88	49	1.8	25	33	1.3	26	14	2.0	72	55	1.3	9	4	2.7	58	14	4.2
Mauritius	–	–	–	–	–	–	–	–	–	–	–	–	–	–	–	–	–	–	94	93	1.0
Mexico	98 x,y	82 x,y	1.2 x,y	–	–	–	11	21	1.9	54	48	1.1	–	–	–	–	–	–	88	74	1.2
Micronesia (Federated States of)	–	–	–	–	–	–	–	–	–	–	–	–	–	–	–	–	–	–	85	49	1.7
Monaco	–	–	–	–	–	–	–	–	–	–	–	–	–	–	–	–	–	–	100	–	–
Mongolia	99	99	1.0	99	99	1.0	8	15	1.7	35	26	1.4	97	94	1.0	26	15	1.7	66	43	1.6
Montenegro	99	100	1.0	99	100	1.0	10	9	1.0	–	–	–	97	99	1.0	47	49	1.0	98	92	1.1
Morocco	97 y	91 y	1.1 y	92	55	1.7	9	21	2.4	23	21	1.1	96 x	83 x	1.2 x	–	–	–	84	66	1.3
Mozambique	51	47	1.1	80	44	1.8	35	46	1.3	65	50	1.3	86	72	1.2	40	24	1.6	42	10	4.2
Myanmar	94	64	1.5	90	63	1.4	27	38	1.4	72	56	1.3	93	89	1.0	–	–	–	84	77	1.1
Namibia	89 y	86 y	1.0 y	95	82	1.2	17	28	1.7	75	69	1.1	95	91	1.0	67	55	1.2	54	17	3.2
Nauru	–	–	–	–	–	–	–	–	–	–	–	–	–	–	–	–	–	–	66	–	–
Nepal	57	58	1.0	90	51	1.8	24	39	1.7	47	44	1.1	80	76	1.1	40	24	1.7	56	43	1.3
Netherlands	–	–	–	–	–	–	–	–	–	–	–	–	–	–	–	–	–	–	97	100	1.0

TABLE 12. DISPARITIES BY RESIDENCE

Countries and areas	Birth registration (%)++ 2010–2015*			Skilled attendant at birth (%) 2010–2015*			Stunting prevalence in children under 5 (%) 2009–2015*			Oral rehydration salts (ORS) treatment for children with diarrhoea (%) 2010–2015*			Primary school net attendance ratio 2009–2014*			Comprehensive knowledge of HIV/AIDS (%) Females 15–24 2010–2014*			Use of improved sanitation facilities (%) 2015		
	urban	rural	ratio of urban to rural	urban	rural	ratio of urban to rural	urban	rural	ratio of rural to urban	urban	rural	ratio of urban to rural	urban	rural	ratio of urban to rural	urban	rural	ratio of urban to rural	urban	rural	ratio of urban to rural
New Zealand	–	–	–	–	–	–	–	–	–	–	–	–	–	–	–	–	–	–	–	–	–
Nicaragua	–	–	–	97	79	1.2	–	–	–	74	57	1.3	76 y	64 y	1.2 y	–	–	–	76	56	1.4
Niger	92	60	1.5	83	32	2.6	30	46	1.6	*47*	*44*	*1.1*	83	45	1.9	31	9	3.3	38	5	8.2
Nigeria	50 y	19 y	2.7 y	67	23	3.0	*26*	*43*	*1.7*	45	28	1.6	87	57	1.5	30	20	1.4	33	25	1.3
Niue	–	–	–	–	–	–	–	–	–	–	–	–	100	100	1.0	–	–	–	100	100	1.0
Norway	–	–	–	–	–	–	–	–	–	–	–	–	–	–	–	–	–	–	98	98	1.0
Oman	–	–	–	–	–	–	–	–	–	–	–	–	–	–	–	–	–	–	97	95	1.0
Pakistan	59	23	2.6	71	44	1.6	37	48	1.3	42	37	1.1	75	59	1.3	–	–	–	83	51	1.6
Palau	–	–	–	–	–	–	–	–	–	–	–	–	–	–	–	–	–	–	100	100	1.0
Panama	98	93	1.1	100	78	1.3	–	–	–	61	44	1.4	97	97	1.0	–	–	–	84	58	1.4
Papua New Guinea	–	–	–	88 x	48 x	1.9 x	35	50	1.4	–	–	–	–	–	–	–	–	–	56	13	4.2
Paraguay	87 y	80 y	1.1 y	–	–	–	12	10	0.8	–	–	–	89 x	87 x	1.0 x	–	–	–	95	78	1.2
Peru	97 y	95 y	1.0 y	97	73	1.3	8	29	3.5	32	21	1.5	92 y	93 y	1.0 y	27 x	8 x	3.3 x	82	53	1.6
Philippines	–	–	–	83	64	1.3	26	35	1.4	54	45	1.2	90 x	87 x	1.0 x	23 x	17 x	1.4 x	78	71	1.1
Poland	–	–	–	–	–	–	–	–	–	–	–	–	–	–	–	–	–	–	98	97	1.0
Portugal	–	–	–	–	–	–	–	–	–	–	–	–	–	–	–	–	–	–	100	100	1.0
Qatar	–	–	–	–	–	–	–	–	–	–	–	–	–	–	–	–	–	–	98	98	1.0
Republic of Korea	–	–	–	–	–	–	–	–	–	–	–	–	–	–	–	–	–	–	100	100	1.0
Republic of Moldova	100	100	1.0	100	99	1.0	4	8	2.2	–	–	–	98	99	1.0	41	32	1.3	88	67	1.3
Romania	–	–	–	–	–	–	14 x	15 x	1.1 x	–	–	–	–	–	–	–	–	–	92	63	1.5
Russian Federation	–	–	–	–	–	–	–	–	–	–	–	–	–	–	–	–	–	–	77	59	1.3
Rwanda	60	64	0.9	97	89	1.1	24	41	1.7	33	27	1.3	91 y	87 y	1.0 y	66	50	1.3	59	63	0.9
Saint Kitts and Nevis	–	–	–	–	–	–	–	–	–	–	–	–	–	–	–	–	–	–	–	–	–
Saint Lucia	91	92	1.0	–	99	–	4	2	0.6	–	–	–	99	100	1.0	57	63	0.9	85	92	0.9
Saint Vincent and the Grenadines	–	–	–	–	–	–	–	–	–	–	–	–	–	–	–	–	–	–	–	–	–
Samoa	68	57	1.2	97	79	1.2	–	–	–	–	–	–	89 y	88 y	1.0 y	5 x	2 x	2.4 x	93	91	1.0
San Marino	–	–	–	–	–	–	–	–	–	–	–	–	–	–	–	–	–	–	–	–	–
Sao Tome and Principe	*76 x*	*74 x*	*1.0 x*	–	–	–	*29*	*29*	*1.0*	–	–	–	*94*	*93*	*1.0*	47 x	38 x	1.3 x	41	23	1.8
Saudi Arabia	–	–	–	–	–	–	–	–	–	–	–	–	–	–	–	–	–	–	100	100	1.0
Senegal	87	63	1.4	80	44	1.8	12	23	1.9	19	25	0.8	79	53	1.5	–	–	–	65	34	1.9
Serbia	100	99	1.0	*100*	*100*	*1.0*	7	5	0.8	50	22	2.3	100	98	1.0	63	41	1.5	98	94	1.0
Seychelles	–	–	–	–	–	–	–	–	–	–	–	–	–	–	–	–	–	–	98	98	1.0
Sierra Leone	80	76	1.1	79	53	1.5	30	40	1.4	86	85	1.0	88	71	1.2	38	22	1.7	23	7	3.3
Singapore	–	–	–	–	–	–	–	–	–	–	–	–	–	–	–	–	–	–	100	–	–
Slovakia	–	–	–	–	–	–	–	–	–	–	–	–	–	–	–	–	–	–	99	98	1.0
Slovenia	–	–	–	–	–	–	–	–	–	–	–	–	–	–	–	–	–	–	99	99	1.0
Solomon Islands	–	–	–	95 x	84 x	1.1 x	23 x	34 x	1.5 x	40 x	37 x	1.1 x	72 x,y	65 x,y	1.1 x,y	34 x	28 x	1.2 x	81	15	5.4
Somalia	6 x	2 x	3.7 x	–	–	–	*32 x*	*48 x*	*1.5 x*	25 x	9 x	2.9 x	39 x	11 x	3.4 x	7 x	2 x	4.1 x	–	–	–
South Africa	–	–	–	–	–	–	*32 x*	*34 x*	*1.1 x*	41 x	32 x	1.3 x	–	–	–	–	–	–	70	61	1.1
South Sudan	45	32	1.4	31	15	2.0	29	32	1.1	44	37	1.2	40	19	2.1	16	7	2.3	16	4	3.7
Spain	–	–	–	–	–	–	–	–	–	–	–	–	–	–	–	–	–	–	100	100	1.0
Sri Lanka	97 x	98 x	1.0 x	99 x	99 x	1.0 x	10	15	1.5	57 x	50 x	1.1 x	–	–	–	–	–	–	88	97	0.9
State of Palestine	99	100	1.0	100	100	1.0	8	8	1.0	30	34	0.9	99	99	1.0	*8*	*6*	*1.3*	93	90	1.0
Sudan	*85*	*50*	*1.7*	41	16	2.5	27	43	1.6	23	22	1.1	86	64	1.4	10	3	3.4	–	–	–
Suriname	100	98	1.0	95	86	1.1	7	12	1.8	33	55	0.6	97	94	1.0	45	33	1.4	88	61	1.4
Swaziland	*62*	*47*	*1.3*	*89*	*80*	*1.1*	23	33	1.4	65	55	1.2	97	96	1.0	70	55	1.3	63	56	1.1
Sweden	–	–	–	–	–	–	–	–	–	–	–	–	–	–	–	–	–	–	99	100	1.0
Switzerland	–	–	–	–	–	–	–	–	–	–	–	–	–	–	–	–	–	–	100	100	1.0
Syrian Arab Republic	97 x	95 x	1.0 x	99 x	93 x	1.1 x	28	28	1.0	56 x	44 x	1.3 x	98 x	96 x	1.0 x	7 x	7 x	1.0 x	96	95	1.0
Tajikistan	88	89	1.0	93	86	1.1	21	27	1.3	58	61	0.9	98	97	1.0	11	8	1.4	94	95	1.0
Thailand	99 y	100 y	1.0 y	100	100	1.0	13	18	1.4	59	57	1.0	96	96	1.0	55	56	1.0	90	96	0.9
The former Yugoslav Republic of Macedonia	100	100	1.0	*98*	*98*	*1.0*	4	6	1.4	–	–	–	98	98	1.0	33 x	18 x	1.8 x	97	83	1.2
Timor-Leste	50	57	0.9	59	20	2.9	39	55	1.4	65	74	0.9	80	70	1.1	14	12	1.2	69	27	2.6
Togo	95	69	1.4	92	41	2.2	16	33	2.1	18	19	0.9	96	85	1.1	28	19	1.5	25	3	8.4
Tonga	92	94	1.0	96	99	1.0	9	8	0.9	–	–	–	92 y	93 y	1.0 y	11	13	0.8	98	89	1.1
Trinidad and Tobago	–	–	–	–	–	–	–	–	–	–	–	–	–	–	–	–	–	–	92	92	1.0
Tunisia	100	98	1.0	100	97	1.0	8	14	1.7	69	59	1.2	99	97	1.0	22	13	1.7	97	80	1.2
Turkey	99 y	98 y	1.0 y	99	92	1.1	8	14	1.8	–	–	–	94 x,y	91 x,y	1.0 x,y	–	–	–	98	86	1.1
Turkmenistan	96 x	95 x	1.0 x	100 x	99 x	1.0 x	17 x	19 x	1.1 x	–	–	–	99 x	99 x	1.0 x	–	–	–	–	–	–
Tuvalu	60 x	38 x	1.6 x	–	–	–	10 x	11 x	1.1 x	–	–	–	98 x,y	99 x,y	1.0 x,y	38 x	41 x	0.9 x	86	–	–
Uganda	38	29	1.3	89	52	1.7	*19*	*36*	*1.9*	46	43	1.1	91	86	1.1	50	35	1.4	29	17	1.7
Ukraine	100	100	1.0	99	99	1.0	*20 x*	*29 x*	*1.4 x*	–	–	–	100	100	1.0	52	45	1.1	97	93	1.1

unicef • 70 YEARS FOR EVERY CHILD

TABLE 12. DISPARITIES BY RESIDENCE

Countries and areas	Birth registration (%)++ 2010–2015*			Skilled attendant at birth (%) 2010–2015*			Stunting prevalence in children under 5 (%) 2009–2015*			Oral rehydration salts (ORS) treatment for children with diarrhoea (%) 2010–2015*			Primary school net attendance ratio 2009–2014*			Comprehensive knowledge of HIV/AIDS (%) Females 15–24 2010–2014*			Use of improved sanitation facilities (%) 2015		
	urban	rural	ratio of urban to rural	urban	rural	ratio of urban to rural	urban	rural	ratio of rural to urban	urban	rural	ratio of urban to rural	urban	rural	ratio of urban to rural	urban	rural	ratio of urban to rural	urban	rural	ratio of urban to rural
United Arab Emirates	–	–	–	–	–	–	–	–	–	–	–	–	–	–	–	–	–	–	98	95	1.0
United Kingdom	–	–	–	–	–	–	–	–	–	–	–	–	–	–	–	–	–	–	99	100	1.0
United Republic of Tanzania	36 y	8 y	4.4 y	83	40	2.0	*30*	*39*	*1.3*	44	44	1.0	91 y	72 y	1.3 y	52	36	1.5	31	8	3.8
United States	–	–	–	–	–	–	–	–	–	–	–	–	–	–	–	–	–	–	100	100	1.0
Uruguay	100	100	1.0	98	98	1.0	–	–	–	–	–	–	97	97	1.0	34	35	1.0	97	93	1.0
Uzbekistan	100 x	100 x	1.0 x	100 x	100 x	1.0 x	18 x	19 x	1.1 x	–	–	–	96 x	94 x	1.0 x	33 x	30 x	1.1 x	100	100	1.0
Vanuatu	51 y	37 y	1.4 y	96	87	1.1	19	32	1.6	38	52	0.7	77 y	77 y	1.0 y	23 x	13 x	1.8 x	65	55	1.2
Venezuela (Bolivarian Republic of)	–	–	–	–	–	–	–	–	–	–	–	–	–	–	–	–	–	–	97	70	1.4
Viet Nam	97	96	1.0	99	92	1.1	*12*	*27*	*2.3*	58	49	1.2	98	98	1.0	54	47	1.1	94	70	1.4
Yemen	48	24	2.0	73	34	2.1	34	51	1.5	24	26	0.9	85	73	1.2	4 x	1 x	6.7 x	–	–	–
Zambia	20	7	3.0	89	52	1.7	36	42	1.2	68	62	1.1	92	84	1.1	50	34	1.5	56	36	1.6
Zimbabwe	57	23	2.4	93	75	1.2	20	30	1.5	45	43	1.1	96	93	1.0	66	51	1.3	49	31	1.6
SUMMARY																					
Sub-Saharan Africa	59	37	1.6	77	40	1.9	26	41	1.5	42	35	1.2	86	68	1.3	34	24	1.4	40	23	1.7
Eastern and Southern Africa	53	37	1.4	79	41	1.9	29	40	1.4	48	40	1.2	87	74	1.2	49	31	1.6	47	26	1.8
West and Central Africa	60	37	1.6	79	41	1.9	25	41	1.6	41	31	1.3	86	62	1.4	28	17	1.7	35	20	1.8
Middle East and North Africa	95	80	1.2	90	65	1.4	17	27	1.6	34	29	1.2	95	84	1.1	–	–	–	93	87	1.1
South Asia	75	57	1.3	69 ‡	41 ‡	1.7 ‡	33	42	1.3	55 ‡	52 ‡	1.1 ‡	85	77	1.1	–	9 ‡	–	65	35	1.8
East Asia and Pacific	84 **	72 **	1.2 **	97	90	1.1	12	23	2.0	49 **	44 **	1.1 **	97	96	1.0	26 **	26 **	1.0 **	86	64	1.3
Latin America and Caribbean	–	–	–	–	–	–	13	26	2.0	51	44	1.1	–	–	–	–	–	–	88	64	1.4
CEE/CIS	–	–	–	99	95	1.0	10 r	16 r	1.6 r	–	–	–	–	–	–	–	–	–	89	81	1.1
Least developed countries	57	40	1.4	77	42	1.8	29	41	1.4	49	41	1.2	85	70	1.2	30	19	1.6	47	33	1.4
World	**83 ****	**60 ****	**1.4 ****	**88 ‡**	**59 ‡**	**1.5 ‡**	**21**	**35**	**1.7**	**45 ‡****	**39 ‡****	**1.1 ‡****	**91**	**79**	**1.1**	**–**	**22 ‡****	**–**	**82**	**51**	**1.6**

For a complete list of countries and areas in the regions, subregions and country categories, see page 112 or visit <data.unicef.org/regionalclassifications>.
It is not advisable to compare data from consecutive editions of *The State of the World's Children*.

DEFINITIONS OF THE INDICATORS

Birth registration – Percentage of children under age 5 who were registered at the moment of the survey. The numerator of this indicator includes children reported to have a birth certificate, regardless of whether or not it was seen by the interviewer, and those without a birth certificate whose mother or caregiver says the birth has been registered.

Skilled attendant at birth – Percentage of births attended by skilled health personnel (doctor, nurse or midwife).

Stunting prevalence in children under 5 – Percentage of children aged 0–59 months who are below minus two standard deviations from median height-for-age of the WHO Child Growth Standards.

Oral rehydration salts (ORS) treatment for children with diarrhoea – Percentage of children under age 5 who had diarrhoea in the two weeks preceding the survey and who received oral rehydration salts (ORS packets or pre-packaged ORS fluids).

Primary school net attendance ratio – Number of children attending primary or secondary school who are of official primary school age, expressed as a percentage of the total number of children of official primary school age. Because of the inclusion of primary-school-aged children attending secondary school, this indicator can also be referred to as a primary adjusted net attendance ratio.

Comprehensive knowledge of HIV – Percentage of young women (aged 15–24) who correctly identify the two major ways of preventing the sexual transmission of HIV (using condoms and limiting sex to one faithful, uninfected partner), who reject the two most common local misconceptions about HIV transmission and who know that a healthy-looking person can be HIV-positive.

Use of improved sanitation facilities – Percentage of the population using any of the following sanitation facilities, not shared with other households: flush or pour-flush latrine connected to a piped sewerage system, septic tank or pit latrine; ventilated improved pit latrine; pit latrine with a slab; composting toilet.

MAIN DATA SOURCES

Birth registration – Demographic and Health Surveys (DHS), Multiple Indicator Cluster Surveys (MICS), other national surveys, censuses and vital registration systems.

Skilled attendant at birth – DHS, MICS and other nationally representative sources.

Stunting prevalence in children under 5 – DHS, MICS, other national household surveys, WHO and UNICEF.

Oral rehydration salts (ORS) treatment for children with diarrhoea – DHS, MICS and other national household surveys.

Primary school net attendance ratio – DHS, MICS and other national household surveys.

Comprehensive knowledge of HIV – AIDS Indicator Surveys (AIS), DHS, MICS, and other national household surveys; DHS STATcompiler, www.statcompiler.com.

Use of improved sanitation facilities – WHO/UNICEF Joint Monitoring Programme for Water Supply and Sanitation (JMP).

Italicized data are from different sources than the data presented for the same indicators in other tables of the report: Table 2 (Nutrition – Stunting prevalence), Table 3 (Health – Diarrhoea treatment), Table 4 (HIV/AIDS – Comprehensive knowledge of HIV), Table 5 (Education – Primary school participation), Table 8 (Women – Skilled attendant at birth) and Table 9 (Child protection – Birth registration).

NOTES

- Data not available.

x Data refer to years or periods other than those specified in the column heading. Such data are not included in the calculation of regional and global averages, with the exception of 2005–2006 data on primary attendance from India. Estimates from data years prior to 2000 are not displayed.

y Data differ from the standard definition or refer to only part of a country. If they fall within the noted reference period, such data are included in the calculation of regional and global averages.

++ Changes in the definition of birth registration were made from the second and third rounds of MICS (MICS2 and MICS3) to the fourth round (MICS4). In order to allow for comparability with later rounds, data from MICS2 and MICS3 on birth registration were recalculated according to the MICS4 indicator definition. Therefore, the recalculated data presented here may differ from estimates included in MICS2 and MICS3 national reports.

* Data refer to the most recent year available during the period specified in the column heading.

** Excludes China.

‡ Excludes India.

r Excludes the Russian Federation.

TABLE 13. DISPARITIES BY HOUSEHOLD WEALTH

Countries and areas	Birth registration (%)++ 2010–2015* poorest 20%	richest 20%	ratio of richest to poorest	Skilled attendant at birth (%) 2010–2015* poorest 20%	richest 20%	ratio of richest to poorest	Stunting prevalence in children under 5 (%) 2009–2015* poorest 20%	richest 20%	ratio of richest to poorest	Oral rehydration salts (ORS) treatment for children with diarrhoea (%) 2010–2015* poorest 20%	richest 20%	ratio of poorest to richest	Primary school net attendance ratio 2009–2014* poorest 20%	richest 20%	ratio of richest to poorest	Comprehensive knowledge of HIV/AIDS (%) Females 15–24 2010–2014* poorest 20%	richest 20%	ratio of richest to poorest	Comprehensive knowledge of HIV/AIDS (%) Males 15–24 2010–2014* poorest 20%	richest 20%	ratio of richest to poorest
Afghanistan	31	58	1.9	16	76	4.9	49	31	1.6	56	52	0.9	40	79	2.0	0	5	23.0	–	–	–
Albania	98 x	99 x	1.0 x	98 x	100 x	1.0 x	27	13	2.1	–	–	–	91	94	1.0	20 x	60 x	3.0 x	10 x	38 x	3.8 x
Algeria	99	100	1.0	95	99	1.0	13	11	1.2	21	31	1.5	96	98	1.0	4	17	3.8	–	–	–
Andorra	–	–	–	–	–	–	–	–	–	–	–	–	–	–	–	–	–	–	–	–	–
Angola	24 x	53 x	2.2 x	–	–	–	–	–	–	–	–	–	63	90	1.4	–	–	–	–	–	–
Antigua and Barbuda	–	–	–	–	–	–	–	–	–	–	–	–	–	–	–	–	–	–	–	–	–
Argentina	99 y	100 y	1.0 y	–	–	–	–	–	–	26	6	0.2	98	99	1.0	29	54	1.8	–	–	–
Armenia	100	100	1.0	99	100	1.0	26	19	1.4	–	–	–	99	100	1.0	–	–	–	–	–	–
Australia	–	–	–	–	–	–	–	–	–	–	–	–	–	–	–	–	–	–	–	–	–
Austria	–	–	–	–	–	–	–	–	–	–	–	–	–	–	–	–	–	–	–	–	–
Azerbaijan	92 x	97 x	1.1 x	90	100	1.1	28	16	1.8	–	–	–	67 y	70 y	1.0 y	1 x	12 x	10.3 x	2 x	14 x	6.3 x
Bahamas	–	–	–	–	–	–	–	–	–	–	–	–	–	–	–	–	–	–	–	–	–
Bahrain	–	–	–	–	–	–	–	–	–	–	–	–	–	–	–	–	–	–	–	–	–
Bangladesh	30	47	1.5	18	73	4.1	50	21	2.4	72	84	1.2	65	81	1.3	2	18	8.9	–	–	–
Barbados	98	99	1.0	–	–	–	8	3	2.4	–	–	–	99	99	1.0	57	66	1.2	–	–	–
Belarus	–	–	–	100	100	1.0	11 x	2 x	5.3 x	–	–	–	93	93	1.0	55	55	1.0	42	43	1.0
Belgium	–	–	–	–	–	–	–	–	–	–	–	–	–	–	–	–	–	–	–	–	–
Belize	95	97	1.0	89	98	1.1	33	9	3.7	43	57	1.3	88	98	1.1	20	53	2.7	–	–	–
Benin	61	95	1.6	60	98	1.6	50 x	29 x	1.7 x	43	57	1.3	57	90	1.6	9 x	26 x	3.1 x	17 x	52 x	3.0 x
Bhutan	100	100	1.0	34	95	2.8	41	21	1.9	60	56	0.9	85	97	1.1	7	32	4.4	–	–	–
Bolivia (Plurinational State of)	68 x,y	90 x,y	1.3 x,y	57	99	1.7	32	9	3.5	18	27	1.5	95 x	99 x	1.0 x	5 x	40 x	8.4 x	11 x	45 x	4.3 x
Bosnia and Herzegovina	100 x	99 x	1.0 x	100	100	1.0	10	10	1.0	–	–	–	93	94	1.0	37	44	1.2	38	45	1.2
Botswana	–	–	–	–	–	–	38 x	20 x	1.9 x	–	–	–	–	–	–	–	–	–	–	–	–
Brazil	–	–	–	–	–	–	7	3	2.1	–	–	–	–	–	–	–	–	–	–	–	–
Brunei Darussalam	–	–	–	–	–	–	–	–	–	–	–	–	–	–	–	–	–	–	–	–	–
Bulgaria	–	–	–	–	–	–	–	–	–	–	–	–	–	–	–	–	–	–	–	–	–
Burkina Faso	62	95	1.5	46	92	2.0	42	19	2.3	13	31	2.5	31	85	2.8	8 x	37 x	4.4 x	–	–	–
Burundi	64	87	1.4	51	81	1.6	70	41	1.7	35	42	1.2	76	92	1.2	–	–	–	–	–	–
Cabo Verde	–	–	–	–	–	–	–	–	–	–	–	–	–	–	–	–	–	–	–	–	–
Cambodia	59	87	1.5	75	98	1.3	42	19	2.3	32	34	1.1	87	98	1.1	27	55	2.1	28	63	2.2
Cameroon	28	89	3.2	19	97	5.1	49	12	4.0	8	36	4.7	60	98	1.6	12 x	50 x	4.0 x	–	–	–
Canada	–	–	–	–	–	–	–	–	–	–	–	–	–	–	–	–	–	–	–	–	–
Central African Republic	46	85	1.8	33	87	2.6	45	30	1.5	11	28	2.5	57	90	1.6	12	21	1.7	19	29	1.5
Chad	6	39	6.5	8	61	7.6	41	32	1.3	14	30	2.2	40	74	1.8	6	18	2.9	–	–	–
Chile	–	–	–	–	–	–	–	–	–	–	–	–	–	–	–	–	–	–	–	–	–
China	–	–	–	–	–	–	–	–	–	–	–	–	–	–	–	–	–	–	–	–	–
Colombia	–	–	–	84	99	1.2	19	7	2.9	47	61	1.3	94	96	1.0	15	32	2.2	–	–	–
Comoros	85	93	1.1	66	93	1.4	38	22	1.7	39	36	0.9	71	95	1.3	–	–	–	–	–	–
Congo	80	99	1.2	78	99	1.3	35	9	3.7	22	37	1.7	94	99	1.1	5 x	12 x	2.4 x	12 x	27 x	2.3 x
Cook Islands	–	–	–	–	–	–	–	–	–	–	–	–	–	–	–	–	–	–	–	–	–
Costa Rica	99	100	1.0	97	99	1.0	–	–	–	–	–	–	94	98	1.0	20	54	2.7	–	–	–
Côte d'Ivoire	44	90	2.0	35	91	2.6	38	16	2.5	6	24	3.7	56	87	1.5	–	–	–	–	–	–
Croatia	–	–	–	–	–	–	–	–	–	–	–	–	–	–	–	–	–	–	–	–	–
Cuba	–	–	–	–	–	–	–	–	–	–	–	–	–	–	–	–	–	–	–	–	–
Cyprus	–	–	–	–	–	–	–	–	–	–	–	–	–	–	–	–	–	–	–	–	–
Czech Republic	–	–	–	–	–	–	–	–	–	–	–	–	–	–	–	–	–	–	–	–	–
Democratic People's Republic of Korea	–	–	–	–	–	–	–	–	–	–	–	–	–	–	–	–	–	–	–	–	–
Democratic Republic of the Congo	16	38	2.4	66	98	1.5	50	23	2.2	31	42	1.4	79	94	1.2	8	24	2.8	–	–	–
Denmark	–	–	–	–	–	–	–	–	–	–	–	–	–	–	–	–	–	–	–	–	–
Djibouti	–	–	–	–	–	–	–	–	–	–	–	–	–	–	–	–	–	–	–	–	–
Dominica	–	–	–	–	–	–	–	–	–	–	–	–	–	–	–	–	–	–	–	–	–
Dominican Republic	65	98	1.5	97	98	1.0	11	4	2.9	47	57	1.2	91	99	1.1	31 x	46 x	1.5 x	21 x	41 x	2.0 x
Ecuador	90	96	1.1	82	100	1.2	37	14	2.6	41	64	1.6	97 y	97 y	1.0 y	–	–	–	–	–	–
Egypt	99	100	1.0	82	99	1.2	24	23	1.0	27	23	0.9	95	98	1.0	2 x	9 x	4.9 x	9 x	28 x	3.1 x
El Salvador	98 x	99 x	1.0 x	–	–	–	31 x	5 x	6.8 x	–	–	–	90 x	92 y	1.0 y	–	–	–	–	–	–
Equatorial Guinea	60	60	1.0	48	88	1.8	28	19	1.5	–	–	–	–	–	–	–	–	–	–	–	–
Eritrea	–	–	–	9	90	10.5	57	27	2.1	42	50	1.2	31 y	84 y	2.7 y	9	37	4.3	21	43	2.0
Estonia	–	–	–	–	–	–	–	–	–	–	–	–	–	–	–	–	–	–	–	–	–
Ethiopia	3 x	18 x	7.0 x	5	56	12.4	47	28	1.7	18	45	2.5	49 y	82 y	1.7 y	–	–	–	–	–	–
Fiji	–	–	–	–	–	–	–	–	–	–	–	–	–	–	–	–	–	–	–	–	–
Finland	–	–	–	–	–	–	–	–	–	–	–	–	–	–	–	–	–	–	–	–	–

TABLE 13. DISPARITIES BY HOUSEHOLD WEALTH

Countries and areas	Birth registration (%)++ 2010–2015*			Skilled attendant at birth (%) 2010–2015*			Stunting prevalence in children under 5 (%) 2009–2015*			Oral rehydration salts (ORS) treatment for children with diarrhoea (%) 2010–2015*			Primary school net attendance ratio 2009–2014*			Comprehensive knowledge of HIV/AIDS (%) Females 15–24 2010–2014*			Comprehensive knowledge of HIV/AIDS (%) Males 15–24 2010–2014*		
	poorest 20%	richest 20%	ratio of richest to poorest	poorest 20%	richest 20%	ratio of richest to poorest	poorest 20%	richest 20%	ratio of poorest to richest	poorest 20%	richest 20%	ratio of richest to poorest	poorest 20%	richest 20%	ratio of richest to poorest	poorest 20%	richest 20%	ratio of richest to poorest	poorest 20%	richest 20%	ratio of richest to poorest
France	–	–	–	–	–	–	–	–	–	–	–	–	–	–	–	–	–	–	–	–	–
Gabon	92	86	0.9	74	95	1.3	30	6	5.2	24	19	0.8	92	97	1.1	–	–	–	–	–	–
Gambia	69	75	1.1	46	82	1.8	30	15	1.9	56	58	1.0	47	82	1.7	20	48	2.4	–	–	–
Georgia	99	100	1.0	–	–	–	–	–	–	–	–	–	92	96	1.0	–	–	–	–	–	–
Germany	–	–	–	–	–	–	–	–	–	–	–	–	–	–	–	–	–	–	–	–	–
Ghana	58	88	1.5	42	94	2.2	25	9	2.9	47	50	1.1	63	84	1.3	18	53	2.9	19	49	2.6
Greece	–	–	–	–	–	–	–	–	–	–	–	–	–	–	–	–	–	–	–	–	–
Grenada	–	–	–	–	–	–	–	–	–	–	–	–	–	–	–	–	–	–	–	–	–
Guatemala	–	–	–	37	96	2.6	66	17	3.8	49	55	1.1	–	–	–	5 x	41 x	7.8 x	–	–	–
Guinea	38	89	2.4	19	92	4.9	34	15	2.2	25	49	1.9	32	89	2.8	–	–	–	–	–	–
Guinea-Bissau	17	35	2.0	23	82	3.6	42	18	2.3	16	37	2.3	56	76	1.4	6	25	4.3	–	–	–
Guyana	84 x	92 x	1.1 x	–	–	–	30	10	3.0	–	–	–	95	98	1.0	37 x	72 x	2.0 x	25 x	65 x	2.6 x
Haiti	71	92	1.3	10	78	8.1	31	7	4.7	52	62	1.2	73	96	1.3	18 x	41 x	2.2 x	28 x	52 x	1.9 x
Holy See	–	–	–	–	–	–	–	–	–	–	–	–	–	–	–	–	–	–	–	–	–
Honduras	92	95	1.0	58	98	1.7	42	8	5.3	63	52	0.8	91	99	1.1	13 x	44 x	3.4 x	–	–	–
Hungary	–	–	–	–	–	–	–	–	–	–	–	–	–	–	–	–	–	–	–	–	–
Iceland	–	–	–	–	–	–	–	–	–	–	–	–	–	–	–	–	–	–	–	–	–
India	57	86	1.5	24 x	85 x	3.6 x	51	27	1.9	19 x	43 x	2.3 x	70 x	96 x	1.4 x	4 x	45 x	11.7 x	15 x	55 x	3.8 x
Indonesia	41	88	2.2	63	98	1.6	48	29	1.7	39	34	0.9	91	97	1.1	–	–	–	–	–	–
Iran (Islamic Republic of)	–	–	–	–	–	–	21	1	17.3	–	–	–	–	–	–	–	–	–	–	–	–
Iraq	98	100	1.0	82	96	1.2	25	22	1.1	19	22	1.1	79	98	1.2	1	8	7.2	–	–	–
Ireland	–	–	–	–	–	–	–	–	–	–	–	–	–	–	–	–	–	–	–	–	–
Israel	–	–	–	–	–	–	–	–	–	–	–	–	–	–	–	–	–	–	–	–	–
Italy	–	–	–	–	–	–	–	–	–	–	–	–	–	–	–	–	–	–	–	–	–
Jamaica	99	100	1.0	97	100	1.0	–	–	–	–	–	–	98	99	1.0	–	–	–	–	–	–
Japan	–	–	–	–	–	–	–	–	–	–	–	–	–	–	–	–	–	–	–	–	–
Jordan	98	100	1.0	99	100	1.0	14	2	7.7	22	21	1.0	97	99	1.0	–	–	–	–	–	–
Kazakhstan	100	100	1.0	100	100	1.0	14	12	1.2	–	–	–	99	100	1.0	25	44	1.8	13	49	3.8
Kenya	52	89	1.7	31	93	3.0	36	14	2.6	52	55	1.0	69	94	1.4	29 x	61 x	2.1 x	42 x	68 x	1.6 x
Kiribati	93 x	94 x	1.0 x	–	–	–	–	–	–	–	–	–	–	–	–	42 x	49 x	1.2 x	38 x	51 x	1.3 x
Kuwait	–	–	–	–	–	–	–	–	–	–	–	–	–	–	–	–	–	–	–	–	–
Kyrgyzstan	96	99	1.0	97	99	1.0	18	11	1.7	–	–	–	99	100	1.0	17 x	29 x	1.7 x	–	–	–
Lao People's Democratic Republic	66	93	1.4	11	91	8.4	61	20	3.1	35	69	2.0	71	97	1.4	6	41	6.5	12	43	3.6
Latvia	–	–	–	–	–	–	–	–	–	–	–	–	–	–	–	–	–	–	–	–	–
Lebanon	–	–	–	–	–	–	–	–	–	–	–	–	–	–	–	–	–	–	–	–	–
Lesotho	42 x	49 x	1.2 x	60	94	1.6	46	13	3.4	–	–	–	89	98	1.1	26 x	48 x	1.8 x	14 x	45 x	3.3 x
Liberia	16 y	31 y	1.9 y	43	89	2.1	35	20	1.8	57	44	0.8	25	65	2.6	14 x	29 x	2.1 x	17 x	37 x	2.2 x
Libya	–	–	–	–	–	–	–	–	–	–	–	–	–	–	–	–	–	–	–	–	–
Liechtenstein	–	–	–	–	–	–	–	–	–	–	–	–	–	–	–	–	–	–	–	–	–
Lithuania	–	–	–	–	–	–	–	–	–	–	–	–	–	–	–	–	–	–	–	–	–
Luxembourg	–	–	–	–	–	–	–	–	–	–	–	–	–	–	–	–	–	–	–	–	–
Madagascar	72	94	1.3	27	73	2.7	48	44	1.1	11	17	1.6	54 y	82 y	1.5 y	10	40	4.1	13	41	3.2
Malawi	4 y	10 y	2.4 y	83	95	1.1	49	34	1.4	60	67	1.1	88	98	1.1	39	50	1.3	48	52	1.1
Malaysia	–	–	–	–	–	–	–	–	–	–	–	–	–	–	–	–	–	–	–	–	–
Maldives	92 x	94 x	1.0 x	–	–	–	22	16	1.4	–	–	–	94	94	1.0	23 x	48 x	2.0 x	–	–	–
Mali	65	96	1.5	35 x	86 x	2.5 x	44 x	22 x	2.0 x	8 x	29 x	3.5 x	36	85	2.4	9	19	2.0	–	–	–
Malta	–	–	–	–	–	–	–	–	–	–	–	–	–	–	–	–	–	–	–	–	–
Marshall Islands	92 x	98 x	1.1 x	–	–	–	–	–	–	–	–	–	–	–	–	12 x	39 x	3.3 x	37 x	58 x	1.6 x
Mauritania	33	84	2.6	27	96	3.6	39	18	2.2	9	33	3.8	45	83	1.9	2	12	7.9	–	–	–
Mauritius	–	–	–	–	–	–	–	–	–	–	–	–	–	–	–	–	–	–	–	–	–
Mexico	–	–	–	–	–	–	26	8	3.2	–	–	–	–	–	–	–	–	–	–	–	–
Micronesia (Federated States of)	–	–	–	–	–	–	–	–	–	–	–	–	–	–	–	–	–	–	–	–	–
Monaco	–	–	–	–	–	–	–	–	–	–	–	–	–	–	–	–	–	–	–	–	–
Mongolia	99	99	1.0	98	99	1.0	25	7	3.9	24	50	2.1	93	98	1.1	17	42	2.5	12	48	4.1
Montenegro	99	99	1.0	99	100	1.0	5	9	0.5	–	–	–	95	100	1.0	39	51	1.3	33	47	1.4
Morocco	–	–	–	38	96	2.5	28	7	4.2	14	23	1.7	77 x	97 x	1.3 x	–	–	–	–	–	–
Mozambique	42	60	1.4	32	90	2.8	51	24	2.1	41	70	1.7	64	95	1.5	41 x	43 x	1.1 x	16 x	45 x	2.7 x
Myanmar	50	96	1.9	51	96	1.9	47	21	2.3	52	75	1.4	81	95	1.2	–	–	–	–	–	–
Namibia	83 y	93 y	1.1 y	73	98	1.4	31	9	3.6	64	70	1.1	88	97	1.1	61 x	69 x	1.1 x	55 x	67 x	1.2 x
Nauru	71 x	88 x	1.2 x	97 x	98 x	1.0 x	52 x	18 x	2.9 x	–	–	–	–	–	–	13 x	10 x	0.8 x	–	25 x	–
Nepal	55	58	1.1	26	93	3.7	55	15	2.2	49	48	1.0	81	82	1.0	12 x	49 x	4.3 x	30 x	59 x	2.0 x
Netherlands	–	–	–	–	–	–	–	–	–	–	–	–	–	–	–	–	–	–	–	–	–

TABLE 13. DISPARITIES BY HOUSEHOLD WEALTH

Countries and areas	Birth registration (%)++ 2010–2015*			Skilled attendant at birth (%) 2010–2015*			Stunting prevalence in children under 5 (%) 2009–2015*			Oral rehydration salts (ORS) treatment for children with diarrhoea (%) 2010–2015*			Primary school net attendance ratio 2009–2014*			Comprehensive knowledge of HIV/AIDS (%) Females 15–24 2010–2014*			Comprehensive knowledge of HIV/AIDS (%) Males 15–24 2010–2014*		
	poorest 20%	richest 20%	ratio of richest to poorest	poorest 20%	richest 20%	ratio of richest to poorest	poorest 20%	richest 20%	ratio of poorest to richest	poorest 20%	richest 20%	ratio of richest to poorest	poorest 20%	richest 20%	ratio of richest to poorest	poorest 20%	richest 20%	ratio of richest to poorest	poorest 20%	richest 20%	ratio of richest to poorest
New Zealand	–	–	–	–	–	–	–	–	–	–	–	–	–	–	–	–	–	–	–	–	–
Nicaragua	–	–	–	–	–	–	–	–	–	–	–	–	–	–	–	–	–	–	–	–	–
Niger	50	89	1.8	12	71	6.0	47	35	1.4	34	49	1.4	35	81	2.3	6	30	5.0	6	42	7.2
Nigeria	7 y	65 y	9.7 y	6	85	15.0	54	18	3.0	20	53	2.6	28	95	3.3	15	33	2.2	23	43	1.9
Niue	–	–	–	–	–	–	–	–	–	–	–	–	100	100	1.0	–	–	–	–	–	–
Norway	–	–	–	–	–	–	–	–	–	–	–	–	–	–	–	–	–	–	–	–	–
Oman	–	–	–	–	–	–	–	–	–	–	–	–	–	–	–	–	–	–	–	–	–
Pakistan	5	71	14.3	30	85	2.9	62	23	2.7	34	48	1.4	39	87	2.2	–	–	–	–	–	–
Palau	–	–	–	–	–	–	–	–	–	–	–	–	–	–	–	–	–	–	–	–	–
Panama	90	97	1.1	72	100	1.4	–	–	–	–	–	–	96	97	1.0	–	–	–	–	–	–
Papua New Guinea	–	–	–	–	–	–	–	–	–	–	–	–	–	–	–	–	–	–	–	–	–
Paraguay	67 y	89 y	1.3 y	–	–	–	28	13	2.2	–	–	–	–	–	–	–	–	–	–	–	–
Peru	94 y	98 y	1.0 y	68	99	1.5	34	4	9.2	23	36	1.6	93 y	96 y	1.0 y	–	–	–	–	–	–
Philippines	–	–	–	42	96	2.3	45	13	3.4	–	–	–	79 x	92 x	1.2 x	14 x	26 x	1.8 x	–	–	–
Poland	–	–	–	–	–	–	–	–	–	–	–	–	–	–	–	–	–	–	–	–	–
Portugal	–	–	–	–	–	–	–	–	–	–	–	–	–	–	–	–	–	–	–	–	–
Qatar	–	–	–	–	–	–	–	–	–	–	–	–	–	–	–	–	–	–	–	–	–
Republic of Korea	–	–	–	–	–	–	–	–	–	–	–	–	–	–	–	–	–	–	–	–	–
Republic of Moldova	99	100	1.0	98	99	1.0	11	3	4.2	–	–	–	98	99	1.0	14	47	3.3	13	40	3.1
Romania	–	–	–	–	–	–	–	–	–	–	–	–	–	–	–	–	–	–	–	–	–
Russian Federation	–	–	–	–	–	–	–	–	–	–	–	–	–	–	–	–	–	–	–	–	–
Rwanda	58	64	1.1	84	97	1.2	49	21	2.3	22	37	1.7	82 y	93 y	1.1 y	–	–	–	–	–	–
Saint Kitts and Nevis	–	–	–	–	–	–	–	–	–	–	–	–	–	–	–	–	–	–	–	–	–
Saint Lucia	–	–	–	–	–	–	–	–	–	–	–	–	–	–	–	–	–	–	–	–	–
Saint Vincent and the Grenadines	–	–	–	–	–	–	–	–	–	–	–	–	–	–	–	–	–	–	–	–	–
Samoa	47	77	1.6	72	94	1.3	–	–	–	–	–	–	85 y	91 y	1.1 y	3 x	3 x	1.0 x	3 x	9 x	2.7 x
San Marino	–	–	–	–	–	–	–	–	–	–	–	–	–	–	–	–	–	–	–	–	–
Sao Tome and Principe	74 x	86 x	1.1 x	–	–	–	38	18	2.2	–	–	–	88	97	1.1	27 x	56 x	2.0 x	39 x	55 x	1.4 x
Saudi Arabia	–	–	–	–	–	–	–	–	–	–	–	–	–	–	–	–	–	–	–	–	–
Senegal	51	93	1.8	30	86	2.8	29	9	3.3	24	24	1.0	50	89	1.8	–	–	–	–	–	–
Serbia	97	100	1.0	98	95	1.0	14	4	3.3	–	–	–	97	100	1.0	28	69	2.4	28	66	2.4
Seychelles	–	–	–	–	–	–	–	–	–	–	–	–	–	–	–	–	–	–	–	–	–
Sierra Leone	77	80	1.0	51	84	1.6	43	28	1.5	87	88	1.0	62	92	1.5	14 x	36 x	2.6 x	–	–	–
Singapore	–	–	–	–	–	–	–	–	–	–	–	–	–	–	–	–	–	–	–	–	–
Slovakia	–	–	–	–	–	–	–	–	–	–	–	–	–	–	–	–	–	–	–	–	–
Slovenia	–	–	–	–	–	–	–	–	–	–	–	–	–	–	–	–	–	–	–	–	–
Solomon Islands	–	–	–	74 x	95 x	1.3 x	34 x	22 x	1.6 x	–	–	–	58 x,y	78 x,y	1.3 x,y	17 x	37 x	2.1 x	35 x	50 x	1.5 x
Somalia	1 x	7 x	6.6 x	–	–	–	52 x	25 x	2.0 x	7 x	31 x	4.8 x	4 x	50 x	13.2 x	1 x	8 x	13.5 x	–	–	–
South Africa	–	–	–	–	–	–	–	–	–	–	–	–	–	–	–	–	–	–	–	–	–
South Sudan	21	57	2.7	8	41	5.1	31	27	1.2	27	52	1.9	10	50	5.1	3	18	6.1	–	–	–
Spain	–	–	–	–	–	–	–	–	–	–	–	–	–	–	–	–	–	–	–	–	–
Sri Lanka	97 x	98 x	1.0 x	97 x	99 x	1.0 x	19	10	2.0	–	–	–	–	–	–	–	–	–	–	–	–
State of Palestine	100	99	1.0	100	99	1.0	8	7	1.1	23	31	1.3	99	99	1.0	5	10	2.1	–	–	–
Sudan	26	98	3.8	6	59	10.5	42	15	2.8	21	16	0.7	48	96	2.0	1	11	13.6	–	–	–
Suriname	98	100	1.0	84	95	1.1	13	6	2.4	–	–	–	92	96	1.1	26	52	2.0	–	–	–
Swaziland	39	73	1.9	65	94	1.4	42	14	3.0	58	60	1.0	95	99	1.0	49	72	1.5	44	64	1.5
Sweden	–	–	–	–	–	–	–	–	–	–	–	–	–	–	–	–	–	–	–	–	–
Switzerland	–	–	–	–	–	–	–	–	–	–	–	–	–	–	–	–	–	–	–	–	–
Syrian Arab Republic	93 x	99 x	1.1 x	–	–	–	–	–	–	45 x	59 x	1.3 x	92 x	99 x	1.1 x	4 x	10 x	2.9 x	–	–	–
Tajikistan	86	90	1.0	74	96	1.3	32	21	1.5	53	62	1.2	95	99	1.0	–	–	–	–	–	–
Thailand	99 y	100 y	1.0 y	98	100	1.0	23	11	2.2	71	53	0.7	94	97	1.0	48	59	1.2	–	–	–
The former Yugoslav Republic of Macedonia	99	100	1.0	98	98	1.0	7	2	3.6	–	–	–	96	99	1.0	9 x	45 x	5.0 x	–	–	–
Timor-Leste	50	56	1.1	10	69	6.9	59	39	1.5	70	71	1.0	60	84	1.4	9	16	1.8	11	35	3.0
Togo	67	97	1.5	27	95	3.6	33	11	3.2	28	25	0.9	80	97	1.2	18	42	2.3	20	55	2.7
Tonga	92	96	1.1	97	99	1.0	7	10	0.7	–	–	–	94 y	94 y	1.0 y	11	16	1.4	13	14	1.1
Trinidad and Tobago	96 x	99 x	1.0 x	–	–	–	–	–	–	–	–	–	95 x	98 x	1.0 x	48 x	62 x	1.3 x	–	–	–
Tunisia	98	100	1.0	94	100	1.1	16	8	2.0	–	–	–	96	98	1.0	10	29	2.8	–	–	–
Turkey	98 y	99 y	1.0 y	91	100	1.1	18	4	4.3	–	–	–	87 x,y	97 x,y	1.1 x,y	–	–	–	–	–	–
Turkmenistan	94 x	97 x	1.0 x	99 x	100 x	1.0 x	21 x	13 x	1.7 x	–	–	–	99	99	1.0	–	–	–	–	–	–
Tuvalu	39 x	71 x	1.8 x	–	–	–	8 x	13 x	0.6 x	–	–	–	99 x,y	100 x,y	1.0 x,y	34 x	39 x	1.2 x	–	67 x	–
Uganda	27	44	1.6	43	88	2.0	37	21	1.8	43	45	1.1	79	92	1.2	20 x	47 x	2.3 x	28 x	47 x	1.6 x

TABLE 13. DISPARITIES BY HOUSEHOLD WEALTH

Countries and areas	Birth registration (%)++ 2010–2015*			Skilled attendant at birth (%) 2010–2015*			Stunting prevalence in children under 5 (%) 2009–2015*			Oral rehydration salts (ORS) treatment for children with diarrhoea (%) 2010–2015*			Primary school net attendance ratio 2009–2014*			Comprehensive knowledge of HIV/AIDS (%) Females 15–24 2010–2014*			Comprehensive knowledge of HIV/AIDS (%) Males 15–24 2010–2014*		
	poorest 20%	richest 20%	ratio of richest to poorest	poorest 20%	richest 20%	ratio of richest to poorest	poorest 20%	richest 20%	ratio of poorest to richest	poorest 20%	richest 20%	ratio of richest to richest	poorest 20%	richest 20%	ratio of richest to poorest	poorest 20%	richest 20%	ratio of richest to poorest	poorest 20%	richest 20%	ratio of richest to poorest
Ukraine	100	99	1.0	99	100	1.0	–	–	–	–	–	–	100	100	1.0	41	53	1.3	40	54	1.3
United Arab Emirates	–	–	–	–	–	–	–	–	–	–	–	–	–	–	–	–	–	–	–	–	–
United Kingdom	–	–	–	–	–	–	–	–	–	–	–	–	–	–	–	–	–	–	–	–	–
United Republic of Tanzania	4	56	12.7	31	90	2.9	*48*	*26*	*1.8*	41	38	0.9	*68*	*95*	*1.4*	*39*	*55*	*1.4*	*34*	*56*	*1.7*
United States	–	–	–	–	–	–	–	–	–	–	–	–	–	–	–	–	–	–	–	–	–
Uruguay	–	–	–	–	–	–	–	–	–	–	–	–	–	–	–	–	–	–	–	–	–
Uzbekistan	100 x	100 x	1.0 x	100 x	100 x	1.0 x	21 x	15 x	1.4 x	–	–	–	93 x	96 x	1.0 x	25 x	33 x	1.3 x	–	–	–
Vanuatu	33 y	59 y	1.8 y	77	95	1.2	40	16	2.4	–	–	–	75 y	80 y	1.1 y	9 x	23 x	2.7 x	–	–	–
Venezuela (Bolivarian Republic of)	–	–	–	–	–	–	–	–	–	–	–	–	86 x	99 x	1.2 x	–	–	–	–	–	–
Viet Nam	91	98	1.1	73	100	1.4	*41*	*6*	*6.7*	–	–	–	94	99	1.0	30	65	2.2	–	–	–
Yemen	17	56	3.3	19	81	4.2	59	26	1.4	27	21	0.8	56	90	1.6	0 x	4 x	–	–	–	–
Zambia	5	29	6.0	45	94	2.1	47	28	1.7	59	68	1.1	75	97	1.3	*24 x*	*48 x*	*2.0 x*	24 x	51 x	2.1 x
Zimbabwe	17	68	3.9	70	96	1.4	33	15	2.2	37	45	1.2	90	98	1.1	47	65	1.4	43	67	1.6
SUMMARY																					
Sub-Saharan Africa	28	68	2.4	29	84	2.9	46	22	2.1	29	45	1.5	55	91	1.7	16	34	2.1	–	–	–
Eastern and Southern Africa	31	61	1.9	32	80	2.5	45	26	1.8	36	48	1.3	64	89	1.4	–	–	–	–	–	–
West and Central Africa	27	70	2.6	27	88	3.2	47	19	2.5	24	45	1.8	46	91	2.0	12	31	2.5	21	44	2.1
Middle East and North Africa	77	95	1.2	62	90	1.5	28	15	1.8	23	23	1.0	78	97	1.2	–	–	–	–	–	–
South Asia	46	79	1.7	24 ‡	81 ‡	3.3 ‡	52	25	2.0	49 ‡	60 ‡	1.2 ‡	65	93	1.4	–	–	–	–	–	–
East Asia and Pacific	57 **	91 **	1.6 **	61 **	97 **	1.6 **	45 **	20 **	2.2 **	44 **	42 **	1.0 **	90 **	97 **	1.1 **	–	–	–	–	–	–
Latin America and Caribbean	–	–	–	–	–	–	22	7	3.3	–	–	–	–	–	–	–	–	–	–	–	–
CEE/CIS	–	–	–	93	99	1.1	19 r	9 r	2.3 r	–	–	–	–	–	–	–	–	–	–	–	–
Least developed countries	34	63	1.9	32	81	2.6	47	24	1.9	38	49	1.3	61	88	1.4	10	26	2.6	–	–	–
World	**57 ****	**84 ****	**1.7 ****	**43 ‡****	**88 ‡****	**2.1 ‡****	**43 ****	**21 ****	**2.1 ****	**34 ‡****	**45 ‡****	**1.3 ‡****	**67 ****	**93 ****	**1.4 ****	–	–	–	–	–	–

For a complete list of countries and areas in the regions, subregions and country categories, see page 112 or visit <data.unicef.org/regionalclassifications>.
It is not advisable to compare data from consecutive editions of *The State of the World's Children*.

DEFINITIONS OF THE INDICATORS

Birth registration – Percentage of children under age 5 who were registered at the moment of the survey. The numerator of this indicator includes children reported to have a birth certificate, regardless of whether or not it was seen by the interviewer, and those without a birth certificate whose mother or caregiver says the birth has been registered.

Skilled attendant at birth – Percentage of births attended by skilled health personnel (doctor, nurse or midwife).

Stunting prevalence in children under 5 – Percentage of children aged 0–59 months who are below minus two standard deviations from median height-for-age of the WHO Child Growth Standards.

Diarrhoea treatment with oral rehydration salts (ORS) – Percentage of children under age 5 who had diarrhoea in the two weeks preceding the survey and who received oral rehydration salts (ORS packets or pre-packaged ORS fluids).

Primary school net attendance ratio – Number of children attending primary or secondary school who are of official primary school age, expressed as a percentage of the total number of children of official primary school age. Because of the inclusion of primary-school-aged children attending secondary school, this indicator can also be referred to as a primary adjusted net attendance ratio.

Comprehensive knowledge of HIV – Percentage of young men and women (aged 15–24) who correctly identify the two major ways of preventing the sexual transmission of HIV (using condoms and limiting sex to one faithful, uninfected partner), who reject the two most common local misconceptions about HIV transmission and who know that a healthy-looking person can be HIV-positive.

MAIN DATA SOURCES

Birth registration – Demographic and Health Surveys (DHS), Multiple Indicator Cluster Surveys (MICS), other national surveys, censuses and vital registration systems.

Skilled attendant at birth – DHS, MICS and other nationally representative sources.

Stunting prevalence in children under 5 – DHS, MICS, other national household surveys, WHO and UNICEF.

Oral rehydration salts (ORS) treatment for children with diarrhoea – DHS, MICS and other national household surveys.

Primary school net attendance ratio – DHS, MICS and other national household surveys.

Comprehensive knowledge of HIV – AIDS Indicator Surveys (AIS), DHS, MICS, and other national household surveys; DHS STATcompiler, www.statcompiler.com.

Italicized data are from different sources than the data presented for the same indicators in other tables of the report: Table 2 (Nutrition – Stunting prevalence), Table 3 (Health – Diarrhoea treatment), Table 4 (HIV/AIDS – Comprehensive knowledge of HIV), Table 5 (Education – Primary school participation), Table 8 (Women – Skilled attendant at birth) and Table 9 (Child protection – Birth registration).

NOTES

- Data not available.

x   Data refer to years or periods other than those specified in the column heading. Such data are not included in the calculation of regional and global averages, with the exception of 2005–2006 data on primary attendance from India. Estimates from data years prior to 2000 are not displayed.

y   Data differ from the standard definition or refer to only part of a country. If they fall within the noted reference period, such data are included in the calculation of regional and global averages.

++ Changes in the definition of birth registration were made from the second and third rounds of MICS (MICS2 and MICS3) to the fourth round (MICS4). In order to allow for comparability with later rounds, data from MICS2 and MICS3 on birth registration were recalculated according to the MICS4 indicator definition. Therefore, the recalculated data presented here may differ from estimates included in MICS2 and MICS3 national reports.

*   Data refer to the most recent year available during the period specified in the column heading.

** Excludes China.

‡   Excludes India.

r   Excludes the Russian Federation.

TABLE 14. EARLY CHILDHOOD DEVELOPMENT

Countries and areas	Attendance in early childhood education 2005–2014*					Adult support for learning ++ 2005–2014*					Father's support for learning ++ 2005–2014*	Learning materials at home 2005–2014*						Children left in inadequate care 2005–2014*				
												Children's books			Playthings ++							
	total	male	female	poorest 20%	richest 20%	total	male	female	poorest 20%	richest 20%		total	poorest 20%	richest 20%	total	poorest 20%	richest 20%	total	male	female	poorest 20%	richest 20%
Afghanistan	1	1	1	0	4	73	74	73	72	80	62	2	1	5	53	52	57	40	42	39	43	27
Albania	40	39	42	26	60	86	85	87	68	96	53	32	16	52	53	57	48	13	14	11	9	16
Algeria	17	17	16	7	31	78	79	78	64	92	79	11	3	23	35	32	36	8	9	8	10	5
Argentina	63	61	66	46	85	84	83	85	73	95	57	61	40	83	61	58	63	8	9	8	10	5
Bangladesh	13	13	14	12	18	78	78	78	64	94	10 y	9	2	23	60	57	60	12	11	12	14	12
Barbados	90	88	91	90 p	97 p	97	97	97	100 p	100 p	46	85	83	89	76	68	77	1	2	1	0	3
Belarus	88	86	89	75	91	96	94	97	90	99	68	92	83	96	79	77	79	4	4	4	4	5
Belize	32	30	34	16	59	86	88	83	73	94	50	40	17	73	57	55	58	2	3	2	4	1
Benin	13	–	–	–	–	28	–	–	–	–	5 y	1	–	–	48	–	–	34	–	–	–	–
Bhutan	10	10	10	3	27	54	52	57	40	73	51	6	1	24	52	36	60	14	13	15	17	7
Bosnia and Herzegovina	13	12	14	2	31	95	95	96	87	100	76	56	39	73	56	58	60	2	2	2	3	1
Botswana	18	–	–	–	–	–	–	–	–	–	–	–	–	–	–	–	–	–	–	–	–	–
Brazil	70 y	–	–	–	–	–	–	–	–	–	–	–	–	–	–	–	–	–	–	–	–	–
Burkina Faso	2	3	1	0	9	14	14	14	12	26	24	–	–	–	–	–	–	–	–	–	–	–
Burundi	5	5	5	4	10	34	35	34	32	38	20	–	–	–	–	–	–	–	–	–	–	–
Cambodia	15 y	12 y	17 y	7 y	38 y	59 y	57 y	62 y	48 y	73 y	9 y	4 y	1 y	12 y	34 y	20 y	53 y	10 y	10 y	10 y	16 y	4 y
Cameroon	28	–	–	–	–	44	–	–	–	–	4 y	4	–	–	53	–	–	34	–	–	–	–
Central African Republic	5	5	6	2	17	74	74	74	70	78	42	1	0	3	49	41	51	61	60	62	58	60
Chad	5	5	4	1	16	70	69	70	64	71	29	1	0	2	43	38	50	56	57	56	58	56
Colombia	37 y	–	–	–	–	–	–	–	–	–	–	–	–	–	–	–	–	–	–	–	–	–
Congo	36	–	–	–	–	59	–	–	–	–	6 y	3	–	–	51	–	–	42	–	–	–	–
Costa Rica	18	17	18	8	40	68	69	66	54	88	52	37	13	70	73	68	74	4	4	4	6	3
Côte d'Ivoire	5	5	5	1	15	50	50	51	55	57	40	5	3	13	39	44	35	59	60	58	62	51
Croatia	72 y	–	–	–	–	–	–	–	–	–	–	–	–	–	–	–	–	–	–	–	–	–
Cuba	76	75	77	–	–	89	89	90	–	–	18 y	48	–	–	78	–	–	4	4	4	–	–
Democratic People's Republic of Korea	98	98	97	–	–	91	88	93	–	–	75	79	–	–	47	–	–	17	17	16	–	–
Democratic Republic of the Congo	7 y	7 y	7 y	1 y	20 y	52 y	55 y	48 y	45 y	64 y	4 y	1 y	0 y	2 y	27 y	18 y	49 y	49 y	50 y	48 y	57 y	29 y
Djibouti	14	12	16	–	–	37 y	38 y	35 y	–	–	28 y	15	–	–	24	–	–	8	8	8	–	–
Dominican Republic	40	–	–	–	–	58	–	–	–	–	6 y	10	–	–	57	–	–	5	–	–	–	–
Egypt	47 y	48 y	47 y	34 y	50 y	–	–	–	–	–	–	–	–	–	–	–	–	4	4	4	7	2
El Salvador	25	–	–	–	–	59	–	–	–	–	8 y	18	–	–	62	–	–	4	–	–	–	–
Gambia	18	17	19	12	32	48	49	47	50	55	21	1	0	4	42	28	50	21	22	19	25	18
Georgia	66	65	67	53	83	84	84	83	67	94	33	51 y	26 y	69 y	38	41	41	8 y	9 y	8 y	4 y	10 y
Ghana	68	65	72	42	97	40	38	42	23	78	30	6	1	23	41	31	51	21	21	21	27	15
Guinea-Bissau	13	–	–	–	–	34	–	–	–	–	0 y	1	–	–	31	–	–	31	–	–	–	–
Guyana	61	–	–	–	–	87	–	–	–	–	16 y	47	–	–	69	–	–	5	–	–	–	–
Honduras	19	17	21	13	28	48	47	49	28	75	59	11	1	34	78	74	81	4	5	4	8	2
Indonesia	17	16	18	–	–	–	–	–	–	–	–	–	–	–	–	–	–	–	–	–	–	–
Iran (Islamic Republic of)	20 y	19 y	22 y	–	–	70 y	69 y	70 y	–	–	60 y	36 y	–	–	67 y	–	–	15 y	15 y	15 y	–	–
Iraq	4	4	4	1	10	58	58	59	40	78	55	5	1	16	34	34	32	8	8	7	9	8
Jamaica	92	92	91	88	100	88	86	90	76	86	28	55	34	73	61	64	56	2	2	2	2	1
Jordan	22 y	21 y	23 y	11 y	39 y	82 y	81 y	83 y	75 y	87 y	72 y	23 y	11 y	40 y	70 y	68 y	74 y	9 y	9 y	9 y	11 y	8 y
Kazakhstan	37	36	38	19	61	92	92	91	84	96	49	48	24	76	45	40	49	4	4	4	5	4
Kyrgyzstan	23	23	23	12	50	72	74	70	63	73	3 y	27	15	54	59	63	54	5	5	4	6	5
Lao People's Democratic Republic	23	21	25	5	73	57	58	57	42	87	52	5	1	24	41	29	50	14	15	13	20	8
Lebanon	62	63	60	–	–	56 y	58 y	54 y	–	–	74 y	29	–	–	16 y	–	–	9	8	10	–	–
Malawi	39	37	41	26	67	29	29	30	22	44	3 y	1	0	6	45	35	66	37	37	37	39	28
Mali	10	10	10	1	40	29	27	30	28	44	14	0	0	2	40	33	49	33	33	33	33	36
Mauritania	14	14	14	2	41	55	54	55	55	64	28	–	–	–	40	42	39	26	27	26	24	25
Mongolia	68	–	–	–	–	60	–	–	–	–	12 y	33	–	–	56	–	–	10	–	–	–	–
Montenegro	40	39	42	7	66	98	97	99	93	98	45 y	73	48	87	60	61	66	3	3	3	2	3
Morocco	39	36	41	6	78	35 y	34 y	35 y	16 y	59 y	58 y	21 y	9 y	52 y	14 y	19 y	7 y	11	–	–	–	–
Mozambique	–	–	–	–	–	47	45	48	48	50	20	3	2	10	–	–	–	33	33	32	–	–
Myanmar	23	23	23	8	46	58 y	58 y	58 y	42 y	76 y	44 y	–	–	–	–	–	–	–	–	–	–	–

unicef 70 YEARS FOR EVERY CHILD

TABLE 14. EARLY CHILDHOOD DEVELOPMENT

Countries and areas	Attendance in early childhood education 2005–2014* total	male	female	poorest 20%	richest 20%	Adult support for learning++ 2005–2014* total	male	female	poorest 20%	richest 20%	Father's support for learning++ 2005–2014*	Learning materials at home 2005–2014* Children's books total	poorest 20%	richest 20%	Playthings++ total	poorest 20%	richest 20%	Children left in inadequate care 2005–2014* total	male	female	poorest 20%	richest 20%
Nepal	51	52	49	41	84	67	70	64	51	90	10 y	5	1	16	59	60	60	21	20	21	30	12
Nigeria	43	42	43	10	84	65	66	64	48	89	37	6	0	19	38	29	48	40	40	40	40	34
Oman	29	–	–	–	–	81	–	–	–	–	22 y	25	–	–	75	–	–	45	–	–	–	–
Panama	37	38	35	28	67	74	73	74	55	89	45	26	7	59	69	67	68	3	3	2	6	1
Qatar	41	41	41	–	–	88	89	88	–	–	85	40	–	–	55	–	–	12	12	11	–	–
Republic of Moldova	71	74	67	50	88	89	86	92	81	95	47	68	33	87	68	75	69	6	6	6	9	5
Saint Lucia	85	87	84	–	–	93	89	96	–	–	50	68	–	–	59	–	–	5	5	5	–	–
Sao Tome and Principe	36	–	–	–	–	63	–	–	–	–	3 y	6	–	–	65	–	–	16	–	–	–	–
Senegal	22 y	23 y	21 y	7 y	43 y	–	–	–	–	–	–	–	–	–	–	–	–	–	–	–	–	–
Serbia	50	52	49	9	82	96	95	96	87	98	37 y	72	44	83	75	78	76	1	2	1	3	2
Sierra Leone	14	13	15	5	42	54	53	55	45	79	42	2	0	10	35	24	50	32	33	32	29	28
Somalia	2	2	2	1	6	79	80	79	76	85	48	–	–	–	–	–	–	–	–	–	–	–
South Africa	37 y	–	–	–	–	–	–	–	–	–	–	–	–	–	–	–	–	–	–	–	–	–
South Sudan	6	6	6	2	13	–	–	–	–	–	–	–	–	–	–	–	–	–	–	–	–	–
State of Palestine	26	27	26	21	38	78	77	78	69	87	12 y	20	13	31	69	64	72	14	14	15	15	12
Sudan	22	–	–	–	–	–	–	–	–	–	–	2	–	–	46	–	–	–	–	–	–	–
Suriname	34	33	35	16	63	73	71	75	56	91	26	25	4	61	59	61	60	7	7	7	9	8
Swaziland	30	–	–	–	–	39	–	–	–	–	2 y	6	–	–	67	–	–	17	–	–	–	–
Syrian Arab Republic	8	8	7	4	18	70	70	69	52	84	62	30	12	53	52	52	51	17	17	17	22	15
Tajikistan	6	–	–	–	–	74	73	74	56	86	23	17	4	33	46	43	44	13	13	12	15	11
Thailand	84	84	85	85	82	93	92	93	87	96	35	43	24	71	71	69	70	5	5	4	7	2
The former Yugoslav Republic of Macedonia	22	25	19	0	56	92	92	91	81	96	71	52	18	81	71	70	79	5	5	5	11	1
Togo	26 y	26 y	26 y	15 y	52 y	25 y	25 y	25 y	20 y	42 y	21 y	1 y	0 y	3 y	34 y	22 y	48 y	29 y	26 y	33 y	36 y	26 y
Trinidad and Tobago	75	74	76	65	87	98	98	98	96	100	63	81	66	93	65	63	72	1	1	1	2	0
Tunisia	44	42	47	13	81	71	68	74	44	90	71	18	3	40	53	46	56	13	13	14	18	9
Turkmenistan	24	23	26	10	64	93	93	92	92	96	66	42	24	65	61	64	48	15	15	16	18	10
Ukraine	52	54	50	30	68	98	97	98	95	99	71	91	92	92	52	61	51	7	6	7	11	5
Uruguay	81	83	80	–	–	93	94	91	–	–	66 y	59	–	–	75	–	–	3	3	3	–	–
Uzbekistan	20	20	19	5	46	91	91	90	83	95	54	43	32	59	67	74	62	5	5	5	6	7
Venezuela (Bolivarian Republic of)	66 y	–	–	–	–	–	–	–	–	–	–	–	–	–	–	–	–	–	–	–	–	–
Viet Nam	71	74	69	53	86	76	76	76	52	96	15 y	26	6	58	52	44	54	7	6	8	14	2
Yemen	3	3	3	0	8	33	34	32	16	56	37	10	4	31	49	45	49	34	36	33	46	22
Zimbabwe	22	20	23	17	34	43	43	43	35	59	3 y	3	1	12	62	48	74	19	19	18	25	7
SUMMARY																						
Sub-Saharan Africa	25	–	–	–	–	51	–	–	–	–	24	4	–	–	–	–	–	–	–	–	–	–
Eastern and Southern Africa	–	–	–	–	–	–	–	–	–	–	–	–	–	–	–	–	–	–	–	–	–	–
West and Central Africa	26	28	21	8	53	52	56	48	43	72	25	4	0	13	38	28	48	41	42	42	44	34
Middle East and North Africa	23	25	21	13	35	63	60	66	–	–	60	16	–	–	45	–	–	11	11	11	14	8
South Asia	–	–	–	–	–	–	–	–	–	–	–	–	–	–	–	–	–	–	–	–	–	–
East Asia and Pacific	34 **	36 **	32 **	–	–	–	–	–	–	–	–	–	–	–	–	–	–	–	–	–	–	–
Latin America and Caribbean	60	–	–	–	–	–	–	–	–	–	–	–	–	–	–	–	–	–	–	–	–	–
CEE/CIS	–	–	–	–	–	–	–	–	–	–	–	–	–	–	–	–	–	–	–	–	–	–
Least developed countries	13	13	12	7	25	57	57	63	50	72	21	–	–	–	–	–	–	–	–	–	–	–
World	–	–	–	–	–	–	–	–	–	–	–	–	–	–	–	–	–	–	–	–	–	–

For a complete list of countries and areas in the regions, subregions and country categories, see page 112 or visit <data.unicef.org/regionalclassifications>.
It is not advisable to compare data from consecutive editions of *The State of the World's Children*.

Attendance in early childhood education – Percentage of children 36–59 months old who are attending an early childhood education programme.

Adult support for learning – Percentage of children 36–59 months old with whom an adult has engaged in four or more of the following activities to promote learning and school readiness in the past 3 days: a) reading books to the child, b) telling stories to the child, c) singing songs to the child, d) taking the child outside the home, e) playing with the child, and f) spending time with the child naming, counting or drawing things.

Father's support for learning – Percentage of children 36–59 months old whose father has engaged in one or more of the following activities to promote learning and school readiness in the past 3 days: a) reading books to the child, b) telling stories to the child, c) singing songs to the child, d) taking the child outside the home, e) playing with the child, and f) spending time with the child naming, counting or drawing things.

Learning materials at home: Children's books – Percentage of children 0–59 months old who have three or more children's books at home.

Learning materials at home: Playthings – Percentage of children 0–59 months old with two or more of the following playthings at home: household objects or objects found outside (sticks, rocks, animals, shells, leaves etc.), homemade toys or toys that came from a store.

Children left in inadequate care – Percentage of children 0–59 months old left alone or in the care of another child younger than 10 years of age for more than one hour at least once in the past week.

Attendance in early childhood education – Demographic and Health Surveys (DHS), Multiple Indicator Cluster Surveys (MICS), and other national surveys.

Adult support for learning – DHS, MICS and other national surveys.

Father's support for learning – DHS, MICS and other national surveys.

Learning materials at home: Children's books – DHS, MICS and other national surveys.

Learning materials at home: Playthings – DHS, MICS and other national surveys.

Children left in inadequate care – DHS, MICS and other national surveys.

– Data not available.

y Data differ from the standard definition or refer to only part of a country. If they fall within the noted reference period, such data are included in the calculation of regional and global averages.

p Based on small denominators (typically 25–49 unweighted cases). No data based on fewer than 25 unweighted cases are displayed.

* Data refer to the most recent year available during the period specified in the column heading.

++ Changes in the definitions of several ECD indicators were made between the third and fourth round of MICS (MICS3 and MICS4). In order to allow for comparability with MICS4, data from MICS3 for the adult support for learning, father's support for learning and learning materials at home (playthings) indicators were recalculated according to MICS4 indicator definitions. Therefore, the recalculated data presented here will differ from estimates reported in MICS3 national reports.

unicef ❤ 70 YEARS FOR EVERY CHILD